Tennyson and Goethe's *Faust*

Tennyson and Goethe's *Faust*

Tom Baynes

EDINBURGH
University Press

Edinburgh University Press is one of the leading university presses in the UK. We publish academic books and journals in our selected subject areas across the humanities and social sciences, combining cutting-edge scholarship with high editorial and production values to produce academic works of lasting importance. For more information visit our website: edinburghuniversitypress.com

© Tom Baynes, 2021, 2023

Edinburgh University Press Ltd
The Tun – Holyrood Road, 12(2f) Jackson's Entry, Edinburgh EH8 8PJ

First published in hardback by Edinburgh University Press 2021

Typeset in 11/13 Adobe Sabon by
IDSUK (DataConnection) Ltd, and
printed and bound by CPI Group (UK) Ltd

A CIP record for this book is available from the British Library

ISBN 978 1 4744 8852 5 (hardback)
ISBN 978 1 4744 8853 2 (paperback)
ISBN 978 1 4744 8854 9 (webready PDF)
ISBN 978 1 4744 8855 6 (epub)

The right of Tom Baynes to be identifiedastheauthorofthisworkhasbeenassertedin accordance with the Copyright, Designs and Patents Act 1988, and the Copyright and Related Rights Regulations 2003 (SI No. 2498).

Contents

Acknowledgements	viii
Preface	xi
Abbreviations	xv
Introduction: *Faust* and British Literature, *c.* 1810–1892	1

I: The Death of Arthur Hallam

1 'I am to die already!': The Gretchen Tragedy	47
2 'To strive onwards': 'Ulysses', Progress and Trances	72
3 'Out of Orcus into Life': Hallam and *Part Two*	95

II: Religion, Nature and Morality

4 'Two souls, alas, dwell in my breast': Religious Doubt	127
5 'Unveil thyself!': *Faust* and the Natural World	153
6 'The kiss of heavenly love': Saints and Sinners	180
'Last words'	200
Conclusion	204
Bibliography	211
Index	224

IN MEMORIAM

M. J. C.

OBIIT MMXII

Acknowledgements

I would like to thank, first and foremost, Kate Shotter. I would also like to express my gratitude to Dr Jane Wright and Dr Samantha Matthews, as well as Dr Stephen Cheeke and Professor Marion Shaw. My thanks are also due to the Arts and Humanities Research Council, which provided me with generous funding. No one whom I met whilst I was writing this book was more helpful than Grace Timmins, formerly the curator of the Tennyson Research Centre, to whom I am indebted for a number of specific discoveries. I would also like to thank Dr David Francis Smith (who gave me access to his thesis) and Martin Blocksidge (who read part of Chapter 1, and suggested a number of improvements). I am grateful to the staff of the University of Bristol, the British Library, Senate House Library, Trinity College Library and the National Library of Scotland. This book would have been difficult – perhaps impossible – to write without *The Poems of Tennyson*, edited by Professor Sir Christopher Ricks, and *The Tennyson Archive*, edited by the same author, and Professor Aidan Day. A big thank you also to the anonymous reviewers, as well as Michelle Houston, Ersev Ersoy and everyone else at Edinburgh University Press.

I would like to thank the following individuals and organisations for permission to reprint, in revised form, material from three different articles: Professor Tom Keymer at Oxford University Press, for '"Out of Orcus into Life": Tennyson's *Princess*, Arthur Hallam, and German Literature', *Review of English Studies*, n.s. 69: 290 (June 2018), 413–29 (see the Introduction, and Chapters 1, 3 and 5); Professor Seamus Perry, also at Oxford University Press, for 'Tennyson and *Werther*', *Essays in Criticism*, 70: 3 (July 2020), 302–25 (Chapters 1 and 2); and Professor Valerie Purton, for 'The Spirit of Goethe Looks Forth: Hallam, Carlyle, and *In Memoriam*', *Tennyson Research Bulletin*, 11: 5 (November 2021) (Chapters 1 and 4).

I would also like to thank Radek Malis, Frank Taylor and the late, great John Porteous, for wit, good company and refreshment. And finally, I would like to express my gratitude to the people of Aldworth in Berkshire, and to the staff and owners of the village's wonderful pub, The Bell. By an odd coincidence, Aldworth was the ancestral home of both Emily Tennyson (née Sellwood) and of Lucy Graves (née Bartholomew). The latter was the wife of Richard Graves, the author of the first English translation of Goethe's *Werther*, which Alfred Tennyson admired so much. Tennyson would never have known, however, that the graves of the Sellwood and Bartholomew families lie just a few yards apart in the churchyard of Aldworth Parish Church.

If you see a great master, you will always find that
he used what was good in his predecessors,
and that it was this which made him great.

Goethe

Preface

The influence on Tennyson of *Faust* spanned the years 1824–55, and was mediated, most notably, by the translations of Abraham Hayward (1801–84). Goethe's masterpiece was of central importance to Tennyson's creative life, and the traces that it left in his work were often combined with those of a sizeable group of closely related texts, by authors such as Schiller, Byron, Shelley and Carlyle (as well as Goethe himself).

This book begins with an introductory account of the literary context of this subject, from the first review of *Faust* in 1810 to the death of Tennyson in 1892. I then examine Tennyson's own engagement with Goethe's drama, which was, I think, too profound and extended to be reduced to any single theme. Instead, at least half a dozen threads can be discerned – and it is these that are explored in my six chapters, which are divided into two groups of three. The first group deals mainly with the highly personal poems that Tennyson wrote in response to the death of Arthur Hallam in 1833. In Chapter 1, I argue that there was a link in his mind between the loss of his friend and the tragedy of Margaret in *Faust: Part One* (an episode which two decades later would be an important influence on *Maud*). Chapter 2 looks at 'Ulysses', in which Tennyson combines four different themes: his trances; his belief in a progressive after-life; his preoccupation with the ship that was carrying Hallam's remains; and the need for forward movement that is expressed in one of Faust's most famous monologues. In Chapter 3, I argue that two other poems from 1833 are influenced by *Faust: Part Two* (as is *The Princess*, in which echoes of Goethe are mingled with echoes of Schiller).

Most of the works discussed in these first three chapters suggest that Tennyson regarded *Faust* with profound admiration. But as I argue in Chapters 4 to 6, that sentiment was mixed, at times, with ambivalence, or even antagonism. The former emotion is increasingly apparent in Tennyson's three major poems on religious doubt, which are discussed in Chapter 4. Carlyle's claim that *Faust* is a dramatisation of that subject is a central influence on these texts, but Tennyson's apparent acceptance of this view ensures that his attitude to Goethe's drama becomes ever more equivocal. A similar pattern can be detected in the numerous works in which Tennyson echoes Faustian Nature poetry (which are dealt with in Chapter 5). A certain amount of ambivalence in relation to both of these topics is already apparent in 1833 or earlier, but it finds its fullest expression in *In Memoriam*, in sections that can be dated to *c*. 1839–50. That is not to say, however, that Tennyson's attitude to Goethe's drama was characterised by any kind of steady overall deterioration. Indeed, as I argue in Chapter 6, his only truly *antagonistic* responses to *Faust* are to be found in a small group of *earlier* poems, most of which are suggestive of deep misgivings about Goethe's sexual morality.

The conception of influence that is employed in this book makes no claims to general applicability, but is intended merely as a useful way of understanding the impact of *Faust* on Tennyson. His engagement with Goethe's drama is examined not in isolation, but in the context of three much broader sources of influence. There are, first of all, the numerous texts that he tended to associate with *Faust*. Second, in many of the poems that I discuss, he is drawing, in addition, on a wide range of Western literature. And third, Tennyson was also subject to other, non-textual forms of influence, such as people, places and personal experience.

My core evidence for the influence on Tennyson of *Faust* is provided by the large number of parallel passages that can be found in his poems. In the words of his friend F. T. Palgrave, '[i]t is among those poets with whom traceable references to their ancestors in art are frequent, allusions which, echo-like, multiply and sweeten their own strains [. . .] that Tennyson, all know, is to be classed' (cited in *Mem.*, II, 497). That insight has been expanded upon by Mustard (1904); Bradley (1910); Loane (1928); Paden (1942); Mattes (1951); Kennedy (1978); Shatto and Shaw (1982); Ricks (1987 and 2002); Douglas-Fairhurst and Perry (2009); Winnick (2019); and Thomas (2019). This considerable body of scholarship leaves little doubt that Tennyson is a very literary kind of poet, our understanding of whom can be enhanced by studying him in conjunction with the authors who helped to provide him with inspiration.

As R. H. Winnick observes, each of the parallel passages in Tennyson's works may be deemed to be either an 'allusion', an 'echo' or 'merely accidental'.¹ Almost all of the parallels with *Faust* belong, I will argue, to the second of these three categories. They can be easily distinguished from the third, which was ably defined by Tennyson himself, when he rejected an alleged influence on his work as being, quite simply, 'not known' to him.² Goethe's drama, however, most certainly *was* known to him – and known, moreover, in considerable detail. It is not, therefore, for 'merely accidental' parallels that I will be arguing.

In contrast to these chance similarities, an 'allusion' is predicated on familiarity with its referent. It is (to quote Sir Christopher Ricks) the opposite of plagiarism, for 'the alluder hopes that the reader will recognize something, the plagiarist that the reader will not'.³ It goes without saying that in drawing inspiration from *Faust*, Tennyson was certainly not plagiarising it, but it would be equally misleading to claim that he was alluding to it. This point can be clarified if we compare a passage in which he *does* make an allusion to one in which he echoes Goethe's drama. In 'Locksley Hall' (*PT*, 271) he writes:

>   this is truth the poet sings,
> That a sorrow's crown of sorrow is remembering happier things.
> (ll. 75–6)

As Tennyson himself informs us (*EE*, II, 342), he wants us to recognise that he is here referring to some famous lines from the *Inferno* ('No greater grief than to remember days | Of joy, when mis'ry is at hand' (*DC*, Vol. I, Canto V, p. 28 / ll. 118–19)). Contrast this clear allusion with these lines from 'Oh! that 'twere possible' (*PT*, 227):

> And to weep, and weep and weep
>   My whole soul out to thee. (ll. 63–4)

---

¹ R. H. Winnick, *Tennyson's Poems: New Textual Parallels* (Cambridge: Open Book Publishers, 2019), p. 1.
² Cited in Robert Douglas-Fairhurst, 'Introduction', in *Tennyson Among the Poets*, ed. Robert Douglas-Fairhurst and Seamus Perry (Oxford: Oxford University Press, 2009), pp. 1–13 (p. 6).
³ Christopher Ricks, *Allusion to the Poets* (Oxford: Oxford University Press, 2002), p. 1.

As I will argue in Chapter 1, when these words are considered in conjunction with other evidence, there can be little doubt that Tennyson is drawing on the following lines from *Faust*:

> I weep, I weep, I weep,
> My heart is bursting within me! (ll. 3606–7 / p. 153)

The resemblance is, however, relatively subtle, so there is no reason to believe that Tennyson is hoping that the reader will recognise the echo. I will not, therefore, be describing him as 'alluding' to *Faust*, but will prefer, instead, such terms as 'to echo' and 'to draw on'.

The textual evidence for the influence of Goethe's drama on Tennyson extends far beyond these parallel passages, for they are typically found in conjunction with similarities of theme, form, imagery and narrative. Additional links to *Faust* are provided by Tennyson's manuscripts, correspondence and marginalia, as well as the writings, letters and journals of those who knew him. And finally, this demonstration of the *fact* of influence would be of little consequence if it did not also provide the basis for an exploration of its *meaning* – and it is that which lies at the heart of this book.

Abbreviations

CG   Sarah Austin (trans.), *Characteristics of Goethe: From the German of Falk, von Müller, &c. With Notes, Original and Translated, Illustrative of German Literature*, 3 vols (London: Wilson, 1833).

DC   *The Vision; or Hell, Purgatory, and Paradise, of Dante Alighieri: Translated by the Rev. Henry Francis Cary, A.M.*, 3rd edn, 3 vols (London: Taylor, 1831) / Dante, *The Divine Comedy: The Vision of Dante*, trans. Henry Cary, ed. Ralph Pite (London: Everyman, 1994). Volume and canto numbers are followed by a page reference to the 1831 edition, and a line reference (or, for prose, a page reference) to the 1994 edition. The text is quoted from the former. Volume I is referred to by the more familiar title the *Inferno*.

EE   Alfred Lord Tennyson, *Works*, annotated Alfred Lord Tennyson, ed. Hallam Lord Tennyson, Eversley Edition, 9 vols (London: Macmillan, 1907–8).

FA   Johann Wolfgang Goethe, *Sämtliche Werke. Briefe, Tagebücher und Gespräche*, ed. Friedmar Apel, Hendrik Birus and others, Frankfurter Ausgabe, 40 vols in 2 parts (Frankfurt am Main: Deutscher Klassiker Verlag, 1987–2013).

Hay. 1   *Faust: A Dramatic Poem, by Goethe. Translated into English Prose, with Remarks on Former Translations, and Notes, by the Translator of Savigny's 'Of the Vocation of Our Age for Legislation and Jurisprudence.'* (London: Moxon, 1833); repr. as Johann Wolfgang von Goethe, *Faust: 1833*, trans. Abraham Hayward (Oxford: Woodstock, 1993).

Hay. 2   [Abraham Hayward], 'ART. IV.—*Goethe's nachgelassene Werke*. (Goethe's Posthumous Works.) Bände I—V. 18mo. Stuttgart and Tubingen [*sic*]. 1833', *Foreign Quarterly Review*, 12: 23 (July 1833), 81–109.

LAHH   *The Letters of Arthur Henry Hallam*, ed. Jack Kolb (Columbus: Ohio State University Press, 1981).

LAT	*The Letters of Alfred Lord Tennyson*, ed. Cecil Y. Lang and Edgar F. Shannon, Jr, 3 vols (Oxford: Clarendon Press, 1982–90).
Mem.	Hallam Lord Tennyson, *Alfred Lord Tennyson: A Memoir by his Son*, 2 vols (London: Macmillan, 1897).
PBS	Percy Bysshe Shelley (trans.), 'Scenes from the Faust of Goethe', in *The Complete Works of Percy Bysshe Shelley*, ed. Roger Ingpen and Walter E. Peck, Julian Edition, 10 vols (London: Benn; New York: Scribner, 1926–30), IV (1928), 322–40.
PT	*The Poems of Tennyson*, ed. Christopher Ricks, Longman Annotated English Poets, 2nd edn, 3 vols (Harlow: Longman, 1987). Numbers refer to poems, not pages. However, in citations from the 'Alternative Drafts' and 'Fragments, Trivia, &c' that are printed in the appendices, the volume number (invariably III) is given, followed by a page number.
S & S	Alfred Lord Tennyson, *In Memoriam*, ed. Susan Shatto and Marion Shaw (Oxford: Clarendon Press, 1982).
SR	*WTC* (see below), I / *Sartor Resartus: The Life and Opinions of Herr Teufelsdröckh*, Introduction and Notes Rodger L. Tarr; text established Mark Engel and Rodger L. Tarr (Berkeley: University of California Press, 2000). Book, chapter and page references to *WTC*, I are followed by page and line references to the 2000 edition. The text is quoted from the latter (and references to its editorial material are given as '*SR*, ed. Tarr').
TA	Christopher Ricks and Aidan Day (eds), *The Tennyson Archive*, 31 vols (New York: Garland, 1987–93).
TRC	The Tennyson Research Centre, Lincolnshire Archives, St Rumbold Street, Lincoln, LN2 5AB, United Kingdom.
W	*Die Leiden des jungen Werthers. Fassung A*, FA (see above), 1, VIII (1994), 10–266 / *The Sorrows of Werter: A German Story* [trans. Richard Graves], 11th edn(?) (London: Dodsley, 1789); repr. as Johann Wolfgang von Goethe, *The Sorrows of Werter: 1789*, trans. Daniel Malthus [*sic*] (Oxford: Woodstock, 1991). Part, page and line references to the German text (together, where applicable, with the date of the individual letter) are followed by a page reference to the translation by Richard Graves. Werther's final, undated letter is referred to as the 'Farewell Letter' (abbreviated to 'F. L.').
WAH	*The Writings of Arthur Hallam*, ed. T. H. Vail Motter (New York: Modern Language Association of America; London: Oxford University Press, 1943).

WM   *Wilhelm Meisters Lehrjahre*, FA (see above), 1, IX (1992), 355–992; *Wilhelm Meisters Wanderjahre. Erste Fassung*, FA, 1, X (1989), 9–259 / *WTC* (see below), XXIII–XXIV. Volume, book, chapter, page and line references to the German text are followed by volume and page references to *WTC*, XXIII or XXIV.

WTC   *The Works of Thomas Carlyle*, ed. Henry Duff Traill, Centenary Edition, 30 vols (London: Chapman and Hall, 1896–9; digitally repr. in Cambridge Library Collection, Cambridge: Cambridge University Press, 2010).

References to *Faust* are preceded, where necessary, by the abbreviation *F*, and consist, firstly, of a line reference to *Faust. Eine Tragödie*, FA, 1, VII / I (1994), 9–464. This is followed by a page reference, which, unless otherwise stated, is to Hay. 1. In references to PBS, the scene number (I or II) is given, followed by a line reference.

Except where otherwise indicated, information on the dating of Tennyson's poems is taken from the relevant headnotes in *PT*. Archaic spellings of Goethe's name (Göthe, Goethé, Goëthe), and of the title of his first novel (*Werter*), have been modernised throughout. The small number of uncredited translations are my own.

Introduction: *Faust* and British Literature, c. 1810–1892

The story of the reception, translation, performance and influence of Goethe's *Faust* in nineteenth-century Britain begins around 1810. Tennyson becomes a part of this narrative at a relatively early stage, for it is probable that he first heard of the work in 1824, and read a substantial translation of *Part One* no later than 1830. By that time, however, Goethe's drama had already attracted the interest of a considerable number of British readers, at least four of whom are major figures: Coleridge, Shelley, Byron and Carlyle. The response to *Faust* of all but the first of these authors provides important context for Tennyson's own engagement with it, and their names will recur on numerous occasions in this book. This Introduction will begin, therefore, by looking at British reactions to Goethe's drama in the years from *c.* 1810 to *c.* 1824. In my discussion of the three decades from the latter date to 1855, an outline of Tennyson's experience of *Faust* will be interwoven with analyses of a number of relevant texts, including Abraham Hayward's *Faust: A Dramatic Poem*, Carlyle's *Sartor Resartus*, Browning's *Paracelsus*, P. J. Bailey's *Festus*, Clough's *Dipsychus*, and poetry and prose by Arnold. The publication of *Maud* in 1855 effectively marks the end of the story of *Faust* and Tennyson, but the drama continued to exert a profound influence on his contemporaries, some of whom – including Lewes, Eliot and Wilde – will be referred to in subsequent chapters. This Introduction will conclude, therefore, by offering a brief summary of developments up to Tennyson's death in 1892.

The Anglo-German dimension of the Faust legend was not a product of the nineteenth century. The first account of the life of Johann Georg Faust (*c.* 1480(?)–*c.* 1540(?)), which was published in Frankfurt in

1587, was quickly translated into English, and provided the source for Marlowe's *Tragical History of Dr Faustus* (early 1590s). English travelling players then re-imported this drama into Germany, where the story became a theatrical staple, enjoying especial popularity in puppet versions. It was through this tradition that the young Goethe (*b.* 1749) first became acquainted with the figure who would preoccupy him intermittently during the whole of his adult life.[1]

The earliest version of his drama – which is known as the *Original Faust* – was probably written between 1773 and 1775 (although it was not published until 1887).[2] *Faust. Ein Fragment* appeared in 1790, but it was not until 1808 that Goethe published *Faust. Der Tragödie erster Teil* (*Faust: Part One*), which began to attract notice in Britain a couple of years later.[3] Act III of the *Zweiter Teil* (*Part Two*) appeared in 1827, and lines 4613–6036 of Act I were published the following year. Goethe's final revisions to his manuscript of *Part Two* date from January 1832, just two months before his death on 22 March, and the completed text was published at Easter of the following year.[4]

In the three decades prior to the appearance of the *Erster Teil* in 1808, Goethe had been known in Britain for a single work, *Die Leiden des jungen Werthers* (1774). This sentimental epistolary novel (which tells of the protagonist's love for the beautiful Charlotte, and his despairing suicide after her marriage to another man) was usually read in the pioneering translation by Richard Graves (1715–1804), which was entitled *The Sorrows of Werther* (1779).[5] Although this work had quickly achieved great popularity, its critical reception had often been hostile, with many readers voicing objections to it on moral and religious grounds. European political developments did much to harden these attitudes, for in the decade and a half from about 1798 to 1812, British readers often associated

---

[1] John R. Williams, *Goethe's 'Faust'* (London: Allen & Unwin, 1987), pp. 3–8, 12–13, 16.
[2] Nicholas Boyle, *Goethe: The Poet and the Age* (Oxford: Clarendon Press, 1991–), I: *The Poetry of Desire (1749–1790)* (1991), I, 143, 185, 222, 218.
[3] Williams, pp. 30–1, 34.
[4] Ibid. p. 37; FA, 1, VII / I, 814.
[5] The anonymous 1779 translation has often been misattributed to Graves's friend Daniel Malthus (see Tom Baynes, 'The Authorship of the First English Translation of Goethe', *Publications of the English Goethe Society*, 90: 2 (September 2021), 91–108).

German literature with the more radical proponents of the French Revolution.⁶

Given this notably unpropitious background, it is hardly surprising that the initial reception accorded to *Faust: Part One* was predominantly negative. It was, therefore, only gradually that the first translations (all of them inadequate and incomplete) began to appear, and a full quarter of a century would elapse before the drama became the object of widespread – but by no means unqualified – admiration.

In the very first review of *Part One*, which was published in August 1810, the prominent German scholar William Taylor dismissed the play as 'impure trash'.⁷ Similarly, the chapter on *Faust* in Germaine de Staël's widely read *De l'Allemagne* (1810) (translated as *Germany* (1813)) is frequently critical, and it concludes with the wish that 'such productions may not be multiplied'.⁸ This judgement was echoed the following year by the *Quarterly Review*, which remarked: 'we neither envy nor admire the talents that produced [*Faust*], at the expense of feeling, morality, and religion'.⁹ In an article in the *London Magazine* in 1820, these concerns were directed, for the first time, at what would prove to be a long-enduring target, the 'Prologue in Heaven' (F, ll. 243–353 / pp. 1–5). The pseudonymous reviewer suggested that this scene, in particular, showed the Germans to be guilty of 'contempt for things which most people consider sacred', for in it, 'the rebellious Spirit of Mischief' Mephistopheles appears 'before the throne of the Almighty'.¹⁰

Despite his knowledge of the German language and its literature, Coleridge's view of *Faust* did not differ significantly from that of most of his contemporaries. His earliest recorded comments on the

---

⁶ Catherine Waltraud Proescholdt-Obermann, *Goethe and his British Critics: The Reception of Goethe's Works in British Periodicals, 1779 to 1855* (Frankfurt am Main: Lang, 1992), pp. 77–88.
⁷ [William Taylor], '*Faust*, &c.; i. e. *Faustus: A Tragedy*, by Goethe. 16mo. pp. 312. Tubingen [*sic*]. 1808', *Monthly Review*, 62 (August 1810), 491–5 (p. 492).
⁸ Baroness Staël Holstein, *Germany* [trans. Francis Hodgson(?)], 3 vols (London: Murray, 1813), Vol. II, Ch. XXIII, pp. 181–226, esp. p. 226; Ben Hewitt, *Byron, Shelley, and Goethe's 'Faust': An Epic Connection*, Studies in Comparative Literature 33 (Oxford: Legenda, 2015), pp. 41–56.
⁹ Anon., 'ART. VI.—*Cours de Littérature Dramatique*. Par A. W. Schlegel. *Traduit d'Allemand*', *Quarterly Review*, 12: 23 (October 1814), 112–46 (pp. 144–5).
¹⁰ Janus Weathercock, 'Sentimentalities on the Fine Arts: To be Continued When he is in the Humour', *London Magazine*, 1: 2 (February 1820), 136–40 (p. 137).

play (which the accomplished Germanist Henry Crabb Robinson wrote down in his diary in August 1812) are notably ambivalent: he 'acknowledged the genius of Goethe as he has never before acknowledged it. At the same time, the want of religion and enthusiasm in Goethe, is in Coleridge's estimation an irreparable defect. [. . .] [He] talks of writing a new Faust!'[11] Coleridge, we are told, would later refer to this unfulfilled project in a conversation in February 1833: '*My* Faust', he declared, 'was Michael Scott' (*c.* 1175–*c.* 1235; a scholar, alchemist and metaphysician).[12] He provided his interlocutors with a lengthy synopsis of this unwritten drama, which would have ended with the protagonist attaining 'the conviction of Redemption of Sinners through God's grace' (Coleridge, *Collected Works*, XIV (1990), I, 337–8). Returning to Goethe's *Faust*, he remarked: 'The German is very pure. But there is no whole in Faust—the scenes are mere magic-lantern pictures—and a large part of the work I think very flat and dull' (ibid. p. 339). He had once been asked to translate it, but had, he said, declined:

> I debated with myself whether it became my moral character to render it into English—and so far certainly lend my countenance to language—much of which I thought vulgar, licentious and most blasphemous. I need not tell you, that I never put pen to paper as translator of Faust. (ibid. p. 343)

Frederick Burwick and James C. McKusick argue that this denial should not be taken at face value, and attribute to Coleridge the anonymous *Faustus: From the German of Goethe* (1821).[13] This translation was occasioned by the popularity of a series of twenty-six illustrations to *Faust* by Moritz Retzsch, which had been published in book form in Germany in 1816. Four years later, these drawings also appeared

---

[11] Henry Crabb Robinson, *Diary, Reminiscences, and Correspondence of Henry Crabb Robinson*, ed. Thomas Sadler, 2nd edn, 3 vols (London: Macmillan, 1869), I, 395, 397. After dining with Tennyson on 31 January 1845, Robinson wrote: 'He is an admirer of Goethe, and I had a long tête-à-tête with him about the great poet' (ibid. III, 260–1).

[12] *The Collected Works of Samuel Taylor Coleridge*, ed. Kathleen Coburn, Bollingen Edition, 16 vols (London: Princeton University Press, 1969–2002), XIV: *Table Talk (I and II). Recorded by Henry Nelson Coleridge (and John Taylor Coleridge)*, ed. Carl Woodring (1990), I, 337.

[13] Samuel Taylor Coleridge (trans.), *Faustus: From the German of Goethe*, ed. Frederick Burwick and James C. McKusick (Oxford: Clarendon Press, 2007), pp. xv–liv.

in two rival British editions: one of these provided only brief captions, but the other, which was entitled *Outlines, Illustrative of 'Faust'*, offered a more comprehensive 'analysis' of the play, together with translations of substantial excerpts.[14] In *Faustus: From the German of Goethe*, Retzsch's illustrations are accompanied by a translation of slightly less than half of the text, the absent passages being represented by sometimes tendentious prose summaries (although the 'Prologue in Heaven' is passed over entirely, as being 'repugnant to notions of propriety such as are entertained in this country' (Coleridge, *Faustus*, p. 7)).

Although the attribution of this work to Coleridge has proven highly controversial, it should be emphasised that it attracted much less attention in the nineteenth century than it has done in the twenty-first. As Burwick himself acknowledges, its appearance 'was not greeted with great public fanfare', and it is notable that in 1833, Sarah Austin (who was a leading British authority on Goethe) professed her ignorance of it.[15] The first edition of *Faustus* did, nevertheless, sell out, and a second was published in 1824.[16] In the meantime, however, a more complete translation had appeared, *Faust: A Drama* (1823; second edition 1825), by Lord Francis Leveson Gower. Although it, too, omitted a number of passages (including most of the 'Prologue in Heaven'), and has long since been acknowledged to have been poor, it was to remain the standard English version for the next ten years.[17] Retzsch's illustrations were, however, widely admired, so many readers purchased copies of both.[18]

One admirer of them was Shelley, who acquired a copy of what might have been either the 1820 *Outlines* or the 1821 *Faustus*: 'What etchings those are!' he wrote from Pisa in April 1822, 'I am never satiated with looking at them.'[19] He had been 'reading over and over again [the German text of] Faust, and always with sensations which no

---

[14] Ibid. pp. xix, 139–222.
[15] Ibid. p. liii; *CG*, III, 43, fn.
[16] Coleridge, *Faustus*, p. liii, and fn.
[17] William Frederic Hauhart, *The Reception of Goethe's 'Faust' in England in the First Half of the Nineteenth Century* (New York: Columbia University Press, 1909), pp. 99–104; Hay. 1, p. x.
[18] Hauhart, p. 39.
[19] *The Complete Works of Percy Bysshe Shelley*, ed. Roger Ingpen and Walter E. Peck, Julian Edition, 10 vols (London: Benn; New York: Scribner, 1926–30), X (1926), Letter no. DLXXXIV, p. 372.

other composition excites' (ibid. p. 371). He deprecated the translation, however, and was spurred by the omission of most of 'May-Day Night', and of the whole of the 'Prologue in Heaven', to produce his own versions of these scenes. The former was published separately in the periodical *The Liberal* in October 1822, and the two scenes first appeared together in *Posthumous Poems* (1824), under the title 'Scenes from the Faust of Goethe'. Although less than perfect, Shelley's 'Scenes' are widely regarded as the finest English translations of the play to have appeared in Goethe's lifetime.

They were not, however, his first translations from *Faust*. At some point early in his career, he had produced a near-complete prose version of about the first quarter of *Part One*, from the 'Dedication' to line 1213.[20] This was clearly written at a very early stage of his acquisition of German: it is likely that he was heavily reliant on a dictionary, and he makes numerous errors. Indeed, it reads more like a crib than a proper translation, for it faithfully preserves the German syntax of the original, and is, therefore, an extremely odd text.

The many hours of hard work that must have gone into this substantial fragment suggest that Shelley (to quote M. Roxana Klapper) felt an 'overriding desire to [. . .] comprehend the entire drama of *Faust*'.[21] It is by no means difficult to see why he was so strongly attracted to the play and its protagonist. In the scene 'Night', there are clear indications that Faust has no conventional religious faith: 'me fails [lacks] belief [. . .] I Fears me neither for Hell nor the Devil' (ll. 765, 369 / *Shelley Manuscripts*, XXI, p. 155, l. 663; p. 131, l. 202). He rejects academic study, and yearns, instead, to 'perceive what the world I In innermost compartments holds' (ll. 382–3 / *Shelley Manuscripts*, XXI, p. 131, ll. 215–16). This impassioned attempt to connect with the divine powers of Nature is a central theme of Shelley's work, and one which is often expressed in terms that are

---

[20] *The Bodleian Shelley Manuscripts: A Facsimile Edition, with Full Transcriptions and Scholarly Apparatus*, ed. Donald H. Reiman, 23 vols (New York: Garland, 1986–2002), XXI: *Miscellaneous Poetry, Prose and Translations from Bodleian MS. Shelley adds. c. 4, etc.*, ed. E. B. Murray (1995), pp. 120–81. The date of this manuscript is disputed; it was written in either 1810–11, or 1815–16 (ibid. p. 476). It includes so many mistakes that they have not been individually noted in quotations.

[21] M. Roxana Klapper, *The German Literary Influence on Shelley*, Salzburg Studies in English Literature: Romantic Reassessment, 43 (Salzburg: Universität Salzburg, 1975), p. 113.

suggestive of the influence of *Faust*.²² Shelley also seems to have taken a strong interest in the provocative subversion of Christian theology that is the 'Prologue in Heaven'. As Jean-Marie Carré observes, the Chorus of the three Archangels with which it opens is a source for the chorus of three spirits that is the 'Ode to Heaven' (1819), whilst F. W. Stokoe points to the influence of the scene as a whole on the discarded 'Prologue to *Hellas*' (1821) (Shelley, *Complete Works*, II (1927), 291–2; III (1927), 11–16).²³

It is in the 'Prologue in Heaven' that Mephistopheles refers to himself as the 'Snake' (l. 335 / PBS, I, l. 95), and this description was adopted by Byron as a nickname for Shelley. This provides, in turn, just one example of the way in which the two poets' experiences of Goethe's drama were closely intertwined. Shelley alludes to Byron's name for him in the opening line of his poem 'To Edward Williams' ('The serpent is shut out from Paradise'), which also includes two near-quotations from *Faust* (1822; Shelley, *Complete Works*, IV (1928), 98–100).²⁴ Similarly, William D. Brewer suggests that in Shelley's translation of the 'Prologue', Mephistopheles' lines are partly modelled on the written and spoken language of Byron, that 'undisputed master of the conversational style'.²⁵

Although Byron had been taught German as a child, he claimed to know 'absolutely nothing' of the language 'except oaths': '[There is

---

²² See Chapter 5, p. 174, fn 54.
²³ Jean-Marie Carré, *Gœthe en Angleterre: étude de littérature comparée* (Paris: Plon-Nourrit, 1920), p. 80; F. W. Stokoe, *German Influence in the English Romantic Period 1788–1818* (Cambridge: Cambridge University Press, 1926), pp. 154–5. In the autumn of 1821, Shelley and his sister-in-law Claire Clairmont read the German text of *Part One*. A few months later she produced, with his encouragement, what would appear to have been the first complete English translation of it, but the manuscript has never been found (see Shelley, *Complete Works*, X (1926), Letter no. DLXXX, p. 366 (Postmark 26 March 1822(?)); Richard Holmes, *Shelley: The Pursuit* (London: Harper Perennial, 2005), pp. 678, 694).
²⁴ Percy Bysshe Shelley, *The Major Works*, ed. Zachary Leader and Michael O'Neill (Oxford: Oxford University Press, 2003), p. 813. When this poem was first published (*Fraser's Magazine*, 6: 34 (November 1832), 599–600), the footnote 'See Faust' (p. 599) was appended to line 35, which echoes lines 3181–4 / pages 130–1. Adolf Droop points out that line 41 draws on lines 1098–9 / page 34 (Adolf Droop, *Die Belesenheit Percy Bysshe Shelley's nach den direkten Zeugnissen und den bisherigen Forschungen* (Weimar: Wagner, 1906), pp. 130–1). See also Carré, p. 79, fn.
²⁵ William D. Brewer, *The Shelley–Byron Conversation* (Gainesville: University Press of Florida, 1994), p. 112.

n]othing I envy [Shelley] so much', he is said to have remarked, 'as to be able to read that astonishing production [*Faust*] in the original'.²⁶ The influence that Goethe's play exerted on him is therefore usually seen as beginning on 14 August 1816, when his acquaintance Matthew Lewis arrived at his home in Cologny, near Geneva.²⁷ As Byron recalled four years later, over the next few days, Lewis 'translated most of [*Part One*] to me *viva voce*' (Byron, *Letters and Journals*, VII (1977), 113, 7 June 1820).

Byron was at this time in a severe state of emotional turmoil. So as he listened to Lewis's oral translation of *Faust*, he might well have identified with the play's tortured central character, who in his pride and isolation resembles, at times, the Byronic hero.²⁸ The two figures are to some extent merged in the protagonist of *Manfred*, which was written between the summer of 1816 and the spring of the following year.²⁹ Byron's debt to *Faust* in this work is widely acknowledged, but it has sometimes been a little exaggerated. As one would expect, given his lack of access to the German text, the influence is generally broad and unspecific, and there are almost no direct verbal echoes. Byron himself admitted that 'The first Scene [. . .] & that of Faustus are very similar' (Byron, *Letters and Journals*, VII (1977), 113, 7 June 1820). In Act I, scene 2 (ll. 100–25), Manfred, like Faust (ll. 686–784 / pp. 19–22), makes an abortive suicide attempt, and his lengthy, lyrical address to the sunset in Act III, scene 2 (ll. 3–30) could owe something to Faust's monologue 'Oh, happy he' (ll. 1064–99 / pp. 33–4). But the accusations of 'gross plagiary' with which the work was greeted in the British press were a gross exaggeration.³⁰

Goethe read *Manfred* in October 1817 and was fascinated. He regarded Byron as the foremost writer of the age, and the British

---

[26] *Byron's Letters and Journals*, ed. Leslie A. Marchand, 13 vols (London: Murray, 1973–94), VIII (1978), 26 (12 January 1821); Thomas Medwin, *Medwin's Conversations of Lord Byron*, ed. Ernest J. Lovell, Jr (Princeton: Princeton University Press, 1966), p. 142.

[27] David Ellis, *Byron in Geneva: That Summer of 1816* (Liverpool: Liverpool University Press, 2011), p. 100.

[28] E. M. Butler, *Byron and Goethe: Analysis of a Passion* (London: Bowes & Bowes, 1956), pp. 29–30.

[29] Lord Byron, *The Complete Poetical Works*, ed. Jerome J. McGann and Barry Weller, 7 vols (Oxford: Clarendon Press, 1980–93), IV (1986), 51–102, 462–5.

[30] Anon., 'The Drama. ART. VIII.—*Manfred: A Dramatic Poem*. By Lord Byron. 8vo. pp. 80. London, Murray, 1817', *Critical Review*, 5: 6 (June 1817), 622–9 (p. 623).

poet took the same view of him.[31] They never met, however, and such interaction as there was between them was initially troubled and distant. In his review of *Manfred* (which was not published until 1820), Goethe, too, argued that it was indebted to his play (FA, 1, XX, p. 454, ll. 18–31 / cited in Butler, p. 58). He had read the work in conjunction with Lady Caroline Lamb's Gothic novel *Glenarvon*, in the mistaken belief that the latter provided a reliable guide to the events of Byron's life, and he therefore expressed the remarkable misapprehension that the poet had once killed a man in Florence.[32] Taken as a whole, though, Goethe's article was by no means unwelcome to the British poet, for it was considerably more positive than the reviews of *Don Juan* which were by then appearing. Dismissing the allegation of murder as simply laughable, Byron responded to the piece with considerable generosity. He proceeded to pen a dedication to Goethe – full of mischievous humour, but essentially friendly – which he intended to use as a preface to *Marino Faliero* (1821). It was omitted on the advice of his publisher John Murray, and the more unequivocally respectful dedication of *Sardanapalus* (1821) also remained unprinted.

Byron's interest in *Faust*, however, showed no sign of diminishing, for both *Cain: A Mystery* and *The Vision of Judgment* (written 1821) bear numerous marks of the play's influence.[33] Like *Part One*, much of the former work consists of lengthy dialogues between the protagonist and the devil, Byron's portrait of whom is – to quote a line from *Don Juan* – 'Much in the mode of Goethe's Mephistopheles' (Byron, *Poetical Works*, V (1986), no. 341, p. 527, XIII. 7. 56). In his study of *Byron, Shelley, and Goethe's 'Faust'*, Ben Hewitt goes further, and argues in considerable detail that *Cain* and *Faust* exhibit 'more complex and far-reaching parallels'.[34] *The Vision of Judgment* was originally intended to be published

---

[31] FA, 1, XXI, p. 504, ll. 21–30 (esp. l. 23) / cited in Butler, p. 85; FA, 2, XII (XXXIX), p. 250, ll. 35–7 / Johann Wolfgang Goethe, *Conversations of Goethe with Eckermann and Soret*, trans. John Oxenford, 2 vols (London: Smith, Elder, 1850), I, 425 (5 July 1827); Byron, *Letters and Journals*, VII (1977), 113 (7 June 1820); X (1980), 213 (22 July 1823).

[32] Butler, pp. 32, 37–41.

[33] See Fred Parker, '"Much in the mode of Goethe's Mephistopheles": *Faust* and Byron', in *International Faust Studies: Adaptation, Reception, Translation*, ed. Lorna Fitzsimmons (London: Continuum, 2008), pp. 107–23 (pp. 111–18); Hewitt, pp. 79–106.

[34] Hewitt, p. 80.

alongside Shelley's translation of the 'Prologue in Heaven', and as Fred Parker observes, in sections 32–5, '[t]he manner of invoking Job, and the idea of polite relations between the devil and his opposite, are unmistakably after Goethe'.[35]

As Byron himself acknowledged, the influence of the German poet is even more perceptible in *The Deformed Transformed* (Byron, *Poetical Works*, VI (1991), no. 388, pp. 517–77), for when this unfinished play was belatedly published in February 1824, it carried the following inscription: '*This production is founded partly on* [. . .] *the "Faust" of the great Goethe*' (ibid. p. 517). According to Thomas Medwin, Shelley did not hesitate to tell Byron that it was merely 'a bad imitation of "Faust"' (Medwin, p. 153),[36] and the description is not, perhaps, entirely unwarranted. As in *Manfred*, the protagonist makes an abortive suicide attempt, which is foiled, on this occasion, by the appearance of the devil (I. 1. 52–93), the portrayal of whom is indebted, once again, to Mephistopheles.[37] Elsewhere, there are echoes of the scenes 'May-Day Night' and 'Before the Gate', and the influence of *Faust* can also be detected in the tetrameter couplets and feminine rhymes of the '*Chorus of Spirits*' which opens Part II (I. 1. 163–4; stage direction before line 481; 2. 123–70; III. 1. 1–22; II. 1. 1–122).

Goethe's fascination with Byron had, in the meantime, been diminished by his reading of *Don Juan*, whose poetry he admired but whose cynicism he deprecated. However, when the unpublished dedication of *Sardanapalus* was forwarded to him towards the end of 1822, he was much moved, and the public dedication to him of *Werner* soon followed.[38] In 1823, he sent Byron a poetic greeting, which reached him aboard the *Hercules*, which was about to depart from Livorno harbour (FA, 1, II, 583–4 / cited in Butler, p. 90). 'I am returning to Greece', explained Byron in his hastily written reply; '[. . .] if ever I come back I will pay a visit to Weimar to offer the sincere homage of one of the many Millions of your admirers' (Byron, *Letters and Journals*, X (1980), 213, 22 July). In Cephalonia shortly before

---

[35] Parker, pp. 115, 116. See also Medwin, p. 130.
[36] See, however, E. J. Trelawny's caveat about Medwin's testimony (Medwin, p. 155, fn 368).
[37] For example, blood is shed at the commencement of his relationship with the protagonist Arnold; he is likened to a snake; and in Part I he has – like Mephistopheles in the 'Prologue in Heaven' – the last words (I. 1. 146–56; 2. 236–40, 289–91, 310–29).
[38] Butler, pp. 72–85.

his death, he discussed German literature with the future historian George Finlay, who reported that the poet was 'perfectly acquainted [. . .] with every passage of "Faust"'.[39] The close relationship between Byron and the drama would subsequently become a reciprocal one: when Goethe came to complete *Part Two*, he alluded to *Sardanapalus* in Act IV, and in Act III he paid a posthumous tribute to Byron, depicting him as the libidinous, dynamic but tragically short-lived character Euphorion.[40]

The enthusiasm of Byron and Shelley notwithstanding, a mainstream acceptance of *Faust* still lay in the future, although from about 1820 onwards, the condemnatory voices became mingled with more appreciative ones.[41] As with the two exiled Romantic poets, however, the favourable appraisals tended to emanate from outside England, with Irish and – in particular – Scottish authors playing a prominent role. The Anglo-Irishman Charles Robert Maturin's Gothic novel *Melmoth the Wanderer*, which appeared in 1820, owes a substantial debt to *Faust*.[42] The same year, John Anster, a native of County Cork, published his translations of extensive excerpts from the play in *Blackwood's Edinburgh Magazine*.[43] Reading them, another Irishman, Byron's friend Thomas Moore, was reduced to tears.[44] In Scotland, interest in German drama had been aroused as early as 21 April 1788, when Henry Mackenzie (author of the sentimental novel *The Man of Feeling*) gave a lecture on the subject at the Royal Society of Edinburgh. In the audience that day was the young Walter Scott, who was spurred to learn German. His translation of Goethe's play *Götz von Berlichingen* appeared in 1799, but he does not appear to have read *Faust: Part One* until 1818, and his verdict on it was ambivalent.[45] However, the man who recorded that verdict for posterity, his

---

[39] Cited in Karl Elze, *Lord Byron: A Biography. With a Critical Essay on his Place in Literature* [n. trans.], (London: Murray, 1872), p. 480.
[40] F, ll. 10176, 9598–938 / *Faust: A Tragedy by J. W. Goethe. Part II, as Completed in 1831* [trans. William Bell Macdonald], 2nd edn (London: Pickering, 1842), pp. 262, 234–50; Williams, pp. 185–6, 163, 175.
[41] Hauhart, pp. 35–8.
[42] Carré, pp. 81–2.
[43] Reprinted in Coleridge, *Faustus*, pp. 223–78.
[44] *Memoirs, Journal, and Correspondence of Thomas Moore*, ed. Lord John Russell, 8 vols (London: Longman, Brown, Green and Longmans, 1853–6), III (1853), 157 (16 October 1820).
[45] Hauhart, pp. 9–10, 75–6.

son-in-law John Gibson Lockhart, published a largely positive article on *Faust* in the *Quarterly Review* in June 1826.[46]

By that time, the most important figure in the early history of British Goethe reception, Lockhart's fellow-Scot Carlyle, had already begun his public advocacy of the drama. Carlyle started learning German in 1819, and he read *Part One* the following year.[47] He recalled the impact it had on him in the first of his many letters to its author:

> when I read your *Faust* among the mountains of my native Scotland, I could not but fancy I might one day see you, and pour out before you, as before a father, the woes and wanderings of a heart whose mysteries you seemed so thoroughly to comprehend and could so beautifully represent.[48]

During the last ten years of Goethe's life, Carlyle worked determinedly to improve his standing in Britain. Although he did occasionally concede that some aspects of the German's writings were 'unfit for the English taste' (*WTC*, XXIII, 10), his more usual tactic was to go on the offensive, and to argue that it was precisely on account of their moral and religious qualities that these works were deserving of attention.[49]

Carlyle launched this project in 1822 in an article for the *New Edinburgh Review*, the title of which suggested that it was an appraisal of the recently published *Faustus: From the German of Goethe*. However, only the first two of its nineteen pages are devoted to this English version of the play, which he quickly dismisses as 'feeble'.[50]

---

[46] [John Gibson Lockhart], 'ART. VII.—1. *Faust: A Drama*, by Goethe. With Translations from the German', *Quarterly Review*, 34: 67 (June 1826), 136–53.

[47] Hauhart, pp. 52–3.

[48] *The Collected Letters of Thomas and Jane Welsh Carlyle*, ed. Charles Richard Sanders, Duke-Edinburgh Edition (Durham, NC: Duke University Press, 1970–), III (1970), 87 (24 June 1824).

[49] Proescholdt-Obermann, p. 156.

[50] [Thomas Carlyle], 'ART. II.—*Faustus: from the German of Goethe*. London. Boosey and Sons. 1821, 8vo. pp. 86', *New Edinburgh Review*, 2: 4 (April 1822), 316–34 (p. 316). Carlyle condemns *Faustus* as a '*caput mortuum*', and expresses his preference for '[a]n avowedly prose translation' (ibid. p. 316). When these words were published in April 1822, Shelley (as is clear from his letter of the 10th) had recently been working on his 'Scenes' (*Complete Works*, X (1926), Letter no. DLXXXIV, p. 371). I propose that Carlyle's article came to his attention, for he appends to his translation of the Archangels' Chorus a footnote, in which he apologises for giving the reader a '*caput mortuum*', and provides, as an alternative, 'a literal translation' (PBS, I, l. 28, fn).

The remainder of the article is concerned with the German text, upon which Carlyle bestows enthusiastic but not unqualified praise, describing it as 'one of the most singular [works] that have ever appeared in Europe' (ibid. p. 331). He also makes his first attempt to turn the tables on Goethe's moralising critics, by advancing the dubious argument (a development, perhaps, of some remarks by de Staël) that *Faust* contains an implicit demonisation of Enlightenment scepticism. 'In many respects', he writes, 'Mephistophiles [sic] resembles some French *philosophe* of the last century. There is the perfection of the intellectual faculties with a total absence of the moral' (ibid. p. 326).[51]

This claim is reiterated in Carlyle's essay on 'Goethe's "Helena"', which was published in the *Foreign Review* in January 1828 (*WTC*, XXVI, 146–97 (pp. 156–8)). Much of this piece consists of his translations of excerpts from *Part Two*, Act III (which had appeared in Germany the previous year under the title 'Helena: Classical–Romantic Phantasmagoria. Interlude to *Faust*'). The commentary with which he intersperses these represents a thoughtful and patient reading of a difficult text. The essay's concluding promise 'to return, in our next Number, to the consideration of [Goethe's] Works and Character in general' was fulfilled in September 1828 by the article 'Goethe' (*WTC*, XXVI, 197, 198–257). Here, the German author is eulogised as a purveyor of 'religious Wisdom', who 'deserves not mere approval as a pleasing poet and sweet singer; but deep, grateful study, observance, imitation, as a Moralist and Philosopher' (ibid. pp. 208, 228). This view is reiterated in two pieces published in 1832, 'Death of Goethe' and 'Goethe's *Works*' (ibid. XXVII, 374–443). The most substantial of Carlyle's many contributions to British Goethe appreciation – his translations of *Wilhelm Meisters Lehrjahre* (1795–6) and *Wilhelm Meisters Wanderjahre* (1821) – appeared in 1824 and 1827, as *Wilhelm Meister's Apprenticeship* and *Wilhelm Meister's Travels* (ibid. XXIII–XXIV). In the coming decades, his publications would play a central role in shaping initial perceptions of Goethe for a great many young British readers.

One of these was Tennyson. Although he would not become proficient in German until about the early 1840s, his interest in Goethe appears to have begun around 1824, during his childhood in the Lincolnshire village of Somersby. In the manuscript that is known as Trinity Notebook 19 – which also includes the text of his rather

---

[51] See Staël Holstein, *Germany*, Vol. II, Ch. XXIII, pp. 182–5; Hewitt, pp. 41–2.

Faustian play *The Devil and the Lady* (*PT*, 2, *c*. 1823–4) – he has written out, in the original language, the first one and a half lines of Goethe's poem *Hermann und Dorothea* (1798).⁵² And as I will argue in Chapter 5, 'Chorus, in an Unpublished Drama, Written Very Early' (*PT*, 101; *c*. 1824) reveals the influence of the first of Shelley's two 'Scenes', which were published in *Posthumous Poems* in 1824.

The first work by Goethe really to capture the young Tennyson's imagination was, however, Richard Graves's translation of *The Sorrows of Werther*.⁵³ This would appear to have influenced two or three of his contributions to the early collaborative venture *Poems by Two Brothers*, which was published in April 1827. Some six months later, Tennyson left his native Lincolnshire to take up a place at Trinity College in Cambridge (where he would remain until the beginning of 1831).⁵⁴ It was, he tells us, around that time that he began to write the most substantial of his early poems, *The Lover's Tale* (*PT*, 153), the plot of which is a free adaptation of *Werther*. Several other works of the Cambridge period also reveal the influence of that novel, including 'Supposed Confessions of a Second-Rate Sensitive Mind' (*PT*, 78) and 'Sonnet [Alas! how weary are my human eyes]' (*PT*, 185).

Tennyson's interest in Goethe was now deepening appreciably, and a number of his university associates might well have contributed to this development. His tutor William Whewell, for example, would later translate *Hermann und Dorothea*, and Tennyson's friend Richard Monckton Milnes was said to be 'ardent in his admiration' for the German poet.⁵⁵ As we will see in Chapter 1, the same can be said of the man who had a greater influence on Tennyson's life than any other single individual, Arthur Henry Hallam (1811–33), whom

---

[52] Alfred Lord Tennyson, Trinity Notebook 0.15.19 (Cambridge, Trinity College Library), folio 73, verso (this page is not reproduced in *TA*); FA, 1, VIII / I, p. 807, ll. 1–2. Tennyson cites, and criticises, lines 1 and 4 of *Hermann* in *Mem.*, II, 11; see also *PT*, 332, l. 5).

[53] For a more detailed account of this subject, see Tom Baynes, 'Tennyson and *Werther*', *Essays in Criticism*, 70: 3 (July 2020), 302–25; 'Alfred Tennyson, Bulwer's *Falkland*, and Graves's *Werther*', *Notes and Queries*, o.s. 265 / n.s. 67: 4 (December 2020).

[54] Robert Bernard Martin, *Tennyson: The Unquiet Heart* (Oxford: Clarendon Press, 1980), pp. 44, 52.

[55] David Francis Smith, 'English Response to Goethe, 1824–1865' (unpublished doctoral thesis, University of Oxford, Exeter College, 1981), p. 330; T. Wemyss Reid, *The Life, Letters, and Friendships of Richard Monckton Milnes, First Lord Houghton,* 2 vols (London: Cassell, 1890), I, 116 (see also p. 201).

he befriended in the spring of 1829.⁵⁶ From October of that year onwards, Tennyson attended the meetings of the secret club that was known as the Apostles, and which was described by another Cantabrigian, Richard Chenevix Trench, as a 'Wordsworthian-Germano-Coleridgian' group.⁵⁷ It was also at Cambridge that Tennyson read Carlyle's 1828 *Foreign Review* essays on 'Goethe's "Helena"' and 'Goethe', as well as his piece on the Romantic poet Novalis (the pseudonym of Friedrich von Hardenberg, 1772–1801), which appeared in the same periodical the following year.⁵⁸

It was probably also around this time that Tennyson discovered Carlyle's translation of the bipartite fictional saga *Wilhelm Meister*. The influence of this text on the young poet's work has been ably explored by Ian H. C. Kennedy, who demonstrates 'the indisputable fact of extraordinary correspondence between parts of Goethe's two novels and a number of Tennyson's poems of the Cambridge period'.⁵⁹ He substantiates this claim with detailed comparisons between passages from Carlyle's *Meister*, and four of the *Poems, Chiefly Lyrical* (1830), as well as such later works as 'Œnone' (*PT*, 164) and 'Mariana in the South' (*PT*, 160).⁶⁰ Kennedy's conclusions have been widely accepted,⁶¹ and they will be cited and expanded upon on a number of occasions in subsequent chapters.

Despite the inadequacy of Gower's translation, *Faust* and its author were now attracting increasing attention in Britain. Noticing a copy of Retsch's illustrations on Julia Manvers's drawing-room table, the protagonist of Disraeli's first novel *Vivian Grey* (1826–7) remarks: 'How beautiful [Goethe's heroine] Margaret is. [...] I always think that this is the only Personification where Art has not rendered

---

⁵⁶ Martin, p. 69. In July 1832, Tennyson and Hallam chose to holiday on the Rhine, but the trip was not a success (ibid. pp. 152–5).
⁵⁷ Cited in Martin Blocksidge, *'A Life Lived Quickly': Tennyson's Friend Arthur Hallam and his Legend* (Brighton: Sussex Academic Press, 2011), p. 119.
⁵⁸ See Chapter 1, pp. 53–4, Chapter 3, pp. 95–7, and Chapter 5, p. 163.
⁵⁹ Ian H. C. Kennedy, 'Alfred Tennyson's *Bildungsgang*: Notes on his Early Reading', *Philological Quarterly*, 57: 1 (Winter 1978), 82–103 (p. 88).
⁶⁰ Ibid. pp. 87–95.
⁶¹ See, for example, *PT*, 73, 78, 91, 113 (headnotes); 153 (II, ll. 194–205, fn); 160 (ll. 37–48, fn; 61–84, fn); 164 (ll. 142–3, fn); 316 (I. 22. 850–923, fn); Alfred Lord Tennyson, *Selected Poems*, ed. Aidan Day (London: Penguin, 2003), pp. 353–4; John Batchelor, *Tennyson: To Strive, to Seek, to Find* (London: Chatto & Windus, 2012), pp. 136, 374, 386.

Innocence insipid.'[62] In Edward Bulwer's novel *Falkland* (1827) (which Tennyson is known to have read), the principal Goethean influence is Graves's *Werther* translation, but its protagonist also learns, 'like Faustus, to find nothing in knowledge but its inutility, or in hope but its deceit; and to bear like him [. . .] the curse and the presence of a fiend'.[63] Thackeray spent much of 1830 in Weimar, where he was able to meet Goethe, and he would later refer to *Part One* in *The History of Pendennis* (1848–50).[64] 'The British world is daily getting readier for a true copy of *Faust*', wrote Carlyle to its author in January 1831 (Carlyle, *Letters*, V (1976), 219; see also p. 194, 15 November 1830).

The turning-point came in the twelve months following Goethe's death in March 1832. The poet's demise led to a new receptivity towards his writings, thus helping to create a favourable climate for posthumous publications. For the small number of British people who could read German, the most significant of these was, of course, *Faust. Der Tragödie zweiter Teil*. However, apart from some extensive excerpts, this would not be translated until 1838.[65] More widespread interest was aroused by the first complete English version of *Part One*, which appeared early in 1833. Although its translator, Abraham Hayward, is little remembered today, he stands alongside Carlyle as one of the two most important intermediaries in the story of Tennyson and *Faust*.

Hayward was born in Wilton, near Salisbury, in 1801, and began learning German whilst still a child. In 1824, he moved to London to read law at the Inner Temple, and in June 1832 was called to the Bar. In the autumn of the previous year, his legal career had taken him to Göttingen, where he met the Brothers Grimm, and several associates of Goethe, which stimulated his interest in German literature. Returning to London, he began work on his translation of *Part One*,

---

[62] Benjamin Disraeli, *Vivian Grey*, ed. Herbert van Thal (London: Cassell, 1968), Bk II, Ch. IX, pp. 45–6, esp. p. 46 (see also p. 49; Bk IV, Ch. IV, p. 142).

[63] *LAT*, I, 23 (18 April [1828]); Kennedy, pp. 95–100; [Edward] Bulwer Lytton, *Falkland*, ed. Herbert van Thal (London: Cassell, 1967), Bk I, pp. 9–10 (see also pp. viii–ix, xi); Baynes, 'Bulwer's *Falkland*'.

[64] Gordon N. Ray, *Thackeray*, 2 vols (London: Oxford University Press, 1955–8), I: *The Uses of Adversity 1811–1846* (1955), pp. 140–7; G. H. Lewes, *The Life and Works of Goethe: With Sketches of his Age and Contemporaries, from Published and Unpublished Sources*, 2 vols (London: Nutt, 1855), II, 442–6; William Makepeace Thackeray, *The History of Pendennis*, ed. Peter L. Shillingsburg (New York: Garland, 1991), Vol. II, Ch. III, p. 22; Ch. IX, p. 93.

[65] Hauhart, p. 144.

which he published (complete with a lengthy 'Preface', and extensive 'Notes') around the end of February 1833.[66] As a reprint was soon required, he visited Germany once again in the autumn of that year, and discussed the play's more difficult passages with a number of eminent figures: Goethe's daughter-in-law; the poets Tieck and von Chamisso; the novelist de la Motte Fouqué; and the illustrator of *Faust*, Moritz Retzsch. The second edition (in which the text of the play was only lightly revised, but the editorial material much expanded) appeared in January 1834.[67]

Faust: A Dramatic Poem, by Goethe represents a significant advance on all previous English translations of *Part One*. Keenly aware of his predecessors' omissions and inaccuracies, Hayward's guiding principle is fidelity to the German text of the play. He deserves considerable credit for refusing to censor this controversial work, which he translates literally, and into prose, presenting it uncut for the very first time: 'I wish', he writes, 'to give as exact a transcript of the mind of Goethe as exhibited in Faust as I can' (Hay. 1, p. 246). Admittedly, the intended exactitude is not fully achieved: some parts of the translation are unidiomatic,[68] whilst others are confusingly *over*-literal. Indeed, two Germans resident in England soon published substantial pamphlets largely devoted to cataloguing Hayward's errors.[69] However, as William Frederic Hauhart points out, *Faust: A Dramatic Poem* needs to be seen in its historical context:

> While the work has some inaccuracies, especially in the first edition, one is after all surprised at the philological accuracy with which he wrought. [. . .] While a prose translation of 'Faust' is not the ideal

---

[66] Hayward's brief introductory note (which is not included in the 1993 facsimile reprint) is dated 25 February (Hay. 1, p. iii).

[67] *A Selection from the Correspondence of Abraham Hayward, Q.C. from 1834 to 1884: With an Account of his Early Life*, ed. Henry E. Carlisle, 2 vols (London: Murray, 1886), I, 1–18; A. Hayward (trans.), *Faust: A Dramatic Poem, by Goethe. Translated into English Prose, with Remarks on Former Translations, and Notes*, 2nd edn (London: Moxon, 1834), pp. v, xxi.

[68] Hauhart, p. 107; Lina Baumann, *Die englischen Übersetzungen von Goethes 'Faust'* (Halle: Niemeyer, 1907), p. 10; Adolf Ingram Frantz, *Half a Hundred Thralls to Faust: A Study Based on the British and the American Translators of Goethe's 'Faust' 1823–1949* (Chapel Hill: University of North Carolina Press, 1949), p. 23.

[69] D. Boileau, *A Few Remarks on Mr. Hayward's English Prose Translation of Goethe's 'Faust'* (London: Treuttel, Würtz, Richter, and Wacey, 1834); W. H. Koller, *'Faust' Papers: Containing Critical and Historical Remarks on 'Faust' and its Translations* (London: Black, Young, and Young, 1835).

version, it served a good purpose in its day. [. . .] Several poor attempts in verse like Gower's had been made. Shelley's fragments, while spirited and poetic, lacked accuracy. Under those conditions about the best thing that could happen for the furtherance of 'Faust' appreciation in England, was an exact literal version like Hayward's.[70]

Early critical verdicts on the translation were mainly positive: in the spring of 1833, it garnered favourable notices in the *Examiner*, the *Edinburgh Review*, the *Athenæum* and *Fraser's Magazine* (the last hailing it as a 'godsend').[71] Coleridge reportedly praised it as 'done in a very manly style', whilst the publication of the second edition is said to have brought letters of congratulation from Southey and Samuel Rogers.[72]

Even if more specific evidence were lacking, it would be reasonable to assume that Tennyson would have been aware of the publication of Hayward's *Faust*, and would have wanted to read it. His writings had already been extensively influenced by English translations of *Werther* and *Meister*, and in later years, his 'six favourite poets' (as commemorated by the six stone shields that adorned the chimney-piece in the study of his Sussex home) were 'Shakespeare, Chaucer, Milton, Wordsworth, Dante, and Goethe'.[73] Apart from the publication of *The Prelude* in 1850, the appearance of *Faust*:

---

[70] Hauhart, p. 112. See also Baumann, pp. 10, 22, 38–9.

[71] Anon., 'The Literary Examiner. *Faust: A Dramatic Poem, by Goethe*', *Examiner*, 1312 (24 March 1833), 180–1; [William Empson], 'ART. VI.—*Faust: A Dramatic Poem, by Goethe*', *Edinburgh Review*, 57: 115 (April 1833), 107–43; Anon., '*Faust: A Dramatic Poem, by Goethe*', *Athenæum*, 287 (27 April 1833), 260–1; [John Abraham Heraud], 'Hayward's Translation of Goethe's *Faust*', *Fraser's Magazine*, 7: 41 (May 1833), 532–54 (p. 532).

[72] Coleridge, *Collected Works*, XIV (1990), II, 200 (see also I, 343, fn 25); Hayward, *Correspondence*, I, 18–19. The editor of the latter work also states that Wordsworth sent his congratulations (ibid. I, 18). However, in his letter to Hayward of 14 May 1833, Wordsworth (who disliked Goethe's writings) merely thanks him politely for sending him a copy of the first edition, and adds: 'the small acquaintance I have with [German] would render any notices of mine upon a Translation of it, utterly insignificant' (*The Letters of William and Dorothy Wordsworth*, ed. Ernest de Selincourt, 2nd edn, ed. Chester L. Shaver, Mary Moorman and Alan G. Hill, 8 vols (Oxford: Clarendon Press, 1967–93), V (1979), no. 761, pp. 615–16 (see also no. 800, p. 676 [1833–4(?)]).

[73] Kennedy, pp. 87–95; James Knowles, 'Aspects of Tennyson: II (A Personal Reminiscence)', *Nineteenth Century*, 33: 191 (January 1893), 164–88 (p. 173). See also William Knight, 'A Conversation with Tennyson (1870)', in *Tennyson: Interviews and Recollections*, ed. Norman Page (Basingstoke: Macmillan, 1983), pp. 177–85 (p. 179); *Mem.*, I, 341; II, 287–8.

A Dramatic Poem in 1833 represents the only time in Tennyson's life that he experienced the arrival of the complete text of a masterpiece by one of these authors. Hayward's *Faust* is likely to have been, for Tennyson, a major event.

It was, moreover, published by Edward Moxon (1801–58), who just twelve weeks earlier had begun his long professional relationship with Tennyson by printing his *Poems* (1832).[74] Hallam was in close contact with the publisher at this time, and his letters reveal that Moxon was in the habit of promptly dispatching to him two copies of each book that appeared under his imprint: one for himself, and one to forward to Tennyson.[75] I propose, therefore, that by early March 1833, Tennyson had in his possession a copy of *Faust: A Dramatic Poem* – probably the volume that is now at the Tennyson Research Centre in Lincoln, which is an 1833 first edition, and which is lightly annotated in his hand. It is likely to be this which is listed as 'Hayward's Faust' in the uncompleted inventory of his books which he drew up around 1861[76] (in which case, it will have been at some point after that date that he gave it to his sister Matilda, who was known to him as 'Maud').[77] In his 'Preface', Hayward writes: 'I had serious thoughts at one time of calling this book "Aids to the understanding of Faust"—a sort of title not unusual in Germany, and indicating the exact light in which I wish my labours to be viewed' (Hay. 1, p. lxxx, fn). Tennyson seems initially to have taken him at his word, for it is clear that he attempted to read the translation in conjunction with the German original: all of his annotations consist of phrases or passages quoted verbatim from Goethe's text, which he inserts in the margin next to their English equivalents. However, apart from an isolated note on page 90, the annotations end on page 35.

---

[74] Martin, p. 160.
[75] *LAHH*, no. 93, p. 380 (4 October 1830); p. 381, fn 8; no. 236, p. 753 ([27 April 1833]), and fn; no. 241, p. 764 ([25 May 1833]). Further evidence that copies of Hayward's *Faust* reached the Hallam household is provided by the fact that Arthur's father Henry is said to have been amongst those who wrote to Hayward to congratulate him on the second edition (Hayward, *Correspondence*, I, 18).
[76] Alfred Lord Tennyson, 'Catalogue of my Books' (TRC, N/25). Listed alphabetically; 'Hayward's Faust' is under 'H'. The conjectural dating of this list is given in Nancie Campbell (ed.), *Tennyson in Lincoln: A Catalogue of the Collections in the Research Centre*, 2 vols (Lincoln: Tennyson Society, 1971–3), I (1971), p. xv.
[77] 'Goethe, Johann Wolfgang, [. . .] Faust: a dramatic poem; trans., with notes, by the Translator of Savigny's "Of the vocation of our age for legislation and jurisprudence." [Abraham Hayward] London: Moxon, 1833. 21.3cm. Inside front board "Maud Tennyson from Alfred"' (ibid., I (1971), 'Books owned by Matilda Tennyson', p. 155, no. 3274 (TRC, AT/3274)).

Harvard Notebook 13 – which also dates from 1833 – provides further evidence that Tennyson was reading *Faust* that year. On the stub of a page that has been cut out, there is a German glossary:

diesen.
    acc[usative]
tisch. ta[ble]
tischen..
schlimm
Gar. very
Neugier
Beflüge[ln(?)]

Fürcht[ten(?)] (*TA*, II, 266)[78]

All but the last of these words occur in the following lines from *Faust*, and in the exact same order:

Wenn *diesen* Langeweile treibt,
Kommt jener satt vom über*tisch*ten Mahle,
Und, was das aller*schlimm*ste bleibt,
Gar mancher kommt vom Lesen der Journale.
Man eilt zerstreut zu uns, wie zu den Maskenfesten,
Und *Neugier* nur *beflügelt* jeden Schritt. (ll. 113–18; italics added)

Whilst one is driven by ennui, the other comes satiated from an overloaded table; and, what is worst of all, very many a one comes from reading the journals. People hurry dissipated to us, as to masquerades; and curiosity only wings every step. (p. 270)[79]

The fact that these lines come from the 'Prologue on the Theatre' (ll. 33–242 / pp. 267–74) with which the play begins confirms the impression that is left by the Lincoln copy of Hayward's *Faust*.[80] It

---

[78] Tennyson's capitalisation of German words does not always conform to present-day norms. These mistakes are so frequent that they have not been noted, either here or in subsequent quotations.
[79] The words 'very many a one comes' are Hayward's slightly awkward translation of 'Gar mancher kommt' ('Quite a lot of them come'). Tennyson, in his glossary, translates 'Gar' as 'very', which may indicate that he was trying to infer the meanings of words by comparing Goethe's text to Hayward's.
[80] The missing word, 'Fürcht[en(?)]', may come from a line in the opening scene of the main action, 'Night' (*F*, l. 369 / p. 7).

would appear that in 1833, Tennyson could only read German literature in translation. However, he also had the original versions to hand, and was trying, at times, to engage with them. On more than one occasion, he seems to have made a thorough attempt to read Goethe's text of *Part One* from beginning to end, but he did not, at this stage, advance very far.

He appears, however, to have been spurred to improve his German, for it was around this time that he drew up a study programme, which begins:

Monday. History, German.
Tuesday. Chemistry, German.
Wednesday. Botany, German.
Thursday. Electricity, German.
Friday. Animal Physiology, German. (*Mem.*, I, Ch. V, '1833–1835', p. 124)

I would suggest that his chief motivation for studying the language was a desire to exchange Hayward's words for Goethe's.

Tennyson would also have wanted to read the recently published *Faust: Part Two*. In the translating of this work, Hayward was, once again, a pioneer. In the April 1833 issue of the *Foreign Quarterly Review*, an anonymous author commended his version of *Part One*, and added: 'Mr. Hayward has now [. . .] an opportunity of crowning his fame by starting first in the field, and giving us a translation of the *new* Faust.'[81] It was, perhaps, in response to this challenge that Hayward, in the very next issue of the *Quarterly*, published a twenty-nine-page article consisting largely of an outline of *Part Two*, interspersed with translations of lengthy excerpts.[82]

It will be a central contention of this book that from early 1833 to early 1834, Tennyson was deeply preoccupied with Hayward's translation of *Part One* (and, from the summer of 1833 onwards, with his article on *Part Two*). About half of the works that he wrote during this period would appear to have been influenced, in one way

---

[81] Anon., 'Miscellaneous Literary Notices, No. XXII: Germany', *Foreign Quarterly Review*, 11: 22 (April 1833), 531–5 (p. 534, fn).

[82] The fact that Tennyson read the *Quarterly* is demonstrated by *LAHH*, no. 195, pp. 652–3 (24 September 1832), and p. 629, fn 6. Hayward felt that '[t]he second part [of *Faust*] presents few (if any) of those fine trains of philosophical thinking, or those exquisite touches of natural pathos, which form the great attraction of the first', so he never translated it in its entirety (Hay. 2, p. 84).

or another, by Goethe's drama, to the extent that this might almost be described as his '*Faust* year'. This influence becomes particularly marked from around June 1833: almost all of the poems dating from between then and early 1834 have either possible or definite links to *Faust*. And right in the middle of this period was the defining event of Tennyson's life: the death in Vienna on 15 September of the twenty-two-year-old Hallam, who suffered a fatal brain haemorrhage.[83]

As well as being profoundly absorbed in Hayward's *Faust* translations, Tennyson was stimulated by them to read, re-read or recollect a number of the closely related works that are referred to in their editorial material. These include Shelley's 'Scenes'; Byron's *Cain* and *The Deformed Transformed*; Carlyle's 'Goethe's "Helena"'; Goethe's *Sorrows of Werther*; and the earliest English translation of his autobiography, *Poetry and Truth* (which was retitled *Memoirs of Goethe* (1824)).[84] Echoes of these works, too, can be found in many of the poems that Tennyson wrote between early 1833 and early 1834.

There is one more text that was of considerable importance to Tennyson during this period: Henry Francis Cary's celebrated translation of *The Divine Comedy* (especially, but not exclusively, the *Inferno*).[85] This poem – which Cary retitles *The Vision of Dante* – does not, of course, have any direct connection with *Faust*. However, in the 'Preface' to his

---

[83] Blocksidge, pp. 215–29.

[84] The study programme cited above may reflect the influence of the *Memoirs*, to which Hayward often refers (although he deprecates, justifiably, the English translation (Hay. 1, p. vi, fn; pp. 214, 220, 228, 235, 237, 238, 241, 244)). In this work, Goethe refers repeatedly to his 'plan of studies' (although there is no precedent for this in the German text), and writes: 'The removal of [my first love] Margaret had annihilated all the joys of my youth. I employed my time in study, endeavouring to repair my loss by making myself a new being' (FA, 1, XIV, Pt II, Bk VI, p. 270, l. 10; p. 263, ll. 20–4 / *Memoirs of Goethe: Written by Himself* [n. trans.], 2 vols (London: Colburn, 1824), I, Ch. VI, pp. 180, 175). Tennyson's own study programme probably dates from shortly after Hallam's death, and it might therefore have had a similar motivation. Goethe refers to his study (or intended study) of Racine and Molière, theology, mechanics, Greek, history and chemistry, all of which are on Tennyson's programme (FA, 1, XIV, Pt I, Bk III, p. 122, l. 7; Bk IV, p. 158, ll. 32–3; Pt II, Bk VI, p. 262, ll. 28–9; p. 264, ll. 15–16; Bk VIII, p. 364, ll. 26–9; p. 375, l. 37–p. 376, l. 3; Bk IX, p. 395, ll. 1–2 / Goethe, *Memoirs of Goethe*, I, Ch. III, p. 87; Ch. IV, pp. 94, 96–7 (translator's interpolation); Ch. VI, pp. 174, 176; Ch. VIII, pp. 246–7, 255–6; Ch. IX, p. 270; *Mem.*, I, 124).

[85] An 1831 copy is at the Tennyson Research Centre (listed in Campbell (ed.), I (1971), p. 44, as no. 827; now AT/826). The Cambridge Apostle Stephen Spring Rice reports that in July 1833, Tennyson was carrying with him a portmanteau 'full of Dantes & dressing gowns' (*LAHH*, p. 768, fn 1). In the study programme cited above, Tennyson's daily acquisition of German in Week One is replaced, in Week Two, by Italian (*Mem.*, I, 124).

translation of *Part One*, Hayward writes: 'in Italy, [. . .] Faust might be expected to inspire a peculiar interest from its being constantly associated by critics with the Divine Comedy of Dante' (Hay. 1, p. lxxviii). He also quotes a similar remark by the German novelist Jean Paul, and a footnote even mentions 'Mr Cary', 'the translator of Dante' (who was Hayward's 'honoured friend' (ibid. pp. lxxiii; lxxviii, fn; lxxix, fn; Hayward, *Faust*, 2nd edn, p. xxv, and fn)).[86] In his article on *Part Two*, Hayward writes: 'Schelling [. . .] stated that Goethe's Faust, like Dante's Divine Comedy, would consist of three parts; the first part [. . .] he took to correspond with the Inferno' (Hay. 2, p. 105). It is possible that these comments were at least partly responsible for Tennyson's simultaneous absorption in *Faust* and the *Comedy*.

Hayward and Tennyson may well have become acquainted at some point in their lives. In the summer of 1852, the poet sent two letters to a 'Miss Hayward' (*LAT*, II, 41–4), whom Cecil Lang and Edgar Shannon describe as 'perhaps one of the nameless sisters of Abraham Hayward, [. . .] who [. . .] knew everyone that Tennyson knew'.[87] Specifically, both men were acquainted with Moxon, Carlyle, Whewell, A. W. Kinglake and Gladstone.[88] Until 1857, the barrister Hayward lived in London's legal district, Temple, where in the 1830s and 1840s, Tennyson stayed regularly, and was often to be found at the Cock Tavern on Fleet Street.[89] From 1835 onwards, Hayward was a member of the Athenaeum Club, which Tennyson also frequented for a time.[90] If they did meet, however, it is clear that they did not form any lasting friendship: in an article in the *Quarterly Review* in 1871, Hayward publicly expressed a low opinion of Tennyson's work, and the Laureate's prestigious name is absent from the long list of Hayward's eminent associates which is provided by the posthumous editor of his letters.[91]

* * *

---

[86] The editorial material in Hayward's *Faust* – which is, for its time, unusually extensive – might have been prompted by the example of Cary's *Vision*.

[87] *LAT*, II, 41, fn.

[88] Carlyle, *Letters*, VI (1977), 86 (10 January 1832); IX (1981), 113–14 ([11 January 1837]); Hayward, *Correspondence*, I, 52 (23 February 1835); p. 67 (2 February 1839); II, 329; Martin, pp. 56, 232, 288.

[89] Hayward, *Correspondence*, I, 53–4 (and p. 54, fn) (29 March 1836); p. 301 (29 December 1856); p. 311 (26 March 1857); Martin, pp. 221–2.

[90] Hayward, *Correspondence*, I, 52 (23 February 1835); Martin, pp. 461–2.

[91] [Abraham Hayward], 'ART. II.—*Lord Byron. Von Karl Elze.* Berlin, 1870', *Quarterly Review*, 131: 262 (October 1871), 354–92, repr. as 'Byron and Tennyson', in A. Hayward, *Sketches of Eminent Statesmen and Writers: With Other Essays*, 2 vols (London: Murray, 1880), II, 305–59; Hayward, *Correspondence*, I, pp. vi–vii, viii–x.

The success of his *Faust* had provided Hayward with an *entrée* into English society, in which he remained a prominent and well-connected figure until his death in 1884.[92] *Faust: A Dramatic Poem* was in print for the remainder of the nineteenth century (an eleventh edition was published in 1890, and a new illustrated one appeared in 1908).[93] It occupies, however, a paradoxical position in the story of *Faust* in Britain, being both central and anomalous, for Hayward's desire to present Goethe's play as faithfully as possible cannot be said to have been widely shared. Indeed, despite the rapidly escalating popularity of *Faust*, an examination of its translation, reception and influence reveals that there was a lingering sense of unease towards it, and a concomitant desire to transform it into something less threatening.

Hayward's pioneering work initiated a remarkable proliferation of British *Faust*s: by 1850, more than a dozen versions of *Part One* had appeared.[94] None was as rigorous as his, however, and in many of them, the censorship or omission of controversial passages such as the 'Prologue in Heaven' was continued.[95] This was true even of the version by John Stuart Blackie (1834), whose most notable admirer was George Henry Lewes.[96] John Anster's translation (1835) vied with Hayward's for popularity, but it is so free that (as Hauhart observes) it 'has sometimes been spoken of as an original poem'.[97]

A similar mixture of enthusiasm and evasiveness can be discerned in the attitudes of the critics. As the authors of *German Literature in British Magazines* observe: 'A sounder and lasting interest in *Faust* begins with Hayward's prose translation of Part I in 1833', but 'the voice of criticism [. . .] continues to be vacillating and contradictory'.[98] Catherine Waltraud Proescholdt-Obermann paints a similarly ambiguous picture:

> The sheer number of translations [. . .] must have convinced readers and critics alike, that this really was a work of extraordinary

---

[92] Hayward, *Correspondence*, I, 19; II, 329.
[93] Frantz, p. 22.
[94] Hauhart, pp. 112–35; Frantz, p. 306.
[95] Hauhart, p. 129; Frantz, pp. 149, 193–4.
[96] Hauhart, pp. 116, 121. The 'Prologue' was restored in the revised edition of 1880 (Frantz, p. 59). Blackie met Tennyson in 1864, and 'got on admirably' with him (*LAT*, II, 367, 10 May).
[97] Hauhart, p. 122.
[98] Walter Roloff, Morton E. Mix and Martha Nicolai, *German Literature in British Magazines 1750–1860*, ed. Bayard Quincy Morgan and A. R. Hohlfeld (Madison: University of Wisconsin Press, 1949), pp. 88, 89.

importance. [...] Although over the years *Faust* had become less controversial, some critics maintained their opposition, and when they did so it was in no uncertain terms. [...] The question of Faust's sin and salvation continued to be seen as problematic even by those [...] with more liberal theological beliefs. [...] English critics continued to dwell on the question of Goethe's moral message.[99]

In short, although *Faust* was now the object of widespread admiration, it remained, for many, a source of considerable unease.

It was against this mixed background that there appeared, between 1833 and 1839, three different works, each of which has been described as an English – or Victorian – *Faust*: Carlyle's *Sartor Resartus* (which was serialised in 1833–4, and published in book form in 1838); Browning's *Paracelsus* (1835); and P. J. Bailey's *Festus* (1839; expanded edition 1845).[100] With the exception of the last-named piece, the description seems a little exaggerated, and is applicable only if greater stress is put on the adjective than on the noun. Each one of these works was, however, part of an ongoing process of assimilation, by means of which the Faustian theme was gradually transformed into something more fully acceptable to Victorian sensibilities. Tennyson (who met Carlyle around 1838, and Browning in 1841, and who seven years later corresponded with Bailey) read all three of these 'Victorian *Fausts*'.[101] As I will argue in Chapters 4 and 5, *Sartor* and *Festus* played a significant role in his developing relationship with the Germanic original, and were important sources for a number of passages in *In Memoriam A. H. H.* (*PT*, 296; written 1833–50).

Sartor Resartus (an acknowledged influence on section CXXIV of that poem)[102] is saturated with the writings of Goethe and other German authors, and *Faust* stands alongside *Werther* and *Meister* as one of its three most significant points of reference. Most notably, the protagonist's 'Philosophy of Clothes' derives primarily from the Chant of the Earth Spirit in the opening scene, 'Night' (*SR*, Bk I,

---

[99] Proescholdt-Obermann, pp. 286–7, 294, 295.
[100] Lore Metzger, '*Sartor Resartus*: A Victorian *Faust*', *Comparative Literature*, 13: 4 (Autumn 1961), 316–31; *The Poems of Browning*, ed. John Woolford, Daniel Karlin and Joseph Phelan (London: Longman, 1991–), I (1991), 103; Alan D. McKillop, 'A Victorian *Faust*', *PMLA*, 40: 3 (September 1925), 743–68.
[101] Martin, pp. 241, 257; *LAT*, I, 283 ([February or March 1848]), p. 294 ([12 September 1848(?)]). See also *LAT*, I, 285 ([5–6 May 1848]).
[102] S & S, p. 284; *PT*, 296, CXXIV, ll. 13–17, fn.

Ch. I, p. 4 / p. 6, l. 2; *F*, ll. 501–9 / p. 12).[103] As in his critical writings, however, Carlyle's response to *Faust* is a very personal one, for as Lore Metzger points out, his translation of this passage includes a subtle alteration, which serves to assimilate Goethe's verse to his own outlook.[104] In like manner, the pivotal conversion experience which is described in Book II, Chapter VII (*SR*, pp. 128–35 / p. 120, l. 1–p. 26, l. 18) is, in Metzger's words, 'filled with echoes from *Faust*', but it expresses, nevertheless, its author's own, very different, sensibility.[105] Even when Carlyle is close to the letter of Goethe's play, he is far indeed from its spirit.

The final instalment of *Sartor* appeared in August 1834.[106] It was probably the following month that Browning began work on *Paracelsus*, which he completed by December, and published in August 1835 (Tennyson's first edition is at the Research Centre in Lincoln).[107] Carré states that Browning 'knew a little German' at this time, having enrolled on a course in it at University College London in June 1828.[108] He was still learning the language eight years later, however,[109] so he would probably have made use of a *Faust* translation – and of those which were available in 1834, Hayward's would have been his most likely choice. He would later recommend it to a friend (Browning, *Correspondence*, VIII, no. 1533, p. 203 [mid-February 1844]), and indeed, he and Hayward must have become acquainted at some point, as Browning was amongst the mourners at his funeral.[110]

The historical Paracelsus (1493–1541) was a Swiss-German contemporary of Johann Georg Faust, and his colourful career as alchemist, physician and astrologer makes him an eminently comparable figure.[111] Browning would certainly have had *Faust: Part One* in

---

[103] Charles Frederick Harrold, *Carlyle and German Thought: 1819–1834* (New Haven, CT: Yale University Press, 1934), p. 79; Smith, p. 51.
[104] Metzger, 'Sartor', p. 326.
[105] Metzger, 'Sartor', p. 323.
[106] *SR*, ed. Tarr, p. xvi.
[107] Browning, *Poems*, I (1991), 98–325 (and see pp. 101–2, 98); Campbell (ed.), I (1971), p. 36, no. 643.
[108] Carré, p. 234, fn.
[109] *The Brownings' Correspondence*, ed. Philip Kelley and Ronald Hudson (Winfield: Wedgestone Press, 1984–), Vol. III, no. 585, p. 278 (19 August 1837).
[110] Anon., 'Funeral of Mr. Hayward, Q.C.', *The Times*, 7 February 1884, p. 7.
[111] Hayward mentions Paracelsus in his 'Notes' (Hay. 1, p. 214), and he is also referred to in part of the May 1833 *Fraser's Magazine* review of Hayward's translation (Heraud, p. 542).

mind when he wrote such passages as Paracelsus' speech in the middle of Part IV (ll. 369–402), which reads, at times, like a summary of the play's opening scenes. He is careful, however, to differentiate his protagonist from Goethe's. Paracelsus is less impious than Faust, and he has, therefore, no need for either magic or Mephistopheles:

> I can abjure so well the secret arts
> These pedants strive to learn—the magic they
> So reverence. I shall scarcely seek to know
> If it exist: too intimate a tie
> Connects me with our God. A sullen fiend
> To do my bidding—fallen and hateful sprites
> To help me—what are these, at best, beside
> God every where, sustaining and directing. (I, ll. 377–84)[112]

Throughout the poem, instead of the tortured, morally ambiguous Faust, Browning portrays a somewhat more optimistic figure, whose repudiation of conventional knowledge is a little less far-reaching, and who remains, to the end, an earnest seeker after truth.

This transformation of *Faust* struck a responsive chord in Philip James Bailey (1816–1902). One of his most treasured possessions was a copy of the first edition of *Paracelsus* (a gift from its author),[113] and it is likely to have been the name of a character from that work, 'Festus', which suggested the title of Bailey's *Festus: A Poem*. In the half-century after its first appearance in 1839, this almost-forgotten work passed through eleven official editions, as well as a further eleven pirated ones (and a remarkable thirty in the United States).[114] Its admirers included Browning, Thackeray, D. G. Rossetti, Edward Bulwer, Samuel Smiles, Matthew Arnold and Tennyson.[115] In a letter to his friend Mary Howitt in November 1846, the last wrote: 'I can scarcely trust myself to say how much I admire it (faulty as it is in construction) for fear of falling into extravagance. This sublimity is Michael-Angelic. Bailey is great' (cited in *LAT*, I, 266

---

[112] See Browning, *Poems*, I (1991), p. 130, ll. 381–2, fn.
[113] J. A. Hammerton, 'Philip James Bailey and his Work', *Sunday Magazine*, 27: 4 (January 1898), 45–52 (p. 49).
[114] McKillop, p. 764; Greta A. Black, 'P. J. Bailey's Debt to Goethe's *Faust* in his *Festus*', *Modern Language Review*, 28: 2 (April 1933), 166–75 (p. 167).
[115] McKillop, pp. 761–2; *The Letters of Matthew Arnold*, ed. Cecil Y. Lang, 6 vols (Charlottesville: University Press of Virginia, 1996–2001), I, 82 ([*c.* 24 February 1848]).

[20 November 1846(?)]). It is clear from the same letter that Tennyson had only just discovered the poem, which he had ordered through Moxon a fortnight earlier, and which he would therefore have been reading in the expanded edition that had appeared the previous year (ibid. I, 263 [5 November 1846]).[116] A copy of it, with marginal pen markings in what is almost certainly his hand, is at the Research Centre in Lincoln.[117] Examining this volume, John O. Waller sheds a considerable amount of light on Tennyson's puzzling enthusiasm for this work.[118] I would argue, however, that his admiration for *Festus* needs to be seen in the context of his continuing preoccupation with its model.

When Bailey's poem first appeared, the *Eclectic Review* declared that 'it is impossible that a more palpable imitation of Goethe's "Faust" could be conceived or executed', whilst the *Athenæum* denounced it as 'a mere plagiarism'.[119] Twentieth-century critics took a milder view, although Alan D. McKillop still argues that Goethe's play provides the 'general scheme of presentation', and is, therefore, the work's 'most obvious source'.[120] Like *Faust*, *Festus* begins with a dedicatory poem, before proceeding to an opening scene in heaven.[121] In the latter, Bailey's hymn of the Seraphim and Cherubim (pp. 1–2) recalls Goethe's Chorus of the Archangels (ll. 243–70 / pp. 1–2), whilst still more obvious similarities are provided by the subsequent intrusion of the devil, and his agreement with God (pp. 2–5).[122] Thereafter, Lucifer and Festus also come to an informal arrangement (pp. 16–23, 38), and as McKillop points out, there are a number of echoes of specific passages of dialogue from *Faust*, as well as plot elements which recall the scenes 'Night', 'Before the Gate' and 'Study [II]'.[123]

However, in creating his Victorian *Faust*, Bailey (rather like Coleridge in his projected drama on Michael Scott) was partly motivated by a

---

[116] See also *LAT*, I, 264 (and fn 3) (12 November [1846]).
[117] Campbell (ed.), I (1971), p. 29, no. 481.
[118] John O. Waller, 'Tennyson and Philip James Bailey's *Festus*', *Bulletin of Research in the Humanities*, 82: 1 (Spring 1979), 105–23.
[119] Anon., 'Art. IV. *Festus, A Poem*. London: Pickering. 8vo. pp. 360', *Eclectic Review*, 6 (December 1839), 654–64 (p. 656); Anon., 'Anthology for 1839', *Athenæum*, 634 (21 December 1839), 958–9 (p. 959). See also Hammerton, p. 49.
[120] McKillop, pp. 749, 746 (see also Black, p. 174).
[121] Philip James Bailey, *Festus: A Poem* (London: Pickering, 1845), pp. iii, 1–13.
[122] McKillop, p. 750.
[123] McKillop, pp. 749–51. Numerous other passages in *Festus* strike me as being reminiscences of – or ripostes to – *Faust* (Bailey, *Festus*, pp. 9, 14–15, 54–5, 85–96, 105–6, 125, 186–7, 210, 293–5, 340, 347, 355, 372, 392).

desire to correct what he saw as the deficiencies of the original. In an interview with the *Sunday Magazine* six decades later, he recalled:

> when I was in my teens, 'Faust' was exercising a great hold on the mind of the public, Goethe's poem was being discussed everywhere. Like the rest, I read it, and was deeply interested in it; interested but not satisfied. [. . .] [T]he whole poem [seemed] too materialistic. [. . .] I was impelled to give utterance to the faith that was in me.[124]

This confident Christianising of Goethe's rather un-Christian drama would have held a considerable appeal for Tennyson, who was frequently plagued by religious doubt. Hence, I would argue, his strong enthusiasm for a poem that (as he himself conceded when recommending it to his friend FitzGerald) is likely to strike most of its readers as 'a great bore' (*LAT*, I, 265, 12 November [1846]).

There is at least one other candidate for the title of 'Victorian *Faust*', Arthur Hugh Clough's *Dipsychus*,[125] and the influence of Goethe's drama is also apparent in a number of poems by his friend Matthew Arnold. Although Tennyson was personally acquainted with both poets, these works cannot be said to have played any role in shaping his response to *Faust*. They deserve, however, to be briefly considered here, for they offer some interesting parallels to his own Faustian poetry. *Dipsychus* reflects its author's familiarity with Carlyle, for it uses Faustian forms and imagery as a vehicle for the largely unrelated theme of the crisis of faith. In Clough's initial draft (which dates from around autumn 1850), the protagonist is called 'Faustulus' and the Spirit 'Mephistopheles',[126] and even in the published text of 1864, the latter is addressed by that name on four separate occasions (IX, l. 44; XIV, ll. 5, 22, 58). His words appear, at times, to reflect the Carlylean view that Goethe's devil is an Enlightenment *philosophe*, a disturbing amalgam of intellectual penetration and ethical negligence:

>   act
> On a dispassionate judgement of the fact;
> Look all your data fairly in the face,
> And rule your conduct simply by the case. (IV, ll. 44–7)

---

[124] Hammerton, p. 50.
[125] *The Poems of Arthur Hugh Clough*, ed. F. L. Mulhauser, 2nd edn (Oxford: Oxford University Press, 1974), pp. 218–99; Metzger, '*Sartor*', p. 316; Lionel Trilling, *Matthew Arnold*, 2nd edn (New York: Columbia University Press; London: Allen & Unwin, 1949), p. 68.
[126] Clough, *Poems*, pp. 681–2.

Elsewhere, however, the imagery of Goethe's play is subjected to a satirical transformation. Whereas Faust is saved from despair by '*The ringing of bells*', and a chorus proclaiming that 'Christ is arisen!', Dipsychus repeatedly declares that 'Christ is not risen', and utters the refrain 'Dong, there is no God; dong!'[127] In passages such as these, *Dipsychus* reads almost like a critique of the Carlylean view of *Faust*: far from providing Clough with a way out of religious doubt, his engagement with Goethe's play seems to be leading him ever more deeply into it.

In a late essay, Arnold quotes the words of the French critic Edmond Schérer, who had opined that '*Faust* stands as one of the great works of poetry; and, perhaps, the most wonderful work of poetry in our century'.[128] 'The *perhaps*', adds Arnold delicately, 'might be away' (ibid. VIII (1972), p. 263, ll. 20–1). His lifelong interest in Goethe had probably begun at Oxford, where much like Tennyson at Cambridge, he had been enthralled by Carlyle's translation of *Meister* (ibid. X (1974), p. 166, l. 29–p. 167, l. 10).[129] Again like Tennyson, it is probable that his early experience of *Faust* was at least partly mediated by Hayward. As James Simpson observes, 'He may well have relied to some extent on translations during his time at Oxford. [...] He must certainly have known Hayward's translation of *Faust I*' (which he would later praise as 'not likely to be surpassed' (*Prose Works*, I, p. 167, l. 36; see also VIII (1972), p. 273, ll. 33–7)).[130] It is reasonable to assume that Arnold would not have written 'A Question: To Fausta' (*c.* 1844) or 'Resignation: To Fausta' (*c.* 1843–8)[131] without thinking of Goethe's play: in the words of Lionel Trilling, this name might have been intended to suggest a 'female Faust'.[132] Faust's own female companion, Margaret (or 'Gretchen'), might herself have been an influence on Arnold's poetry. In 'The Forsaken Merman' (*Poems of Matthew Arnold*, pp. 100–5; *c.* 1847–January 1849) Arnold adapts

---

[127] *F*, l. 737 and preceding stage direction; ll. 757, 797 / pp. 20, 21, 23; *Dipsychus*, I, ll. 11, 12, 15, 33, 79 (see also VIII, l. 15); VI, ll. 14, 26, 45, 58, 72, 92, 107, 119.

[128] *The Complete Prose Works of Matthew Arnold*, ed. R. H. Super, 11 vols (Ann Arbor: University of Michigan Press, 1960–77), VIII: *Essays Religious and Mixed* (1972), 'A French Critic on Goethe', p. 263, ll. 19–20.

[129] See also James Simpson, *Matthew Arnold and Goethe*, Texts and Dissertations, 2 (London: Modern Humanities Research Association, 1979), p. 17.

[130] Simpson, p. 20.

[131] *The Poems of Matthew Arnold*, ed. Kenneth Allot, 2nd edn, ed. Miriam Allott (London: Longman, 1979), pp. 38, 88–100.

[132] Trilling, p. 99.

a Danish ballad about a woman called Grethe (whom he refers to as Margaret (ll. 13, 22, 77)). He adds a passage in which she sits at her spinning wheel; recalls her separation from a loved one; and is overcome with sorrow (ll. 87–107) – which is a fairly clear reminiscence of the scene in *Faust* entitled 'Margaret's Room' (ll. 3374–413 / pp. 141–2). This is not, it should be added, the only Margaret in Arnold's work. The name of the 'Marguerite' who is the subject of his 'Switzerland' lyrics (which are heavily influenced by Goethe)[133] is known only from the works themselves, and it may well be the poet's own invention.[134] In his discussion of *Faust* in the 'Preface' to *Poems* (1853), Arnold refers admiringly to 'the unsurpassed beauty of the scenes which relate to Margaret' (*Prose Works*, I: *On the Classical Tradition* (1960), p. 8, l. 21). I would suggest that his high opinion of this section of Goethe's play is either the cause or the consequence of the name of his 'Marguerite'.

Returning to Tennyson, we find that by 1838, he appears to have been making progress with his German: on 25 December, his friend John Heath gave him a copy of *Wilhelm Meisters Lehrjahre*,[135] and he was also given *Hermann und Dorothea*,[136] and *Rabenhorst's Pocket Dictionary of the German and English Languages*.[137] On four different pages of the last-named work, Tennyson has written the word 'Faust', alongside a word from Goethe's drama that he has looked

---

[133] *Poems of Matthew Arnold*, p. 124, ll. 11–16 and fn; p. 133, l. 56 and fn; pp. 138–9, ll. 45–80 (and see fns to ll. 51–2, 61–2, 65–6, 72, 79–80); p. 145, ll. 9–10, 13, 17 and fns; p. 147, ll. 1–4 and fn; p. 150, ll. 31–2 and fn; p. 153, l. 4, fn. Arnold's evident preoccupation with Goethe during his second stay in Thun in September 1849 would almost certainly have been prompted by the fact that 28 August had marked the centenary of the German poet's birth.

[134] *Poems of Matthew Arnold*, p. 121, headnote.

[135] Johann Wolfgang Goethe, *Wilhelm Meisters Lehrjahre. Ein Roman*, 4 vols (Berlin: Unger, 1795–6) (TRC, AT/1017). My examination of this book suggests that it was originally the property of John Balfour (see *LAHH*, no. 42, p. 182, 30 October [1827], and p. 183, fn 8). Balfour seems to have given it to Heath, who subsequently gave it to Tennyson. Volume I is inscribed 'A. Tennyson. Xmas day 1838' in the poet's hand, and Tennyson has also compiled extensive German-English glossaries at the end of each of the four volumes.

[136] Campbell (ed.), I (1971), p. 52, no. 1013 (inscribed 'A. Tennyson. Xmas day 1838'; bound together with Johann Heinrich Voß, *Luise. Ein ländliches Gedicht in drei Idyllen* (Stuttgard and Tübingen: [n. pub.], 1828).

[137] G. H. Noehden (ed.), *Rabenhorst's Pocket Dictionary of the German and English Languages, in Two Parts*, 3rd edn (London: Longman, 1829) (TRC, AT/1846) (same inscription as *Hermann*). See also Campbell (ed.), I (1971), p. 101, no. 2217.

up. For example, on page 65 of Part II of the dictionary, next to the verb *bieten* ('to offer'), is the annotation 'die wette biet' ich. Faust'. This means 'I offer the wager', and is a quotation from the famous pact scene (*F*, l. 1698 / p. 58).[138]

Another Christmas gift that year was *Characteristics of Goethe* (1833) by Sarah Austin (1793–1867).[139] This lengthy compendium consists of memoirs of the poet written by a number of different German authors, which have been translated into English, and interspersed with copious notes. Austin herself describes the book as 'too long', and 'defective and ill-constructed' (*CG*, III, 318; I, p. xxxviii), but like Hayward's *Faust* it needs to be seen in its historical context. The first genuine English biography of Goethe would not appear until 1855 (see below), so until then, *Characteristics* provided his British admirers with a welcome source of otherwise scarce information. In terms of its importance in the story of Tennyson and *Faust*, it stands not far behind the work of Carlyle and Hayward (both of whom Austin knew; she also spent some time with Tennyson in October 1858, although it is not clear whether this was their first meeting).[140] As I will argue in Chapters 4 and 5, the combined evidence of at least two of Tennyson's poems – and, also, of his letter to his fiancée Emily Sellwood of 24 October 1839 (*LAT*, I, 174–5) – leaves no doubt that he read *Characteristics* at some point that year.

---

[138] The other entries that include the word 'Faust' are in Part II, pages 20, 90 and 308. These probably relate, respectively, to line 2110 / page 75; line 847 / page 26; and line 90 / page 269. A letter of December 1842 confirms that Tennyson was reading German by then, although four years later, he wrote: 'Would that my acquaintance were more perfect with German' (*LAT*, I, 214 [*c*. 10 December]; p. 262, 5 November [1846]). Citing these words, his son adds: 'He could read German with ease at this time' (*Mem.*, I, 271, fn; see also pp. 277–8; II, 463–4). Henry Sewell Stokes (with whom Tennyson stayed in 1848) states that he was 'a good German scholar, [. . .] and could recite whole passages from Goethe's *Faust*' (cited in J. Cuming Walters, *Tennyson: Poet, Philosopher, Idealist* (London: Kegan Paul, Trench, Trübner, 1893), p. 157; but see also Walters's caveat about Stokes's testimony, p. 156). Charles Villiers Stanford (who first met Tennyson in 1879) reports that he pronounced German 'with a strong English accent', although he adds that 'Goethe himself would have acknowledged his reading of "Kennst du das Land" to be a masterpiece' (Sir Charles Villiers Stanford, 'A Composer Remembers', in *Interviews and Recollections*, ed. Page, pp. 127–30 (p. 129)).

[139] Campbell (ed.), I (1971), p. 29, no. 469 (inscribed 'A Tennyson Xmas day 1838').

[140] Hay. 1, p. lxxxvi; Carlyle, *Letters*, VII (1977), 82–5 (21 January 1834); pp. 204–5 ([9 June 1834]); p. 229 ([3 July 1834]); *Lady Tennyson's Journal*, ed. James O. Hoge (Charlottesville: University Press of Virginia, 1981), pp. 123, 124, 125 (2, 12, 18 October).

It was probably also in 1839 that Tennyson began work on *The Princess: A Medley* (*PT*, 286; first edition 1847), which draws quite heavily on *Faust: Part Two*. It seems to me very likely that he was reading this text in German, but also making use of an English translation. This was probably the one by William Bell Macdonald, which had been published in Dumfries in 1838, a second edition of which was printed in London four years later.[141] Tennyson's next two major works, *In Memoriam* (1850) and *Maud: A Monodrama* (*PT*, 316; 1855), are strongly influenced by *Faust: Part One*. It should be added, however, that the latter poem effectively marks the end of his long creative engagement with Goethe's drama, for in the remaining thirty-seven years of his life, he produced only three short pieces that are suggestive of its influence.

The story of *Faust* in Britain during those years is, however, every bit as rich as it had been in the preceding four and a half decades. It seems appropriate, therefore, to conclude this Introduction with a brief overview of developments up to 1892.

Tennyson, it should be emphasised, never experienced any kind of comprehensive disillusionment with either *Faust* or its author.[142] For example, on 17 February 1858, his wife Emily wrote in her journal: 'We begin *Faust* as we have neither of us read it or anything German for a long time' (Emily Tennyson, *Journal*, p. 109). Clear evidence of Tennyson's continuing enthusiasm for Goethe is also provided by his library, of which Lang, writing in 1971, remarks:

> Hardly any conclusion to be drawn from the catalogue of these libraries is more striking than what must be inferred from the sheer number of German books, and among these authors Goethe's name of course leads all the rest. It is not a revelation that Goethe was one of the great formative influences on Tennyson, but very much more remains to be done.[143]

---

[141] *Part Two* was enjoying something of a vogue in these years, with five different translations appearing between 1838 and 1843 (see Frantz, pp. 132–47, 195–204, 306).

[142] See *Mem.*, II, 287–8, 376–7, 422–3, 464, 504. In ibid. I, 118 (and II, 337), Tennyson would appear to be echoing line 13 of Goethe's sonnet 'Nature and Art' (FA, 1, II, 838–9 / Johann Wolfgang Goethe, *Selected Verse: With Plain Prose Translations of Each Poem*, ed. and trans. David Luke (Harmondsworth: Penguin, 1964), p. 197).

[143] C. Y. Lang, 'Introduction', in Campbell (ed.), I (1971), pp. ix–xiv (p. xi).

This judgement was based, however, on just a small fraction of Tennyson's Goethe collection. It was probably at some point in the first half of the 1850s – as he became more settled, and more financially secure – that he acquired a forty-volume edition of Goethe's *Sämmtliche Werke* (*Complete Works*). (Documents kept at the Tennyson Research Centre show that this was part of his library by 1855. It was still in the collection as late as 1957, although it had disappeared by *c.* 1963.)[144] It would seem, therefore, that during the second half of his life, Tennyson owned more books by Goethe than by any other single author.

In 1851, Carlyle had given Tennyson a copy of John Oxenford's English version of *Conversations of Goethe*, which he appears to have read immediately (marking, amongst others, two passages relating to *Faust*).[145] His library also included two of the most distinguished of the twenty-two *Faust* translations[146] that were published in Britain and the United States between 1855 and his death: Theodore Martin's (1865), and the American Bayard Taylor's (1871).[147] It is likely, however, that both were unwanted gifts from their

---

[144] Listed in: [Emily and Alfred Tennyson], 'Loose Sheets from a Catalogue of Tennyson's Library 1855–56' (N/19), item 3, 'May 1855', p. 1; item 4, 'May 1855', p. 4; Anon., 'Catalogue of Books in Tennyson's Library. 1856–59' (N/20), '1857', p. 1; 'Drawing Room. 1858', p. 1; [Emily Tennyson], 'Catalogue of Books in Alfred Tennyson's Library 1874' (N/22), '1874', p. 7; [Audrey Tennyson], 'Farringford Library Catalogue 1887' (N/23), '1887', p. 5; 'Inventory of the Library, the Property of Hallam, Lord Tennyson Trust Ltd. Stored at Messrs Shoolbred's Depository Harrow Road. W. June 1957. R. Ridgill Trout. F.V.I. 37 Tavistock Square. London. W.C.I.' (no ref. no.), p. 25. Absent from: 'Catalogue of the Library of Alfred Lord Tennyson, C-GRE', "Robin" Binder No. 582½ R, probably compiled by Lawrence Elvin, Local Studies Librarian (no ref. no.; *c.* 1963).

[145] *Conversations of Goethe with Eckermann and Soret*, trans. John Oxenford, 2 vols (London: Smith, Elder, 1850) (TRC, AT/1008). On the title page of Volume I is 'Alfred Lord Tennyson from Thomas Carlyle', and on the fly-leaf of Volume II is 'Tennyson from T. Carlyle 1851'. The marked passages relating to *Faust* are: I, 415; II, 392. The marginal markings in this book are undoubtedly Tennyson's: many of the marked passages chime with his own opinions, such as his belief in personal immortality, and his hostility towards source-hunters (I, 135; II, 109, 110). Also marked is a passage in which Goethe, referring to the Napoleonic period, remarks 'I did not hate the French' (II, 259). In January 1852, Tennyson published an attack on Napoleon III (*PT*, 304), in which he twice declares 'We hate not France' (ll. 17, 19). See also Chapter 1, p. 67.

[146] Frantz, pp. 306–7.

[147] Campbell (ed.), I (1971), p. 52, nos 1010, 1011 (vol. 2 only).

translators.[148] Of much greater interest to Tennyson was *The Life and Works of Goethe* by George Henry Lewes (whom he would later befriend).[149] This pioneering biography was published in November 1855. Tennyson was given a copy by the academic Alexander Grant on 27 December,[150] and a couple of years later, Emily recorded in her journal that her husband was reading passages from it out loud to her (Emily Tennyson, *Journal*, p. 111, 16 March 1858; p. 120, 27 August 1858). The *Life* stands alongside Carlyle's various publications of 1822–32 as one of the two most influential contributions to British Goethe studies to appear in the nineteenth century, and its impressive scholarship ensured that it was still widely read in the twentieth. As David Francis Smith observes, it would be a mistake to regard Lewes as 'a paragon of rationality and objectivity, at an opposite extreme from the brilliant but madly self-deceiving misinterpreter, Carlyle'.[151] However:

> Lewes has a much stronger claim to an authentic community of spirit with Goethe than Carlyle has, and for that reason [. . .] he gives, by and large, a more accurate idea of what Goethe was like to the British reader than Carlyle did.[152]

The many qualities of the *Life* were quickly recognised by both critics and public, and it was, therefore, a deserved success. It should be added, however, that the chapter on *Part Two* is unworthy of the book as a whole: much of Lewes's plot summary is paraphrased (without acknowledgement) from Hayward's *Foreign Quarterly Review* article, and his translation of Faust's dying speech is taken almost verbatim from the same source (Lewes, II, 428–35; Hay. 2, pp. 84–105, esp. p. 100).

---

[148] The pages of the version by Martin (whom Tennyson had met on 2 June 1859 (Emily Tennyson, *Journal*, p. 135)) are mostly uncut. Taylor got on well with Tennyson during his visits to Farringford in 1857 and 1867, but they subsequently fell out (*Mem.*, I, 418; Emily Tennyson, *Journal*, p. 94, 19 June 1857; pp. 258–9, 21 February 1867; Martin, pp. 468–9). The copy of his *Faust* might have been an unsuccessful peace offering.

[149] Martin, pp. 490, 527–8.

[150] Emily Tennyson, *Journal*, p. 57 (27 December 1855); F. B. Pinion, *A Tennyson Chronology* (Basingstoke: Macmillan, 1990), p. 73; Campbell (ed.), I (1971), p. 67, no. 1389.

[151] Smith, p. 171.

[152] Ibid. p. 253.

Many of the other translations of German texts that Lewes provides in the *Life* were the work of his partner, Mary Ann Evans, who in 1854–5 had accompanied him on his research trip to Weimar (in the course of which she read extensively in Goethe's works).[153] The future George Eliot had begun learning German as early as 1840, and had discovered *Faust* by 1845.[154] The protagonist's pact with Mephistopheles seems to have been of particular interest to her: she alludes to it in a letter from Germany in August 1854, and again in 'The Lifted Veil' (1859) and *Daniel Deronda* (1876).[155] It was, however the heroine Margaret who meant the most to Eliot: her widower John Walter Cross recalled that 'Nothing in all literature moved her more than the pathetic situation and the whole character of Gretchen. It touched her more than anything in Shakspeare [sic]'.[156] It was during a second trip to Germany (and Austria) in 1858 that Eliot wrote much of *Adam Bede*.[157] Rosemary Ashton points out that in this novel, Hetty Sorrel is a kind of cousin to Margaret: both women have a sexual relationship with a social superior; become pregnant; give birth; commit infanticide; and are subsequently sentenced to death.[158]

Goethe's heroine exercised an equally potent hold over the imagination of Dante Gabriel Rossetti, the influence on whom of *Faust: Part One* spanned almost his entire lifetime. He discovered Retzsch's illustrations to the play whilst still a child, and later 'read and re-read' Lewis Filmore's little-known 1841 translation, which seems to have inspired what may have been his first literary effort (a lost prose tale which he wrote at the age of fifteen).[159] The influence of

---

[153] Rosemary Ashton, *The German Idea: Four English Writers and the Reception of German Thought, 1800–1860* (Cambridge: Cambridge University Press, 1980), pp. 134, 166–7.

[154] Rosemary Ashton, *George Eliot: A Life* (London: Hamilton, 1996), pp. 31, 59–60; *The George Eliot Letters*, ed. Gordon S. Haight, 9 vols (New Haven, CT: Yale University Press, 1954–78), VIII, 10 ([June(?) 1845]).

[155] Eliot, *Letters*, II, 173 (and fn 4); George Eliot, 'The Lifted Veil', in *The Lifted Veil; Brother Jacob*, ed. Helen Small (Oxford: Oxford University Press, 1999), pp. 1–43 (Ch. I, pp. 20–1; see also p. 93, endnote); George Eliot, *Daniel Deronda*, ed. Graham Handley (Oxford: Clarendon Press, 1984), Bk II, Ch. XVI, p. 167 (see also Bk I, Ch. I, p. 3; Ch. V, p. 39; Bk V, Ch. XXXVII, p. 424; Ch. XXXIX, p. 452; Bk VI, Ch. XLVIII, p. 555).

[156] *George Eliot's Life: As Related in her Letters and Journals*, ed. J. W. Cross, 3 vols (Edinburgh: Blackwood, 1885), III, 421.

[157] Ashton, *Eliot*, pp. 195–8.

[158] Ibid. pp. 196–7.

[159] *Dante Gabriel Rossetti: His Family-Letters. With a Memoir by William Michael Rossetti* [ed. William Michael Rossetti], 2 vols (London: Ellis and Elvey, 1895), I, 59, 60, 103.

Faust is also apparent in the poems 'Lilith: From Goethe' (written 1866), 'Sonnet LXXVIII: Body's Beauty' (*c.* 1866) and 'Eden Bower' (1869).[160] Rossetti's many Faustian drawings and paintings include *Faust: Mephistopheles outside Gretchen's Cell* (1846), *Faust and Margaret in Prison* (*c.* 1856), *Lady Lilith* (1868) and the now-lost *Risen at Dawn* (1878–80).[161]

Two authors with links to Rossetti – his erstwhile friend Ruskin, and his memorialist Pater – took a more mixed view of Goethe's drama. 'I entirely dislike Faust,' declared the former in 1857, although five years later, he acclaimed *Part Two* as 'a perfect treasure-house of strange knowledge and thought'.[162] In *The Renaissance* (1873), Pater denigrates *Part Two* as 'a mass of science which has almost no artistic character at all', but this does not prevent him from using its symbolism to support his argument on two separate occasions later on in the book.[163]

No such doubts assailed Henry James, who regarded Goethe's drama as 'one of the greatest productions of the human mind'.[164] James is known to have met Abraham Hayward, and Susie Ellis argues that *Faust* influenced some half a dozen of his works, from *Watch and Ward* (1871) to *The Bostonians* (1885–6).[165] Another Victorian novelist, Thomas Hardy (who owned a copy of Hayward's translation), depicts, in seven works of fiction dating from 1872 to 1887, a series of characters whom J. O. Bailey terms 'Mephistophelian visitants'.[166] Grace Stevenson Haber demonstrates that *The Mayor of Casterbridge* (1886) contains echoes of Carlyle's essay on

---

[160] Dante Gabriel Rossetti, *Collected Poetry and Prose*, ed. Jerome McGann (New Haven, CT: Yale University Press, 2003), pp. 304 (and see p. 409), 161–2, 43–8. See *F*, ll. 4119–23 / p. 175.

[161] Eva Krüger, *Bilder zu Goethes 'Faust'. Moritz Retzsch und Dante Gabriel Rossetti* (Hildesheim: Olms, 2009), pp. 53–105, 162–7, 169, 171–2, 174, 179.

[162] *The Works of John Ruskin*, ed. E. T. Cook and Alexander Wedderburn, Library Edition, 39 vols (London: Allen, 1903–12), XIV (1904), 129; XXXVI (1909), 422 (17 August [1862]).

[163] Walter Pater, *The Renaissance: Studies in Art and Poetry*, ed. Adam Phillips (Oxford: Oxford University Press, 1986), pp. 72, 133, 145–6.

[164] Henry James, *The Scenic Art: Notes on Acting and the Drama 1872–1901*, ed. Allan Wade (London: Hart-Davis, 1949), p. 220.

[165] Susie Ellis, 'The Influence of Goethe's *Faust* on the Fiction of Henry James' (unpublished doctoral thesis, University of Ulster, 1992), esp. p. 52.

[166] Walter F. Wright, *The Shaping of 'The Dynasts': A Study in Thomas Hardy* (Lincoln: University of Nebraska Press, 1967), p. 19; J. O. Bailey, 'Hardy's "Mephistophelian Visitants"', *PMLA*, 61: 4 (December 1946), 1146–84 (p. 1146).

'Goethe's "Helena"', and a number of critics have detected the influence of *Faust* in *The Dynasts* (published 1904–8), which Hardy was already planning and researching in 1886–7.[167]

It was around that time that *Part One* belatedly became an English theatrical sensation. Henry Irving's production of *Faust* opened at the Lyceum Theatre in London on 19 December 1885.[168] The Prince and Princess of Wales were in the audience, and the attendees at subsequent performances included such luminaries as Liszt and Gladstone.[169] Irving had travelled to Germany to research the scenic aspects of the production, which was very much a vehicle for his own portrayal of Mephistopheles (Ellen Terry was Margaret, and in the title role, the ineffectual H. B. Conway was quickly replaced by George Alexander).[170] Irving's biographer Jeffrey Richards describes his *Faust* as 'one of the great landmarks of Victorian spectacular theatre', and '[p]erhaps the crowning achievement of [his] regime in both artistic and economic terms'.[171] It received scores of notices and reviews, and was revived in the 1886–7 season; again in 1888; and twice thereafter.[172] All in all, it was performed a total of 792 times in Britain and America, and grossed an estimated £250,000.[173] Such was its popularity that it gave rise to numerous spoofs, including *Mephisto*; *Faust and Loose; or, Brocken Vows*; and *Faust up to Date*.[174] The satirical publication *Judy* even depicted Gladstone as Mephistopheles.[175]

---

[167] Grace Stevenson Haber, 'Echoes from Carlyle's "Goethe's 'Helena'"' in *The Mayor of Casterbridge*, *Nineteenth-Century Fiction*, 12: 1 (June 1957), 89–90; Bailey, 'Mephistophelian Visitants', pp. 1170, 1183; F. B. Pinion, *A Thomas Hardy Dictionary: With Maps and a Chronology* (Basingstoke: Macmillan, 1989), pp. 6, 86, 113–14.

[168] Jeffrey Richards, *Sir Henry Irving: A Victorian Actor and his World* (London: Hambledon and London, 2005), p. 415.

[169] Ibid. p. 415; Laurence Irving, *Henry Irving: The Actor and his World* (London: Faber and Faber, 1951), pp. 468, 471–2.

[170] Richards, pp. 415, 416; Irving, pp. 462–3, 466, 469–70.

[171] Richards, pp. 416, 415.

[172] William Heinemann, 'The Lyceum *Faust*: A List of Press Notices and Reviews', *Publications of the English Goethe Society*, o.s. 2 (1887), 112–14; Richards, p. 415.

[173] Richards, p. 415.

[174] Anon., 'Our Omnibus-Box', *The Theatre*, n.s. 8 (July 1886), 47–58 (pp. 47–9); Anon., 'Drama: The Week', *Athenæum*, 3042 (13 February 1886), 241; Anon., '*Faust and Loose*', *Saturday Review*, 61: 1581 (13 February 1886), 229; Anon., '*Faust up to Date*', *Saturday Review*, 66: 1724 (10 November 1888), 554.

[175] Anon., 'Scene from *Faust and Loose*', *Judy, or the London Serio-Comic Journal* (14 April 1886), 170.

But if the popular impact of the Lyceum *Faust* was unprecedented, its approach to its literary source was not. With the exception of a German production at St James's in 1852, and an adaptation performed at Drury Lane in 1866, none of the London stage versions of *Faust* had been faithful to the original, and some had been deliberate travesties.[176] Victorian theatre managers and playwrights – much like the critics and translators of the period – tended to transform *Faust* into something more compatible with the moral and religious values of their audiences. For example, in W. S. Gilbert's *Gretchen: A Play, in Four Acts* (1879), Faustus is a monk, whose 'chaste and sober life' is disrupted by his affair with the heroine, who in the last act lectures him as she dies: 'Thou shalt atone, for thou hast greatly sinned — | Thou shalt atone with worthy deeds lifelong.'[177] The adaptation that Irving commissioned from W. G. Wills was similarly didactic: 'Such a picture as Irving gives us of "Mephistopheles"', enthused Lewis Carroll, 'must surely have a healthy influence. Who can see it and not realise [. . .] the utter *hatefulness* of sin?'[178] Others were more critical, however: 'It is not for these things that we go to see the great Goethe', wrote Henry James in his review.[179]

Many members of the Lyceum audience were nevertheless encouraged by what they had seen to take a greater interest in *Faust*. In June 1887, William Heinemann (the founder of the publishing house) observed that 'there has been in the last eighteen months [. . .] an unprecedented demand for copies of the various translations', and in

---

[176] The available sources on these productions are sometimes mutually contradictory, but the chronology would appear to have been as follows: *Faustus* (Drury Lane, 1825); a *Faust* ballet (Haymarket, 1833); *The Devil and Doctor Faustus: A Drama, in Three Acts* (Theatre Royal, 1841); *Faust, or, the Demon of Drachenfels* (Sadler's Wells, 1842); *Faust* (St James's Theatre, 1852); *Faust and Marguerite: A Magical Drama* (Princess Theatre, 1854); *Faust and Marguerite* (St James's Theatre, 1864); *Faust and Marguerite; or, the Devil's Draught* (Drury Lane, 1866); *Gretchen: A Play, in Four Acts* (Olympic Theatre, 1879) (William Heinemann, 'Goethe on the English Stage', *Publications of the English Goethe Society*, o.s. 4 (1888), 24–7 (pp. 24–5); Carré, pp. 231–2; Proescholdt-Obermann, pp. 167 (and fn), 294; Richards, p. 415; Carlyle, *Letters*, XXVII (1999), 147 (and fn 1), 20 June 1852; p. 148, 22 June 1852).

[177] W. S. Gilbert, *Gretchen: A Play, in Four Acts* (London: Newman, 1879), Act I, p. 4; Act IV, p. 120.

[178] Lewis Carroll, 'The Stage and the Spirit of Reverence', *The Theatre*, n.s. 11 (June 1888), 285–94 (p. 292).

[179] James, p. 222.

the words of H. S. Bluhm, Irving's production also provoked a 'flood of articles' in the press.[180] This atmosphere of heightened interest may help to account for the fact that in the three years from 1887 to 1890, at least four different British authors published works that were influenced by *Faust*.

More than half a century after *Paracelsus*, Robert Browning returned to the Faustian theme in 'Fust and Friends', which forms the epilogue to *Parleyings* (1887).[181] The following year, Tennyson's friend Roden Noel (1834–94) published *A Modern Faust* (parts of which Hallam Tennyson read to his father during his illness in January 1889 (*LAT*, III, 389)).[182] Noel appears to have seen Goethe's drama in Carlylean terms, for he argued that 'the familiar name of Faust' was 'not altogether inappropriate' to a poem on 'the speculative difficulties peculiar to our day and generation'.[183] However, apart from a couple of brief references to *Faust* (Noel, pp. 88, 151), it would not be easy to deduce the title of this almost-forgotten work from its contents.

A more tangible connection with Goethe's drama is provided by Arthur Conan Doyle's *The Sign of the Four*. In Chapter II, Sherlock Holmes's client Miss Morstan receives an anonymous letter that instructs her to 'Be at the third pillar from the left outside the Lyceum Theatre to-night at seven o'clock.'[184] By the time that she, Holmes and Dr Watson arrive there in Chapter III, 'the crowds', we are told, 'were already thick at the side-entrances' (p. 19). I would suggest that

---

[180] Heinemann, 'English Stage', p. 26; H. S. Bluhm, 'The Reception of Goethe's *Faust* in England after the Middle of the Nineteenth Century', *Journal of English and Germanic Philology*, 34: 2 (April 1935), 201–12 (p. 208).

[181] *The Complete Works of Robert Browning: With Variant Readings & Annotations*, ed. Roma A. King, Jr and others, 17 vols (Athens: Ohio University Press, 1969–2012), XVI (1998), 130–54.

[182] Noel sent Tennyson inscribed copies of several of his books (Campbell (ed.), I (1971), p. 79, nos. 1696–9; p. 167, no. 3462). He was one of the earliest members of the Metaphysical Society, which Tennyson co-founded in 1869, so their meeting on 9 October 1873 was not, presumably, their first (*Mem.*, II, 167; Emily Tennyson, *Journal*, p. 363). Tennyson's letters to Noel are all cordial (*LAT*, III, 61 [late June 1873]; p. 206, 13 February 1881; p. 310 [7 February 1885]).

[183] Roden Noel, *A Modern Faust and Other Poems* (London: Kegan Paul, Trench, 1888), p. xiv. Noel is probably echoing the discussion of religious doubt in the 'Preface' to Carlyle's translation of *Wilhelm Meister's Travels*, which refers to 'difficulties peculiar to the time' (*WTC*, XXIII, 25).

[184] Arthur Conan Doyle, *The Sign of the Four*, ed. Christopher Roden (Oxford: Oxford University Press, 1993), p. 14.

these theatre-goers were gathering for a performance of the hugely popular *Faust*, and that it is this episode that prompts Holmes, in Chapter VI, to quote lines 1205–6 from the scene 'Study [I]' in *Part One* (p. 48 (see also Ch. XII, p. 119); Hay. 1, p. 39). Faust – less than seventy lines later – utters the words 'the spell of the four' (l. 1272 / p. 42), and at the Lyceum, the equivalent phrase was accorded a good deal more prominence by being placed in the opening scene: 'The mighty Spell of Four will I pronounce. [. . .] | By the sign and by the spell'.[185] It is quite possible that these words helped to suggest the title of Conan Doyle's novel.

The Sign of the Four appeared in *Lippincott's Magazine* in February 1890. The influence of the Lyceum *Faust* may also be discernible in a novel that an acquaintance of Doyle's published in the same periodical five months later. '[I]t is a pity', declared Oscar Wilde, 'that Goethe never had an opportunity of reading [*The Picture of*] *Dorian Gray* [expanded edition 1891]. I feel quite certain that he would have been delighted by it'.[186] It can be safely assumed that the erudite Wilde had by this time read *Faust* (which a few years later would be amongst the books that he would ask to be sent to him in Reading Gaol).[187] Critics have detected a number of resemblances between the two works: in both, the protagonist has a love affair with a young woman, which leads to her death; her brother (a soldier in *Faust*, a sailor in *Dorian*) seeks revenge, but is himself killed instead.[188] It is notable that all of these similarities relate to the Gretchen tragedy in *Part One*, which had provided the focus

---

[185] [W. G. Wills], *Faust, in a Prologue and Five Acts: Adapted and Arranged for the Lyceum Theatre by W. G. Wills, from the First Part of Goethe's Tragedy* ([n.p., n. pub., 1886]; British Library, System number 001447891; General Reference Collection 11747.f.5.(4.).; bound together with three German plays), p. 3.

[186] *The Complete Letters of Oscar Wilde*, ed. Merlin Holland and Rupert Hart-Davis (London: Fourth Estate, 2000), p. 446 (13 August 1890).

[187] Ibid. p. 673 (and fn 3) (16 December [1896]).

[188] *The Complete Works of Oscar Wilde*, ed. Russell Jackson and Ian Small (Oxford: Oxford University Press, 2000–), III: *The Picture of Dorian Gray: The 1890 and 1891 Texts*, ed. Joseph Bristow (2005) (all references are to the 1891 version), Chs IV–X, pp. 208–75; Chs XVI–XVIII, pp. 324–45; Dominick Rossi, 'Parallels in Wilde's *The Picture of Dorian Gray* and Goethe's *Faust*', *CLA Journal*, 13: 2 (December 1969), 188–91; Norbert Kohl, *Oscar Wilde: The Works of a Conformist Rebel*, trans. David Henry Wilson (Cambridge: Cambridge University Press, 1989), p. 162. See also Ted R. Spivey, 'Damnation and Salvation in *The Picture of Dorian Gray*', *Boston University Studies in English*, 4: 3 (Autumn 1960), 162–70 (p. 162, fn).

of the Lyceum adaptation.[189] Also, in the pivotal scene of Wilde's novel, Dorian exclaims: 'If it were I who was to be always young, and the picture that was to grow old! [. . .] I would give my soul for that!' (Ch. II, p. 189, ll. 32–3, 35).[190] The oft-cited resemblance between these words and the Faustian pact[191] is strengthened considerably if they are compared to the Lyceum script, in which Faust sells his soul not (as in Goethe) to seek an elusive perfect moment, but in order to regain his youth (Wills, pp. 7–8).

Like Wilde, Tennyson was a friend of Ellen Terry, and an acquaintance of Henry Irving.[192] It is hardly surprising, therefore, that he attended a performance of the Lyceum *Faust* in July 1886.[193] His son and biographer Hallam Tennyson states that he looked upon this 'melodramatic representation' as a 'degradation of the drama' (ibid. IV, 141), and this was, in all probability, a fair appraisal. By that time, Goethe's masterpiece had long since ceased to be a major influence on Tennyson's work – although as I will argue in Chapter 5, 'The Dreamer' (*PT*, 461), which was '[t]he last poem he finished' before his death in October 1892, includes a few faint echoes of *Faust* (*Mem.*, II, 419).

Two conclusions are suggested by the preceding discussion. First, it seems clear that in Victorian Britain, Goethe's drama was a central text. '*Faust*, which rivals [*Hamlet*] in popularity, rivals it also in prodigality', asserted Lewes confidently in 1855 (Lewes, II, 282). It stood alongside the plays of Shakespeare, and just a handful of other works – *The Iliad*, *The Odyssey*, *The Divine Comedy*, *Paradise Lost* and the poetry of the Romantics – which were seen as comprising the canon of British and European literature. *Faust* still tends to be placed in this company today, but sometimes with more of a sense of duty than enthusiasm. By contrast, during most of the nineteenth century, it was very much a *living* work: regularly performed;

---

[189] In Goethe's text, Gretchen does not make her entrance until halfway through *Part One* (stage direction before l. 2605 / p. 101). In the Lyceum adaptation, which is in a 'Prologue' and five acts, she first appears as early as the second scene of the 'Prologue' (Wills, p. 16).

[190] See also *Dorian Gray*, Ch. XVI, p. 329, l. 11; p. 332, ll. 28–9; Ch. XIX, p. 350, ll. 8–10.

[191] Rossi, p. 188; Kohl, p. 162.

[192] Martin, pp. 448, 511–12, 523–5; Richard Ellmann, *Oscar Wilde* (London: Hamilton, 1987), pp. 114, 229 (see also p. 15).

[193] [Hallam Lord Tennyson], *Materials for a Life of A. T.: Collected for my Children*, 4 vols ([n.p., n. pub., 1895]), IV, 141.

endlessly retranslated; widely read and discussed; and an important source of inspiration for dozens of creative writers, from Shelley to Wilde. If – as I will argue repeatedly in the following chapters – Tennyson was deeply influenced by *Faust*, he was by no means alone.

Second, it seems equally clear that British attitudes to *Faust* were anything but straightforward. Although the reading public gradually realised that Goethe's drama was not the 'impure trash' that its first reviewer had taken it to be, the moral and religious misgivings that it aroused never entirely disappeared. Only a few individuals were immune to these concerns, and significantly, they were often the targets of moral and religious disapproval themselves: one thinks of Shelley, Byron, Lewes, Eliot, Rossetti and Wilde. For the majority, admiration for *Faust* was attended by a certain discomfort, which tended to vent itself through sometimes far-reaching attempts at modification or re-interpretation.

As we have seen, this dual response is discernible in the translation, reception, performance and influence of Goethe's drama. And as I will argue in the next six chapters, it is also discernible in at least two dozen of Tennyson's poems, including several of the very greatest.

Part I

The Death of Arthur Hallam

Chapter 1

'I am to die already!': The Gretchen Tragedy

The pattern of the influence of *Faust* on Tennyson reveals that there was a link in his mind between the death of Arthur Hallam in September 1833, and the tragedy of Margaret (or 'Gretchen') that comprises the second half of *Part One*. This episode consists of the nineteen scenes from 'The Street' to 'Dungeon', which chart the course of a love affair between the protagonist and a young woman, which turns rapidly from idyll to disaster (*F*, ll. 2605–4612 / pp. 101–203).

At least two of Tennyson's poems of the Cambridge period (as well as one by Hallam) appear to reflect an interest in the character and situation of Goethe's heroine. Around the time of Hallam's death, this interest was renewed and intensified, and this is borne out by several of the elegies that Tennyson wrote for his friend in 1833–4, including 'Hark! the dogs howl!' and 'Oh! that 'twere possible'. These two poems are linked, respectively, to *In Memoriam* and *Maud*, in both of which Tennyson turns, once again, to the Gretchen tragedy. The paucity of documentation – only two dozen letters from Hallam to Tennyson survive, and none at all from the poet to his friend – means that the biographical roots of the connection between Hallam and *Faust* are largely a matter for speculation. However, given the central role of literature in the two men's friendship, it seems possible that their enthusiasm for Goethe was an important shared experience.

It has not been widely acknowledged that Hallam was an enthusiastic Germanophile. His editor, T. H. Vail Motter, writes:

> in his death literature lost a scholarly critic whose especial competence in Italian studies would have furnished the Victorians a valuable

counterweight for the disproportionate reverence which the leadership of Coleridge and Carlyle bestowed upon things German.[1]

This judgement has been echoed, to a greater or lesser extent, by later commentators.[2] It dates, however, from 1943, and although the first part of it is basically sound,[3] the latter part may bear the imprint of contemporary events. Apart from a few sceptical remarks about Hegel and his followers, the only evidence that Hallam deprecated 'things German' is a passage in his 'Oration, on the Influence of Italian Works of Imagination on the Same Class of Compositions in England' (*WAH*, p. 250, and fn; pp. 213–34, esp. 232–3). This, however, was written to be read out in Trinity College Chapel in December 1831, and speaking in this sacred environment, just a short time after a further outbreak of political upheaval in Europe, Hallam is likely to have been mindful of German culture's lingering association with immorality, irreligion and revolution.[4] The suspicion that his words should not be taken at face value would appear to be confirmed, moreover, by the oration's most famous remark: 'Rhyme has been said to contain in itself a constant appeal to Memory and Hope' (*WAH*, p. 222, fn). In *De l'Allemagne* (1810), translated as *Germany* (1813), Germaine de Staël writes:

la rime [. . .] est l'image de l'espérance et du souvenir. Un son nous fait désirer celui qui doit lui répondre, et quand le second retentit il nous rappelle celui qui vient de nous échapper.

Rhyme [. . .] is the image of hope and of memory. One sound makes us desire another corresponding to it; and when the second is heard, it recals [sic] that which has just escaped us.[5]

---

[1] *WAH*, p. 115.
[2] See, for example, Richard Cronin, 'Goethe, the Apostles, and Tennyson's "Supposed Confessions"', *Philological Quarterly*, 72: 3 (Summer 1993), 337–56 (p. 343).
[3] 'To me nothing else in the world resembles the delight I take in Italian literature', writes Hallam to Emily Tennyson in 1831. Tellingly, however, he adds: 'Perhaps [. . .] I owe this to early associations, which you have not: perhaps German would lay stronger hold on your imagination' (*LAHH*, no. 118, pp. 456–7, 5 August). During his nine-month stay in Italy in 1827–8, the teenage Hallam had met his first love, Anna Wintour (Blocksidge, pp. 56–79).
[4] *WAH*, p. 213; Ashton, *German Idea*, pp. 1, 5–8, 13, 30–1, 64.
[5] Mme la Baronne de Staël Holstein, *De l'Allemagne*, 3 vols (Paris: Nicolle, 1810; repr. London: Murray, 1813), Vol. I, Pt II, Ch. IX, p. 270 / *Germany*, I, 289. De

It would appear, therefore, that even as Hallam was making a public show of distaste for German culture, he was alluding to a work that is dedicated to its praise. Perhaps this circumstance served to colour the dismissive appraisal of his own essay that he was to offer in a letter to his father a few weeks later: 'A Chapel Oration', he declared, 'is a vile mould of composition' (*LAHH*, no. 136, p. 504, [10 January 1832]).

It is Hallam's correspondence that provides the most reliable guide to his opinion of German culture, and that opinion was strongly positive both before and after he delivered his chapel address. By September of 1829, although he had 'always had some previous knowledge of the language', he was reading it 'with great diligence' (ibid. no. 81, p. 334 [11 October 1829]; no. 76, p. 314, 1 September [1829]).[6] The following month he declared, 'I really think learning German a branch of moral duty', and at the end of the year he reported, 'I have been making way in that divine language' (ibid. no. 81, p. 334

Staël's novel *Corinne ou l'Italie* (1807) had had a powerful effect on Hallam when he read it in 1828 (*LAHH*, no. 50, pp. 210, 212, 214, fn, 25 June). In a letter of October 1829, he remarks: 'It has seemed to me that Religion never gains by being, as Mdme. de Stael [sic] expresses it, "conduite hors du cercle des connaissances humaines, à force de Reverences"' (*Letters*, no. 79, pp. 329–30). This is an allusion to the following passage in *Germany*, from the chapter 'Of French Philosophy':

> une des causes de l'affoiblissement du respect pour la religion, c'est de l'avoir mise à part de toutes les sciences, [. . .] c'est pour ainsi dire la reconduire hors du cercle de l'esprit humain à force de révérences.
>
> one of the causes of the diminution of respect for religion, is this custom of setting her apart from all the sciences; [. . .] it is, if we may so express ourselves, to bow her out of the circle of the human mind. (de Staël Holstein, *De l'Allemagne*, Vol. III, Pt III, Ch. III, p. 31 / *Germany*, III, 33; the last four words of the French text have been omitted by the English translator.)

In the preceding chapter, 'Of English Philosophy', de Staël discusses Locke and Dugald Stewart (1753–1828), and both chapters include references to Newton (de Staël Holstein, *De l'Allemagne*, Vol. III, Pt III, Ch. II, pp. 18–21, 25–6, 29; Ch. III, p. 37 / *Germany*, III, 19–22, 27–8, 30–1, 39). In a letter dating from a couple of weeks prior to the one cited above, Hallam writes: 'My morning companions are mostly Aristotle, or Locke, or [Dugald] Stewart,' and he concludes: 'Send me word how you like Sir Isaac [Newton]? Have you read the fine closing chapter of the Principia yet?' (*LAHH*, no. 78, pp. 322, 326 [16 September 1829]).

[6] See also ibid. no. 75, p. 309 (September 1829); no. 87, pp. 357–8 (14 March 1830).

[11 October]; no. 83, p. 343, 12(?) December). A letter to his friend Robert Robertson of March 1830, in which Hallam outlines unrealised holiday plans, is worth quoting at length:

> I [. . .] intend being very happy at Bonn, Heidelberg or such like fine place. I am promised an introduction to the principal Burschen [Student] Clubs, in which I will drink beer, and clash swords for fatherland. [. . .] A friend of mine has lately returned from Deutschlands [*sic*], and made me rather mad by singing the patriotic songs of our brethren on the other side of the sea. I can conceive nothing equal to the delight and Schwärmerei [enthusiasm] of hearing [the poet and dramatist Karl Theodor] Körner's divine war melodies[7] hurled forth from eight hundred voices on the plain of Jena, an event, thank Heaven, which is now a matter of history. [. . .] Come what will there must ever be communion of heart between an Englishman and German, [more] than we can have with any other people on the face of the Globe. Their literature has of late mightily and nobly influenced our own. They almost vindicate to themselves our Shakespeare, less understood by any than Schlegel and Tieck. Let a man go further back and, taking up the English translation of the Bible then think of Luther, the greatest Northern mind that ever shone. [. . .] Let us go back further still, read our glorious old ballads along with the Nibelungen Lied—or let him ponder over the republican spirit which makes us properly Englishmen—and straightway the old Saxon forests will ring out a witness to our primeval and inviolate alliance. (ibid. no. 87, p. 356)[8]

This enthusiasm does not appear to have diminished during the remaining three years of Hallam's life. In a book review written in September 1832, he argues that 'the Teutonic languages' have greater expressive power than 'those of the South', and in his letters of that month, he twice reports that he is reading German (*WAH*, pp. 236–7; *LAHH*, no. 188, p. 638; no. 191, p. 646). In November, he recommends the study of it to his fiancée, Emily Tennyson (the poet's

---

[7] See Lord Francis Leveson Gower (trans.), *Faust: A Drama, by Goethe. With Translations from the German*, 2nd edn, 2 vols (London: Murray, 1825), II, 'War Song'; 'War Song: Written before the Battle of Danneberg' (pp. 189–199). Compare 'English Warsong' (*PT*, 116).
[8] Elsewhere in this letter, Hallam uses the phrase 'blowing out my brains' (ibid. p. 358). This could be an echo of *Werther*, the protagonist of which is 'so mad as to blow out his brains' (W, Pt I, p. 94, ll. 3–4, 12 August [1771] / p. 77).

sister): 'there is no language—hardly your own—that you would like as well. It would be a new world for you' (*LAHH*, no. 205, p. 681).⁹

Hallam's own acquisition of German was partly motivated by a desire to experience at first hand what he called 'the glory of Goethe' (ibid. no. 83, p. 343, 12(?) December 1829).¹⁰ A letter dating from 16 September 1829 reveals that he had by that time at least some familiarity with *Faust: Part One*, which he seems to have regarded as Goethe's chief work: 'I have taken up German eagerly', he writes; '[. . .] I hope to walk with Kant, and the author of Faust in another year' (ibid. no. 78, p. 322). In a letter from Somersby the following April, he alludes to the play once again: 'what an amalgamate of Mephistophilisms that London society is!' (ibid. no. 88, pp. 360–1). And in September 1832, he writes to Tennyson to suggest that Goethe is suitable company for a pre-eminent Greek, and two of the greatest of all Italians (referring to the line 'Plato, Petrarca, Livy, and Raphaël' in 'The Palace of Art',¹¹ he comments: 'I would hint a change of Livy into some other body. What think you of "Goethe and Raffael"?' (ibid. no. 195, p. 652; see also no. 113, p. 441, 15 July 1831)).

It does not seem unreasonable to assume that Hallam would have talked about Goethe's work with Tennyson. Although these discussions are lost, a number of passages in the two men's writings provide evidence of them – and might even be said to be a continuation

---

⁹ See also *LAHH*, no. 202, pp. 669–70 (23 October [1832]); no. 203, p. 675 (30 October 1832); no. 220, p. 717 (25 January [1833]); no. 246, p. 778 (30 August [1833]).

¹⁰ The seeds of Hallam's interest in Goethe could have been sown early on: his house-master at Eton, Edward Craven Hawtrey, was 'proficient and widely read in [. . .] German' (Blocksidge, p. 30; see also *Auswahl von Goethes lyrischen Gedichten* [ed. Edward Craven Hawtrey], 2nd edn (Eton: Williams, 1834)). Alternatively, Hallam could have been introduced to Goethe's work by his sister Ellen, or his friend John Kemble (both of whom spoke German), or by his classical tutor at Cambridge, Julius Hare (*LAHH*, no. 78, p. 322 [16 September 1829]; Blocksidge, p. 139; *Mem.*, I, 36). In an anthology of German and classical verse published in 1847, all of the translations from Goethe, and all but one of those from Schiller, are either by Hare, or by Tennyson's Cambridge tutor William Whewell (J[ohn] F[rederick] W[illiam] H[erschel], W[illiam] W[hewell], J[ulius] C[harles] H[are], E[dward] C[raven] H[awtrey] and J. G. L. (unidentified; probably John Gibson Lockhart) (trans.), *English Hexameter Translations from Schiller, Goethe, Homer, Callinus, and Meleager* (London: Murray, 1847), pp. 1–240).

¹¹ Deleted in 1842 (*PT*, 167, ll. 137–64, fn).

of them. In seeking to uncover something of this literary 'conversation', one sometimes has the sense that one is intruding into a private dialogue, whose frame of reference is not readily accessible to outsiders. Ricks's comments on Tennyson could also be applied to Hallam:

> Tennyson [. . .] does not most characteristically *allude*. Or rather, the world of those readers who are to take Tennyson's allusions is in one respect [. . .] a smaller circle than what might be called the usual world of educated common readers. [. . .] [S]ome of [his] strongest and deepest poetical reminiscences [. . .] are of words which only a tiny circle within the large circle of [his] original readers could ever have recognized and participated in. There is here one kind of privacy, the privacy of intimates.[12]

Hallam's 'Lines Addressed to Alfred Tennyson' may provide an early example of these 'confidential allusions'.[13] This poem was written in the late summer of 1829, in response to its author's recent visit to a mental asylum.[14] But the 'Lines' may also reflect the influence of Keats's 'Isabella',[15] and of 'Dungeon' in *Faust: Part One* (ll. 4405–612 / Gower, II, 65–78). In this scene (which will be discussed in greater detail later on in this chapter), Gretchen's love affair with the protagonist has led to disaster: she has killed their baby, been incarcerated, and gone insane. In his 'Lines', Hallam chooses to focus on one specific mad young woman, about whose love-life he speculates, and whom he imagines to be '[t]he sufferer of a penal life', who is guilty of an unnamed crime (*WAH*, p. 67). The poem is dated 'Malvern, September, 1829' (ibid. p. 66), and it was there, in a letter that he wrote on the 16th of that month, that Hallam announced his intention to 'walk with [. . .] the author of Faust'. The same letter strongly suggests that he was studying *De l'Allemagne*,[16] whose chapter on Goethe's drama includes a translation of 'Dungeon' (Vol. II, Pt. II, Ch. XXIII, pp. 206–16).

The 'Lines' were first published in Hallam's *Poems* (1830), which had at one stage been intended to comprise a single volume with

---

[12] Ricks, *Allusion*, p. 181. In the last two sentences quoted here, Ricks is referring specifically to *In Memoriam*.
[13] Ibid. p. 181 (again with reference to *In Memoriam*).
[14] *LAHH*, no. 76, pp. 311–12 (1 September [1829]); Blocksidge, p. 109.
[15] Keats writes: 'And so she pined', and three lines later, he uses the words 'pity' and 'ditty' in consecutive lines (*The Poems of John Keats*, ed. Jack Stillinger (Cambridge, MA: Belknap Press of Harvard University Press, 1978), 'Isabella; or, The Pot of Basil', pp. 245–63, ll. 497, 500–1). Hallam rhymes 'pity' with 'ditty', and in the following stanza he writes: 'So pined the maiden' (*WAH*, p. 67).
[16] See pp. 48–9, fn 5.

Tennyson's *Poems, Chiefly Lyrical* of the same year.[17] In the best-known piece from the latter collection, 'Mariana' (*PT*, 73), the lonely female character whom Tennyson describes is broadly reminiscent of the forlorn young woman of Hallam's lyric, and the two works may also be linked by 'Isabella',[18] and by *Faust*.

There can be little doubt that Goethe was somewhere in Tennyson's mind when he wrote this famous poem. As Kennedy demonstrates, his Mariana owes as much to her namesake in the *Apprenticeship* as she does to the Mariana of *Measure for Measure*.[19] And as Ricks observes, line 15 of the poem ('She could not look on the sweet heaven') would appear to echo a line from the *Aeneid* ('she is weary of gazing on the arch of heaven'),[20] the Latin original of which provides the epigraph for the title page of Graves's *Werther* translation. The form and mood of both 'Mariana' and 'Mariana in the South' (*PT*, 160) may also draw on the scene 'Gretchens Stube' (or 'Margaret's Chamber') in *Part One* (ll. 3374–413 / Coleridge, *Faustus*, p. 57).[21] In *Faust* – much as in *Werther* and *Meister* – what seems to resonate for Tennyson is the figure of the despairing heroine, abandoned by her lover and longing for death. In 'Margaret's Chamber', the pervasive atmosphere of world-weariness is expressed in a quatrain refrain (ll. 3374–7, 3386–9, 3402–5), and the same can be said of both of the Mariana poems ('Mariana', ll. 9–12 etc.; 'Mariana in the South', ll. 9–12 etc.). Also, in a similar scene, 'Zwinger' (or 'The Fausse-Braye'),[22] Margaret prays to the Virgin Mary (ll. 3587–619 / Coleridge, *Faustus*, p. 61), and Mariana does the same after her relocation to the South (ll. 21–30, 59–60).

In August 1831, *Poems, Chiefly Lyrical* became the subject of a celebrated review by Hallam, in which his literary 'conversation' with Tennyson can be seen to be continued.[23] He alludes early on in this

---

[17] Martin, p. 102.
[18] See *PT*, 73, headnote.
[19] Kennedy, pp. 93–5.
[20] *PT*, 73, l. 15, and fn.
[21] The similarities between the Mariana poems and *Faust* are especially noticeable if one compares them to the translation attributed to Coleridge. But this does not necessarily indicate that Tennyson read it: like Byron, his early experience of the play might have come at least partly through the *viva voce* translations of German-speaking friends (such as Hallam).
[22] Modern translations of *Faust* render the title of this scene as 'A Shrine in the Ramparts', 'By the Ramparts' or 'By the City Wall'.
[23] For a more detailed account of this subject, see Tom Baynes, 'The Spirit of Goethe Looks Forth: Hallam, Carlyle, and *In Memoriam*', *Tennyson Research Bulletin*, 11: 5 (November 2021).

piece to a passage from the *Apprenticeship*,[24] and a detailed comparison reveals that the article as a whole is loosely modelled on Carlyle's 1828 essay 'Goethe'. Specifically, his discussions of the role of the poet, the need for critical fairness, and a number of other topics have identifiable precedents in the earlier piece. Hallam is implicitly arguing that his youthful friend can already bear comparison with Goethe, the man on whom Carlyle had showered almost boundless praise. For both its author and its subject, therefore, the article is likely to have had a significance that it has never possessed for any of its numerous other readers. When he received his copy of 'On Some of the Characteristics of Modern Poetry, and on the Lyrical Poems of Alfred Tennyson', the individual named in its title is likely to have been much gratified by Hallam's public advocacy of his work. Of still greater value, however, would have been the bold subliminal comparison that his friend had made between himself and Carlyle's 'first genius of our times' (*WTC*, XXVI, 229), which is conveyed via a multitude of private allusions to their shared literary culture.

In the bleak months after Hallam's death two years later, Tennyson turned again and again to Hayward's *Faust* to help him to express his loss. I would suggest that this provided him with a way of continuing at least something of the 'conversation' that has been sketched out above, thus prolonging his sense of spiritual contact with his late friend. The evidence indicates that *Faust* was, for Tennyson, the most important of a number of works by Goethe and other German authors, all of which had been admired by Hallam. The German glossary that is in Harvard Notebook 13 (and which relates, as was mentioned in the Introduction, to *Faust* (*TA*, II, 266)) is one of three that Tennyson compiled *c*. late 1833. The one in Harvard Notebook 14 relates to an essay by Schiller, 'On the Sublime', and the one in Harvard Notebook 17 shows that Tennyson was also attempting to read the same author's play, *The Maid of Orleans* (*TA*, II, 279, 280, 283; III, 36).[25] Hallam, it should be noted, was a great admirer of Schiller: he refers to him repeatedly

---

[24] *WAH*, p. 186 (refers to *WM*, Vol. IX, Bk V, Ch. VI, p. 670, ll. 29–35 / XXIII, 340).

[25] Friedrich Schiller, *Werke und Briefe*, ed. Otto Dann, Axel Gellhaus and others, 12 vols (Frankfurt am Main: Deutsche Klassiker, 1988–2004), VIII (1992), 822–40; V (1996), pp. 151–4, 'Prolog'. 1., 2. 1–95. The first of Tennyson's two glossaries relates to the complete text of Schiller's essay, which would seem to indicate that he read it from beginning to end in German. The second, however, follows the pattern already noted in the Introduction: it deals with the first two scenes of the play, and then quickly peters out.

in his letters, and he published translations of three of his poems.[26] Looking ahead a little to 1838, we find that Tennyson's annotations in his copy of *Rabenhorst's German Dictionary* (which he was given for Christmas that year) reveal that he used it to help him to read not just *Faust*, but also the *Apprenticeship* and *The Bride of Messina*.[27] The last-named work, which was Schiller's least-known play,[28] seems like a surprising choice, until one recalls that Hallam had singled it out for praise ('Oh the glories of Schiller's Braut von Messina!' he exclaims in a letter (*LAHH*, no. 76, p. 314, 1 September [1829])). Another Christmas gift in 1838 was the *Poems* of Ludwig Tieck (TRC, AT/2217), one of whose lyrics Hallam had translated, and to whom he refers in the passage from the letter of March 1830 that was cited earlier (*WAH*, pp. 312–13; *LAHH*, no. 87, p. 356). In short, by walking with Tieck, Schiller and 'the author of Faust', Tennyson was following in Hallam's footsteps, and tempering his bereavement with a consoling sense of literary intimacy.

Goethe's drama is likely to have stood out amongst these works because of its powerful resonances with Hallam's death: the Gretchen tragedy is a tale of passionate attachment, which is abruptly sundered by loneliness and abandonment. This may explain why shortly after he received the news from Vienna in early October, Tennyson returned to 'Gretchens Stube' (which in Hayward's translation becomes 'Margaret's Room' (pp. 141–2)). Gretchen is here describing her lost lover:

The smile of his mouth,
The power of his eyes,

And of his speech
The witching flow,
The pressure of his hand,
And ah! his kiss! (ll. 3396–401 / p. 142)

---

[26] *LAHH*, no. 78, p. 322 ([16 September 1829]); no. 82, p. 337 ([18 November 1829]); no. 83, pp. 344–45 (12(?) December 1829); no. 113, p. 441 (15 July 1831); no. 180, p. 614 (16 July 1832); *WAH*, pp. 308–11.

[27] Tennyson wrote the relevant lines from Goethe or Schiller in the margin, followed by the abbreviations 'W. M.', or 'B. v. M.' (Noehden (ed.) (TRC, AT/1846), II, 34, 43, 44, 64, 151, 185, 187, 311, 363, 389, 416, 425). In the case of *Meister*, he often provides volume and page references to his copy of the novel (Goethe, *Meister* (TRC, AT/1017)). In Part II, page 43 of the dictionary, he has written 'Iph.' next to line 1003 of Goethe's play *Iphigenia in Tauris*, and on page 356 we find part of line 3 of Goethe's poem 'To the Favoured' (FA, 1, V, 584; II, 11).

[28] Thomas Rea, *Schiller's Dramas and Poems in England* (London: Unwin, 1906), p. 91.

Although this passage needs to be balanced against other possible sources,[29] Margaret's anatomising of the departed Faust into 'mouth', 'eyes', 'speech', 'the pressure of his hand' and 'his kiss' is echoed by Tennyson in at least three of his elegies for Hallam. In 'Hark! the dogs howl!' (*PT*, 214; late 1833), he writes:

> I seek the voice I loved – ah where
> Is that dear hand that I should press,
> Those honoured brows that I would kiss? (ll. 7–9)

Similarly, in 'Break, break, break' (*PT*, 228), he exclaims: 'O for the touch of a vanished hand, | And the sound of a voice that is still!' (ll. 11–12).[30] And in the fragment 'Let Death and Memory keep the face' (*PT*, Vol. III, pp. 596–7; date unknown; 1833–4?), he mentions 'voice', 'lips' and 'eye', before concluding with a verbatim reiteration of Margaret's words: 'the pressure of his hand' (ll. 6, 7, 9, 10, 12).[31]

---

[29] These include: the Song of Songs (which also influenced 'Margaret's Room': see Otto Pniower, 'Goethes *Faust* und das hohe Lied', *Goethe-Jahrbuch*, 13 (1892), 181–98 (pp. 185–8)); Shakespeare, Sonnet 106, line 6; Byron, *Childe Harold*, Canto III (*The New Oxford Shakespeare: The Complete Works, Modern Critical Edition*, ed. Gary Taylor, John Jowett and others (Oxford: Oxford University Press, 2016), pp. 2819–82; Byron, *Poetical Works*, II (1980), III. 2. 514–15).

[30] This poem may also reflect the influence of *Cain* (which is referred to on the opening page of the 'Notes' to Hayward's *Faust* (Byron, *Poetical Works*, VI (1991), 227–95; Hay. 1, p. 207)). Compare, for example, the lines cited above, and Byron's 'Oh! for a word more of that gentle voice [. . .]!' (III. 1. 356). Also similar are 'Thoughts which arise within me' (*Cain*, I. 1. 177), and 'thoughts that arise in me' ('Break, break, break', l. 4).

[31] Tennyson had already used the phrase 'The pressure of the hand' in *The Devil and the Lady* (I. 4. 106), but further evidence of a link to *Faust* is provided by the scene 'Garden', in which Gretchen half-yields to Faust's advances:

> FAUST.
> [. . .] [L]et this pressure of the hand, say to thee what is unutterable.
> [. . .]
> (MARGARET *presses his hands, extricates herself from his embrace, and runs away.* [. . .]) (ll. 3189–90; stage direction before l. 3195 / p. 131)

'The Gardener's Daughter: Or, The Pictures' (which dates at least partly from 1833–4) portrays, like 'Garden', two pairs of lovers, and a romantic encounter in a garden. In some unused passages, Tennyson refers to 'the warm | Love-pressure of half-yielded hands'; 'the pressure of halfyielded hands'; and 'the warm pressure of half-yielded hands' (*PT*, 208, ll. 252–5, fn; *PT*, Vol. III, p. 587; *TA*, II, 243; III, 156; XI, 293, 296; XXIX, 47; XIII, 41). See also *LAT*, III, 6 (26 June 1871).

Both of these pieces have links to Tennyson's longest and greatest elegy for his friend. Hallam Tennyson describes 'Hark! the dogs howl!' as 'the germ of "In Memoriam" [*PT*, 296]' (*Mem.*, I, 107), whilst 'Let Death and Memory keep the face' provided the basis of section CXIX.[32] But the Gretchen tragedy also leaves its mark on XCVII. This section was not included in the trial edition of *In Memoriam* that was published in mid-March of 1850, and it might, therefore, have been written at some point between that date, and the publication of the finished work on 1 June.[33] During this ten-week period, Tennyson and Emily Sellwood were themselves about to become 'Two partners of a married life' (XCVII, l. 5). And in March 1850, Emily was given a German copy of *Faust: Part One* by her acquaintance Ellen Lushington.[34] Although the chronology is rather tight, it may be that she talked about the play with her fiancé, and these discussions might have helped to inspire XCVII.

The opening stanza of this section takes us straight into the world of *Faust*:

> My love has talked with rocks and trees;
>   He finds on misty mountain-ground
>   His own vast shadow glory-crowned;
> He sees himself in all he sees. (ll. 1–4)

Tennyson himself remarked of line 3 that it is '[l]ike the spectre of the Brocken' (EE, III, 253). The area around that mountain – which provides the setting for the scene 'May-Day Night' in *Part One* – is famed, as Hayward explains in his 'Notes', for an eerie 'optical deception': the visitor can sometimes see 'his own shadow extending to the length of five or six hundred feet' (Hay. 1, p. 251).[35] Lines 1 and 4 of this stanza are reminiscent, moreover, of the scene 'Forest and Cavern', in which Faust addresses Nature (amidst a 'giant pine',

---

[32] *PT*, 296, CXIX, fn.
[33] Ibid. 296, XCVII, fn; S & S, pp. 22, 23, 257, 258; Martin, pp. 332–3; Batchelor, p. 188.
[34] Campbell (ed.), I (1971), p. 160, no. 3334; Ann Thwaite, *Emily Tennyson: The Poet's Wife* (London: Faber and Faber, 1996), p. 191.
[35] Tennyson had already referred to this natural phenomenon in his early poem 'On Sublimity' (*PT*, 26, l. 94, and fn). See W. D. Paden, *Tennyson in Egypt: A Study of the Imagery in his Earlier Work* (Lawrence: University of Kansas, 1942), pp. 24–5; p. 122, endnote 51.

and 'wall-like rocks'): 'thou showest me to myself', he declares, 'and deep mysterious wonders of my own breast reveal themselves' (ll. 3229, 3237, 3232–4 / p. 135).

It is possible that the remainder of XCVII contains echoes of the earlier, happier scenes of the Gretchen tragedy. For example, the 'gift' in line 25 may be loosely adapted from Faust's present to her in 'Evening', whilst the words 'to him she sings | Of early faith and plighted vows' suggest the song 'There was a king in Thule, faithful even to the grave', which Margaret intones (not, admittedly, in Faust's presence) in the same scene (*F*, ll. 2783–804, 2759–82 / pp. 108–9, 108; *In Memoriam*, XCVII, ll. 29–30).

It was, however, the very last scene of the Gretchen tragedy, 'Dungeon' (*F*, ll. 4405–612 / pp. 195–203), that resonated most strongly with Tennyson. Its influence upon him was sometimes combined with that of *Werther* – the closing stages of which, in particular, held an especial fascination for him (*W*, Pt II, pp. 198–266 / pp. 179–219). The two texts are, in fact, closely related, for both are harrowing portrayals of extreme emotions, and both have their origins in Goethe's 'Storm and Stress' period of the 1770s.[36]

In 'Dungeon', the severely traumatised Margaret has succumbed to madness. Her mother and brother have both died, and she has been abandoned by Faust, whom she has not seen for about a year. She has killed their baby, and is due to be executed for this crime the following day. Faust enters her prison cell and implores her to escape with him, but she is too distracted to comprehend. The two lovers can do no more than share a last kiss and a passionate embrace, before their final, agonised parting, which takes place as day begins to break.

Daybreak also provides a recurrent backdrop to the sorrows of Werther, and as in 'Dungeon', death is a tangible presence in the novel's closing pages, for they deal with the anguished final days of the protagonist's life. He too is close to madness, for he has been abandoned by his beloved Charlotte. Like Faust and Gretchen, the lovers meet, kiss and embrace before separating forever, and the despairing Werther shoots himself the following night.

It seems likely that Tennyson sensed these affinities, for he echoes both 'Dungeon' and *Werther* in three texts that date, I would argue, from late 1833, or early 1834: 'Love's latest hour is this' (*PT*, 224);

---

[36] *Faust* and *Werther* 'sprang up', Goethe tells us, 'at the same time' (FA, 2, XII (XXXIX), p. 304, l. 23, 10 February 1829 / Goethe, trans. Oxenford, II, 126).

a number of passages in 'The Flight' (*PT*, 259);[37] and the Harvard Notebook 13 draft of 'Oh! that 'twere possible' (*TA*, II, 267–8) (which is immediately preceded by the glossary for *Faust* that was analysed in the Introduction (*TA*, II, 266)).[38] All three of these works might be described as 'lines addressed to Arthur Hallam', and they may be partly a response to the similarly titled piece that was discussed earlier – which, as I have argued above, may represent, in turn, Hallam's own response to 'Dungeon'.[39]

However, in contrast to his friend's poem, Tennyson's three lyrics make no reference to the prison setting of this scene (and the madness of its central character influences only lines 57–60 of 'The Flight').[40] What matters most to Tennyson are, instead, the broad similarities between 'Dungeon', *Werther* and the death of Hallam: in the denouements of both texts, Goethe depicts an impassioned farewell between a young man and woman, which takes place as the sudden, premature death of one of them draws ever closer. Reading these works in 1833–4, Tennyson would have been greatly moved

---

[37] Ricks dates 'The Flight' to '*c.* 1836 (?)' (*PT*, 259, headnote), but the draft of it in Trinity Notebook 21 is preceded by 'The Rosebud' (*PT*, 244) and 'Tithon' (*PT*, 218) (poems that Ricks himself dates to *c.* 1834 and late 1833). It is followed, moreover, by 'Oh! that 'twere possible' (lines 1–4 and 5–6 of which resemble, respectively, lines 45 and 79–80 of 'The Flight') (*TA*, XII, 206–9, 213–19). Line 51 of 'The Flight' ('The Fiend would yell, the grave would yawn, my mother's ghost would rise') recalls both the Gretchen tragedy, and another poem of 1833, 'The Mother's Ghost' (*PT*, 221).

[38] The Harvard Notebook 13 draft corresponds to *PT*, 227, ll. 1–16, 23–5, 42–8, 58–64. There are few, if any similarities to Goethe's drama in the additional material that is in the various other versions of the poem. 'Oh! that 'twere possible' may also be influenced by the passage in Goethe's autobiography that gives an (at least partly apocryphal) account of the loss of his first love, who – as Hayward mentions in his 'Notes' – 'was called Margaret' (Hay. 1, p. 243; FA, 1, XIV, Pt II, Bk VI, p. 244, l. 21–p. 245, l. 32 / Goethe, *Memoirs of Goethe*, I, Ch. VI, pp. 161–3; see Boyle, I (1991), 57).

[39] The rhyme of 'pity' with 'ditty' in Hallam's poem is repeated in 'Oh! that 'twere possible' (ll. 29, 32).

[40] Both motifs are present in Browning's response to 'Dungeon', Part V of *Paracelsus*, which was written less than a year later (Browning, *Poems*, I (1991), 273–308). This closing scene takes place in a 'stifling cell' with 'casement-bars' (ibid. ll. 30, 2). Festus – like his near-namesake Faust(us) – initially goes unrecognised by the cell's inmate, Paracelsus (ibid. ll. 85–93). The latter sings distractedly; seems very close to madness; cannot be persuaded to leave; and feels himself to be the target of public hostility (ibid. ll. 84–6, 98–103, 137–40). All of these details invite comparison with Margaret in 'Dungeon', as does Paracelsus' death at the end of the scene (ibid. l. 894).

by such lines as Werther's 'Adieu! my dear, my dearest friend!' (Pt II, p. 216, l. 30, 20 December [1772] / p. 184), or Gretchen's 'I am yet so young, so young! and am to die already!' (ll. 4432–3 / p. 196).

All three of Tennyson's poems are blackened, therefore, by the powerful sense of impending doom that pervades both 'Dungeon' and *Werther* – but they can also be said to be brightened, more fleetingly, by their false and poignant dawns. '[I]t is growing day!' declares Margaret; '[. . .] The bell tolls! [. . .] Judgement of God! I have given myself up to thee!' (ll. 4580, 4590, 4605 / pp. 202, 203). '[T]he morning grows apace', exclaims the female speaker of 'The Flight'; '[. . .] the clock [. . .] strikes the hour– I I bide no more, I meet my fate, whatever ills betide!' (ll. 93–5). These lines should also be compared to the words that are uttered by the despairing Werther just seconds before he shoots himself: 'the clock strikes twelve — I go [. . .]!', he exclaims (Pt II, p. 264, l. 1 / p. 216). In a letter dating from a couple of months earlier, Werther hopes 'never to wake again!' (Pt II, p. 176, l. 21, 3 November [1772] / p. 159), for 'in the morning', he tells us, 'torrents of tears flow from my oppressed heart! and bereaved of all comfort, I weep over the woes to come' (Pt I, p. 108, ll. 16, 22–4, 21 August [1771] / p. 93; misdated 20 August [1771]). The equally tearful speaker of 'The Flight' wishes, like Werther, to 'wake no more' (l. 7), and is bereft of all comfort as the day begins to dawn: 'Come, speak a little comfort! all night I prayed with tears, I And yet no comfort came to me, and now the morn appears' (ll. 17–18; see also ll. 1–4). In line 72, she contemplates suicide, and in line 98 – taking her cue, perhaps, from Werther's vision of 'the church-yard which contains my grave' (Pt. II, p. 224, ll. 23–4, F. L. / p. 191) – she 'seems[s] to see [her] new-dug grave'.

The title of 'Love's latest hour' refers, as Ricks points out, to the hour of death, and line 13 of this poem evokes the dawn: 'I go: the day steals on.'[41] Its speaker longs to grow 'stiff and cold', and adds that 'The world is nothing worth', and ''Twere better far to die!' (ll. 20, 25, 28). These words seem to echo Werther's desire to lie 'cold and stiff', as well as his phrase 'the whole world is now nothing to me', and his ominous remark ''twere better far that I should depart!'[42] In line 23 of the draft of 'Oh! that 'twere possible', we find the words 'Half the night', which are taken from Werther's Farewell Letter (Pt II, p. 250, l. 10 / p. 204), and ten lines later, the phrase 'the

---

[41] *PT*, 224, l. 1, fn.
[42] Pt II, p. 248, l. 12 (F. L.); Pt I, p. 54, ll. 28–9 (9 June [1771]); Pt II, p. 196, l. 23 (17 December [1772]) / pp. 202, 42, 179.

shuddering dawn' (l. 33) evokes 'Dungeon': 'My horses shudder; the morning is gloaming up', says Mephistopheles impatiently to Faust, during his brief appearance in that scene (ll. 4599–600 / p. 202). Tennyson also draws on 'Dungeon' towards the end of this poem, where he writes:

> I loathe the squares and streets,
> And the faces that one meets,
> Hearts with no love for me. (ll. 58–60)

These lines echo the grim moment when Margaret imagines the hostile crowd that will soon be gathering for her execution: 'The square, the streets, cannot hold them', she exclaims (ll. 4588–9 / p. 202).

However, filled as he is with anguished love for Hallam, Tennyson reads 'Dungeon', in particular, as a love scene – and one which conveys, perhaps, the consolatory message that love can triumph even over mortality. In line 3 of 'Oh! that 'twere possible' – and, also, in line 2 of 'Love's latest hour' – the speaker refers to their 'true-love'. It may not be entirely a coincidence that Margaret uses the same term to refer to Faust on two different occasions towards the beginning of 'Dungeon' (ll. 4435, 4461 / pp. 196, 197). Belatedly recognising his 'sweet' voice (l. 4469 / p. 197), she clasps him to her (stage direction before l. 4471 / p. 198), and exclaims:

> What! you can no longer kiss? So short a time away from me, my love, and already forgotten how to kiss? Why do I feel so sad upon your neck? when, in other times, a whole heaven came over me from your words, your looks; and you kissed me as if you were going to smother me! Kiss me! or I will kiss you!
> *(She embraces him.)* (ll. 4484–92 / p. 198)

'I will press thee to my heart with thousandfold warmth', replies Faust (l. 4499 / p. 199). Tennyson draws on this passionate exchange in line 5 of 'The Flight'; in lines 8–10 of 'Oh! that 'twere possible'; and, in particular, in 'Love's latest hour', where he writes:

> Sweet! let me feel thine heart.
> One Kiss! one Kiss! One Kiss!
> Cling, clasp me heart to heart!
>
> One Kiss! I scarce can speak,
> And thy lips tremble now.
> Yet let me kiss thy cheek,

Ah! let me kiss thy brow!
One on thy neck, thy cheek,
Another on thy brow! (ll. 4–12)

In a letter to W. B. Donne, in which he cited this poem, Tennyson's friend John Kemble noted wryly that its ardour had no obvious biographical source: 'Wouldn't verses like these make one half believe that Ælfred [sic] has had nothing to think about all his life, but illicit loves?' (cited in *PT*, 224, headnote). The 'illicit love' which had inspired Tennyson was, however, a literary one, which he had fused with his love of Hallam. This process might have been helped by the fact that Faust's Christian name, Henry, is the same as Hallam's middle name.[43] Perhaps Tennyson was especially moved by the closing line of 'Dungeon', in which Margaret's voice is heard '*from within, dying away*': 'Henry! Henry!' she cries (l. 4612 / p. 203).

It may be, however, that the bleakness of this ending was too potent for Tennyson to engage with it directly: both 'Oh! that 'twere possible' and 'Love's latest hour' conclude, instead, by echoing earlier scenes from the Gretchen tragedy. In 'Zwinger' (which in Hayward's translation becomes 'Place Devoted to Religious Exercises'), Margaret had declared: 'I weep, I weep, I weep, | My heart is bursting within me!' (ll. 3606–7 / p. 153). All of the six surviving manuscripts of 'Oh! that 'twere possible' conclude: 'And to weep, and weep and weep | My whole soul out to thee' (ll. 63–4; *TA*, II, 268; III, 134; IX, 184; XII, 219 (omits 'to' in line 63); XXIX, 49, 69). In 'Zwinger', Margaret's anguish had already been very deep, but she was, at least, neither mad, condemned nor incarcerated. By taking her back to this earlier scene, Tennyson is following the impulse that lies right at the heart of 'Oh! that 'twere possible': a deep desire to turn back the clock, and return to a previous, more benign state of affairs.

Towards the end of 'Love's latest hour', Gretchen seems to be transported even further back, to 'Margaret's Room', which had concluded:

Ah! could I enfold him
And hold him! and kiss him
So as I would!
On his kisses
I should die away! (ll. 3408–13 / p. 142)

---

[43] Tennyson might also have noticed that Abraham Hayward's initials, 'A. H.', were the same as Arthur Hallam's (Hay. 1, pp. lxxxvii, 205).

In the penultimate stanza of 'Love's latest hour', we find the words 'folding thy dear waist', and the speaker twice laments that they 'no more shall fold' it (ll. 21, 22, 24).[44] The poem concludes:

> 'Twere better far to die!
> Lay lip to lip! Pluck forth
> My heart that I may die! (ll. 28–30)[45]

Even as he was echoing Gretchen's morbid sentiments, Tennyson might have been able to derive some faint consolation from them, for in 'Margaret's Room' (unlike 'Dungeon'), the heroine's premonitions of death prove to be premature, and she later finds the arms of her true love around her once again.

After drafting 'Oh! that 'twere possible' in 1833–4, Tennyson returned to it not once but twice: in 1837, and again in 1854–5. The circumstances that surrounded each of these three phases of work would seem to indicate that although this lyric contains no reference to Margaret's madness, that connection was there in the mind of the poet. With regard to the 1833–4 period, there can be little doubt that at that time, Tennyson was deeply preoccupied with insanity. In January of the latter year, he wrote to his uncle about the deteriorating mental health of his brother Septimus, and expressed the grave fear that 'his mind [would] prove as deranged' as that of another brother, Edward (who had himself gone mad the previous year (*LAT*, I, 106; see also p. 92, 27 May 1833)). When Tennyson revised 'Oh! that 'twere possible' for publication in *The Tribute* in September 1837, he might have recently visited the environs of Dr Matthew Allen's lunatic asylum in High Beech in Essex.[46] And when he returned to the poem in 1854–5, he developed it into a longer work, the original title of which was *Maud or the Madness* (*Mem.*, I, 402).

---

[44] Compare also l. 23 and *F*, ll. 3394–401 / p. 142 (and see also 'Oh! that 'twere possible', l. 25).

[45] Compare 'The Flight', lines 46–8 and, also, the famous words of Marlowe's Faustus: 'Her lips suck forth my soul' (cited in Hay. 2, p. 94). Although Tennyson was, we are told, 'very fond' of Marlowe (*Mem.*, II, 292), this is one of only two or three occasions when he appears to echo *The Tragical History of Dr Faustus*.

[46] Lang and Shannon conjecturally date Tennyson's letter to Milnes – in which he enclosed the manuscript of 'Oh! that 'twere possible' – to March 1837, but the poem was not published until September (*LAT*, I, 149; *PT*, 227, headnote). Tennyson first visited his future home Beech Hill House (a short walk from Allen's mental asylum, which he later frequented), at some point between March and May of that year, and the Tennyson family moved there from Somersby in June (Pinion, *Tennyson Chronology*, pp. 26–7).

The procedure that Tennyson adopted in expanding 'Oh! that 'twere possible' into *Maud* (*PT*, 316) seems appropriate for a piece that draws its principal inspiration from the *closing* scene of *Part One*, and the *latter* stages of *Werther*. As his friend Aubrey de Vere recalled:

> to render the poem fully intelligible, a preceding one was necessary. He wrote it; the second poem too required a predecessor; and thus the whole work was written, as it were, *backwards*. (cited in *Mem.*, I, 379)

Tennyson himself compared the new material to *Hamlet* (EE, IV, 270–1), and others have detected similarities to *Romeo and Juliet*, *The Bride of Lammermoor*, the poetry of Wordsworth and *Alton Locke*.[47] The influences on *Maud* may also include the literary movement known as the Spasmodic School, and an anonymous ballad that was published alongside 'Oh! that 'twere possible' in *The Tribute*.[48] But although this list already comprises a considerable number of sources, the Gretchen tragedy needs to be added to it. Like at least two other major Victorian narratives – *Adam Bede* and *Dorian Gray* – *Maud* is strongly indebted to this section of *Faust*.

Although this influence is most readily apparent in Part II of the poem, it can also be detected in Part I, which exhibits a number of similarities to the first six scenes of the Gretchen tragedy. And as in the lyric from which *Maud* was developed, these are mingled, at times, with similarities to *The Sorrows of Young Werther*.[49] Like both Margaret and Charlotte, Maud sings a song to herself: it is, we are told, a 'chivalrous [. . .] song', 'of men that in battle array' (I. 5. 162–72; I. 10. 382–4, esp. 383; 5. 162–89, esp. 169). It resembles, therefore, the piece that is sung by Gretchen in the scene 'Evening' (already referred to above), which tells of the King of Thule, his mistress and his knights (ll. 2759–82 / p. 108). However, the outdoor *setting* of Maud's performance ('In the meadow under the Hall! | She is singing an air' (I. 5. 163–4; see also II. 4. 180–3)) is more redolent of *Werther*, in which Charlotte remarks: 'when any thing

---

[47] *PT*, 316, headnote; Jayne Thomas, *Tennyson Echoing Wordsworth* (Edinburgh: Edinburgh University Press, 2019), pp. 121–62.

[48] *PT*, 316, headnote. The Spasmodic School had been initiated by Bailey's *Festus*.

[49] In this respect, *Maud* looks back not just to 'Oh! that 'twere possible', but, also, to two other *Werther*-influenced poems, *The Lover's Tale* (*PT*, 153) and 'Locksley Hall' (*PT*, 271) (see Baynes, 'Tennyson and *Werther*', pp. 319–20).

disturbs my temper, I go into the garden, I sing a lively air, and it vanishes' (Pt I, p. 64, ll. 32–4, 1 July [1771] / p. 52). Similarly, in Tennyson's description of the encounter that sparks the two lovers' infatuation (I. 6. 196–200), it is *Werther* that suggests the time of year (spring) (W, Pt I, p. 12, ll. 24–5, 4 May 1771 / p. 3; *Maud*, I. 6. 198), whilst the Gretchen tragedy contributes the place and circumstances (a chance meeting on a street) (F, ll. 2605–18 / p. 101; *Maud*, I. 5. 199–200). The very last passage in Part I, 'Come into the garden, Maud', is perceptively compared by Kennedy to an episode in the *Apprenticeship*, but it may also derive inspiration from the highly romantic scene 'Garden' in *Faust* (*Maud*, I. 22. 850–923; F, ll. 3073–204 / pp. 125–32).[50]

The next six scenes of Goethe's play include the consummation of Faust and Margaret's love, and her subsequent pregnancy. It is this part of the drama which, just four years later, would leave such notable traces in George Eliot's debut novel, but Tennyson, in contrast, passes over it entirely. This is, in fact, the principal difference between *Faust* and *Maud*: in the latter work, the tragedy is caused not so much by the unleashing of Eros, as by the constraints that have been imposed by Mammon. Although infanticide is mentioned briefly at I. 1. 44, it is placed in a financial context, thus encapsulating in miniature Tennyson's shift of focus: 'a Mammonite mother kills her babe for a burial fee', he writes.

As Part II begins, the love scene in the garden is, accordingly, cut short, by a brusque intrusion of money-mindedness: Maud 'had hardly spoken a word, | When her brother ran in his rage to the gate' (II. 1. 11–12). In terms of the poem's Faustian analogues, we now jump forwards to the *last* seven scenes of Goethe's play, in which the extramarital liaison of Faust and Gretchen brings tragic consequences for the latter and her family. In the first of these scenes ('Night.—Street before Margaret's Door'), the protagonist is confronted by his lover's angry brother, and kills him in a duel (ll. 3698–775 / pp. 156–60). Much the same thing happens in *Maud* (II. 1. 1–30). The 'terms of disgrace' that are heaped upon Tennyson's weeping heroine (II. 1. 14–15) have a precedent in the dying Valentine's invective against the tearful Margaret (ll. 3726–75, esp. l. 3771 / pp. 158–60, esp. p. 160). In both works, the killer flees ('to the Brocken [mountain]' in *Faust*; to the 'Breton strand' in *Maud*), and is haunted by an apparition – not of his victim, but of his victim's sister, who is, at this point, still

---

[50] Kennedy, p. 92; WM, Vol. IX, Bk I, Ch. XVII, p. 424, l. 32–p. 427, l. 24 / XXIII, 101–4.

alive.⁵¹ It is consistent with Tennyson's shift in focus from Eros to Mammon that this 'fratricide' of the greedy prospective brother-in-law brings the same psychological consequences as the infanticide of the innocent love-child in *Faust*: the protagonist of *Maud* finds himself confined, much like Margaret, to 'cells of madness' (III. 6. 2), and he echoes her desperate words in 'O that 'twere possible' (II. 4. 141–238).⁵²

Like *Faust*, *Maud* does not end there, and it may be that the brief Part III owes something to *Faust: Part Two* (Act III of which Tennyson read out to Emily shortly after *Maud* had been all but completed (Emily Tennyson, *Journal*, p. 44, 2 April 1855; *Mem.*, I, 384)). Tennyson remarks of his protagonist that he is here 'giving himself up to work for the good of mankind' (EE, IV, 271). Perhaps he was recalling a line from Austin's *Characteristics*: 'exhortations to labour for the good of mankind, are thickly scattered through [Goethe's] works' (*CG*, I, p. xxi). A similar thought is expressed in the concluding words of the chapter on *Faust: Part Two* in Lewes's *Life*: 'man lives for man, and [. . .] only in as far as he is working for Humanity can his efforts bring permanent happiness' (II, 435). Lewes is referring to Act V, in which the erstwhile individualist Faust oversees a land reclamation project, declaring:

A space to many millions would I give,
[. . .]
Plains green and fertile; men and herds as well,
Soon happy on the newest soil would dwell. (ll. 11563, 11565–6 /
　Macdonald, p. 328)

In the previous act, however, Faust – in order to be granted this land by the Emperor – has fought on his behalf in a war. In Part III of

---

⁵¹ F, ll. 3711–15, 4032, 4183–208 / pp. 157, 171, 178–9; *Maud*, II. 1. 30; 2. 120; 2. 77; 1. 31–40; 2. 81–90. Both heroines subsequently die (*Maud*, II. 3. 139; 5. 239–40; Margaret's death is not represented on stage, but it is implicit in the action of 'Dungeon'). All of the incidents in *Maud* that have been recounted here take place in the same order as their Faustian equivalents, with only two slight exceptions: in *Faust*, the song comes just *after* the lovers' meeting in the street, and the reproaches which the brother directs at the heroine are uttered just *after* he is wounded. Note, also, that the mothers of both heroines die – although Maud's (unlike Margaret's) is already deceased by the time the work begins (I. 4. 159).

⁵² The distracted speaker of *Maud*, who sits 'Plucking the harmless wild-flower on the hill' (II. 1. 3), also resembles the madman 'looking for flowers' who appears towards the end of *Werther* (Pt II, p. 186, ll. 9–10, 30 November [1772] / p. 167).

Maud, the speaker enlists in the armed forces, and it may be that Tennyson (who was also responding, of course, to the outbreak of the conflict in the Crimea) has conflated Faust's bellicose means with his beneficent end. Perhaps he was also glancing back at Werther's letter of 25 May 1772, in which he writes: 'I had a scheme in my head, which I intended to conceal from you till it was accomplished;—now that it has failed I may as well tell it to you. I had a mind to go into the army' (Pt II, p. 154, ll. 11–13 / p. 141).

A further influence on Part III of *Maud* is the very last scene of *Faust: Part Two*, 'Mountain Defiles', in which the departed Margaret reappears in heaven. Here, Goethe's heroine is surrounded by ethereal 'spirit-choirs', including 'Bands of boys that are blest' (ll. 12084, 11971–2 / Macdonald, pp. 350, 345). At the conclusion of *Maud*, Tennyson's dead heroine (whose role in the poem is, as we have seen, broadly analogous to that of Margaret in *Faust*) makes a similar reappearance: 'She seemed to divide in a dream from a band of the blest' (III. 6. 10).

Unlike her Faustian prototype, however, the spirit of *this* heroine is a prophet of war (III. 6. 11–14), and Tennyson introduces a similarly belligerent note into what is the poem's final echo of Goethe. In the copy of the English edition of *Conversations of Goethe* with which Carlyle presented him in 1851,[53] Tennyson marked the following words: 'He who will work aright must never rail, must not trouble himself at all about what is ill done, but only do well himself' (FA, 2, XII (XXXIX), p. 147, l. 34–p. 148, l. 1 / Goethe, trans. Oxenford, TRC, AT/1008, I, 208). In what is, very nearly, the closing line of *Maud*, the protagonist declares: 'It is better to fight for the good than to rail at the ill' (III. 6. 57).[54] Somewhat improbably, Goethe's deep aversion to strife and negativity has here been transformed into a kind of poetic rallying-cry.

As well as providing sources for much of its plot, *Werther* and *Faust* may also have exercised a *formal* influence on *Maud*. As John R. Williams observes, '[t]here can scarcely be another work with a greater profusion of metrical forms' than *Faust*, and it is unlikely to be a coincidence that the same can be said of *Maud* in relation to

---

[53] See Introduction, p. 34, and ibid. fn 145.
[54] These words were added in 1856 (*PT*, 316, III. 6. 54–9, fn). In January of that year, Emily Tennyson wrote in her *Journal* (pp. 59, 60): '[Alfred] read me some of Eckermann's conversations with Goethe' (9 January); 'Molière these evenings and a little Eckermann' (14th); 'read some of Eckermann' (25th).

the œuvre of Tennyson.⁵⁵ The words of A. Dwight Culler, too, are of considerable relevance here:

> In Goethe's [. . .] works [the vogue for monodrama] may be seen most clearly in *Werther* and the early *Faust*. *Werther* is in some ways the greatest of the European monodramas, and it is obvious that its epistolary form, in which the individual letters correspond to the sections of the monodrama, is ideally suited for following out all the turns and twists of the hero's highly mercurial spirit.⁵⁶

It should be recalled that all of the letters that comprise the text of *Werther* are written by a single individual: the impassioned protagonist himself. This makes the novel at least broadly comparable, I think, to *Maud: A Monodrama*, of which Tennyson remarks: 'The peculiarity of this poem [. . .] is that different phases of passion in one person take the place of different characters' (*Mem.*, I, 396).

There is one more piece by Tennyson that deserves to be mentioned here, for it is possible that it, too, creates a link between the death of Hallam and the tragedy of Margaret. In the scene 'Evening' (ll. 2678–804 / pp. 105–9), Gretchen sings a memorable song about 'a king in Thule' and 'his dying mistress' (ll. 2759, 2761 / p. 108). I have already suggested above that Tennyson was interested in this passage, and this supposition would appear to be confirmed by a letter to him from his friend John Heath, which Lang and Shannon date to around mid-February 1835:

> I have copied [and am sending to you] a Teutonic song which [our friend John] Kemble has imported[,] which I would respectfully offer to the sweetest siren of the family. You know the mood of mind in which Gretchen sings it in Faust and I think there is something well suiting in the wildness and simplicity of the air. (*LAT*, I, 128)⁵⁷

Lang and Shannon argue that the 'siren' to whom Heath refers was '[p]resumably Mary Tennyson, to whom he became engaged', and they further observe that '[h]er sister Emily',

---

⁵⁵ Williams, p. 220. The April 1855 entry in Emily Tennyson's *Journal* (p. 44) confirms that her husband was by this time reading *Faust* in German.

⁵⁶ A. Dwight Culler, 'Monodrama and the Dramatic Monologue', *PMLA*, 90: 3 (May 1975), 366–85 (p. 372).

⁵⁷ See also *Mem.*, II, 504, fn: 'The [. . .] songs in *Faust* [Tennyson] often quoted with lavish praise.'

writing from Somersby on 22 February to Ellen Hallam, whom she had been visiting, noted that Heath had sent 'a play written by Taylor (I never heard of him before)' and also 'at the same time a Song from Faust, Es war ein König in Thule' ['There was a king in Thule'].[58]

Coincidentally, it is another encounter between Ellen and Emily that raises the possibility of Margaret's song having played at least some role in the gestation of one of Tennyson's greatest poems. In October 1834, Ellen wrote in her diary: 'My dear Emily read to me this morning a little poem of Alfred's—a kind of ballad upon the death of King Arthur.'[59] As Robert Bernard Martin observes, 'If this was the "Morte d'Arthur" [*PT*, 226], the description is a strange one.'[60] I propose that Ellen was actually referring to a now-lost piece resembling 'The King in Thule'.[61] This little ballad describes how a woman gave a priceless metal object (in this case, 'a golden goblet') to a king; years later, 'when he came to die, [. . .] with his knights around him, [. . .] on the sea', that object was thrown into the water, and he promptly expired (ll. 2762, 2767, 2772, 2774, 2775–82 / p. 108).

The dramatic context of this song may have left a faint trace in the finished 'Morte d'Arthur', for immediately after she sings it, young

---

[58] *LAT*, I, 128, fn 5. For two reasons, Lang and Shannon's interpretation of Heath's letter might be questioned. First, the letter may actually date from early 1834, at the tail-end of Tennyson's period of intense absorption in *Faust*. This suggestion is supported by the fact that the four poems that Heath mentions in the letter can all be dated to between September 1833 and the beginning of 1834 (and the two books to which he refers were both published in 1833 – 'Mrs Austin' (ibid. I, 128) can be confidently identified as *Characteristics*, of which Tennyson would have been made aware through Hayward's repeated references to it (Hay. 1, p. 236; Hay. 2, pp. 86–7, fn; 106, 107)). Second, the song that Heath enclosed with the letter might actually have been a setting of 'Margaret's Room': the 'wildness' to which he refers would be far less appropriate to 'The King in Thule' than to this passage, in which the heroine's 'mood of mind' is much more pronounced. One would then have to assume that the setting of 'Thule' mentioned by Emily Tennyson in her letter to Ellen Hallam was a *separate* gift, made the following year. This, in turn, would account for the fact that Heath's letter makes no reference to 'a play written by Taylor' (which, as Emily clearly states, he sent 'at the same time' as the song).

[59] Cited in Martin, p. 195.

[60] Ibid. p. 195.

[61] The little ballad that was originally entitled 'How King Cophetua wooed the beggar-maid' (which in the Heath MS is dated September 1833) exhibits a number of similarities to both 'Evening' and, in particular, the preceding scene, 'The Street' ('The Beggar Maid', *PT*, 211, and headnote; *TA*, XXIX, 28; *F*, ll. 2605–77 / pp. 101–4).

Margaret finds and opens the casket full of jewellery which Faust has left for her: 'Good heavens! look!' she exclaims. 'I have never seen any thing like it in all my born days! A set of trinkets, a countess might wear on the highest festival. [. . .] [A]ll presses after gold,— hangs on gold' (ll. 2790-3, 2802-4 / p. 109).[62] In Malory, Arthur simply tells Sir Bedivere 'thou wouldest for my rich sword see me dead',[63] but in Tennyson's poem he accuses him of acting 'from lust of gold', and likens him to '[. . .] a girl | Valuing the giddy pleasure of the eyes' (ll. 127-8)[64] – words that might easily serve as a description of Margaret in 'Evening'. It should probably be added, however, that in contrast to most of the other pieces discussed above, the resemblances between 'Morte d'Arthur' and the Gretchen tragedy cannot be said to be conclusive. And when the poem was absorbed into the much longer *Idylls of the King* (*PT*, 463-76; published 1859-85), they disappeared almost without trace, like the King of Thule's goblet sinking into the sea.

The poems of 1833-4 that have provided the focus of this chapter represent Tennyson's response to Goethe's drama at its most direct and visceral. In the midst of the most tragic episode of his life, he turned repeatedly to the most tragic episode in *Faust*. It is likely that during Hallam's lifetime, he and Tennyson had discussed Goethe's works, and had made 'confidential allusions' to them in their own writings. However, the snatches of the Gretchen tragedy that we find in such pieces as 'Hark! the dogs howl!', 'Let Death and Memory keep the face', 'Love's latest hour' and 'Oh! that 'twere possible' cannot be fairly described as allusions – perhaps not even confidential ones. Bereaved of their only comprehending auditor, they seem, at times, mere echoes, which are wasted – like the poet's sighs – 'in the air' ('Hark!', l. 12). But if a longing for Hallam in his capacity as listener is discernible here, his sudden absence as speaker is no less keenly felt. Devastated by the fact that his friend has been prematurely silenced, Tennyson memorialises him in a manner that allows

---

[62] In other words, 'everyone desires and clings to gold'.
[63] Sir Thomas Malory, *La Morte d'Arthur: The Most Ancient and Famous History of the Renowned Prince Arthur, and the Knights of the Round Table*, 3 vols (London: Wilks, 1816), III, Ch. CLXVII, p. 359.
[64] '[T]he spectre of the Brocken' that appears in the 'Notes' to Hayward's *Faust*, and *In Memoriam*, XCVII, may haunt line 183 of 'Morte d'Arthur' ('Larger than human on the frozen hills'), as well as lines 20-1 of 'Hark! the dogs howl!' ('Larger than human passes by | The shadow of the man I loved').

the doomed Margaret (the analogous character in *Faust*) to speak, for it is she whom he echoes.[65] The recurrent yearning for the voice of the dead that is expressed in these lyrics is touchingly – but inadequately – fulfilled in the echoes of a dying voice that they contain. In other words, in these poems, a voice that is still is lamenting its own extinction, and offering, thereby, the implicit hope of immortality. As I will argue in the next chapter, that same hope is of central importance to what is, perhaps, the greatest of all the works that Tennyson wrote in the immediate aftermath of Hallam's death.

---

[65] Only once in the poems of 1833–4 that have been discussed above is there an echo that relates to Faust: his retreat to a tranquil 'Forest and Cavern' (ll. 3217–373 / pp. 135–40) apparently helps to suggest lines 61–2 of 'Oh! that 'twere possible' ('Always I long to creep | To some still cavern deep').

Chapter 2

'To strive onwards': 'Ulysses', Progress and Trances

In 'Ulysses' Tennyson responds to the loss of Hallam by combining three literary sources – and two themes from his own experience – to express his belief in an 'after-life [. . .] of progress' (*Mem.*, II, 365). The groundwork for this synthesis was laid in March 1833, when he wrote, in the village of Mablethorpe, the little-known poem 'Mechanophilus', which echoes *Faust*, the *Inferno* and Carlyle. The same locale – and the same literary sources – would later leave their mark on 'Locksley Hall' (*c.* 1838–9), in which Tennyson is looking back to the earlier poem.[1] Both pieces combine his visionary trances with a strong sense of the need for progress, or forward movement.[2] These two themes had an especial significance for Tennyson in relation to the death of Hallam, for they provided him, once again, with a much-needed sense of communion with his late friend. This is expressed in two interlocking series of poems, which intersect in 'Ulysses' (October 1833) – a work which combines, like 'Mechanophilus' and 'Locksley', echoes of *Faust*, the *Inferno* and Carlyle.

Tennyson's trance experiences inform more than a dozen of his lyrics, spanning virtually the whole of his career, from 'Armageddon' (*PT*, 3) (which may be his first surviving original poem) to the late

---

[1] For the dating of this poem, and a detailed discussion of its close relationship to another earlier piece, *The Lover's Tale* (*PT*, 153), see Tom Baynes, 'Three New Sources for "Locksley Hall": Goethe, Byron, and Dickens', *Notes and Queries*, o.s. 266 / n.s. 68: 4 (December 2021); 'Tennyson and *Werther*', pp. 316–19.

[2] Throughout this chapter, these two terms will be used interchangeably (the latter is the meaning of the Latin *progressus* (<http.//www.oed.com>; last accessed 2 February 2021)).

piece 'The Ancient Sage' (*PT*, 415).³ These works form a recognisable group, with their own distinctive themes and vocabulary (although an abiding sense of the inadequacy of words is also a part of the pattern).⁴ The trance – or 'vision'⁵ – is sometimes described in terms of contact with an angel,⁶ and there are numerous references to wings and flight.⁷ Tennyson often mentions the sun⁸ (or the moon),⁹ and the whole experience has a radiant quality, with repeated use of such words as 'gleam[s]',¹⁰ 'shining',¹¹ 'light', 'bright[ness]',¹² and 'flash[ed]' or 'flashing'.¹³ Some of these poems also refer to the departure of the spirit from the body,¹⁴ and the transcendence of Time and Place.¹⁵

Tennyson provides a detailed description of the experiences that inspired these lyrics in his son's *Memoir* of him:

> A kind of waking trance I have frequently had, quite up from boyhood, when I have been all alone. This has generally come upon me thro' repeating my own name two or three times to myself silently, till all at once, as it were out of the intensity of consciousness of individuality, the individuality itself seemed to dissolve and fade away into boundless being, and this not a confused state, but the clearest of the clearest, [. . .] utterly beyond words, where death was an

---

³ Stephen Allen Grant, 'The Mystical Implications of *In Memoriam*', *Studies in English Literature, 1500–1900*, 2: 4 (Autumn 1962), 481–95 (pp. 482–3); S & S, p. 254; *In Memoriam* (*PT*, 296), XII, l. 6, fn.

⁴ 'The Two Voices' (*PT*, 209), l. 384; *In Memoriam*, XCV, ll. 45–6; 'Sage', ll. 238–9. See also *Mem.*, I, 320 (cited below), and II, 473.

⁵ 'Armageddon', III, l. 20; IV, l. 2; 'Timbuctoo' (*PT*, 67), ll. 182, 202; 'Sage', l. 285.

⁶ 'Armageddon', II, ll. 2, 19, 51; 'The Mystic' (*PT*, 96), l. 1; 'What did it profit me that once in Heaven' (*PT*, Vol. III, p. 620), l. 2.

⁷ 'Armageddon', II, l. 41; 'Stanzas [What time I wasted youthful hours]' (*PT*, 198), l. 2; 'This Earth is wondrous, change on change' (*PT*, 201), l. 13; 'Hark! the dogs howl!' (*PT*, 214), ll. 3–4; *In Memoriam*, XLI, l. 10; 'What did it profit', ll. 4–5.

⁸ 'Armageddon', II, l. 9; 'Timbuctoo', l. 107; 'This Earth', l. 25; *In Memoriam*, XLI, l. 17; 'Sage', l. 238.

⁹ 'Armageddon', II, ll. 32–6; 'Timbuctoo', l. 108; 'This Earth', ll. 11, 17, 27.

¹⁰ 'Voices', l. 380; 'Sage', ll. 214–15, 240, 246.

¹¹ 'Armageddon', II, l. 5; 'Mystic', l. 27; 'Stanzas', l. 2.

¹² 'Armageddon', II, l. 18; 'Timbuctoo', ll. 62, 74, 105; 'Mystic', l. 28; 'Stanzas', l. 4; 'This Earth', l. 2; *In Memoriam*, XLI, l. 11.

¹³ 'Armageddon', II, l. 28; 'Timbuctoo', l. 62; 'This Earth', l. 9; *In Memoriam*, XLI, l. 12; XCV, l. 36.

¹⁴ 'Armageddon', II, ll. 14–16; 'Mystic', ll. 36–8; 'Sage', ll. 234–5. See also *Mem.*, II, 90.

¹⁵ 'Armageddon', II, ll. 43–5 (see also *TA*, XII, 17); 'Mystic', ll. 5–6; 'To — [As when with downcast eyes]' (*PT*, 179), l. 12.

almost laughable impossibility, the loss of personality (if so it were) seeming no extinction but the only true life. [. . .] This might [. . .] be the state which St Paul describes, 'Whether in the body I cannot tell, or whether out of the body I cannot tell' [2 Corinthians 12: 2]. [. . .] I am ashamed of my feeble description. Have I not said the state is utterly beyond words? But in a moment, when I come back to my normal state of 'sanity,' I am ready to fight for *mein liebes Ich* [my own dear self], and hold that it will last for æons of æons. (I, 320; see also II, 90, 473–4)

Tennyson appears to have associated these experiences with the writings of both Dante and Goethe. In the passage cited above, the words 'A kind of waking trance' may be an echo of a phrase from Cary's *Divine Comedy*: 'our Poet, in a kind of waking dream' (*DC*, Vol. II, Canto XV, p. 78 / p. 441). This translation is entitled *The Vision of Dante*, and both its editorial material and the poem itself include numerous references to visions and trances.[16] Tennyson's phrase '*mein liebes Ich*' is a quotation from Goethe's lyric 'Higher and Highest Things', which exhibits some noticeable parallels with the English poet's trances (FA, 1, III / I, p. 132, l. 9 / Goethe, trans. Luke, p. 268).[17] Also, Kennedy cites two descriptions of mystical experiences from *Wilhelm Meister*, and suggests that they influenced 'The Mystic', 'Hark! the dogs howl!' and 'This Earth is wondrous, change on change'.[18]

Of still greater relevance, however, is Faust's superb speech 'Oh, happy he', which he delivers in the scene 'Before the Gate'. In 'Armageddon', Tennyson had written:

The sun went down; [. . .]
[. . .]

---

[16] *DC*, Vol. I, pp. xxxii, xl, fn (four times), xli, fn (twice), xlii, fn; Canto III, p. 13 / p. 432; Canto XXIV, p. 130 / l. 113; Vol. II, Canto IX, p. 45 / l. 17; Canto XII, p. 62 / l. 33; Canto XV, p. 81 (twice) / ll. 84, 91; Canto XVII, p. 91 / l. 33; Vol. III, Canto XXIX, p. 155 / l. 80; Canto XXXI, p. 164 / p. 448; Canto XXXII, p. 173 / l. 125; Canto XXXIII, p. 176 / l. 58; p. 177 / l. 105.

[17] '[M]en and angels make intimate acquaintance. [. . .] [T]he transfigured spirit will pass more decisively into a consciousness of its own infinity. [. . .] And I shall then everywhere penetrate more easily through the eternal spheres, which are permeated by the pure living speech of God. [. . .] [W]e soar out of sight and disappear' (FA, 1, III / I, pp. 132–3, ll. 22, 31–2, 37–40, 44 / Goethe, trans. Luke, pp. 269, 270).

[18] Kennedy, pp. 89–90, 92 (refers to *WM*, Vol. IX, Bk VI, p. 788, ll. 1–8; p. 766, l. 13–p. 767, l. 28 / XXIII, 454, 433–5).

[There was a] rustling of white wings! The bright descent
Of a young seraph! [. . .]
[. . .]
I felt my soul grow godlike [. . .]
[. . .]
    [. . .] my mental eye grew large
With such a vast circumference of thought,
That, in my vanity, I seemed to stand
Upon the outward verge and bound alone
Of God's omniscience. [. . .]
[. . .]
My mind seemed winged with knowledge and the strength
Of holy musings and immense Ideas,
Even to Infinitude. All sense of Time
And Being and Place was swallowed up and lost
Within a victory of boundless thought. (I, l. 108; II, ll. 1–2, 21, 23–7, 41–5)

It is not difficult to imagine that the author of these lines would have responded strongly when he subsequently read 'Oh, happy he', in which the 'godlike' Faust experiences, just after sundown, a visionary departure from the body. Much of the vocabulary – 'bounds', 'knowledge' and 'wings of the mind' – is similar to that of 'Armageddon':

WAGNER.
[. . .] If, in youth, you honour your father, you will willingly learn from him: if, in manhood, you extend the bounds of knowledge, your son may mount still higher than you.

FAUST.
Oh, happy he, who can still hope to emerge from this sea of error! Man desires what he knows not, and cannot employ what he knows. But let us not embitter the blessing of this hour by such melancholy reflections. See, how the green-girt cottages shimmer in the setting Sun! He bends and sinks, the day is overlived. Yonder he hurries off, and quickens other life. Oh! that I have no wing to lift me from the ground, to struggle after, for ever after, him! I should see, in everlasting evening beams, the stilly world at my feet,—every height on fire,—every vale in repose,—the silver brooks flowing into golden streams. The rugged mountain, with all its dark defiles, would not then break my godlike course.— —Already the sea, with its heated coves, opens on my enraptured sight. The god seems at last to sink away. But the new impulse wakes. I hurry on to drink his everlasting light,—the day

before me and the night behind,[19]—the heavens above, and under me the waves.—A beauteous dream! as it is passing, he is gone. Alas, no bodily wing can keep pace with the wings of the mind. Yet it is the inborn tendency of our being for feeling to strive upwards and onwards. (ll. 1060-93 / pp. 33-4)

This speech certainly has numerous similarities to poems such as 'Armageddon'. But it is, at the same time, profoundly different. Faust's soul does not just *depart* from his body: it embarks on a purposeful, progressive journey. This strong sense of forward movement is, prior to 1833, almost entirely absent from Tennyson's poems, the greatest of which describe characters who are psychologically static and physically isolated.

This pattern changes in 'Mechanophilus (In the Time of the First Railways)' (*PT*, 197), and this can be partly attributed, I think, to the influence of 'Oh, happy he'.[20] Ricks dates 'Mechanophilus' to *c*. 1833, and the draft in Trinity Notebook 17 suggests that it was written during Tennyson's stay in the Lincolnshire seaside village of Mablethorpe in early March of that year: interpolated into the draft is another piece, 'Lines [Here often, when a child, I lay reclined]', which was first published in the *Memoir* under the title 'Mablethorpe' (*TA*, XI, 208; *Mem.*, I, 161; *PT*, 202).[21] If this dating is correct, there is a strong possibility that when Tennyson wrote 'Mechanophilus', he had just acquired a copy of Hayward's *Faust*, which had been published around the end of February. Like 'Armageddon', 'Mechanophilus' describes a visionary flight, but its novel, progressive tone can be plausibly traced to 'Oh, happy he' (it also appears to echo Wagner's reference to sons who surpass their fathers, and who extend, thereby, 'the bounds of knowledge'):

---

[19] Compare 'The night behind and only the day before' (Emily Tennyson, *The Letters of Emily Lady Tennyson*, ed. James O. Hoge (University Park: Pennsylvania State University Press, 1974), no. 53, p. 100, 10 June 1856).

[20] Tennyson did not revise 'Mechanophilus' and prepare it for publication until 1892.

[21] This is almost certainly where it was written: Tennyson repeatedly refers to the place that he is describing as 'here' (ll. 1, 3, 4, 5). Hallam Tennyson dates 'Lines' to 1837 (*Mem.*, I, 161), but as Ricks points out, this cannot be correct, as all the other poems in Trinity Notebook 17 date from 1833 (*PT*, 202, headnote). Ricks further observes that Tennyson was in Mablethorpe in March of that year (ibid. 202, headnote). Tennyson's wintry description of the area in 'Lines' (ll. 7-8) is not dissimilar to the one in his letter to his aunt, Elizabeth Russell, which he wrote on 10 March, shortly after his return to Somersby (*LAT*, I, 88).

> Bring me my horse! Bring me my wings
>   That I may soar the sky,²²
> [. . .]
> To those still-working energies
>   I see no term or bound.
>
> As we surpass our father's skill
>   Our sons will shame our own,
> A thousand things are hidden still
>   And not a hundred known
> [. . .]
> Deep under deep for ever goes,
>   Heaven over heaven expands. (*TA*, XI, 205, 207; corresponds to *PT*, 197, ll. 9–10, 19–24, 35–6)

Standing, I would argue, on the Lincolnshire coast, the erstwhile poet of stasis and isolation is now moving resolutely forwards, with Faust, across the ocean: 'Meantime push forward work & wield', writes Tennyson (*TA*, XI, 207).

Throughout 'Mechanophilus', these Faustian echoes are mingled with echoes of two other works: Cary's *Inferno*, and Carlyle's 'Signs of the Times' (*WTC*, XXVII, 56–82; 1829).²³ In two of the three manuscripts of 'Mechanophilus', the poem is called 'Æonophilus' ('the lover of the age'), and when the two titles are combined, they evoke Carlyle's 'Mechanical Age' (*TA*, XI, 204; III, 28; *WTC*, XXVII, 59). Carlyle also writes: 'We remove mountains, and make seas our smooth highway' (*WTC*, XXVII, 60), and in his drafts of lines 5–6, Tennyson combines this sentiment with echoes of a number of phrases from Dante: 'Dash back those breakers with a pier! | Strow yonder mountain flat!' (*TA*, XI, 205).²⁴ At line 11, he combines a

---

²² Compare also *F*, ll. 2064–6 / p. 71; *WM*, Vol. IX, Bk IV, Ch. XII, p. 604, ll. 13–14 / XXIII, 277.

²³ Tennyson cites the Italian text of the *Inferno* in his letter from Somersby of 10 March 1833 (already referred to above (*LAT*, I, 88)). The influence of both that work and 'Oh, happy he' may be reflected in 'Stanzas', which follows 'Mechanophilus' in Trinity Notebook 17 (*TA*, XI, 209). The tristichs in which this poem is written are highly unusual for Tennyson (compare also *DC*, Vol. II, Canto XXV, p. 139 / ll. 113–14; Vol. III, Canto XXIX, p. 154 / l. 63, and 'Stanzas', l. 9).

²⁴ See *DC*, Vol. I, Canto VII, p. 35 / ll. 22–3; Canto XV, p. 79 / ll. 5–6; for references to 'pier[s]', see Canto XV, p. 79 / p. 435; l. 4; p. 80 / l. 16; Canto XVI, p. 84 / p. 435; Canto XVIII, p. 97 / l. 99; Canto XIX, p. 100 / l. 43; p. 103 / l. 131; Canto XXI, p. 111 / l. 63; p. 113 / l. 134. Tennyson associated breakers with Mablethorpe (*LAT*, I, 171, [July 1839(?)]; p. 172 [July 1839(?)]).

variation on Dante's 'Thine eye discover quickly that, whereof | Thy thought is dreaming' with Carlyle's repeated use of the word 'outward': 'Thought into the outward springs | I see her with the eye' (*DC*, Vol. I, Canto XVI, p. 88 / ll. 120–1; *WTC*, XXVII, 59, 60, 66, 68, 72, 73, 81; *TA*, XI, 205). The words 'vantage ground' from Canto XXII crop up in line 18, and in a draft of line 29, the 'resistless engines' of Carlyle become 'strong engines' (*DC*, Vol. I, p. 118 / l. 115; *WTC*, XXVII, 60; *TA*, XII, 201).[25]

Perhaps Tennyson was led to create this amalgam of the *Inferno*, 'Signs' and 'Oh, happy he' by a recognition of the broad similarities between these three texts. For if the first-named work has the visionary quality that we also find in Faust's monologue, a passage in Carlyle's essay shares Faust's sense of forward movement: 'the happiness and greatness of mankind at large have been continually progressive', he writes; '[. . .] only in resolutely struggling forward, does our life consist' (*WTC*, XXVII, 80).

Tennyson would appear to be looking back to 'Mechanophilus (In the Time of the First Railways)' in 'Locksley Hall' (*PT*, 271) (the seed of which was provided by a line that he made as he embarked on his first railway journey in 1830 (l. 182; *EE*, II, 344)).[26] The coastline depicted in this poem is, he tells us, 'Lincolnshire', and his friend FitzGerald is more specific, remarking of lines 3–6: 'This is all Lincolnshire coast: about Mablethorpe, where A. T. stayed much' (*Mem.*, I, 195; *EE*, II, 342).[27] In lines 11–12, Tennyson writes:

> Here about the beach I wandered, nourishing a youth sublime
> With the fairy tales of science, and the long result of Time.

This is, I propose, a recollection of Tennyson's youthful visit to Mablethorpe in March 1833, during which the hymn to science and technology that is 'Mechanophilus' was probably written. In that poem,

---

[25] Compare also *WTC*, XXVII, page 56 and 'Mechanophilus', lines 31–2, as well as 'but a preface, shadowy' (*DC*, Vol. III, Canto XXX, p. 161 / l. 80) and 'but the shade— | The preface' (*TA*, XI, 'Mechanophilus', p. 204).

[26] See also 'Mechanophilus', l. 7 and 'Locksley', l. 166 (and see also the important observations in Blocksidge, p. 146).

[27] Mablethorpe may even have provided one of several models for Locksley Hall itself: 'About a mile from the village was once the seat of the [. . .] family of Fitzwilliam, part of whose mansion, converted into a farm house, is standing within a spacious moated area, and is still denominated the Hall' ([Thomas Allen], *The History of the County of Lincoln: From the Earliest Period to the Present Time*, 2 vols (London: Saunders, 1834), II, 154).

he had celebrated the potential of 'the Present'; looked enthusiastically into 'the Future'; and – amidst numerous echoes of *The Vision* – had marvelled at '[t]he wonders' that the latter was to bring (ll. 31, 17, 27). All of these elements can be found in lines 14–16 of 'Locksley':

When I clung to all the present for the promise that it closed:

When I dipt into the future far as human eye could see;
Saw the Vision of the world, and all the wonder that would be.

When the last two lines cited here are reiterated (almost verbatim) at lines 119–20, they are preceded by the following couplet:

Men, my brothers, men the workers, ever reaping something new:
That which they have done but earnest of the things that they shall do. (ll. 117–18)

This, too, is suggestive of 'Mechanophilus', in the published version of which, Tennyson writes:

Meanwhile, my brothers, work, and wield
  The forces of today,
And plow the Present like a field,
  And garner all you may! (ll. 29–32)

Lines 121–4 of 'Locksley' reveal that the 'Vision' referred to in lines 16 and 120 relates to aviation. The link back to 'Mechanophilus' (in which Tennyson had declared: 'Bring me my wings | That I may soar the sky') is a little clearer in two unused lines from the Yale Manuscript of the poem: 'I had visions in my head of all the wonders that would be: | When a man shall range the spaces, using unimagin'd sails' (*TA*, XXIV, 47).[28]

As in 'Mechanophilus', this visionary atmosphere is combined with a strong sense of the need for forward movement. In expressing this, Tennyson appears to turn, once again, to both Goethe and Carlyle. In the heavily Goethean Book II of *Sartor Resartus* (which is a prominent influence on 'Locksley'),[29] there is a paragraph in which

---

[28] See also *PT*, 271, l. 141, fn.
[29] See William Darby Templeman, 'Tennyson's "Locksley Hall" and Thomas Carlyle', in *Booker Memorial Studies: Eight Essays on Victorian Literature in Memory of John Manning Booker 1881–1948*, ed. Hill Shine (Chapel Hill: University of North Carolina Press, 1950), pp. 34–59; Baynes, 'Tennyson and *Werther*', pp. 316–19.

Carlyle emphasises – on five different occasions – the overriding need to move 'forward[s]': 'A nameless Unrest [. . .] urged me forward', he writes; 'forward must I'; 'still Forward!'; 'Forwards!'; 'Forwards!' (I, Ch. VI, pp. 125–6 / p. 118, ll. 2–3, 6, 16, 17, 18). And in the second of Shelley's two 'Scenes from the Faust of Goethe', we find the words 'Forward, onward, far away!' and, also, 'Let the great world rage!' (l. 4042 / PBS, II, ll. 89 (interpolated by Shelley); 240). Both texts are likely influences on Tennyson's expression of his faith in progress in lines 181–2 of 'Locksley': 'Forward, forward let us range,' he writes, 'Let the great world spin forever'. The poem can be seen to combine, therefore, some very similar influences to 'Mechanophilus', for in addition to these echoes of Goethe and Carlyle, lines 75–6 are (as was discussed in the Preface) a clear allusion to the *Inferno*.[30]

The combined evidence of 'Mechanophilus' and 'Locksley Hall' suggests that Tennyson's visit to Mablethorpe in March 1833 was marked by a spiritual experience of some intensity. Although its precise nature can only be guessed at, it seems to have combined trances, progress, Goethe, the *Inferno* and Carlyle.

All of these elements are also present in 'Ulysses' (*PT*, 217). This visionary piece expresses, Tennyson tells us, the need for progress in the face of adversity: it 'was written soon after Arthur Hallam's death, and it gives the feeling about the need of going forward and braving the struggle of life' (EE, II, 339). That is also what Faust expresses in 'Oh, happy he' in 'Before the Gate', so as I will argue below, this speech is an important influence on the poem. 'Ulysses' draws, in addition, on three of the next four scenes in *Faust*: 'Study [I]', 'Study [II]' and 'Witches' Kitchen'.[31] As in 'Mechanophilus' and

---

[30] EE, II, 342 (refers to *DC*, Vol. I, Canto V, p. 28 / ll. 118–19). As Lang observes, lines 33–4 of 'Locksley' draw on *Meister* (Lang, 'Introduction', in Campbell (ed.), I (1971), p. xi (refers to *WM*, Vol. IX, Bk I, Ch. XVII, p. 426, ll. 12–15 / XXIII, 102–3)).

[31] 'Ulysses' has been linked to Goethe's drama in brief comments by six different critics: Paull F. Baum, *Tennyson Sixty Years After* (Chapel Hill: University of North Carolina Press, 1948), p. 300; E. J. Chiasson, 'Tennyson's "Ulysses" – A Re-interpretation' (1954), in *Critical Essays on the Poetry of Tennyson*, ed. John Killham (London: Routledge & Kegan Paul, 1960), pp. 164–73 (p. 168, and fn 1); Georg Roppen, '"Ulysses" and Tennyson's Sea-quest', *English Studies*, 40: 2 (April 1959), 77–90 (p. 79); John Pettigrew, 'Tennyson's "Ulysses": A Reconciliation of Opposites', *Victorian Poetry*, 1: 1 (January 1963), 27–45 (p. 39); Kenneth M. McKay, *'Many Glancing Colours': An Essay in Reading Tennyson, 1809–1850* (Toronto: University of Toronto Press, 1988), pp. 117–18, 121; Harry Levin, 'A Faustian Typology', in *Faust through Four Centuries: Retrospect and Analysis. Vierhundert Jahre Faust. Rückblick und Analyse*, ed. Peter Boerner and Sidney Johnson (Tübingen: Niemeyer, 1989), pp. 1–12 (p. 6).

'Locksley', echoes of Goethe are mingled with echoes of Carlyle – in this case, the essay 'Faustus', and the description of Faust's character in 'Goethe's "Helena"' (WTC, XXVI, 158–62). The trio of literary influences is completed by the Ulisse episode in Canto XXVI of the *Inferno*, which is widely acknowledged to be the lyric's most important source.[32]

Before we look in detail at the relationship between these texts and Tennyson's poem, it will be helpful to examine its biographical and philosophical background, and to situate it within two interrelated series of works. I would suggest that the death of Hallam served to strengthen – perhaps even to *forge* – what was, quite probably, the core of Tennyson's outlook: his faith in an 'after-life [. . .] of progress', and his corresponding abhorrence of the possibility that death leads to extinction, damnation or stagnation. Half a century later, Queen Victoria recorded his comments on this subject in her journal:

> He talked of the many friends he had lost, and what it would be if he did not feel and know that there was another world, where there would be no partings; and then he spoke with horror of the unbelievers and philosophers who would make you believe there was no other world, no Immortality. [. . .] He quoted some well-known lines from Goethe whom he so much admires. (*Mem.*, II, 457, 7 August 1883; see also I, 263–4; II, 420, 474)

Tennyson 'never would believe that Christ could preach "everlasting punishment"' (ibid. I, 322; see also II, 352–3), and with an apparent echo of Ulysses (who has 'suffered greatly' and 'wrought, and thought' (ll. 8, 46)), he remarked: 'I can hardly understand, [. . .] how any great, imaginative man, who has deeply lived, suffered, thought and wrought, can doubt of the Soul's continuous progress in the after-life' (*Mem.*, I, 321). Indeed, he once declared that he would kill himself 'if I thought there was no future life', and it is likely that this deep dread of mortality exacerbated his sombre state of mind in late 1833–4, when a 'cloud of [. . .] overwhelming sorrow [. . .] for a while blotted out all joy from his life, and made him long for death' (ibid. II, 35; I, 109).

An important focus for that sorrow was provided by the image of a ship upon the ocean, which appears in a number of poems that

---

[32] *Mem.*, II, 70; EE, II, 338–9; PT, 217, headnote (line 64 of 'Ulysses', 'the great Achilles, whom we knew', echoes Canto V: 'the great | Achilles, who [. . .]' (DC, Vol. I, p. 26 / ll. 64–5)). Reminiscences of numerous other poets have been identified in 'Ulysses', including Homer, Virgil, Horace, Shakespeare, Wordsworth and Shelley (PT, 217, fns; Thomas, pp. 52–79; Winnick, pp. 107–9).

date from this period (and later). As Susan Shatto and Marion Shaw point out, it can be traced to a phrase in the letter through which Tennyson learned of Hallam's demise: 'He died at Vienna, [. . .] and I believe his Remains come by Sea from Trieste' (*LAT*, I, 93, 1 October 1833).[33] Shortly after Tennyson read these words, he composed an address to the 'Fair ship [. . .] from the Italian shore', which was bringing his friend's 'loved remains' back to England (*In Memoriam*, IX, ll. 1, 3). In the Heath Manuscript, this is dated 'Oct. 6. 1833', and it was therefore written shortly before 'Ulysses', which is dated 'Oct. 20' (*TA*, XXIX, 30, 33). It later became the first in a series of sections in *In Memoriam* (IX–XVII), almost all of which express an intense emotional engagement with the ship from Trieste. As Martin suggests, 'Ulysses' needs to be read in conjunction with these:

> If one were in doubt about the connection of the poem with Hallam, it would be obvious from the linking of the pervading images of death with the vessel and the dark broad seas ['Ulysses', ll. 44–5]. The Italian ship and its 'dark freight' [*In Memoriam*, X, l. 8] [. . .] clearly obsessed Tennyson during the long wait for the arrival of the body.[34]

Martin's observation can be expanded upon by pointing out that in *In Memoriam*, IX–XVII, Tennyson is repeatedly anxious lest 'the roaring wells | Should gulf' Hallam's body (X, ll. 17–18; see also IX, ll. 9–16; XV (and EE, III, 229); XVII, ll. 1–20).[35] The threat of shipwreck is also a theme in both 'Ulysses' (in which it is represented, similarly, by 'the gulfs' (l. 62)),[36] and in lines 37–48 of 'The Flight' (*PT*, 259) (which have numerous affinities with the former piece, and which are clearly inspired by the voyage of the ship from Trieste).[37]

The copy of Cary's *Inferno* that is at the Research Centre in Lincoln may provide an insight into Tennyson's deep concern for the Italian ship. Alongside the following words from Dante's philosophical

---

[33] S & S, p. 173.
[34] Martin, p. 186.
[35] See also *LAT*, I, 105 (30 December [1833]).
[36] Tennyson almost certainly takes this image from Cary's *Inferno*, in which it occurs repeatedly.
[37] Compare also the suicidal speaker of 'The Flight' ('all my life was darkened, as I saw the white sail run' (l. 39)), and Tennyson's comment on the death of Hallam ('I suffered what seemed to me to shatter all my life so that I desired to die' (*LAT*, II, 290 [c. 23 December 1861])). A further connection to Hallam's death is suggested by lines 33–6 of 'The Flight' (see Blocksidge, p. 221).

essay *The Banquet* (which are cited by Cary in his comments on Canto XXVII, which follows the Ulisse episode) there is a marginal pencil marking, which is, presumably, Tennyson's:

> As it hath been said by Cicero in his treatise on old age, natural death is like a port and haven to us after a long voyage; and even as the good mariner, when he draws near the port, lowers his sails, and enters it softly with a weak and inoffensive motion, so ought we to lower the sails of our worldly operations, and to return to God with all our understanding and heart, to the end that we may reach this haven with all quietness and with all peace. And herein we are mightily instructed by nature in a lesson of mildness; for in such a death itself there is neither pain nor bitterness; but as ripe fruit is lightly and without violence loosened from its branch, so our soul without grieving departs from the body in which it hath been.[38]

This passage is of obvious relevance to 'Ulysses', in which the speaker embarks, in '[o]ld age' (l. 50), on a long voyage, which he has resolved to continue until he dies (ll. 59–61). In describing this scenario, Tennyson is, I think, attenuating the pain and bitterness of Hallam's death by imaginatively extending his short life into seniority – and, also, into eternity. The threat of shipwreck is suggestive, therefore, of the brutal suddenness of his friend's demise, and the challenge to his beliefs that it represents. However, as long as Hallam's body is progressing across '[t]he trenchèd waters' (those '[e]mblems or glimpses of eternity' ('Ode to Memory: Addressed to—' (*PT*, 84), ll. 104, 103 (and fn); 1830 text)),[39] it provides a temporal symbol of the progress of his

---

[38] *The Vision; or Hell, Purgatory, and Paradise, of Dante Alighieri: Translated by the Rev. Henry Francis Cary, A.M.*, 3rd edn, 3 vols (London: Taylor, 1831) (TRC, AT/826), I, 260 (this passage is not reproduced in the 1994 edition).

[39] See also 'Mechanophilus', l. 35 (cited above); Roppen, p. 87; and Werther's letter of 9 May 1772:

> When I looked at the water as it flowed, and formed romantic ideas of the countries it was going to pass through, my imagination was soon exhausted; but the water continued flowing farther and farther, till I was bewildered in the idea of invisible distance. Exactly such, my dear friend, were the thoughts of our good ancestors. And when Ulysses talks of the immeasurable sea, and the unlimited earth, is it not more natural, more true, more according to our feelings, than when, in this philosophic age, every school-boy thinks himself a prodigy, because he can repeat after his master that the earth is round? (Pt I, p. 152, ll. 16–28 / pp. 139–40)

soul through the after-life, thus fortifying Tennyson's imperilled faith in immortality. It is that same faith which enables the poet to move forwards himself, and in doing so, he experiences a welcome feeling of communion with his late friend.

Tennyson is able to intensify this emotion by drawing on his trances. As we saw earlier, these would habitually culminate in a strong conviction of eternal life, and his description of them in the *Memoir* is immediately followed by this comment by his son: 'In the same way he said that there might be a more intimate communion than we could dream of between the living and the dead, at all events for a time' (*Mem.*, I, 320; compare *In Memoriam*, XCIV, ll. 1–4). Indeed, if 'Ulysses' is part of Tennyson's series of poems inspired by the Italian ship, it is also part of a second series, in which he repeatedly overcomes his fear of death – often expressed through echoes of the *Inferno* – by means of a vision.[40] Poems describing trance-like flights precede both of the two surviving holographs of 'Ulysses',[41] and a notebook containing one of these also includes the piece beginning 'Hark! the dogs howl! the sleetwinds blow' (*TA*, III, 19–20; *PT*, 214). It is possible that this line contains traces of the sufferings that are described at the start of Canto VI of the *Inferno* (which includes references to 'a dog', 'Howling' and 'sleety flaw' (*DC*, Vol. I, pp. 29, 30 / ll. 13, 18, 9)). In 'Hark!', Tennyson overcomes this nightmare by embarking on what Ricks calls a 'visionary journey', which culminates in an imagined reunion with Hallam (ll. 3–26).[42] Comparable experiences are portrayed in *In Memoriam*, XCV (ll. 16–48) and, also, in XLI. With a possible echo of the words 'to strive upwards and onwards' in 'Oh, happy he', Tennyson (so his son implies) describes the latter section as evoking 'the upward and onward progress of life'

---

[40] The earliest of these poems is probably 'Pierced through with knotted thorns of barren pain' (*PT*, 190; *c.* 1832). Compare 'Pierc'd through with pain' (*DC*, Vol. I, Canto XXVII, p. 142 / l. 10), and see *PT*, 190, headnote; *TA*, XII, 19–20.

[41] 'What did it profit me that once in Heaven' (*TA*, XII, 231; *PT*, Vol. III, p. 620) and 'This Earth is wondrous, change on change' (*TA*, III, 9–10; *PT*, 201). The first four words of the latter piece recall a phrase from 'Signs': 'this wondrous planet, Earth' (*WTC*, XXVII, 82). This poem is also influenced by Shelley's 'Scenes' (which are discussed in some detail in Hay. 1, pp. lix–lxiv). The opening stanza is reminiscent of the Archangels' Chorus (ll. 243–70 / *PBS*, I, ll. 1–28); the phrase 'Jack-a-lantern' (l. 3869 / *PBS*, II, l. 37) prompts Tennyson's two references to 'Jack' of beanstalk fame (ll. 14, 17); and as Ricks points out, the words 'giant-snouted crags' are echoed in 'monstrous rocks from craggy snouts' (*F*, l. 3879 / *PBS*, II, l. 49; *PT*, 201, l. 23, and fn).

[42] *PT*, 296, XII, l. 6, fn.

(EE, III, 236), and he places this sense of forward movement in firm opposition to the horrors of mortality:

> my nature rarely yields
> To that vague fear implied in death;
> Nor shudders at the gulfs beneath,
> The howlings from forgotten fields. (XLI, ll. 13–16)

The threatening 'gulfs' recall Dante, and Tennyson glosses the last line cited here as 'The eternal miseries of the Inferno', his son adding: 'More especially, I feel sure, a reminiscence of Dante's *Inferno*, Canto iii. lines 25–51' (EE, III, 236).

These two series of poems intersect in *In Memoriam*, XII and CIII; in 'The Voyage' (*PT*, 257); and in 'Ulysses', all of which combine the image of a ship with a sense of victory over death through visionary forward movement. In the first-named piece,[43] Tennyson embarks on an imagined flight '[o]'er ocean-mirrors' towards the ship from Trieste: '[I] forward dart [. . .], and play | About the prow' (ll. 9, 17–18). Ricks compares line 6 ('I leave this mortal ark behind') to line 3 of 'Hark!' ('I leave the dreaming world below'),[44] and the visionary character of this section is clearly indicated by the poet's own comment on that line: 'My spirit flies from out my material self' (EE, III, 228). In CIII, Tennyson experiences 'a vision of the dead' (l. 3), and sees

> The shape of him I loved, and love
> For ever: then flew in a dove[45]
> And brought a summons from the sea. (ll. 14–16)[46]

Much as in 'Ulysses', the speaker leads a group of companions to 'a little shallop [. . .] | At anchor in the flood below' (ll. 19–20), and Tennyson remarks that the subsequent voyage (which ends as he sails with Hallam towards a sinking star (ll. 41–56)) evokes '[t]he great progress of the age as well as the opening of another world'.[47] A further visionary sea journey is portrayed in 'The Voyage' (which

---

[43] Like 'Pierced through', this draws on Genesis 8: 8–9 (*PT*, 190, l. 34, fn; *PT*, 296, XII, fn).
[44] *PT*, 296, XII, l. 6, fn.
[45] Compare, once again, Genesis 8: 8–9.
[46] Tennyson glosses 'sea' as 'eternity' (EE, III, 255).
[47] Cited in Knowles, p. 186.

Ricks compares to both *In Memoriam*, XII and 'Ulysses'):[48] 'one fair Vision ever fled | Down the waste waters day and night', writes Tennyson (ll. 57–8). In this piece, there is one member of the vessel's crew who lacks the progressivist outlook of his fellows, and who succumbs, therefore, to death: 'overboard one stormy night | He cast his body, and on we swept' (ll. 79–80). The poem's concluding lines suggest, however, that for the speaker and his surviving shipmates, the journey will stretch out into eternity: 'We know the merry world is round, | And we may sail for evermore' (ll. 95–6).

A comparable victory over mortality is achieved – albeit by a much narrower margin – in 'Ulysses'. It should be noted, first of all, that the speaker's journey resembles the contemporaneous voyage of Hallam's remains. Three days before he wrote the poem, Tennyson had a meeting with his late friend's father, who may have given him the news that although the ship would be departing fairly soon, she had not yet done so.[49] This is the situation during at least the first fifty-seven of the seventy lines of 'Ulysses'. Also, Tennyson would have known that once the ship had passed south of the Italian Peninsula, her route would, for a time, have duplicated that of Ulisse's vessel, heading westwards towards the Pillars of Hercules.[50]

The poem's sense of communion with Hallam is further reinforced by what John Pettigrew calls 'the unusually insistent presence of echoes from other works of literature'.[51] As Ricks observes: 'To the loneliness of the poet or of the man, [allusions] offer company, the company of dear dead poets. [. . .] All language holds communion with the dead'.[52] These words seem especially applicable to 'Ulysses', two of the principal sources of which have demonstrable links to the dead Hallam (he had greatly admired Goethe, and Dante was his favourite poet).[53]

An affirmation of eternal life may also be implicit in the dramatic monologue *form* of 'Ulysses'. Ulisse delivers his narration retrospectively, from amidst the fires of hell: his shipwreck and damnation are,

---

[48] *PT*, 257, headnote; ll. 40–1, fn (and see *TA*, XII, 211). Compare, especially, line 16 of 'The Voyage' and line 60 of 'Ulysses' (and compare also line 68 of the former poem to the words of Ulisse (*DC*, Vol. I, Canto XXVI, p. 141 / l. 117)). Also, *contrast* the sea journey of 'The Voyage' with that of 'The Flight' (a draft of which follows 'The Voyage' in Trinity Notebook 21 (*TA*, XII, 210–15)).
[49] *LAT*, I, 94 ([10 October 1833]); Blocksidge, p. 224.
[50] These are mentioned in the visionary poems 'Timbuctoo' (ll. 1–3; 11–12, and fn; l. 247) and 'The Poet' (l. 15, and fn).
[51] Pettigrew, pp. 42–3.
[52] Ricks, *Allusion*, pp. 188, 189 (refers to *In Memoriam*, XCIV, l. 4).
[53] Martin, p. 71; Blocksidge, p. 64.

quite literally, a foregone conclusion. For the Faust of 'Oh, happy he', however, events are unfolding as he speaks, and the outcome is open. This is also the case in 'Ulysses', and by fusing his ostensible source with Goethe's drama, Tennyson rescues Ulisse from damnation, and extends to him the possibility of redemption. This crucial alteration represents, in turn, a further similarity to *Faust*, for as Carlyle had foreseen in 'Goethe's "Helena"', that work effects a comparable transformation of its own source material: 'it might seem as if the action was not intended, in the manner of the old Legend, to terminate in Faust's perdition' (*WTC*, XXVI, 161).

'Ulysses' is divided into four verse paragraphs. The first of these can be usefully compared to *In Memoriam*, IX (which, as we have seen, was written just a fortnight earlier). In that piece, Tennyson had been so preoccupied with the 'Fair ship' – and the prospect of reunion with his late friend in the after-life (ll. 1–18) – that his family relationships had seemed to pale by comparison: Hallam, he writes, is 'More [dear] than my brothers are to me' (l. 20). Ulysses expresses a similar feeling of alienation from those to whom he should be closest, describing himself as 'Matched with an agèd wife' (and disparaging the people amongst whom he lives as 'a savage race' (ll. 3, 4)).[54] As in *In Memoriam*, IX, however, the emotional focus of the poetry lies far away across the ocean, for Ulysses is already contemplating his voyage. It is likely, therefore, that in both texts, the speaker's coldness towards his family is also Tennyson's warmth towards his friend.

The opening words of paragraph one may also contain a first, faint echo of *Faust*, and there is a second, less equivocal one at the start of paragraph two. If read in conjunction with the contexts from which they are drawn, they can be seen as an attempt to place progress in opposition to death. When Tennyson writes the words 'It little profits' (l. 1), he may be thinking of the scene 'Night', in which Faust declares: 'What one does not profit by, is an oppressive burthen; what the moment brings forth, in that only can it profit us' (ll. 684–5 / pp. 18–19).[55] It is at that moment that he notices a phial of poison, which he then grasps, with the intention of committing suicide. As he does so, he seems very similar to the self-destructive Ulisse, for he

---

[54] Compare 'Locksley', line 177, and, also, one of Hallam's last letters to Somersby: 'The Tyrolese are an uncivilised race, possessing apparently the virtues & vices of the savage state' (*LAHH*, no. 245, p. 776, 24 August [1833]).

[55] Compare the opening words of the trance-influenced fragment that precedes 'Ulysses' in Trinity Notebook 22: 'What did it profit me' (*PT*, Vol. III, p. 620).

describes his feelings in terms of an ocean voyage: 'I am beckoned out into the wide sea; the glassy wave glitters at my feet; another day invites to other shores' (ll. 699–701 / p. 19). For Faust, however, death is merely a transition to a progressive after-life (or 'new spheres of pure activity'), and as he *'places the goblet to his mouth'*, he is in any case interrupted by the *'singing of chorusses'* (l. 705; stage direction before l. 737 / pp. 19, 20). In the later scene 'Witches' Kitchen', he lifts a second chalice, which is filled not with poison, but with a magical potion that takes thirty years off his life (stage direction before l. 2583; ll. 2341–2 / pp. 99, 88). 'Hand us thy drink, and fill the cup to the brim', Mephistopheles tells the witch, before urging Faust onwards: 'Now forth at once! You must not rest' (ll. 2578–9, 2587 / pp. 99, 100). It is *this* scene, not 'Night', that Tennyson echoes in lines 6–7: 'I cannot rest from travel: I will drink | Life to the lees'.[56]

This shared restlessness is probably the most important similarity between Ulysses and Faust. As Tony Robbins observes, 'Ithaca, the goal of all Odysseus' striving, in Tennyson's poem is the objective correlative of Ulysses' discontent'.[57] The speaker's disillusioned attitude towards his homeland bears a close resemblance to Faust's relationship to 'the passing moment' (l. 1699 / p. 58): although Faust's ostensible goal is to raise that moment to perfection, it brings, in practice, only dissatisfaction, and the renewal of his onward striving. For both Faust and Ulysses, it is not the *attainment* of the ideal that is meaningful, but the *pursuit* of it. This outlook is powerfully dramatised in 'Oh, happy he': Faust does not yearn to *reach* the setting sun, but simply 'to struggle after, for ever after' it. The goal that is pursued by Ulysses – which seems to be both earthly and transcendent – is similarly elusive:

> all experience is an arch wherethrough
> Gleams that untravelled world, whose margin fades
> For ever and for ever when I move. (ll. 19–21)

For both characters, this never-ending forward movement keeps extinction at bay. 'If ever I lie down, calm and composed, upon a

---

[56] This echo may well be more appropriate than Tennyson himself could have realised. Goethe wrote most or all of 'Witches' Kitchen' in Rome in 1788, and '[t]he motif [of the magical potion] may derive from Annibale Carracci's fresco, in the Palazzo Farnese, of Circe offering the cup to Ulysses' (Boyle, I (1991), 527; see also p. 563).

[57] Tony Robbins, 'Tennyson's "Ulysses": The Significance of the Homeric and Dantesque Backgrounds', *Victorian Poetry*, 11: 3 (Autumn 1973), 177–93 (p. 181).

couch, be there at once an end of me', declares Faust (ll. 1692–3 / p. 58). Ulysses, too, equates rest with death: 'How dull it is to pause, to make an end' (l. 22).

The language that Tennyson uses as his speaker begins to contemplate the resumption of his travels has numerous overlaps with both *Faust* and his own descriptions of his trances. 'I am become a name', says Ulysses at line 11, which is suggestive, I think, of the poet's concentration on his name at the commencement of his visions. In 'Goethe's "Helena"', Carlyle writes: 'Faust, [. . .] like [Homer's] Bellerophon, wanders apart, "eating his own heart". [. . .] A ravenous hunger for enjoyment haunts him everywhere' (*WTC*, XXVI, 159, 160). The words 'always roaming with a hungry heart' (l. 12) seem to look back to those lines – and, also, forwards to *In Memoriam*, XCV, in which the trance episode is prefaced with the phrase 'A hunger seized my heart' (l. 21). Perhaps Tennyson also read a visionary quality into the words of Mephistopheles in 'Study [I]': 'I am a part of the part, which in the beginning was all' (l. 1349 / p. 44). This could help to explain why he echoes them at line 18, where he writes: 'I am a part of all that I have met'. Nine lines later, Carlyle's 'silence of the blank bygone Eternity' (*WTC*, XXVI, 'Goethe's "Helena"', p. 166) may well help to suggest Tennyson's 'eternal silence' (l. 27).

As Georg Roppen observes, the words that bring paragraph two to a close 'carry strong connotations of spiritual quest and transcendent existence'.[58] As in 'Mechanophilus', Tennyson draws on Wagner's reference to 'the bounds of knowledge', as well as Faust's subsequent pursuit, in 'Oh, happy he', of 'the setting Sun' as it 'bends and sinks'.[59] And once again, he mingles Goethe with Carlyle, who in his essay on *Part One*, had described the protagonist as having 'allowed his desires to reach beyond the boundaries', thus arriving at 'the utmost limits of human research' (Carlyle, '*Faustus*', pp. 333, 322):

> yearning in desire
> To follow knowledge like a sinking star,
> Beyond the utmost bound of human thought. (ll. 30–2)[60]

---

[58] Roppen, p. 86.
[59] Note that like 'Oh, happy he', Ulisse's voyage across the ocean is a 'flight', in which he and his companions, he informs us, 'Made our oars wings' (*DC*, Vol. I, Canto XXVI, p. 141 / ll. 121–2).
[60] Compare also 'follow but thy star' (*DC*, Vol. I, Canto XV, p. 81/ l. 55), as well as '[Faust's] sleepless pilgrimage towards Knowledge and Vision' (*WTC*, XXVI, 'Goethe's "Helena"', p. 159). See also *PT*, 217, ll. 31–2, fn; Winnick, pp. 108–9.

These lines should also be compared to the 'victory of boundless thought' in the earlier 'Armageddon', in which the entranced poet had

> seemed to stand
> Upon the outward verge and bound alone
> Of God's omniscience. (II, ll. 45, 25–7)

It is reasonable to suppose, however, that by the time Tennyson wrote 'Ulysses' in October 1833, these experiences had acquired a new import for him. To quote, once again, from his description of them in the *Memoir*: when individuality fades into 'boundless being, [. . .] utterly beyond words', death becomes 'an almost laughable impossibility'. It is, I would suggest, this visionary affirmation of immortality that is being enacted in Ulysses' journey beyond the bounds.

Paragraph three consists of a father's comments on his son. This suggests a further similarity to 'Mechanophilus', for as in the earlier poem, Tennyson may be responding to Wagner's remark about fathers and sons, which precedes 'Oh, happy he'. Ulysses' language is now a little gentler than it had been in paragraph one, but there is still a clear sense that his family relationships have ceased to be the emotional focus of his life.

That focus is provided, instead, by the image in the opening line of paragraph four: 'There lies the port; the vessel puffs her sail' (l. 44). In *In Memoriam*, IX, X and XVII, Tennyson implicitly invests the ship with life by addressing her directly, and he creates the same effect here by making her the subject of a verb. Paragraph four might also be compared to section LXXXIV, in which the poet crowns Hallam's head with 'silver hair', and then goes 'hovering o'er the dolorous strait' with him, 'To the other shore, [. . .] | [. . .] as a single soul' (ll. 32, 39–40, 44). In 'Ulysses', however, the affirmation of longevity and immortality that the old man's sea voyage represents is repeatedly challenged by the spectre of decease, the verse being subject to numerous shifts of mood and ambiguities of meaning. For example, in line 45, the darkening seas can be seen (as Martin suggests in the passage cited earlier) as being redolent of death. But it may be that the dusk here described is intended to evoke not the *end* of life, but – in the words of Douglas Bush – 'the evening of life',[61] of which

---

[61] 'Alfred, Lord Tennyson', ed. Douglas Bush, in *Major British Writers*, ed. G. B. Harrison, 2nd edn, 2 vols (New York: Harcourt, Brace, 1959), II, 369–466 (p. 396, fn) (Bush refers, specifically, to ll. 54–5).

Hallam had been robbed. (Old age is not, of course, the same thing as death. 'Old age hath yet his honour and his toil' (l. 50).) A further layer of meaning is provided by the fact that this twilight scene also resembles 'Armageddon', 'Timbuctoo', 'This Earth is wondrous' and *In Memoriam*, XCV, in all of which, a description of visionary illumination is set against a backdrop of nightfall. As in the last-named piece, it is more plausible to regard the gathering darkness not as a metaphor for despair, but, instead, as an apposite backdrop, which helps to ensure that Hallam's 'living soul' can be 'flashed' all the more brightly onto Tennyson's (XCV, l. 36).

'[T]he feeling of [Hallam's] loss' is,[62] to be sure, clearly discernible in the words 'Death closes all', which begin line 51. However, as in line 26 (and, also, 69), this reference to mortality is immediately followed by the qualifying conjunction 'but'. And in line 51, Tennyson effectively brings his friend back to life, for the words 'ere the end' are taken from one of Hallam's 'Four Translations from the German'.[63] Another work that might be loosely described as a translation from the German – the heavily Faustian *Deformed Transformed* – would appear to be echoed at line 53. In Part I, scene 2 of Byron's play, a reference to men who are 'like the Gods' is followed, two lines later, by the phrase 'men who war with mortals' (Byron, *Poetical Works*, VI (1991), I. 2. 185, 187). Tennyson's words 'men that strove with Gods' read like a conflation of these two phrases – although tellingly, the allusion to mortality has now been elided. Elsewhere in the same scene of *The Deformed*, the protagonist Arnold asks, 'What! are there | New Worlds?' (ll. 10–11), a question that would appear to be answered in line 57 of 'Ulysses', with its hopeful evocation of 'a newer world'.

Tennyson was probably led to this little-known play by the reference to it in the 'Notes' to Hayward's translation of *Part One*, and

---

[62] Tennyson (with reference to 'Ulysses'); cited in Knowles, p. 182.
[63] *WAH*, 'III. FROM SCHILLER ["*Die Theilung der Erde.*" 1795.]', pp. 310–11 (p. 311, stanza III) (there is no precedent for these words in the German text: see Schiller, *Werke und Briefe*, I (1992), p. 24, l. 11; p. 442, l. 11). Perhaps Tennyson responded to the news of his friend's death by re-reading some of his writings (and one can well imagine that these three words would have stuck in his mind). If this is indeed what happened, Motter's comment on the next of the 'Four Translations' (*WAH*, 'IV. FROM TIECK ["*Wie lieb und hold ist Frühlingsleben.*"], pp. 312–13) may gain in significance: 'It is interesting that the metre Hallam has used, taken from the German, produces a stanza like that of "In Memoriam"' (ibid. p. 312, fn). In other words, it is possible that even the *form* of Tennyson's poem is in memoriam A. H. H.

the same text mentions both *Cain* and *Manfred* (pp. 207, 214).[64] It is these two dramatic poems – along with *Faust* itself, and Carlyle's comments on it – that are echoed in the magnificent six-line sentence with which 'Ulysses' concludes (ll. 65–70). In 'Study [II]', Mephistopheles tells the protagonist: 'Thou art in the end—what thou art. [. . .] [T]hou abidest ever what thou art' (ll. 1806, 1809 / p. 61). Byron may well be drawing on these words in both *Manfred* and *Cain*, whose somewhat Faustian protagonists declare, respectively, 'I I Am what I am', and 'That which I am, I am' (Byron, *Poetical Works*, IV (1986), III. 1. 151–2; VI (1991), III. 1. 509).[65] All three of these texts – but especially *Cain* – would appear to be echoed in the concluding sentence of 'Ulysses'. Although it begins with a further

---

[64] '[I]n some sense', writes Hayward, 'almost every thing [Byron] wrote might be called Faustish' (Hay. 1, p. 214). This comment could help to explain the echoes of Canto III of *Childe Harold* that are detected in 'Ulysses' by Pettigrew (p. 44), Ricks (*PT*, 217, l. 18, fn) and B. J. Leggett ('Dante, Byron and Tennyson's Ulysses', *Tennessee Studies in Literature*, 15 (1970), 143–59). There are at least four other reasons why Tennyson should have combined echoes of Goethe with echoes of Byron – and done so, moreover, in this particular poem. First, if he had read Thomas Moore's recently published *Letters and Journals of Lord Byron* (1830) (an 1866 copy of which is at TRC (AT/1623)), he would have learned that its subject had briefly corresponded with the German poet shortly before his departure for Greece (Thomas Moore, *Letters and Journals of Lord Byron: With Notices of his Life* (London: Murray, 1830), pp. 457–8). Second, Moore also recounts that not long before his death, Byron undertook 'a journey to Ithaca', during which he 'paid a visit to the mountain cave in which, according to tradition, Ulysses deposited the presents of the Phaecians' (p. 459). Third, as Leggett observes (p. 156), when Tennyson received the news of Hallam's death in October 1833, it might well have stirred memories of April 1824, when another young British writer had met with a premature end on the Continent. Fourth, Tennyson would certainly have been aware that Byron's body had been transported back to England by sea (Moore, *Byron*, p. 494) – and along a route, moreover, which overlapped with those taken by both Ulysses' vessel, and the ship from Trieste.

[65] Compare also Exodus 3: 14: 'And God said unto Moses, I AM THAT I AM'. Byron's *Cain* continues:

> I did not seek
> For life, nor did I make myself; but could I
> With my own death redeem [Abel] from the dust –
> And why not so? let him return to day,
> And I lie ghastly! (III. 1. 509–12)

Compare Tennyson's feelings for the dead Hallam (whom he had described, just two weeks before he wrote 'Ulysses', as 'More [dear] than my brothers are to me' (*In Memoriam*, IX, l. 20)).

acknowledgement of death, this is followed, once again, by a resolute assertion of enduring life:

> Though much is taken, much abides; and though
> We are not now that strength which in old days
> Moved earth and heaven;⁶⁶ that which we are, we are. (ll. 65–7)

'Faust', remarks Carlyle, 'will not yield, for his heart, though torn, is yet unweakened' (*WTC*, XXVI, 'Goethe's "Helena"', pp. 160–1). Tennyson transforms this comment into one last allusion to the blow which fate had recently dealt him, but he then expresses (like Faust in the concluding sentence of 'Oh, happy he') his continuing determination 'to strive':⁶⁷

> One equal temper of heroic hearts,
> Made weak by time and fate, but strong in will
> To strive, to seek, to find, and not to yield. (ll. 68–70)

If Tennyson had intended his speaker to be little more than an anglicised Ulisse, he would have ended 'Ulysses' at lines 62–4, which are a (heavily attenuated) version of that character's fate. However, this grand concluding sentence has no precedent in the *Inferno*, and is, instead, conspicuously Faustian.

This raises the significant question of the relative importance of Faust and Ulisse for Tennyson's portrayal of his speaker. Some might argue that the two characters are, in any case, very similar: in both '*Faustus*' and 'Goethe's "Helena"', Carlyle places considerable emphasis on 'Faust's criminality', thus making him sound much like the nefarious Ulisse (Carlyle, '*Faustus*', p. 333). However, he also argues that 'Faust, [. . .] wild and wilful as he is, cannot be regarded as a wicked, much less as an utterly reprobate man' (*WTC*, XXVI, 'Goethe's "Helena"', pp. 161–2). In contrast to Ulisse, he does not belong in the inferno:

> To send him to the Pit of Woe, to render such a character the eternal slave of Mephistopheles, would look like making darkness triumphant over light. [. . .] Our seared and blighted yet still noble Faust will not end in the madness of horror, but in Peace grounded on better Knowledge. (ibid. XXVI, 'Goethe's "Helena"', p. 162)

---

⁶⁶ The words 'earth and heaven' are used by Cain shortly after the phrase that has just been quoted (III. 1. 530), and by Faust after 'Oh, happy he' (l. 1119 / p. 35).
⁶⁷ See also *WTC*, XXVI, 'Goethe's "Helena"', p. 158.

Perhaps it was this crucial difference between *Faust* and the Ulisse episode that led Tennyson to use both of them as sources for 'Ulysses'. Throughout this poem, he seems deeply troubled by the fear of death that is represented to him by the *Inferno*. Ultimately however, he transcends these anxieties, and goes soaring into the sunset with Faust. Much like Goethe's protagonist, Ulysses' defining characteristic is his unremitting striving, which is closely linked to the attainment of immortality. Although Canto XXVI of the *Inferno* remains its most obvious source, 'Ulysses' is, in spirit, the most Faustian poem that Tennyson ever wrote.

The interpretation of the relationship between 'Ulysses' and *Faust* that has been offered above will be greatly strengthened if it can be demonstrated that in October 1833, Tennyson knew that Carlyle's prediction had proven correct, and that *Part Two* concludes with Faust's ascension to heaven. The most likely source of this knowledge would have been Hayward's *Foreign Quarterly Review* article, which had appeared three months earlier. As I will argue in the next chapter, Tennyson draws on this in the other two dramatic monologues on classical themes that he was working on in late 1833, and he would return to *Part Two* in the long narrative poem that he published in 1847.

Chapter 3

'Out of Orcus into Life': Hallam and *Part Two*

In later life, Tennyson shared the widely held view that *Faust: Part Two* is a lesser work than *Part One*. 'The poem', he remarked in 1886, 'is full of splendid imagery, but far inferior on the whole to the first part' (*Mem.*, II, 325).[1] In 1833, however, he had drawn on it in two of his poetic responses to the death of Hallam, 'Tithon' and 'Tiresias'.[2] He renewed his preoccupation with *Part Two* in *The Princess*, and this work, too, reflects his feelings about his late friend (most notably in 'Come down, O maid, from yonder mountain height'). In all of these poems, Tennyson is responding to *Part Two* in a manner that appears to be strongly influenced by his knowledge of the life of its author – a life which both resembled, and differed from, his own experience.

Tennyson's interest in *Part Two* was first aroused during his time at Cambridge. It was in January 1828 (just two months after his arrival there) that Carlyle's essay 'Goethe's "Helena"' was published in the *Foreign Quarterly Review*. This provides a full summary – illustrated with extensive excerpts – of *Part Two* Act III (which was first published under the title 'Helena', and which is set entirely in Greece). Tennyson seems to have made a connection between Carlyle's article and the two Greek tragedies that would later provide him with sources for

---

[1] Tennyson appears to echo Lewes (II, 423): 'the *Second Part of Faust* [. . .] [is] very far inferior to the *First Part*'.

[2] 'Tithon' was written in late 1833; revised as 'Tithonus' in 1859; and published in 1860 (*Mem.*, I, 443, and fn; p. 459; II, 9). 'Tiresias' was begun in 1833, prior to death of Hallam, and was continued shortly after it. Tennyson revised and completed the poem in 1883, and published it in 1885 (David F. Goslee, 'Three Stages of Tennyson's "Tiresias"', *Journal of English and Germanic Philology*, 75 (1976), 154–67).

'Tiresias': Euripides' *Phoenician Women* and Aeschylus' *Seven against Thebes*.³ Evidence of this link is provided by a little-known text: the eight-line fragment 'Refulgent Lord of Battle tell me why' (*PT*, Vol. III, p. 608). Tennyson wrote this poem on the inside back cover of his copy of William Trollope's *Pentalogia Graeca* (1825), which is now at the Research Centre in Lincoln. The *Pentalogia* is an anthology, in the original Greek, of five tragedies, including *Seven against Thebes* and *Phoenician Women*. In the front of the book, the poet has written 'A. Tennyson | Somersby | July 6th 1825', and all of the plays have annotations in his hand. It would appear that Tennyson subsequently gave this volume to the future clergyman David Hillcoat Leighton, who was a student at Cambridge from 1826 to 1830 (Tennyson's inscription has been obscured by the words 'D. H. Leighton | Trinity College').⁴

As Aidan Day points out, 'Refulgent Lord' draws on lines 784–92 of *Phoenician Women*.⁵ But it also draws on Carlyle's translation of an important episode from *Part Two* Act III: the brief life of Faust and Helena's son, Euphorion (ll. 9598–938 / *WTC*, XXVI, 190–3). 'Our readers', remarks Carlyle,

> are aware that this Euphorion, the offspring of Northern Character wedded to Grecian Culture, frisks it here not without reference to modern Poesy, which had a birth so precisely similar. Sorry are we that we cannot follow him through these fine warblings and trippings on the light fantastic toe: to our ears there is a quick, pure, small-toned music in them, as perhaps of elfin bells when the Queen of Faery rides by moonlight. (*WTC*, XXVI, 191)

Evidence that Tennyson read this passage was provided as long ago as 1903, when D. Laurance Chambers suggested that lines 32–6 of 'Sir Launcelot and Queen Guinevere' (*PT*, 205) contain 'a faint recollection' of the second of the two sentences cited above.⁶ In a footnote

---

[3] *PT*, 219, headnote.
[4] William Trollope (ed.), *Pentalogia Græca* (London: Rivington, 1825) (TRC, AT/3550); Aidan Day, 'Notable Acquisitions by the Tennyson Research Centre: Tennyson's Annotated Copy of William Trollope's *Pentalogia Græca* and an Unlisted MS Poem', *Tennyson Research Bulletin*, 3: 5 (November 1981), 203–8 (pp. 203–6).
[5] Day, pp. 205–6.
[6] D. Laurance Chambers, 'Tennysoniana', *Modern Language Notes*, 18: 8 (December 1903), 227–33 (p. 231).

to the paragraph from which this passage is drawn, Carlyle writes that 'certain sagacious critics among the Germans have hit upon the wonderful discovery of Euphorion being—Lord Byron!' (the mocking tone is misplaced, for most authorities today would uphold this judgement (*WTC*, XXVI, 193)).[7] Euphorion, Carlyle tells us, 'begins to talk of courage and battle', and the essay also includes repeated allusions to the refulgence that emanates from his brows (ll. 9620, 9623–4; stage directions before ll. 9901, 9903 / *WTC*, XXVI, 191–3, esp. 192). He 'takes to dancing and romping with the Chorus [. . .] in a style of tumult' – but his 'life-dance' soon comes to an end: 'to die in strife', he declares, 'Is the law of life' (ll. 9888–9 / *WTC*, XXVI, 192). Tennyson brings all of these elements together in his poetic fragment:

> Refulgent Lord of Battle tell me why
>   Thy joy is in the tumult and the strife
>   And the purple tide of life
> [. . .]
> Nor ever do thy martial feet advance
>   In the mazes of the dance (ll. 1–3, 7–8)

In one of the scenes which Carlyle translates, Goethe writes, 'The Seven also before Thebes bore carved work | Each on his Shield', and a couple of pages later, Carlyle himself likens this scene to '*Seven before* [sic] *Thebes*' (ll. 9032–3 / *WTC*, XXVI, 179, 181). Perhaps it was these words which led Tennyson from 'Goethe's "Helena"' to the *Pentalogia*.

Tennyson took up these connections again shortly after the death of Hallam. The first complete English translation of *Part Two* was not published until 1838,[8] so when he sought to gain access to the play in late 1833, Tennyson – with his limited German – is likely to have turned to 'Goethe's "Helena"', and Hayward's recent *Foreign Quarterly Review* article. The latter piece includes numerous translations of extracts, and gives a fairly detailed outline of the plot (although Hayward passes over Act III, directing the reader, instead, to Carlyle (Hay. 2, p. 96)).

In 'Tithon' and 'Tiresias', Tennyson echoes a similar combination of sources to those on which he had drawn in 'Ulysses': *The Divine*

---

[7] Williams, pp. 163, 175; FA, 1, VII / I, 789.
[8] Frantz, pp. 137, 306.

Comedy, Carlyle and *Faust*.⁹ Here, however, he turns not to *Part One* but to *Part Two*. It should be noted that when Goethe began his masterpiece, he did not intend it to be a bipartite work: in the *Original Faust* of the 1770s, the closing scene, 'Dungeon', has a crushing sense of finality (FA, 1, VII / I, 535–9). His subsequent decision to continue the drama beyond this point left him facing what Nicholas Boyle describes as '[t]he unspeakably difficult task of engineering a transition from what had once been [his] version of the last despairing midnight moments of Dr Faust's earthly existence to some new beginning of a new life'.¹⁰ Goethe's solution to this dilemma was the powerful opening scene of *Part Two*, 'A pleasant neighbourhood' (which Hayward singles out for praise, and translates in its entirety (ll. 4613–727 / Hay. 2, pp. 84–6)).¹¹ As the curtain goes up, we see 'Faust bedded upon flowery turf, tired, restless, endeavouring to sleep.—[It is] [t]wilight.—A circle of spirits [is] hovering round' (stage direction before l. 4613 / Hay. 2, p. 84). These spirits are instructed by their master to 'cleanse [Faust's] heart's core of the horrors it has felt' (l. 4625 / Hay. 2, p. 85). He awakens, and the rest of the scene is taken up by his monologue, 'The pulses of life beat with renewed vigour', which includes a rapturous description of the sunrise (ll. 4679–727 / Hay. 2, pp. 85–6). 'A pleasant neighbourhood' depicts, both literally and figuratively, a new dawn.

As discussed in Chapter 1, Tennyson, in late 1833, appears to have been deeply moved by 'Dungeon', and to have identified the

---

⁹ Tennyson compares the words 'I earth in earth' ('Tithon', l. 63) to Dante's 'Terra in terra' (cited in EE, II, 340; translated by Cary as 'Earth my body is, | In earth'; DC, Vol. III, Canto XXV, p. 135 / ll. 124–5). There is also a clear echo of *The Divine Comedy* in the earliest version of 'Tiresias'. In Canto X of the *Inferno*, Dante describes an encounter with two men, who – like the blind Greek prophet – 'have knowledge of future things' (p. 50 / p. 434). The words of one of them, 'Strikes not on his eye | The blessed daylight?', are echoed in 'the blessèd daylight made itself | Ruddy within the eaves of sight' (DC, Vol. I, Canto X, p. 52 / ll. 67–8; TA, XI, 166; corresponds to PT, 219, ll. 2–3). Both Tithonus and Tiresias are mentioned in *The Divine Comedy*, and Dante also refers to the seven against Thebes (DC, Vol. II, Canto IX, p. 45 / l. 1; Vol. I, Canto XX, p. 104 / p. 436; p. 105 / l. 37; Vol. II, Canto XXII, p. 122 / l. 112; Vol. I, Canto XIV, p. 75 / ll. 64–5. Compare also DC, Vol. I, Canto XXVII, p. 144 / l. 75; Vol. I, Canto I, p. 5 / l. 71; Vol. II, Canto XIV, p. 77 / ll. 149–51 to, respectively, 'Tithon', ll. 7, 53 and 62–4, and see, in addition, F, l. 8817). As McKay observes (p. 264), in Trinity Notebook 20, which includes drafts of both 'Tithon' and 'Tiresias', Tennyson has copied out, in German, the first three and a half lines of Goethe's poem 'Lili's Park' (Alfred Lord Tennyson, Trinity Notebook 0.15.20 (Trinity College Library, Cambridge), folio 2, verso (this page is not reproduced in TA); FA, 1, I, p. 293, ll. 1–4).
¹⁰ Boyle, II: *Revolution and Renunciation (1790–1803)* (2000), p. 534.
¹¹ See also Chapter 5, pp. 158–61.

protagonist's loss of Gretchen with his own loss of Hallam. It is likely, therefore, that as he struggled to come to terms with the death of his friend, Faust's hopeful emergence from the darkness of that scene into the bright light of 'A pleasant neighbourhood' would have interested him profoundly. This seems to be borne out by the fact that he echoes the opening of *Part Two* in both 'Tithon' and 'Tiresias'. What is more, 'A pleasant neighbourhood' appears to have set the pattern for his engagement with the rest of the play, for elsewhere in these two poems, he draws on a couple of episodes from Acts III and V, both of which deal, once again, with the experience of intense light. In human terms, however, these later scenes are altogether gloomier than their optimistic precursor, and this is reflected in what Tennyson makes of them. Indeed, although 'Tithon' and 'Tiresias' are full of splendid imagery, their subject matter includes thraldom, darkness and death. The brilliant surface of 'A pleasant neighbourhood' is being married, involuntarily perhaps, to the murky depths of 'Dungeon': Tennyson is trying to use *Part Two* to help him put Hallam's death behind him, but his distress is so deep that even an inspirational new dawn can cast some lengthy shadows. As I will argue later on, the crux of his engagement with Goethe's play may lie, moreover, in two important (but deeply sombre) passages on which he chooses *not* to draw.

Tennyson's portrayal of Tithon – who is '[b]eloved by Aurora' (EE, II, 340) – is indebted not just to the poem's acknowledged sources,[12] but also to two characters in *Part Two*, both of whom can be said to be enamoured of the dawn: Faust himself in Act I, and Lynceus in Act III. Tennyson takes from the 'Pulses of life' speech the phrase 'glimmering haze of morn' (l. 4686 / Hay. 2, p. 86), and turns it into 'gleaming halls of morn' ('Tithon', l. 10). There are also more than thirty individual words that occur in both the 115 lines of 'A pleasant neighbourhood', and the sixty-four lines of 'Tithon' (as Ricks observes, when suggesting the influence of a passage from Shakespeare on one by Keats: 'Although no single shared word is unusual, the density achieves a cumulative plausibility').[13] However, Tennyson also seems to draw on the more disconcerting daybreak that is described in Act III. Lynceus, who is the Warder of Faust's

---

[12] Ricks cites one of the *Homeric Hymns*, 'To Aphrodite', and Horace's *Odes* (*PT*, 324, headnote; see also *PT*, 99, l. 5).

[13] Ricks, *Allusion*, p. 176. The words include the following (line references to *Faust* (Hay. 2, pp. 84–6) are here followed by those for 'Tithon'): 'mist[s]' (ll. 4636, 4688 / ll. 10, 53); 'everlasting' (ll. 4697, 4707 / l. 11); 'tremulous' (l. 4693 / l. 18); 'twilight' (stage direction before l. 4613; l. 4637 / l. 37); and 'airy' (l. 4621 / l. 51).

Tower, is enthralled by the beautiful Helena, who is so radiant that her appearance on the horizon resembles a sunrise:

> Watching o'er the course of morning,
> Eastward, as I mark it run,
> Rose there, all the sky adorning,
> Strangely in the south a sun.
>
> Draws my look towards those places,
> Not the valley, not the height,
> Not the earth's or heaven's spaces;
> She alone the queen of light. (ll. 9222–9 / WTC, XXVI, 183)

This sunrise does not bring revival, but imprisonment, and a death sentence (which are, of course, the themes of 'Dungeon'): Faust casts Lynceus into fetters, and threatens to have him killed for failing to warn of the approach of 'so august a visitor' (ll. 9192–212; WTC, XXVI, 182). As Carlyle points out, Lynceus has also been 'taken captive' by the ravishing Helena: 'Let me kneel and let me view her, | Let me live, or let me die', he pleads, but when he offers her a gift of plundered treasure, Faust tells him to 'take back the bold-earn'd load' (ll. 9218–19, 9333 / WTC, XXVI, 183, 185). Tithon, too, is enthralled by a beautiful female sun-figure, and when he, like Lynceus, begs for death, he does so in language which may contain echoes of this scene: 'Release me: let me go: take back thy gift' (l. 19).

When Lynceus reappears in Act V, he is witness to a fierce conflagration. On page 98 of his article, Hayward prints a stage direction from the previous act, 'A cloud comes down and breaks apart' (before l. 10039), and on the facing page, he translates Lynceus' beautiful descriptive passage from Act V, which includes the following words: 'the darkened world! I see fire-sparks sprouting, [. . .] and [. . .] a glow, fanned by the air current' (ll. 11307–8, 11310–11 / Hay. 2, p. 99). This blaze spreads to the manuscript of 'Tithon':

> A soft air fans the cloud apart; there comes
> A glimpse of that dark world. [. . .]
> [. . .]
> Spreading a rapid glow with loosened manes,
> [. . .] trampling twilight into flakes of fire.[14]
> 'Tis ever thus: thou growest more beautiful. (ll. 28–9, 36–8)

---

[14] The *Inferno* is, I think, a more likely source for the words 'flakes of fire' (*DC*, Vol. I, Canto XIV, pp. 73, 74 / p. 435; l. 26) than the one suggested by Charles R. Forker ('Tennyson's "Tithonus" and Marston's *Antonio's Revenge*', Notes and Queries, o.s. 204 / n.s. 6: 11 (December 1959), 445).

The last line quoted here echoes Carlyle, who remarks in 'Goethe's "Helena"' that *Part Two* 'grows [. . .] more beautiful' with repeated readings (*WTC*, XXVI, 197). However, in Act V as in Act III, Goethe's poetry, for all its brilliance, is blackened with suffering: the intense glow that Lynceus observes is the work of Mephistopheles, who 'has set fire to the cottage [of two minor characters, the Ovidian Philemon and Baucis], and the old couple perish in the conflagration' (Hay. 2, p. 99). A disquieting mixture of luxuriant description and deep distress also characterises the passage from 'Tithon' cited above, in which the ever-renewed beauty of the sunrise brings no renewal of vigour for the steadily declining speaker.[15]

The echoes of *Part Two* in 'Tiresias' are fewer and fainter, and are found only in the manuscripts dating from 1883. But these could include revised versions of passages drafted half a century earlier, and now lost[16] (the late 1833 text of the poem, which is in Trinity Notebook 20, is interspersed with three stubs). 'Tiresias' certainly appears to have been influenced by the same scenes from Acts I and III as are drawn upon in 'Tithon'. For both Faust and Lynceus, the experience of intense sunlight leads to temporary blindness. In 'A pleasant neighbourhood', the effects are no more than momentary: Faust is briefly 'dazzled', and rues what he refers to metaphorically as his attempt to light the 'torch of life' (ll. 4702, 4709 / Hay. 2, p. 86) – a phrase which crops up in line 154 of 'Tiresias'. However, when Lynceus, in Act III, is 'blinded with excess of light' by the sunlike Helena, his 'extraordinary obscuration of vision' lasts for some time (*WTC*, XXVI, 183, 187):

> Eye and heart I must surrender
> Drown'd as in a radiant sea;
> That high creature with her splendour
> Blinding all hath blinded me. (ll. 9238–41 / *WTC*, XXVI, 183)

Lynceus' disturbing experience may have provided a source for 'Tiresias', in which the speaker's glimpse of Pallas Athene's 'Ineffable beauty' causes *his* eyes to grow 'dark | For ever', leaving him 'Henceforth [. . .] blind' (ll. 54, 46–8). In what is usually regarded as the principal source for this passage (Callimachus' *Hymns*, 5. 73–81),

---

[15] Compare also 'Man comes and tills the earth' ('Tithon', l. 3) and the numerous references to the tilling of the earth in the biblical *Cain* (Byron, *Poetical Works*, VI (1991), II. 2. 104–5, 125; III. 1. 217, 474, 504).

[16] Goslee ('Three Stages', p. 159, fn) is inclined to reject this possibility, but Ricks (*PT*, 219, headnote) leaves it open.

this blinding is a straightforward punishment,[17] but in Tennyson's poem, it is associated with 'a dreadful light', which emanates – as with Goethe's Helena – from the 'golden' goddess herself (ll. 42–5).[18]

It seems reasonably clear, therefore, that 'Tithon' and 'Tiresias' echo a number of scenes from *Part Two*. Surprisingly however, Tennyson also *ignores* a couple of scenes in which one might have expected him to have taken an especial interest. In order to understand why he neglected them, it may be helpful to look at the events which occurred around the time of the play's publication. It is likely that for Tennyson, *Part Two* was associated with two deaths, one of which occurred just before its appearance, and the other a short time afterwards.

On 22 March 1832 Goethe died in Weimar at the age of eighty-two. Carlyle had of late portrayed him as a serenely happy individual, and he was certainly a fulfilled one, a man whose life's task was now complete. The most tangible sign of this was, of course, *Part Two* itself, which (as Tennyson would have known from Hayward's article) had been finished shortly before Goethe's death (Hay. 2, p. 106). In Britain, there was a further reason why his passing had an element of fortuitousness, for it marked the turning-point of his reputation, and the dawning realisation that he was one of the giants of European culture. Hallam's suggestion that Tennyson should mention the German poet in 'The Palace of Art' along with Plato, Petrarch and Raphael was symptomatic of the emerging feeling that Goethe – in every sense – had joined the immortals (*LAHH*, no. 195, p. 652, 24 September 1832).

On 15 September 1833, Hallam himself died in Vienna. Tennyson always regarded him as a genius of the first rank, a man who, had he lived, would have been capable of a similar level of achievement to Goethe.[19] But Hallam had died not at eighty-two, but twenty-two. What is more, his brief life had been marred by instability and unhappiness, and his vast potential was almost entirely unfulfilled.

---

[17] Douglas Bush, *Mythology and the Romantic Tradition in English Poetry* (New York: Pageant, 1957), p. 216; Callimachus, *Hymns and Epigrams; Lycophron; Aratus*, with translations by A. W. Mair and G. R. Mair, 2nd edn (Cambridge, MA: Harvard University Press; London: Heinemann, 1955), pp. 118, 119.

[18] Compare also l. 8924 / *WTC*, XXVI, 176 and 'Tiresias', l. 104. The source for 'Semele' (*PT*, 220; 1833) (which is in Trinity Notebook 20 with drafts of 'Tithon' and 'Tiresias' (*TA*, XII, 198–9)) is likely to be either the quotation from Marlowe's *Dr Faustus* in Hay. 2 ('Brighter art thou than flaming Jupiter, | When he appear'd to hapless Semele' (p. 94)), or the two references to Semele in *DC* (Vol. I, Canto XXX, p. 157 / l. 2; Vol. III, Canto XXI, p. 109 / l. 5).

[19] See *In Memoriam*, LXXIII, ll. 5–6; CXIII, ll. 8–12; *Mem.*, II, 496.

When Tennyson read the available translations of *Part Two* in late 1833, he might have detected a painful congruity between these real-life events, and the action of the play itself. It, too, includes two important death scenes: that of the '*beautiful Youth*' Euphorion in Act III, and the death, 'in extreme old age', of Faust himself in Act V (stage directions before ll. 9903 and 11143 / *WTC*, XXVI, 193; Hay. 2, p. 99). The 'little life of Euphorion' is, as we have seen, tumultuous, and his early demise – which lacks the idealism of Missolonghi – seems like a sad and wasteful end for a man who is at one point referred to as a 'Genius' (*WTC*, XXVI, 191; *F*, l. 9603 / *WTC*, XXVI, 190). In strong contrast, the 'greybeard' Faust (l. 11592 / Hay. 2, p. 100) expresses, in his dying speech, a belated sense of fulfilment, and looks forward to the kind of immortality that was also achieved by his creator:

> here, hemmed round by danger, bring childhood, manhood and old age their well-spent years to a close. I would fain see such a busy multitude,—stand upon free soil with free people. I might then say to the moment—'Stay, thou art so fair!' The trace of my earthly days cannot perish in centuries. In the presentiment of such exalted bliss I now enjoy the most exalted moment.
> *(Faust sinks back [. . .].)* (ll. 11577–86 / p. 100)

One might have expected that as he read *Part Two* in late 1833, these death scenes would have provided the focus of Tennyson's attention. But there are no clear verbal echoes of them anywhere in either 'Tithon' or 'Tiresias'. They may, however, have exercised a more subtle influence on these works. In both poems, Tennyson seems to be taking aspects of these two deaths and transforming them, so that their poignancy is turned into consolation. Far from echoing these scenes, he seeks, instead, to mute them.

Like 'Ulysses', 'Tithon' and 'Tiresias' are poems about the lives of old men, which were written in response to the death of a young one. However, their approach to this theme differs sharply from that of the first-named piece. It is, I think, revealing to compare these three poems to *In Memoriam*, LXXXIV. In this section, Tennyson (as mentioned in the previous chapter) envisages Hallam's survival into old age, and their simultaneous entry into the after-life. In the closing stanza, however, he abruptly retracts what he has just written:

> What reed was that on which I leant?
>   Ah, backward fancy, wherefore wake
>   The old bitterness again, and break
> The low beginnings of content. (ll. 45–8)

A comparable sentiment underlies 'Tithon', for although Tennyson describes it as 'a pendent to [. . .] "Ulysses"' (*Mem.*, I, 459), it might, with equal justice, be called a palinode. As Ricks observes, the poem 'meets Hallam's death at a different angle [from that of "Ulysses"]: by envisaging a situation in which immortality is no blessing'.[20] Indeed, the 'Life piled on life' that 'Were all too little' for Ulysses (ll. 24–5) is all too much for Tithon, whose old age has neither honour nor toil. In both this poem and 'Tiresias', it is *youth* that is celebrated and immortalised, whilst age is implicitly denigrated. It might seem puzzling that Tennyson should have written such strongly contrasting works within so short a space of time. No less than 'Ulysses', however, 'Tithon' and 'Tiresias' provide the poet with much-needed solace: seen through the prism that they create, Hallam's early death begins to seem not tragic but fortuitous.

In 'Tithon' and 'Tiresias', old age is certainly not a time of Goethean fulfilment, or Ulyssean endeavour. It brings, instead, an intense yearning for oblivion:

> Release me! so restore me to the ground;
> Thou seest all things, thou wilt see my grave. ('Tithon', ll. 60–1)
>
> I would that I were gathered to my rest. ('Tiresias', l. 162)

In both poems, immortality belongs properly to the young. For the aged Tithon, it is, paradoxically, 'fatal' (l. 5). For the youthful Menœceus, however, it is fate: it represents, that is to say, the fulfilment of his destiny. The 'exalted bliss' of the elderly Faust, '[t]he trace of [whose] earthly days cannot perish in centuries', is transferred to him. Menœceus' name is to be amongst those which, when 'Graven on memorial columns,'

>   are a song
> Heard in the future; few, but more than wall
> And rampart, their examples reach a hand
> Far through all years, [. . .]
> [. . .]
>   Fairer thy fate than mine, if life's best end
> Be to end well! ('Tiresias', ll. 120–3, 126–7)

Whereas Euphorion (and Hallam) had appeared to forfeit their potential by dying young, Menœceus fulfils his by the same means.

---

[20] Christopher Ricks, *Tennyson*, 2nd edn (Basingstoke: Macmillan, 1989), p. 119.

'He will achieve his greatness', observes Tiresias, as the boy goes off to his death (l. 161).

It was not until the 1840s that Tennyson wrote and published a poem in which the Euphorion episode is clearly echoed: *The Princess: A Medley* (*PT*, 286). Shortly before his death, Goethe's refulgent Lord of Battle tells the (female) chorus:

> I am the hunter,
> Ye are the game. (*F*, ll. 9771–2 / Macdonald, p. 242)

As previously discussed, Euphorion's resemblance to Lord Byron is then spelled out. In the words of Carlyle:

> he takes to dancing and romping with the Chorus; and this in a style of tumult which rather dissatisfies Faust. The wildest and coyest of these damsels he seizes with avowed intent of snatching a kiss; but, alas, she resists, and, still more singular, *'flashes up in flame into the air'* [stage direction before l. 9808]. [. . .] Euphorion shakes off the remnants of the flame, and now, in a wilder humour, mounts on the crags, begins to talk of courage and battle. [. . .] From his high peak, he catches the sound of war, and fires at it, and longs to mix in it, let Chorus and Mother and Father say what they will. (*WTC*, XXVI, 192)

In Part V of *The Princess*, the Prince's father tells his son:

> Man is the hunter; woman is his game:
> The sleek and shining creatures of the chase,
> We hunt them for the beauty of their skins;
> They love us for it, and we ride them down.
> Wheedling and siding with them! Out! for shame!
> Boy, there's no rose that's half so dear to them
> As he that does the thing they dare not do,
> Breathing and sounding beauteous battle, comes
> With the air of the trumpet round him, and leaps in
> Among the women, snares them by the score
> Flattered and flustered, wins, though dashed with death
> He reddens what he kisses: thus I won
> Your mother, a good mother, a good wife
> Worth winning; but this firebrand – gentleness
> To such as her! (ll. 147–61)

Does this 'hard old king' (V, l. 456) represent what Euphorion would have become had he lived? If he does, this passage might be seen – like

'Tithon' and 'Tiresias' – as a somewhat equivocal portrayal of longevity. But this is not the only affinity between these lines and those two poems. All three texts take the form of an address by an old man to a youth (or a personification thereof), and in each case, the elder figure is calling for death or violence. In the lines from *The Princess* quoted here, the family relationships of the Euphorion episode – a father, a mother and their son – are preserved. Once again, however, Tennyson adapts his source in order to favour the younger man, for the more reckless characteristics of Euphorion are now transferred to the elderly father. And whereas in *Faust* it is the parents who call for prudence,[21] it is, in this text, the son: '"Yea but Sire," I cried, | "Wild natures need wise curbs. The soldier? No [. . .]"' (V, ll. 164–5). The whole passage appears, at first glance, to have no connection with the death of Hallam. When read in conjunction with its Faustian source, however, it reveals a bias towards youth, and this may be traceable to the fact that the wisest man whom Tennyson had ever known was now frozen in time at the age of just twenty-two.

The influence of Goethe on *The Princess* goes far beyond this individual passage. And although some critics have pointed to connections between the poem and the death of Hallam,[22] the full extent of such links has, I think, been underestimated. Here too, it may help us to understand Tennyson's response to Goethe better if we look beyond the two men's writings, and draw a comparison between the events of their lives.

It is likely that Tennyson conceived the idea of *The Princess* in 1839.[23] And on Christmas Day of the previous year, he had been given a copy of Austin's *Characteristics*. As I argued in Chapter 1, Tennyson had five years earlier found consolation for the death of Hallam by turning to *Faust*, for his engagement with Goethe's drama in 1833–4 enabled him to continue something of his ongoing 'conversation' with his late friend. As he read *Characteristics*, he would have learned in detail that the author of *Faust* had himself had a similar experience. Austin cites Goethe:

---

[21] ll. 9717–22, 9729–34, 9737–42, 9877–83, 9891–2; WTC, XXVI, 192.
[22] See Jerome Hamilton Buckley, *Tennyson: The Growth of a Poet* (Cambridge, MA: Harvard University Press; London: Oxford University Press, 1960), p. 269, endnote 24, as well as Douglas Bush's observations on 'Tears, idle tears' (referred to below).
[23] *Mem.*, I, 248, fn; *PT*, 286, headnote. *The Princess* was published in 1847, but it was repeatedly revised thereafter, not reaching its final form until 1853 (*PT*, 286, headnote).

> In the beginning of May [1805, Schiller and I] [...] parted before his house-door—never to meet again. [...] He departed on the ninth; I [had been dangerously ill, and] was now doubly and trebly attacked by all my maladies. When I had manned myself, I looked around for some important definite occupation: my first thought was to finish [the play on which Schiller had been working at the time of his death,] *Demetrius*. [...] I burned with desire to carry forward our intercourse in despite of death; to preserve his thoughts, views, and designs even in their details; and to show here, for the last time, the highest pitch to which a common labour could be carried, by the redaction of the matter I had inherited together with that I could originate. By thus carrying forward his existence I seemed to find compensation for his loss. (FA, 1, XVII, pp. 141–2, paragraphs 450–1 / CG, II, 325–6)

It was only when Goethe abandoned this plan that his grieving began in earnest:

> I dare not, even now, think of the state into which I felt myself plunged. Now was Schiller indeed torn from me—now had I first lost his society. [...] [I]ntolerable grief seized me; and, as bodily suffering cut me off from all society, I was secluded in most melancholy solitude. My journal bears no record of that time; the blank leaves tell of the void in my existence. [...] How often must I inwardly smile in after times, when sympathizing friends looked in vain for Schiller's monument in Weimar; then and ever I bethought me that I could have founded the noblest [monument], the most satisfactory to him and to our companionship. (FA, 1, XVII, pp. 142–3, paragraph 451 / CG, II, 327–8)

I propose that in *The Princess*, Tennyson is, in a broad sense, taking up Goethe's abandoned plan. For just as the completed *Demetrius* would have been, in effect, a collaboration between Goethe and Schiller, echoes of the two men's work are brought together in Tennyson's poem. In *The Princess*, Goethe and Schiller are, figuratively speaking, reunited.

So, too, perhaps, are Tennyson and Hallam, for the former appears to have felt a sense of identification with Goethe, and his loss of Schiller.[24] F. T. Palgrave recounts that in July 1853 (just two

---

[24] It should be noted that whereas Tennyson undoubtedly preferred Goethe to Schiller, Hallam may have had greater esteem for the latter author (see *Mem.*, I, 277; Chapter 1, pp. 54–5).

months before the twentieth anniversary of Hallam's death), Tennyson read out to him Goethe's poem 'upon the sight of Schiller's skull', which he 'valued for its stately beauty and tender feeling for a friend' (*Mem.*, II, 504).[25] And in August 1865, Tennyson visited Weimar, where – as Emily recorded in her journal – 'we tried to impress upon our driver that we wanted to see all which concerned' Goethe and Schiller:

> A. and the boys [were taken] inside the Fürstengruft [Royal Tomb], where they saw Goethe's and Schiller's coffins lying beside those of the Royal Family. Lionel had a leaf of bay given him for A. from Goethe's coffin. [...] Afterwards we drove to Schiller's house. [...] [O]n [his bed was] a portrait of himself, said to be good, taken soon after death. The 'other-world' peace of it struck A. and me. [...] [We w]ent [...] to Goethe's town-house. [...] The Director [...] took us into the sacred study. One cannot explain in words the awe and sadness with which this long dark room filled A. (Emily Tennyson, *Journal*, pp. 231, 232; 12 August, 1 September 1865)

'I touched Goethe's coffin', Tennyson told his friend William Allingham in October, declaring Weimar to be 'the most interesting place in Europe'.[26]

The links between *The Princess*, and Goethe and Schiller – and beyond to Tennyson and Hallam – are most clearly revealed in its most celebrated passage, the beautiful self-contained lyric 'Come down, O maid, from yonder mountain height' (VII, ll. 177–207). There is a considerable amount of biographical material (relating to all four individuals) which is relevant to our understanding of this lyric. Tennyson wrote it in German-speaking Switzerland in August 1846 (*Mem.*, I, 252). Many of the details of this tour (which he recorded in a journal, in a manuscript book of *The Princess*) suggest that Goethe, Schiller and Hallam were on his mind (*Mem.*, I, 230–3). This was only Tennyson's second lengthy visit to the Continent since he and Hallam had travelled to Germany in 1832, and he chose to retrace the route of that trip by journeying, once again, down the Rhine: Nonnenwerth and Drachenfels brought 'sad recollections'

---

[25] Palgrave is referring to 'In the solemn burial-vault' (FA, 1, II, 684–5 / Goethe, trans. Luke, pp. 326–7). Carré (p. 256) makes the connection with Hallam.

[26] *William Allingham's Diary: 1847–1889*, ed. H. Allingham and D. Radford (London: Macmillan, 1907; repr. London: Centaur Press, 2000), p. 125 (19 October 1865). See also *Mem.*, II, 235.

(ibid. I, 232). On 6 August he spent the night in Mannheim, which from 1783 to 1785 had been the home of Schiller (ibid. I, 232).[27] In Lucerne on the 8th, he spoke to an 'agreeable Swiss young lady to whom I quoted Goethe and she spouted [Schiller's] *William Tell*' (which is set in the area (*Mem.*, I, 232; see also p. 233)).

Tennyson's journal ends on 12 August, as he heads 'over the hills to Meyringen' in the Bernese Alps, but the *Memoir* informs us that 'Come down, O maid' was written elsewhere in that region, 'chiefly at Lauterbrunnen and Grindelwald' (ibid. I, 233, 252). There is evidence to suggest that Tennyson would have associated this whole area with Goethe, Hallam and Schiller. The celebrated Reichenbach Falls near Meiringen and, in particular, the Staubbach Falls above Lauterbrunnen (which are the highest in Switzerland) can be confidently identified as the principal sources of inspiration for Tennyson's 'thousand wreaths of dangling water-smoke' (VII, l. 198). In October 1779, Goethe, too, had visited the Bernese Alps, and had been inspired by these same waterfalls to write his 'Song of the Spirits over the Waters'.[28] If Tennyson at some point had a look at Karl Bädeker's newly published guide to *Die Schweiz* (*Switzerland*) (1844), he might have been aware of this connection, for in his description of the Staubbach, Bädeker cites ten lines from Goethe's poem.[29]

In September 1816, Byron had toured the region: he kept an 'Alpine Journal', and was inspired by the magnificent scenery to set his *Manfred* there. A more significant visitor – at least from Tennyson's point of view – arrived in June 1822: the eleven-year-old Arthur

---

[27] H. B. Garland, *Schiller* (London: Harrap, 1949; repr. Westport, CT: Greenwood, 1976), pp. 79–94.

[28] Boyle, I (1991), 309; FA, 1, I, 318–19 / Goethe, ed. Luke, pp. 58–59. This lyric is included in Goethe's *Gedichte* [*Poems*], 2 vols (Stuttgart: Cotta'schen, 1829), a copy of which Tennyson owned (TRC, ET/3336). (In Campbell (ed.), it is listed as 'Vol. 2 only' (I (1971), p. 160, no. 3336), but this is incorrect. Also, although this book is catalogued as having belonged to the Sellwood family, Vol. I has 'A Tennyson | Somersby' on the title page, and both volumes are annotated in the poet's hand. 'Song of the Spirits' has two glosses (I, 292–3).) The *Memoir* informs us that Goethe's *Gedichte* were probably one of Tennyson's 'usual travelling companions' (I, 341).

[29] [Karl Bädeker], *Die Schweiz. Handbüchlein für Reisende, nach eigener Anschauung und den besten Hülfsquellen bearbeitet* (Koblenz: Bädeker, 1844), p. 150. This guide includes more than a dozen quotations from Goethe (many of them lengthy), and an almost equal number from Schiller. Goethe's lines 'Keep not standing fix'd and rooted', which Tennyson would have known from *Meister*, are cited on the title page (*WM*, Vol. X, Ch. XV, p. 173, ll. 1–8 / XXIV, 345).

Hallam, who was on holiday with his parents. His mother Julia kept a journal of the trip:

> 30th [June]: we proceeded up the narrow picturesque valley of the Luschinen [*sic*] to Lauterbrunnen where we spent the day. Henry walked with his guide to see the fall of the Smadribach [*sic*]. Arthur & I mounted the char horses & rode part of the way – the fall of the Staubbach near the inn is worth seeing from its singularity – the volume of water is not large; but it falls entirely in a sheet of foam, which has a beautiful effect.[30]

The next day, she writes, 'Arthur & I went in the Char to Grindelwald', and the day after, the family 'descended 6 hours to Meyringen', passing 'the fine fall of the Reichenbach' on their way (ibid. pp. 13, 15). This spectacular journey would certainly have been a memorable experience for an eleven-year-old boy, so it is possible that Hallam would have described it years later to Tennyson.[31]

Unlike Goethe and Hallam, Schiller never visited the Bernese Alps, but the fact that Tennyson associated him with this region can be clearly demonstrated. As was mentioned in Chapter 1, the glossary in Harvard Notebook 17 reveals that *c*. late 1833, Tennyson was attempting to read the German text of the 'Prologue' to *The Maid of Orleans* (1801) (*TA*, III, 36). He returned to this play a few years later: in the copy of Schiller's *Sämmtliche Werke* (*Complete Works*) that is at the Research Centre in Lincoln, *The Maid* is the only text in this 1,304-page volume that is heavily annotated, with numerous English glosses of German words in the poet's hand.[32] Beneath one of these notes, Tennyson has written 'Noehden', and under another, 'Noeh' (pp. 460, 496). These are references to G. H. Noehden, the editor of the German dictionary that he was given for Christmas in 1838, and his glosses have clearly been made with the help of that work. This – and the level of German which the annotations suggest – would seem to indicate that Tennyson read *The Maid of Orleans* at some point between 1839 and his trip to Switzerland in 1846.

---

[30] Julia Maria Hallam, [*Travel Journal*, 17 May–1 September 1822], British Library, *Hallam Papers*, Additional Manuscripts, 81293–305 (81295A, pp. 12–13).

[31] As Kolb points out, Hallam echoes Byron's 'Alpine Journal' in a letter to Emily Tennyson (*LAHH*, no. 184, p. 626 [28 August 1832], and p. 627, fn 3).

[32] *Schiller's sämmtliche Werke in einem Bande* (Stuttgart: Cotta'schen, 1834) (TRC, AT/1947), pp. 459–98.

The maid of the title is, of course, Joan of Arc, and scene 2 of the 'Prologue' is played out between herself, her father Thibaut and the young shepherd who is in love with her, Raimond. When Thibaut laments the fact that Joan is unresponsive to Raimond's attentions, the latter defends her in fifteen lines of verse (from which Tennyson noted down two words in his 1833 glossary, annotating the same two words again years later in the *Collected Works*).[33] They include the following:

> Yet loves she on the mountain heights to rove,
> And from the dewy heath fears she to come
> Down to the haunts of men, where eating cares
> And low-born passions dwell. Oft from the vale
> Wondering have I beheld her noble form,
> Upon the upland pastures, as she stood
> In towering dignity, tending her flock.[34]

The theme of these pentameters recurs in those of Tennyson:

> 'Come down, O maid, from yonder mountain height:
> What pleasure lives in height (the shepherd sang)
> In height and cold, the splendour of the hills? [. . .]' (VII, ll. 177–9)

In an alternative draft of the first two lines, Tennyson wrote: 'O Daughter of the height & of the cold | Come to us, mountain shepherdess' (*TA*, XXVI, 222). Schiller's opening stage direction refers to Joan as one of Thibaut's '*three daughters*', and the words of Raimond

---

[33] The two words are *allmählich* (which Tennyson translates as 'by degrees') and *Trift* ('drove' or 'pasture') (Schiller, *Werke und Briefe*, V (1996), p. 153, 'Prolog'. 2. 68, 74; *TA*, III, 36; TRC, AT/1947, p. 459).

[34] Schiller, *Werke und Briefe*, V (1996), p. 153, 'Prolog'. 2. 69–75; Rev. H. Salvin (trans.), *Mary Stuart, A Tragedy; The Maid of Orleans, A Tragedy: From the German of Schiller, with a Life of the Author* (London: Longman, 1824), p. 208. (All subsequent references to *The Maid of Orleans* are to these two editions, with act, scene and line references to Schiller's text being followed by page references to Salvin's. Note that Salvin divides the play into fewer scenes than Schiller.) As discussed in the Introduction, in late 1833, Tennyson's command of German was limited, so he might well have been approaching *The Maid of Orleans* in the same way as he did *Faust: Part One*, by trying to read the original text in conjunction with a translation. Salvin's was the only complete one that was available at that time (R. Pick, *Schiller in England 1787–1960: A Bibliography* (London: [n. pub.], 1961), pp. 1–27, esp. p. 19, no. 207). There is considerable evidence to suggest that Tennyson was familiar with it (see below).

cited above make it clear that she is a mountain shepherdess ('Prolog', 1, stage direction before l. 1 / p. 205).

'Come down, O maid' may have begun to germinate in Tennyson's mind on 11 August 1846, when (as he recorded in his journal) he saw 'far off [the] Jungfrau [mountain] looking as if delicately pencilled' (*Mem.*, I, 233; see also II, 65). The Jungfrau (which means 'virgin') is the highest peak in the Bernese Alps, and it dominates the region. As Julia Hallam wrote in 1822: 'The Jungfrau is the great ornament of this spot – from the Inn window [in Lauterbrunnen], we had a magnificent view of it, embellished with the various tints of the setting sun' (p. 13, 30 [June]). The German title of *The Maid of Orleans* is *Die Jungfrau von Orleans*, and the word *Jungfrau* is used on more than fifty different occasions in the text. It is not difficult to make the necessary inference: Tennyson linked the Jungfrau of the Alps to the Jungfrau of Schiller's play. The close bond between maid and mountain in this lyric can be partly attributed to their shared name.[35]

It is likely, therefore, that Tennyson associated his shepherd with Goethe (who had stood in the valley where the poem was written), and his maid with Schiller (to whose play she can be traced). Tennyson might, in turn, have identified himself with the former, and Hallam with the latter.[36] This interpretation could help to explain why he made two important changes to his source. In Schiller's play, the mountain heights are portrayed as a refuge, but the poem associates them, instead, with death: the maid lives 'In height and cold', moving 'so near the Heavens', and walking 'With Death and Morning' (VII, ll. 179, 180, 189). Even the high Alpine waterfall, with its 'thousand wreaths', is abundantly mournful (VII, l. 198). In some of Tennyson's drafts, these suggestions of mortality are stronger still: 'there is death among the silver horns', he writes; 'leave the cold, the death'; 'Descend, descend & move no more in Heaven' (*TA*, XXVI, 223, 227). So whereas Schiller's Raimond is happy to accept Joan's wanderings, Tennyson's shepherd – right from his opening word – addresses the maid in the imperative, gently pleading with her to cross the 'threshold', and return to life and love (*The Maid*, 'Prolog'.

---

[35] See Paul Turner, *Tennyson* (Routledge & Kegan Paul, 1976), p. 102; Leonée Ormond, *Alfred Tennyson: A Literary Life* (Basingstoke: Macmillan, 1993), p. 92. Adjacent to the Jungfrau is another peak, the Silberhorn ('Silver Horn'), to which Tennyson refers in line 189 of the lyric (see *PT*, 286, VII, l. 189, fn).

[36] In August 1846, Hallam's father was staying in Lausanne; Tennyson may have visited him there just a few days after he wrote 'Come down, O maid' (Martin, p. 308).

2. 65–8 / p. 208; *The Princess*, VII, l. 185). The poem can be seen as Tennyson's attempt to entice the dead Hallam down from 'the lifelessness of those high places', and into the valley, an environment which is strongly suggestive of the most treasured episode of their friendship (*LAT*, II, 49, [mid-November 1852(?)]). In the words of Martin:

> Recurrently sounding through the poetry written after the Pyrenean trip [of 1830] is the word 'valley', always connected with love, usually with youth, and frequently with Arthur Hallam. [. . .] As [Tennyson] was to write in *The Princess*, nearly two decades later, 'Love is of the valley' [VII, ll. 183, 184; see also l. 195]. [. . .] Much of ['Come down, O maid'] rings with echoes of his stay with Hallam in Cauteretz.[37]

Like Tennyson's late friend, the maid has entered the deathly region she now inhabits at an early age (the literal translation of *Jungfrau* – or *junge Frau* – is 'young woman'). The shepherd confidently expects that she will eventually descend and rejoin him in the valley (which, with its maize, vines and red wine, is more redolent of southern France than of high-altitude Lauterbrunnen, where 'little fruit can be grown' (*The Princess*, VII, ll. 186–8; Bädeker, p. 149)). Tennyson – who in 'Ulysses' thirteen years earlier had imaginatively prolonged the existence of the recently deceased Hallam – is now trying to bring his long-dead friend back to life.[38]

This imaginative reunion of Goethe and Schiller – and of Tennyson and Hallam – may also be perceptible in the 'medley' that is *The*

---

[37] Martin, pp. 120, 307. See also 'In the Valley of Cauteretz' (*PT*, 326), the concluding lines of which (ll. 7–10) may owe something to the concluding lines of the 'Dedication' which opens *Faust: Part One* (ll. 31–2 / p. 266). Like Tennyson's poem, the 'Dedication' evokes 'the dear ones, who, cheated of fair hours by fortune, have vanished away before me' (ll. 15–16 / p. 265). Tennyson quotes line 22 of it in an 1887 letter to Queen Victoria (*LAT*, III, 351, 12 March).

[38] The other poem which the Princess reads out in section VII, 'Now sleeps the crimson petal' (ll. 161–74), may be influenced by Goethe's *West-Eastern Divan* (W. D. Paden, 'Tennyson and Persian Poetry, Again', *Modern Language Notes*, 58: 8 (December 1943), 652–56 (p. 654)). The *Memoir* describes Tennyson as 'especially praising' this work (II, 233), and an 1828 copy of it is at TRC. (*Goethe's Werke. Vollständige Ausgabe letzter Hand* (Stuttgart: Cotta'schen, 1828) (AT/1016). In Campbell (ed.), this is listed as 'Vols 1 and 5 only' (I (1971), p. 52, no. 1016), but this is incorrect: Vol. 1 has now been recatalogued as *Gedichte*, I (ET/3336), and 'Vol. 5' actually consists of Vols 5 and 6 bound together. Vol. 5 is the *Divan*, Vol. 6 is Goethe's commentary on it.)

Princess as a whole, for the poem interweaves elements from *Faust: Part Two* and *The Maid of Orleans*.[39] Tennyson could have been led to couple these two works by a passage in Act IV of the latter, in which Joan's father accuses her of being a kind of female Faust: 'to the foe of man | Did she make over her immortal part' (ll. 2992–3 / p. 350). There is, however, a further link between the two plays, and it is this which provides, I believe, the key to Tennyson's response to them. As discussed above, *The Maid* inspired him to write a lyric in which a man attempts to entice a woman down from 'the Heavens', thus bringing her, implicitly, back to life.[40] This is also the relationship between the sixteenth-century Faust and the ancient Greek Helena in Acts I to III of *Part Two* – although here, the home of the dead is not the Christian heaven, but the classical underworld. In his essay on 'Helena', Carlyle quotes Goethe:

> The old Legend tells us, [. . .] that Faust, in his imperious pride of heart, required from Mephistopheles the love of the fair Helena of Greece; in which demand the other, after some reluctance, gratified him. [. . .] [He] found means to bring back the individual Helena, in person, out of Orcus into Life. (FA, 1, XXII, p. 391, ll. 23–7, 32–4 / WTC, XXVI, 165)[41]

---

[39] It may be significant that both works are mentioned repeatedly in *Characteristics* (II, 85, 86, 87, 94, 317; III, 43–5, 87–8, 94, 256, 296–7, 303–4, 305). Also, it was only in the years 1838–43 that *Part Two* really came into its own in Britain, with translations appearing at the rate of about one a year, and its new-found popularity overlapped with a comparable vogue for *The Maid*, seven translations of which were published between 1841 and 1848 (see Pick, pp. 34–44).

[40] Tennyson's attention might also have been caught by Joanna's brief resurrection in the play's closing scene:

> SOREL.
>   She opes her eyes!
> She lives!
>
>   BURGUNDY (astonished).
>   How! does she come back from the grave?
> Does she subdue the all-destroyer, death?
> See, see! she rises up! she stands! (V. 14. 3517–19 / p. 380)

[41] If *Faust* can be linked to *The Maid*, the latter can be linked, in turn, to Schiller's sometimes free translation of Carlo Gozzi's play *Turandot*, which John Killham cautiously suggests as an influence on *The Princess* (Schiller, *Werke und Briefe*, IX (1995), 371–465; John Killham, *Tennyson and 'The Princess': Reflections of an Age* (London: Athlone Press, 1958), pp. 222–9). 'Schiller', he observes, '[. . .] goes

A similar resurrection is implicitly described in *The Princess* – which can, in this respect, be usefully compared to *In Memoriam*.[42] In both works, the expression of love is also an encounter with mortality: in order for passion to be fulfilled, it must surmount the barrier between life and death. This theme – which is clearly stated in *In Memoriam* – is no more than hinted at in *The Princess*. There is, however, a broad similarity between the two poems, which may be significant: in both works, the speaker yearns to be reunited with an individual with whom he had once had a close bond, but who has now undergone a sudden and unexpected change.

Some of the details of these two transformations seem comparable. In section LXXXIV of *In Memoriam* (already cited above), Tennyson looks back to 1833, and addresses his dead friend:

> the day was drawing on,
> When thou shouldst link thy life with one
> Of mine own house. (ll. 10–12)

That day never came, however, for whilst holidaying in 'Imperial' Vienna, Hallam was seized by a 'sudden frost', and 'turned to something strange' (XCVIII, l. 29; LXXXI, l. 10; XLI, l. 5). In section I of *The Princess*, the speaker recalls that 'when the days drew nigh that I should wed', unexpected news arrived from a 'foreign court' (ll. 40, 74). His 'affianced' had become as cold as the east wind, and was now a 'strange Poet-princess' (III, ll. 338, 215 (and fn), 256). When the Prince sets forth to reverse this change, his journey suggests a transition from one form of existence to another. First, he crosses a frontier, and then, in section II, he passes through a gate, on which is written: 'LET NO MAN ENTER IN ON PAIN OF DEATH' (I, l. 108; II, l. 178).

The Prince's subsequent courting of Ida has a number of similarities to *Part Two* (in Act III of which, Faust is twice described as

---

much further [than Gozzi]. [. . .] [W]e cannot fail to notice that [in his version of the play,] the original heroine of the fairy tale has been changed into an ardent supporter of women's rights' (ibid. pp. 227, 228). *Turandot* (which is included in the edition of Schiller's *Complete Works* that is at TRC) is based on the oriental tales which Killham cites as the foremost influences on *The Princess* (TRC, AT/1947, pp. 597–624; Killham, pp. 198–211). The various sources of Tennyson's poem might be seen, therefore, as comprising a chain of interrelated works.

[42] The gestation periods of these two poems overlap substantially: from 1839 to 1850, Tennyson was working – albeit intermittently – on both. For the theme of resurrection, see *In Memoriam*, XXXI, XXXII.

a 'prince', whilst Helena is at one point referred to as a 'princess' (ll. 9191, 9491, 9385 / Macdonald, pp. 216, 229, 225)). As John Killham points out, the speaker of Tennyson's poem resembles the protagonists of two oriental stories, both of whom fall in love with images of their future wives before they have even met them.[43] But Faust – who in Act I of *Part Two* is entranced by an apparition of Helena – provides another precedent (ll. 6487–500, 6549–59 / Macdonald, pp. 86, 90). Act I also includes a lengthy masquerade, in which Nymphs and goddesses appear (ll. 5065–986 / Macdonald, pp. 20–58).[44] The Prince's idea of donning 'female gear' is suggested by his recollection of 'how we three presented Maid | Or Nymph, or Goddess [. . .] | In masque or pageant' (I, ll. 196, 193–95). Faust undertakes a magical flight southwards – from Germany to Greece – in search of Helena (l. 7056 and preceding stage direction / Macdonald, p. 115), and as mentioned above, their subsequent marriage represents 'Northern Character wedded to Grecian Culture' (*WTC*, XXVI, 191). Tennyson's blond, blue-eyed Prince twice expresses his yearning for the dark-haired Ida by identifying himself with a southward-flying bird, and there are numerous passages in which the two characters are associated with North and South.[45]

The relationship between Raimond and Joan in *The Maid* also leaves its mark on *The Princess*. In section II of Tennyson's poem, Joan is one of the female role models who are invoked by Ida's colleague Lady Psyche. Significantly, this reference is preceded by a mention of Elizabeth I, who is one of the two central characters in Schiller's preceding play, *Mary Stuart* (1800):

> in arts of government
> Elizabeth and others; arts of war
> The peasant Joan and others. (ll. 145–7)[46]

---

[43] *The Princess*, I, ll. 37, 89–99; Killham, pp. 203, 205, 209–10.

[44] One of these goddesses is Aglaia, whose name is inherited by the child in *The Princess* (and later on in *Part Two*, the name of her mother, Psyche, is used as well (ll. 5299–300, 11660 / Macdonald, pp. 30, 333)).

[45] I, ll. 1–3, 38; IV, l. 257; III, ll. 193–5; IV, ll. 70–98; I, ll. 4, 35, 165–6, 235; II, l. 246; III, ll. 102, 230; IV, ll. 411–12.

[46] As mentioned earlier, Salvin's volume comprises translations of *Mary Stuart* and *The Maid*, and in the copy of Schiller's *Complete Works* that is at TRC, these two plays are printed consecutively (AT/1947, pp. 415–98). The 'lady [. . .] that armed | Her own fair head' who is described in the 'Prologue' to *The Princess* (ll. 32–48, esp. ll. 32–3) resembles Joan very closely, right down to her 'eyes', which are 'on fire' (l. 41) (Joan has 'eyes of fire' (II. 6. 1570 / p. 277)). See also 'A Dream of Fair Women' (*PT*, 173), ll. 267–8.

Both Joan and Ida have taken on a traditionally masculine role, whilst shunning involvement with men. As the former declares:

> I did not put this iron harness on,
> To deck with bridal wreaths my braided hair.
> 'Tis to a work far different I am called,
> Which none but a pure maid [*Jungfrau*] can bring to pass.
> I fight the battles of the Lord of Hosts,
> Nor must an earthly man call me his bride. (III. 4. 2199–204 / p. 307; see also III. 4. 2257–64 / p. 309)

Ida seems like a scholarly version of Joan:

>   when we set our hand
> To this great work, we purposed with ourself
> Never to wed. (II, ll. 45–7; see also I, ll. 47–9)

In both texts, however, the heroine's resolve is tested by a group of male invaders from the North: 'saucy islanders' in *The Maid* ('Prolog'. 3. 322 / p. 217), and 'a rout of saucy boys' in *The Princess* (V, l. 384).[47]

The leader of this group, the Prince, is determined to break down the barriers between Ida and himself. She, however, is associated with death, being 'as grand as doomsday and as grave' (I, l. 185). His two attempts to create a greater intimacy with her seem to carry him, therefore, to the frontiers of existence. The first of these efforts – which takes place during the geological excursion in sections III and IV – is tentative and unsuccessful. When, in section III, the trip is about to begin, the Prince experiences one of his bouts of 'catalepsy',[48] in which he seems 'to move among a world of ghosts' (I, ll. 20, 17):

>   On a sudden my strange seizure came
> Upon me, [. . .]
> The Princess Ida seemed a hollow show,
> [. . .]
> And I myself the shadow of a dream,
> For all things were and were not. (ll. 167–9, 172–3)

These words lend an air of unreality – or non-existence – to what follows. Setting out, the Prince and Ida ride side by side (l. 181), and

---

[47] See also 'Prologue', l. 78; VII, l. 323. Compare also 'hadst thou bereaved | The lioness of her whelps', and 'The old lion, glaring with his whelpless eye' (Salvin, p. 278; *The Princess*, VI, l. 83).

[48] These were added in 1851 (*PT*, 286, headnote).

as they gradually draw closer to one another, references to death proliferate: 'let the topic die'; 'you will shock him even to death'; 'perchance your life may fail' (ll. 189, 196, 220). Alluding to the days before she founded her university, the Princess states quite explicitly that she sees herself as having died: 'We touch on our dead self, nor shun to do it, | Being other' (ll. 205–6). She would, moreover, be happy to die again, eagerly contemplating a 'single act | Of immolation, any phase of death' (ll. 267–8). As in *In Memoriam*, the looming presence of mortality makes Nature herself seem redolent of extinction: the scarpéd cliff reveals 'The bones of some vast bulk that lived and roared | Before man was' (ll. 277–8).[49] Ida compares the fields where she and the Prince walk to 'the Elysian lawns', whilst above them, 'the Sun | Grew broader toward his death' (ll. 324, 345–6). Even the intercalated lyric which follows this section reiterates the words 'dying, dying, dying' (III ∧ IV, ll. 6, 12, 18; see also l. 13).

Like that other female death-figure – the beloved woman of 'Come down, O maid' – Ida is closely identified with the heights. As Paul Turner observes, she takes her name from the mountain in 'Œnone' (*PT*, 164).[50] Physically lofty, she is addressed, of course, as 'your Highness', and she exhorts her students to 'lift [their] natures up'.[51] At the beginning of section IV, however, she unwittingly adumbrates the maid's descent into the valley: 'let us down and rest', she declares, before she and the Prince come 'Down from the lean and wrinkled precipices' (ll. 3, 4). As they do so, a tentative intimacy is created: 'Once she leaned on me, | Descending; once or twice she lent her hand' (ll. 8–9). This longed-for touch of a hand is a recurrent image in *In Memoriam* (VII, ll. 4–5; XIV, l. 11; CXIX, l. 12). Perhaps Ida's return to earth is also, implicitly, Hallam's.

This faintly Schillerian descent from the heavens is quickly followed by a Goethean ascent from the underworld. In *Part Two* Act I, Faust journeys into the bowels of the earth: 'A glowing tripod then will tell you this', Mephistopheles informs him, 'That you have reached the deepest deep abyss' (ll. 6283–4 / Macdonald,

---

[49] Compare these words – and the mention two lines earlier of 'the woods' – to *Cain*: 'the wild habitants | Of the deep woods of earth, the hugest which | Roar nightly in the forest' (Byron, *Poetical Works*, VI (1991), II. 2. 135–7).

[50] Turner, p. 102. Tennyson 'wrote part of Œnone in the valley of Cauteretz' with Hallam (EE, I, 358). In section V of *The Princess*, Ida is described as 'standing like a stately Pine | Set in a cataract on an island-crag' (ll. 336–7). This image, Tennyson tells us, is 'Taken from a torrent above Cauteretz' (EE, IV, 261).

[51] II, l. 27; III, ll. 162–3, 186, 195, 215; VI, ll. 305–6, 309; II, l. 74 (see also III, ll. 207–8; V, ll. 271, 276, 499–503; VI, l. 14).

p. 75). Faust retrieves this magical object, which is needed in order to conjure up an apparition of Helena (already mentioned above). An observer describes his return to the surface: 'A tripod rises with him from the cave, | I see the censer's holy incense wave' (ll. 6423–4 / Macdonald, p. 82). Music is played, and the illusory Helena appears (l. 6444; stage direction before l. 6479 / Macdonald, pp. 83, 85). In *The Princess*, as the Prince and Ida enter the tent together, the imagery and actions are similar to those in *Faust*:

> on a tripod in the midst
> A fragrant flame rose, and before us glowed
> Fruit, blossom, viand, amber wine, and gold.
>
> Then she, 'Let some one sing to us: lightlier move
> The minutes fledged with music.' (ll. 15–19)

The 'mournful' (VI, l. 298) song which follows, 'Tears, idle tears' (ll. 21–40), can be seen as the equivalent of Faust's attempt to conjure up the dead. It includes numerous references to death (ll. 33, 36, 40), and Tennyson even mentions 'a sail, | That brings our friends up from the underworld' (ll. 26–7). 'Tears, idle tears' was written at Tintern Abbey, which Tennyson described as being 'full for me of its bygone memories' (*Mem.*, I, 253). As Bush points out, one of these might well have been the memory of Hallam, whose resting-place is nearby.[52]

The song displeases Ida (as does that of the Prince which follows), and Cyril's 'careless tavern-catch' brings the whole episode to a disastrous close (l. 139). The Prince's second attempt to restore his bond with his 'betrothed' (I, l. 119) is the contest in section V, and its aftermath in VI and VII. This, too, is an encounter with death: more literal, more intense, and, ultimately, more successful. Once again, it is not just the Prince and Ida, but also Goethe and Schiller who are brought into proximity. Section V of *The Princess* is indebted to the battle scenes in Act IV of *Part Two*: the compound noun 'War-music' (l. 256), for example, may well be Tennyson's translation of '*Kriegsmusik*'

---

[52] Bush (ed.), 'Alfred, Lord Tennyson', p. 408. Bush compares the lyric to section XIX of *In Memoriam* (ibid. p. 408). Tennyson also remarked that 'Tears, idle tears' evokes 'the abiding in the transient', a phrase which could easily serve as a translation of the title of one of Goethe's best-known poems, 'Dauer im Wechsel' (which David Luke renders as 'Permanence in Change' (*Mem.*, I, 253; see also II, 70, 288; FA, 1, II, 493–4 / Goethe, trans. Luke, pp. 195–6)).

(stage direction before l. 10297). Goethe's 'three mighty men' are, perhaps, the ancestors of the king's 'three broad sons', whilst '[t]he Emperor's Tent' becomes Tennyson's 'imperial tent' (*F*, stage directions before ll. 10323 and 10345 / Macdonald, pp. 269, 271; *The Princess*, ll. 259, 9). Also, in both Act IV of *Part Two* and section V of *The Princess*, the ruler wishes to take part in the fighting, but is dissuaded from doing so by one or more of his subjects (*F*, ll. 10407–22, 10473–86 / Macdonald, pp. 274, 277; *The Princess*, ll. 342–8).

Earlier, in section IV, the Prince and Ida had experienced a brief moment of physical closeness whilst one of them was near to death.[53] Their *spiritual* rapprochement in VI and VII takes place in a similar context, and here, Tennyson draws, once again, on Schiller. The dramatic turning-point of *The Maid* comes at the end of its third act, when Joan encounters the English general Lionel on the battlefield, and is about to kill him, when she is overcome with pity (III. 10.; ll. 2454–517 / pp. 320–5). In the similarly medieval setting of a formal tournament, Ida's 'noble heart [is] molten in her breast' at the sight of the wounded Prince (VI, l. 103). The Princess is now ready to embark on her second descent – a much more far-reaching one than that which had taken her from the quarry to the tent in section IV. Once again, Tennyson's language anticipates that of 'Come down, O maid' (with its 'cold', 'ice' and 'azure pillars of the hearth', which beckon its addressee (VII, ll. 179, 191, 201)):

> we will scatter all our maids
> Till happier times each to her proper hearth:
> [. . .]
>   [. . .] speak to the king:
> Thaw this male nature to some touch of that
> Which kills me with myself, and drags me down
> From my fixt height. (VI, ll. 283–4, 286–9; see also VII, ll. 16–17, 20–1, 28)

This 'killing' of Ida is really a return to life, for her earlier transformation is now being reversed by a more 'truthful change' (VII, l. 329). But it is only in section VII, when the Prince, too, is at the

---

[53] As Killham points out (pp. 207–8), the Prince's rescuing of Ida from the river (IV, ll. 157–71) may derive from the poem's oriental sources. But it also resembles Chiron's account of how he rescued Helena from the swamps of Eleusis in *Faust: Part Two* (ll. 7403–25 / Macdonald, pp. 132–3).

threshold of life and death, that the barriers between them are finally overcome:

> Last I woke sane, but well-nigh close to death.
> [. . .]
>   '[. . .]I shall die tonight.
> Stoop down and seem to kiss me ere I die.'
> I could no more, but lay like one in trance,
> That hears his burial talked of by his friends,
> And cannot speak, nor move, nor make one sign,
> But lies and dreads his doom. She turned; she paused;
> She stooped; and out of languor leapt a cry;
> Leapt fiery passion from the brinks of death;
> And I believed that in the living world
> My spirit closed with Ida's at the lips. (ll. 104, 134–43)

'Stoop down and seem to kiss me': this resembles Tennyson's initial draft of line 13 of *In Memoriam*, XCIII (which is addressed to Hallam's spirit): 'Stoop soul & touch me: wed me' (*TA*, XVI, 58). The similarity may well be significant, for it suggests, once again, that the reunion of Ida and the Prince is also a reunion of Tennyson and Hallam.

Indulging this 'sweet dream' (VII, ll. 130, 134) may have helped to fortify Tennyson to face the harsh realities of the later sections of *In Memoriam*. As discussed above, in LXXXIV, he revisits the territory of 'Ulysses' by imagining Hallam as an old man, but the section concludes with a firm rejection of this 'backward fancy', which serves only to reawaken '[t]he old bitterness' (ll. 46, 47). And in XCII–XCIV, he explicitly rejects the possibility that his friend will ever come back to life.[54] Like the main narrative of *The Princess*, *In Memoriam* ends with marriage, the anticipation of childbirth, and the hope of better things, but even as it looks to the future, it finds space for one final, poignant, look back:

>   a closer link
> Betwixt us and the crowning race
> [. . .]

---

[54] As Alfred Gatty observes, lines 13–16 of XCII contain an echo of Coleridge's translation of Schiller's *Death of Wallenstein* (Alfred Gatty, *A Key to Lord Tennyson's 'In Memoriam'*, 4th edn (London: Bell, 1894), p. 100, fn). Ricks points out that Hallam may be alluding to this passage in his letter to Emily Tennyson of 20 December 1832 (*PT*, 296, XCII, ll. 13–16, fn; *LAHH*, no. 215, p. 706).

> For all we thought and loved and did,
>   And hoped, and suffered, is but seed
> Of what in them is flower and fruit;
>
> Whereof the man, that with me trod
>   This planet, was a noble type. ('Epilogue', ll. 127–8, 134–8)

Section VII of *The Princess* employs similar language, but in this case, the loss with which the poem began has been entirely cancelled out, and the sometimes bitter complexities of *In Memoriam* are, therefore, absent:

> '[. . .] Dispensing harvest, sowing the To-be
> [. . .]
> Then springs the crowning race of humankind.
> [. . .]
>   [. . .] let us type them now
> In our own lives,
> [. . .]
>   O we will walk this world,
> Yoked in all exercise of noble end,
> And so through those dark gates across the wild
> That no man knows. [. . .]' (ll. 273, 279, 281–2, 339–42)

This is an optimism unqualified by any past tragedy. Helena, it would seem, has been brought up from Orcus, and Joan has descended from the heights. Goethe and Schiller are reunited – and so too, I think, are Tennyson and Hallam.

The full title of Goethe's masterpiece is sometimes given as *Faust: First and Second Parts of the Tragedy*. The strict applicability of the last word of this description is much disputed by critics. It is, however, far more appropriate to *Part One* than it is to *Part Two*. The latter work places the fate of the protagonist (and of Gretchen) in a larger, more hopeful context: it begins with renewal, and ends in redemption, thus fulfilling the hinted promise of the 'Prologue in Heaven'. And although Faust's dying speech may be tragic in a broad sense, he still comes across as a much happier individual than he had been in the anguished monologue he delivered when we first met him (ll. 11559–86, 354–417 / Macdonald, pp. 328–9; Hay. 1, pp. 7–9).

This trajectory is reflected in the poems that we have looked at in the last three chapters. In the works discussed in Chapter 1, Tennyson is often looking death in the face. But he is also seeking, at times, to attenuate his loss, by placing physical extinction in the context of metaphysical survival. As I argued in Chapter 2, this impulse finds its most powerful expression in the seventy lines of 'Ulysses'. And a recontextualisation of mortality is also present – in sometimes surprising ways – in the poems that have been discussed in the present chapter. In 'Tithon', death is desirable; in 'Tiresias', laudable; in *The Princess*, reversible.

In most of the poems that have been dealt with so far, Tennyson's attitude towards *Faust* is, essentially, an admiring one. Goethe's drama certainly provided him with a fertile source of inspiration for the works that he wrote in response to his deep personal loss of 1833. However, when Tennyson deals with more general themes – religion, Nature and morality – a contrasting, but largely concurrent story emerges. It is his Faustian poems on these three topics that will provide the subject matter of the second half of this book.

Part II

Religion, Nature and Morality

Chapter 4

'Two souls, alas, dwell in my breast': Religious Doubt

Tennyson's trance experiences – which were discussed in detail in Chapter 2 – formed what W. D. Paden justly describes as 'the personal basis of his faith'.[1] It should be added, however, that this basis was, in fact, an extremely narrow one. For although Tennyson's visions gave him a strong conviction of immortality, they gave him little else besides, and his relationship with Christianity was uneasy. In his less exalted states of mind, he was often plagued by religious doubt, and in his blackest moods, even his belief in the after-life would sometimes waver. His poetic descriptions of these depressions suggest that they were scarcely less intense or perennial than his trances: in questions of faith, Tennyson was very much a divided soul. He wrote three major poems on religious doubt: 'Supposed Confessions of a Second-Rate Sensitive Mind', 'The Two Voices' and *In Memoriam*.

Often linked by critics,[2] these works are also linked by the influence of *Faust*, and of Carlyle's Goethe criticism. The former contributed significantly to these three poems' atmosphere of mental division, and in this respect they form part of a broader group of nineteenth-century texts (which also includes works by Byron, Clough, Arnold, Roden Noel and Wilde). Equally important to these poems are the articles on Goethe that Carlyle published between 1822 and 1832, which include the claim that *Faust* is a portrayal of the crisis of faith. This interpretation of the drama (expressed, as it was, in the author's forceful and confident prose) won a great many converts, but its basic untenability ensured that its prestige was only

---

[1] Paden, *Tennyson in Egypt*, p. 71.
[2] See Ormond, p. 16; A. Dwight Culler, *The Poetry of Tennyson* (New Haven, CT: Yale University Press, 1977), p. 151; *PT*, 78, 209, headnotes.

transitory. This background is reflected in Tennyson's three poems, in which an implicit adherence to the Carlylean view of *Faust* gradually gives way to ambivalence. Tennyson seems, though, to have avoided open disillusionment by shifting his focus: in the passages on religious doubt in *In Memoriam*, he turns away from Goethe's drama itself, and looks, instead, to the reinterpretations of it that had been offered by Carlyle and others.

The most succinct expression of Faust's mental division is his famous 'Two souls' speech, in which he declares:

> Two souls, alas, dwell in my breast: the one struggles to separate itself from the other. The one clings with obstinate fondness to the world, with organs like cramps of steel: the other lifts itself majestically from the mist to the realms of an exalted ancestry. (ll. 1112–17 / p. 35)

The evocation of inner conflict in *Faust* extends, however, far beyond this single passage. Elsewhere in the drama, the protagonist repeatedly engages in tense dialogues with interlocutors who seem to be, in one way or another, aspects of himself: his fellow scholar Wagner in his first two scenes, and thereafter Mephistopheles, to whom he is bound by the pact. In 1827, Goethe assented to the view of the French critic J. J. Ampère that both Faust and Mephisto were really two different aspects of his own personality, and seven years earlier, the anonymous author of the 'Introduction' to the *Outlines, Illustrative of 'Faust'* (1820) had suggested that the reader should 'consider Faust and Mephistopheles as one person' (FA, 2, XII (XXXIX), Pt III, p. 607, ll. 33–7, 3 May; Coleridge, *Faustus*, p. 181).

This particular aspect of Goethe's drama is likely to have been of considerable interest to Shelley, whose biographer Richard Holmes remarks: 'the image of the pursuing fiend [. . .] [is] a central motif in many [of his] individual works. [. . .] The sense [is] of a doubleness in the mind'.[3] For example, in 'To—' ('O! there are spirits in the air'), which dates from around 1815, the poet refers to 'This fiend, whose ghastly presence ever | Beside thee like thy shadow hangs' (Shelley, *Complete Works*, I (1927), pp. 201–2, ll. 31–2). And in 'Alastor' – which was written in the same year, and which is known to have been influenced by *Faust*[4] – the protagonist is at one point 'Startled by his own thoughts', and looks hurriedly around, but finds

---

[3] Holmes, p. 65.
[4] See, for example, Hay. 1, p. 217.

that 'There was no fair fiend near him, not a sight | Or sound of awe but in his own deep mind' (Shelley, *Complete Works*, I (1927), pp. 175–98, ll. 296–8).

Charles E. Robinson assumes that it is the *Outlines, Illustrative of 'Faust'* to which Shelley refers in a letter from Pisa of 12 January 1822, and he argues that the 'Introduction' to that work was an important influence on *The Deformed Transformed*, which Byron began writing the following month (Shelley, *Complete Works*, X (1926), 345–6).[5] Although the *Faust* translation that the two poets were reading could just as easily have been the one attributed to Coleridge, the assumption that it was the *Outlines* is made more plausible by the fact that Byron's play explores what Robinson calls the 'devil as doppelgänger' theme.[6] He argues that Byron is referring to *The Deformed* in the following comments (which were attributed to him by Thomas Medwin):

> The hero of the piece is [attended by] [. . .] his second self [. . .] [who] at every turn [. . .] intrudes like the demon in Faust in his solitude. [. . .] One voice like the voice of his own soul whispers in his ears.[7]

Some three decades later, Clough would explore similar territory in *Dipsychus*:

> What is this persecuting voice that haunts me?
> What? whence? of whom? How am I to detect?
> Myself or not myself? My own bad thoughts,
> Or some external agency at work [. . .]?
> [. . .]
> How shall I call him? Mephistopheles?
> [. . .]
>   [. . .] O double self! (II, ll. 17–20; IX, 44; XI, l. 63)

Clough's friend Matthew Arnold, in his 'Preface' to *Poems* (1853), refers to 'the dialogue of the mind with itself; [. . .] the doubts, [. . .] the discouragement, of Hamlet and of Faust' (*Prose Works*, I (1960),

---

[5] Charles E. Robinson, 'The Devil as Doppelgänger in *The Deformed Transformed*: The Sources and Meaning of Byron's Unfinished Drama', in *The Plays of Lord Byron: Critical Essays*, ed. Robert Gleckner and Bernard Beatty (Liverpool: Liverpool University Press, 1997), pp. 321–45 (p. 328).
[6] Ibid. p. 328.
[7] Cited in ibid. pp. 331–2.

p. 1, ll. 24–7; see also *Poems of Matthew Arnold*, p. 140, ll. 93–6). Roden Noel, in his 'Preface' to *A Modern Faust* (1888), explains that it portrays a 'divided nature, [. . .] enfeebled by internal dissensions, through the warfare of higher and lower selves. [. . .] My Satan [. . .] is chiefly, though not entirely, the man's own worse self' (pp. xiv, xv; see also p. 151). In Wilde's *Picture of Dorian Gray* (1890–1), 'the divided self of Dorian corresponds', argues Norbert Kohl, 'to Faust's cry of: "Zwei Seelen wohnen, ach! in meiner Brust" [Two souls, alas, dwell in my breast]'.[8] 'Supposed Confessions of a Second-Rate Sensitive Mind', 'The Two Voices' and *In Memoriam* are part of an identifiably Faustian strand of nineteenth-century British literature.

These three poems should be compared, in particular, to *Dipsychus* and *A Modern Faust*, for they reveal, like them, the influence of Carlyle, who had linked Goethe's evocation of mental division to the theme of religious doubt. When he first read *Part One* in 1820, Carlyle saw in it a depiction of his own inner torment, much of which was bound up with his lengthy battle against atheism (Carlyle, *Letters*, III (1970), 87, 24 June 1824). In his article on '*Faustus*' (1822), he not only hints that Faust and Mephistopheles represent different aspects of a single psyche, but argues, also, that this split is indicative of an ongoing struggle against Enlightenment scepticism:

> In many respects Mephistophiles [*sic*] resembles some French *philosophe* of the last century. There is the perfection of the intellectual faculties with a total absence of the moral. [. . .] Faust [. . .] has been born with the head of a sceptic and the heart of a devotee. [. . .] [He] and Mephistophiles personify the two propensities [. . .] which by their combination, in different proportions, give rise to so many varieties of moral disposition among men. (Carlyle, '*Faustus*', pp. 326, 332)

In 'Goethe's "Helena"' (1828), Carlyle adds:

> Goethe's Devil [. . .] is a *philosophe*. [. . .] If Mephistopheles represent the spirit of Denial, Faust may represent that of Inquiry and Endeavour: the two are, by necessity, in conflict; the light and the darkness of man's life and mind. [. . .] It is this conflicting union of the higher nature of the soul with the lower elements of human life [. . .] that the poet has [. . .] proposed to delineate [in *Part One*]. (*WTC*, XXVI, 156–7, 158, 161)

---

[8] Kohl, p. 162. See also Hans-Peter Gerhardt, 'Oscar Wildes *Dorian Gray* als Faustdichtung', *Faust-Blätter*, 25 (1973), 669–75 (p. 671).

Carlyle develops these arguments in his 'Preface' to *Wilhelm Meister's Travels* (1827), and in the essays 'Goethe' (1828), 'Death of Goethe' and 'Goethe's *Works*' (both 1832). In these pieces, he argues that *Part One* should be placed alongside *The Sorrows of Young Werther* as a product of the tempestuous early phase of the German poet's development, which had eventually given way to the wisdom and serenity of his later years. Carlyle gradually shifts his emphasis from the works themselves to their author, whom he portrays as a man who has shaken off his youthful scepticism and emerged, after much trial and error, as 'a Believer' (*WTC*, XXVI, 210). Goethe becomes, for Carlyle, nothing less than 'the Redeemer of the time' (ibid. XXVII, 379).

Today, Carlyle's view of *Faust* and its author is widely regarded as untenable. It represents, to a great extent, a projection of his own preoccupations onto the writings of the German poet. This insight has been elaborated by numerous critics,[9] but the most revealing comment of all comes from Carlyle himself, in a letter to Goethe in 1827: 'your works', he writes, 'have been a mirror to me' (Carlyle, *Letters*, IV (1970), 248, 20 August). The strongly personal character of Carlyle's interpretation did not, however, prevent it from exercising a considerable influence during the whole of the second quarter of the nineteenth century (and to some extent beyond). By arguing that Goethe's life and works offered a solution to the widespread crisis of faith, Carlyle greatly enhanced the German poet's attractiveness for those many readers who felt uncertain of their spiritual beliefs. Tennyson can be confidently said to have been one of them, for as I will argue below, 'Confessions', 'Voices' and *In Memoriam* all reveal that he associated *Faust* with religious doubt. However, the latter two poems also suggest that the Carlylean view of Goethe's drama was deeply problematic for him, for it raised hopes that the work itself was unable to fulfil.

The details of this process are not easy to pinpoint, partly because Tennyson, Carlyle and Goethe all held religious beliefs that could be fairly described as vague, elusive and inconsistent. There are, however, a number of observations that can be made with a reasonable degree of certainty. Tennyson felt at least some sense of allegiance to

---

[9] Carré, pp. 144, 157–60, 177–9; Louis Cazamian, *Carlyle*, trans. E. K. Brown (New York: Macmillan, 1932), pp. 42–7; William Rose, 'Goethe's Reputation in England during his Lifetime', in *Essays on Goethe*, ed. William Rose (London: Cassell, 1949), pp. 141–85 (pp. 183–5); Metzger, '*Sartor*', pp. 326–7; Ashton, *German Idea*, pp. 89–90; Smith, pp. 6–8, 22–4.

Christianity: although he acknowledged that it needed to change and develop, he did not expect it to disappear ('Ring in the Christ that is to be', he writes in *In Memoriam*, which refers, he explains, to '[t]he broader Christianity of the future' (CVI, l. 32; EE, III, 256)).[10] This outlook serves to differentiate him from Carlyle and Goethe, both of whom (for all their manifold differences) believed in God, but not in Christ. Indeed, Goethe's attitude towards Christianity was, from around 1770 onwards, frequently hostile. As early as 1773, he bluntly declared 'I am not a Christian', and eighteen months later, he described 'the whole teaching about Christ' as 'such a damned filthy affair'.[11] It is certainly not realistic, therefore, to regard him as a Christian poet, and his masterpiece, although it makes use of Christian symbolism, is not a Christian work (Faust offers no objection when Margaret tells him that he has 'no Christianity' (ll. 3468–9 / p. 145; see also ll. 369, 765, 1660–70 / pp. 7, 21, 56–7)). Contrary to the claims of Carlyle, then, *Faust* could offer Tennyson no real solution to his crisis of faith, which was, at least to some extent, a specifically Christian one. Swept along, however, by Carlyle's powerful language – which is both broad and biblical, and open, therefore, to misinterpretation – it is likely that he would have been unable, at least initially, to recognise this.

This assumption is lent considerable support by 'Supposed Confessions of a Second-Rate Sensitive Mind Not In Unity With Itself' (*PT*, 78; published 1830).[12] Kennedy demonstrates that the title of this poem echoes the words 'the Confessions of some mind not yet in unity with itself', which come from Chapter VIII of *Wilhelm Meister's Travels* (*WM*, Vol. X, p. 60, ll. 10–11 / XXIV, 235).[13] We gain a better understanding of why Tennyson latched on to this particular

---

[10] See also 'Confessions', ll. 18–32, 98–106; 'Voices', ll. 400–11, 460–2; *In Memoriam*, 'Prologue'; *Mem.*, I, 325–7; II, 231.

[11] FA, 2, I (XXVIII), p. 331, l. 3 (second half of November 1773); p. 451, ll. 17–18 (*c.* 12 May 1775) / cited in Boyle, I (1991), 150, 189 (with italics added to the latter). See also Boyle, I (1991), 93, 352–3, 659–60; II, 161–2; David Luke, '"Vor deinem Jammerkreuz": Goethe's Attitude to Christian Belief', *Publications of the English Goethe Society*, n.s. 59 (1989), 35–58. Goethe may even have gone through a period of atheism, which lasted from *c.* 1788 to *c.* 1792 (see Boyle, I (1991), 558–9; II, 144–5).

[12] This was the title in *Poems, Chiefly Lyrical*; the last five words were dropped in 1884 (*PT*, 78, headnote).

[13] Kennedy, p. 87.

phrase if we look at a passage in Carlyle's 'Preface' to this novel,[14] in which he alludes to it:

> Goethe's [. . .] world seems once to have been desolate and baleful as that of the darkest sceptic: but he has covered it anew with beauty and solemnity, derived from deeper sources, over which Doubt can have no sway. [. . .] To reconcile these contradictions is the task of all good men, each for himself, in his own way and manner; a task which, in our age, is encompassed with difficulties peculiar to the time; and which Goethe seems to have accomplished with a success that few can rival. *A mind so in unity with itself*, even though it were a poor and small one would arrest our attention, and win some kind regard from us; but when this mind ranks among the strongest and most complicated of the species, it becomes a sight full of interest, a study full of deep instruction. (*WTC*, XXIII, 24, 25; italics added)

The title of 'Confessions' signals Tennyson's interest in the Carlylean notion that Goethe had triumphed over religious doubt, and this interest would appear to be confirmed by both the text of the poem, and Tennyson's comments on it. The insights of Smith are relevant here:

> there are influential aspects of Carlyle's thought which would not have been the same if he had not known and admired Goethe. Above all two large ideas, neither of them new but both given special impetus by Carlyle's propagation of them, stem from Carlyle's encounter with Goethe: that there is an enormous moral and religious value in work, and that belief can co-exist with, indeed flow out of, a spirit of sceptical inquiry.[15]

The first of these two ideas can be partly traced to some words from the *Apprenticeship* that Carlyle often quotes: 'doubt of any kind can be removed by nothing but activity' (*WM*, Vol. IX, Bk V, Ch. XVI, p. 716, ll. 36–7 / XXIII, 386).[16] A comparable remedy for mental division is proposed by Tennyson in his comment on the speaker of 'Confessions': 'If some kind friend had taken him by the hand and said, "Come, work" [. . .] he might have been a happy man, though

---

[14] Note that in *WTC* (XXIII, 12–33), this is printed before the *Apprenticeship*, *not* the *Travels*.
[15] Smith, p. 55.
[16] See also *WTC*, XXIII, 17; *SR*, Bk II, Ch. IX, p. 156 / p. 145, ll. 15–16; Carlyle, *Letters*, VI (1977), 122 (16 February 1832); XII (1985), 106 (12 April 1840).

sensitive' (EE, I, 336–7). The second idea – which may also owe something to Coleridge – is expressed in Carlyle's essay 'Goethe', in which he argues that the German poet 'believes, [. . .] not by denying his unbelief, but by following it out', and is, therefore, qualified to 'stand forth [. . .] as the Teacher and exemplar of his age' (*WTC*, XXVI, 210, 208). Or as Tennyson puts it in 'Confessions':

> 'It is man's privilege to doubt,
> If so be that from doubt at length,
> Truth may stand forth unmoved of change. [. . .]' (ll. 142–4)[17]

Elsewhere in the text of this poem, Tennyson is thinking not just of Goethe as an individual, but of *The Sorrows of Werther*, and also perhaps of *Faust: Part One*. In his Farewell Letter, the protagonist of the former work expresses his defiant scorn for mortality: 'What is death?' he asks, 'We do but dream when we talk of it. [. . .] How can we be annihilated!' (Pt II, p. 248, ll. 13–14, 18–19 / pp. 202, 203). It is in much the same spirit that he goes on to recollect the funeral of a friend:

> I stood by the side of the grave when the coffin was let down; when I heard the creaking of the cords as they were let down and drawn up, when the first shovelful of earth was thrown in, [. . .] my heart was smitten, grieved, rent; but I neither knew what had happened, nor what was to happen to me.—Death! Grave!—I understand not the words. (Pt II, p. 248, ll. 24–7, 29–32 / p. 203)

Tennyson draws on this scene in the second verse paragraph of 'Confessions', but he heightens the emotionalism of Werther's account by introducing a number of modifications. Here, the speaker's indifference to mortality – and his relative composure as the earth is thrown onto the coffin – are no longer the memory of a real event, but

---

[17] Compare also Coleridge, *Aids to Reflection* (1825) (which incorporates writings by the seventeenth-century Archbishop of Glasgow Robert Leighton): 'Never be afraid to doubt, if only you have the disposition to believe, and doubt in order that you may end in believing the Truth' (Coleridge, *Collected Works*, IX: *Aids to Reflection*, ed. John Beer (1993), p. 107). Tennyson, we are told, 'never much cared' for Coleridge's prose works (*Mem.*, I, 50), but Hallam read *Aids* in 1828, and described it as 'amply rewarding a deeper search' (*LAHH*, no. 55, p. 233 [26 August]).

become, instead, an elusive, yearned-for possibility. And the wound that is sustained by his heart is now a good deal more graphic, for it is directly inflicted by those malevolently creaking cords:

> How sweet to have a common faith!
> To hold a common scorn of death!
> And at a burial to hear
> The creaking cords which wound and eat
> Into my human heart, whene'er
> Earth goes to earth, with grief, not fear,
> With hopeful grief, were passing sweet!
> [. . .]
> To stand beside a grave. (ll. 33–9; fn to ll. 39 ∧ 40, l. 5)

It says much about Tennyson's troubled state of mind that he seems, in these lines, to be envying a man who is on the verge of taking his own life. This passage also reveals how strong an influence Carlyle's portrayal of Goethe was exerting on him: at this early stage of his career, he appears to have believed that even in the despairing conclusion of *The Sorrows of Werther*, a solution to the crisis of faith might be profitably sought.

Prior to 1833, Tennyson would probably have been reading *Faust: Part One* in the version by Gower, whose deliberate mistranslations of a number of passages would have made Carlyle's interpretation of it appear more plausible. For example, lines 777–8 (which Hayward would later render faithfully as 'amidst a thousand burning tears, I felt a world rise up to me') are transformed by Gower into 'I form'd myself a new creation, | While tears of christian fervour ran' (Hay. 1, p. 22; Gower, I, 43).[18] Despite its many inaccuracies, Gower's translation does at least make some attempt to preserve the verse forms of the German text of *Part One*. And although these are highly diverse, they do not vary quite as widely as they would later come to do in *Part Two*: the tetrameter is Goethe's preferred line-length; the iamb is his most typical choice of metrical foot; and the couplet is a recurring constituent of his rhyme schemes. The fact that all of these characteristics can be found in 'Confessions' might be seen as being indicative of the influence of Gower's *Faust*. Tennyson uses iambic tetrameters throughout the poem, and all but two of its first sixteen lines are in couplets (which makes this passage

---

[18] Contrast also *F*, l. 765 / Hay. 1, p. 21, and Gower, I, 43.

very much an anomaly amongst the *Poems, Chiefly Lyrical*).¹⁹ Also, in Gower's translation of the 'Two souls' speech – which is the obvious Faustian analogue of the 'mind not yet in unity with itself' of *Meister* – the protagonist uses the phrase 'the grosser earth', and his assistant Wagner's subsequent response includes the words, 'I know whose frosty fang | Vexes, who fret me with their arrowy tongues' (ll. 1114, 1130–1 / Gower, I, 62, 63). Tennyson may be echoing this exchange towards the end of 'Confessions', in which (shortly after a reference to '[o]ur double nature' (l. 175)), the speaker expresses his fear of 'the busy fret | Of that sharp-headed worm [. . .] | In the gross blackness underneath' (ll. 185–87).²⁰

In June 1833, Tennyson's friend J. M. Kemble wrote to W. B. Donne, informing him that the poet was at work on a new piece, in a similar vein to 'Confessions'. He had drafted 'some superb meditations on Self destruction',

> called *Thoughts of a Suicide* wherein he argues the point with his soul and is thoroughly floored. These are amazingly fine and deep, and show a mighty stride in intellect since the *Second-Rate Sensitive Mind*. (cited in *PT*, 209, headnote)

It is possible that the working title of this piece is indicative, once again, of the influence of Carlyle's Goethe criticism, which includes references to the 'suicidal Night-thoughts of *Werther*',²¹ and 'the destruction of [Faust's] spirit by the force of its own thoughts; a suicide of the mind' (*WTC*, XXVI, 'Goethe', 234; Carlyle, '*Faustus*', 332). The title under which the poem was eventually published, 'The Two Voices' (*PT*, 209), might have been intended as a sort of counterpart to the 'two souls' of Faust. As Culler observes:

> one feels that the final version of the poem [. . .] reflects [Tennyson's] decision to abandon the Romantic confessional mode in favor of

---

[19] Twenty years later, Clough would make iambic tetrameter couplets the most frequently used verse form for the words of the 'Spirit' in *Dipsychus*, thus heightening the similarity to *Faust* (although the phrase 'I am not quite in union with myself' (VII, l. 133) suggests that he might also have been thinking back to *Meister*, 'Confessions' or Carlyle's Goethe criticism).

[20] See also *PT*, 98, ll. 9–10.

[21] Carlyle is also alluding to Edward Young's *The Complaint: or, Night Thoughts* (1742–5), which Tennyson knew (*PT*, 2, I. 1. 63, fn; Ricks, *Allusion*, p. 197).

the more formal debate with one's soul or with a Mephistophelean tempter. It was no doubt the growing popularity of *Faust*, whose hero also says, 'Two souls, alas, are housed within this breast,' which led him to this conclusion.[22]

In addition to the broad formal similarity that is noted by Culler, 'Voices' repeatedly echoes a number of passages from *Part One*. It draws on three of the four 'university scenes' ('Night', 'Before the Gate' and 'Study [II]'), as well as 'May-Day Night' (which Tennyson appears to have consulted in the translations of both Hayward and Shelley).[23] What is more, the speaker's encounter with Nature in the poem's conclusion (which will be discussed separately in Chapter 5) is extensively influenced by Hayward's *Foreign Quarterly Review* article on *Part Two*. Indeed, although 'Ulysses' is, in spirit, Tennyson's most Faustian poem, for sheer quantity of specific verbal echoes, it is far surpassed by 'Voices'.

But if the influence of Goethe's drama is much stronger in 'Voices' than it had been in 'Confessions', this new intensity of engagement is accompanied by an emerging sense of estrangement. In the earlier poem, there had been nothing to indicate that Tennyson's scepticism had extended to Carlyle's highly idealised portrayal of Goethe. Indeed, when he wrote 'Confessions', Tennyson might even have been a little in awe of the German poet (in comparison with whom, his own, more discordant mind might have seemed to him inferior, or 'second-rate'). In 'Voices', however, the *details* of his response to *Faust* tend to belie the Carlylean view of the work that is suggested by the poem's *form*. Specifically, one would expect the nihilistic 'voice' to correspond – as in *The Deformed Transformed* and *Dipsychus* – to Mephistopheles, and the speaker, therefore, to be a Faustian figure. But the 'voice' actually combines elements of both Mephisto *and* Faust (with the latter, in fact, predominating), whilst the speaker might be more plausibly identified with Tennyson himself.[24] In other words, 'Voices' does not portray the interaction between Goethe's devil and his protagonist, but Tennyson's own interaction with both. It is not a dialogue with Mephistopheles, but with *Faust*.

As we have seen above, Carlyle had claimed that Goethe's protagonist possesses, in spite of his scepticism, 'the heart of a devotee'.

---

[22] Culler, *Tennyson*, p. 152.
[23] The university scenes comprise the first four scenes of the main action of *Part One* (ll. 354–2072 / pp. 7–72).
[24] Or perhaps Hallam: see Pinion, *Tennyson Chronology*, p. 10; Blocksidge, p. 225.

In Tennyson's poem, however, Faust's emotional outpourings are repeatedly used by the 'voice' in his attempts to persuade the speaker to commit the impious crime of suicide. For example, in 'Study [II]', Faust laments that 'at the approach of night, I must stretch myself in anguish on my couch; here, too, no rest is vouchsafed to me' (ll. 1562–4 / p. 53). 'Thine anguish will not let thee sleep', observes Tennyson's 'voice' tauntingly (l. 49). In 'Night', Faust uses the words 'Thou hast not gained', whilst in 'Study [II]', he declares: 'I am not a hair's breadth higher, nor a whit nearer the Infinite' (ll. 568, 1814–15 / pp. 14, 62). The 'voice', as part of his relentless attempt to undermine the speaker, combines echoes of both phrases:

'Thou hast not gained a real height,
Nor art thou nearer to the light,
Because the scale is infinite. [. . .]' (ll. 91–3)

Out in the Harz Mountains on May-Day Night, Faust describes how 'the light [. . .] | [. . .] within that narrow corner | Masses itself into intensest splendour' (ll. 3921, 3926–27 / PBS, II, ll. 102, 108–09). The 'voice' appropriates this lucent image, but uses it to argue that illumination is fleeting and limited: 'Sometimes a little corner shines', he declares mockingly (l. 187).

Only rarely does the 'voice' echo Mephistopheles. 'I will go forward', says Mephisto in 'May-Day Night' (l. 4053 / p. 172). The 'voice' uses these words verbatim at line 190, but attributes them, sarcastically, to the optimistic speaker: 'I will go forward, sayest thou'. Elsewhere in 'May-Day Night', an *Ignis-fatuus* declares: 'Our course, you know, is generally zigzag', to which Mephisto replies: 'Go straight on' (ll. 3862, 3864 / PBS, II, ll. 30, 32). The 'voice' uses this exchange to argue, once again, that his adversary's intellectual wanderings are all in vain: 'If straight thy track, or if oblique, | Thou know'st not' (ll. 193–4).[25]

Given that the 'voice' is, one presumes, inside the head of the speaker, it might seem misplaced to differentiate between them. They

---

[25] 'Voices' may also contain echoes of another dialogue with the devil, *Cain*. Compare, for example, Byron's observation that 'the world had been destroyed several times before the creation of man', and Tennyson's lines 'When first the world began, | Young Nature through five cycles ran, | And in the sixth she moulded man' (Byron, *Poetical Works*, VI (1991), 'Preface', p. 229, ll. 55–6; 'Voices', ll. 16–18). Also similar are Byron's references to 'The Mammoth' and 'wild habitants | Of the deep woods' (II. 2. 143, 135–6), and Tennyson's 'Mammoth, in the primal woods' (unadopted passage; see fn to ll. 268–318 / TA, XI, 163).

present, however, a much greater contrast than their prototypes in Goethe's drama (in which, paradoxically, Faust and Mephisto are, at least nominally, two separate individuals). Tennyson's speaker is an upright, somewhat idealised figure, and a very different character, therefore, to the often desperate Faust of the university scenes. In marked contrast to the sinister 'voice', he echoes Goethe's drama only once. In 'May-Day Night', the protagonist remarks: 'Many a riddle must there be untied', to which Mephisto replies: 'And many a riddle is also tied anew' (ll. 4040–1 / pp. 171–2). In what might be seen as a weary concession to the arguments of the 'voice', Tennyson's speaker declares:

> 'in seeking to undo
> One riddle, and to find the true,
> I knit a hundred others new. [. . .]' (ll. 232–4)[26]

This echo of *Faust* – and the creeping frustration that it expresses – are, however, untypical. More usually, the speaker responds to the arguments of the 'voice' with considerable determination, and in doing so, he draws on a broad range of literary works, including the Bible, Horace's *Odes*, *Hamlet*, *Paradise Lost*, Wordsworth and the writings of Hallam.[27] Admittedly, the 'voice' echoes other texts as well,[28] but *he* does so far less often, thus reversing the pattern that is displayed by the poem's echoes of Goethe (most of which occur in the words of the 'voice' rather than those of the speaker). So although 'Voices' follows Carlyle in associating *Faust* with the problems of unbelief, its relationship to the full range of its sources suggests that Tennyson is beginning to look for solutions elsewhere.

---

[26] In lines 208–13 of 'Voices', Tennyson may be picking up on Shelley's rhymes of 'striven' and 'Heaven', and 'dream' and 'Gleam' (*F*, ll. 3997–8, 3871, 3873 / PBS, II, ll. 192–3, 40, 42). Compare also *W*, Pt II, p. 256, ll. 34–5 / p. 209 and 'Voices', l. 290.

[27] *PT*, 209, ll. 1, 5–6, 52–3, 119–20, 142, 152, 210, 236–7, 239, 277–9, 280, 301–3, 304–6, 378, 395–6, 399, fns; Winnick, pp. 99–100, 101–3. Winnick (p. 100) suggests an echo of *Purgatory* at line 67, and the echo of Acts 7: 55 that Ricks identifies in his footnote to lines 222–5 also includes an echo of the *Inferno*: the words 'smote him on the face' (l. 225) are taken from Canto XXX (p. 160 / l. 103; compare also 'put forth thy strength', and 'put not forth her power' (*DC*, Vol. II, Canto IV, p. 21 / l. 45; 'Voices', l. 160)). The tristich form of 'Voices' (which is highly unusual for Tennyson) might have been partly inspired by the Italian text of the *Comedy*.

[28] *PT*, ll. 196–9, 228, 243, 256–7, 264, fns; Winnick, pp. 99, 100–1, 103.

A similar complexity is evinced in the transition from the main body of 'Voices' to its conclusion. Towards the end of 'Night', the despairing Faust greets 'the morn' by raising a poisoned chalice to his lips, but he is interrupted by the *'ringing of bells and singing of chorusses'* (l. 736 and subsequent stage direction / p. 20). These recall to him 'the solemn stillness of the Sabbath', and in the next scene, 'Before the Gate', a depiction of the townspeople enjoying their springtime day of rest is followed by Faust's great monologue 'River and rivulet are freed from ice', which describes how 'the mass is scattering itself through the gardens and fields' in celebration of Easter (ll. 772, 808–902; ll. 903–48, esp. ll. 929–30 / pp. 22, 24–8; pp. 28–9, esp. p. 29). On the 'Sabbath morn' that is described in 'Voices', the speaker puts thoughts of suicide behind him:

>   the light increased,
> With freshness in the dawning east.
>
> Like softened airs that blowing steal,
> When meres begin to uncongeal,
> The sweet church bells began to peal. (ll. 402, 404–8)

The speaker then leaves his home; mingles with the townspeople; and goes 'forth into the fields', which are filled with spring flowers (ll. 409–24, 448, 451–3).

This passage represents what is probably the most obvious similarity to Goethe's drama that can be found anywhere in Tennyson's work (Paull F. Baum may well be thinking of it, when he refers to the poem's 'borrowing from "Faust"').[29] However, as in the main body of the piece, Tennyson's echoes of Goethe – numerous though they are – should not be seen as expressions of agreement. When Faust hears the church bells, he is on the point of committing suicide, but at the analogous moment in 'Voices', the speaker is affirming, as never before, his will to live. Instead of placing *'the goblet to his mouth'* (*Faust*, stage direction before l. 737 / p. 20), he seems, instead, to be throwing down the gauntlet to Goethe's protagonist:

> 'Whatever crazy sorrow saith,
> No life that breathes with human breath
> Has ever truly longed for death.

---

[29] Baum, p. 97.

"Tis life, whereof our nerves are scant,
Oh life, not death, for which we pant;
More life, and fuller, that I want.' (ll. 394–9)[30]

In contrast to Faust – who is revitalised by the bells, the dawn and the arrival of spring – the victory over despair that is achieved by the speaker of 'Voices' *precedes* his emergence from his mental labyrinth, and comes, therefore, from within. Tennyson is here moving *away* from Goethe (who argued that 'All pleasure in life is founded on the regular return of external things', such as '[t]he alternations of day and night, [and] of the seasons' (FA, 1, XIV, Pt III, Bk XIII, p. 628, ll. 34–7 / WTC, XXVI, 'Goethe', 220)). But he is also moving *closer* to Carlyle (who in 'Signs of the Times' had argued that 'our happiness depends on the mind which is within us, and not on the circumstances which are without us' (WTC, XXVII, 67)).

This shift – *away* from Goethe himself, and *towards* his Victorian re-interpreters – is even more perceptible in what is the final part of Tennyson's trio of poems on religious doubt, *In Memoriam*. This work is also linked to 'Voices' in a more specific way, for it includes numerous evocations of church bells.[31] These resound for the first time in XXVIII, in which, as David Goslee observes, they 'evoke enough associations with Tennyson's past and his surroundings that he, like Faust on hearing the Easter chorus, can renounce suicide'.[32] However, in both this section and the similarly nocturnal IV, Tennyson is drawing not only on 'Night', but also on an even more famous Goethean portrayal of self-destruction: *Werther*. In the *Memoirs of Goethe*, the German poet gives an account of his reaction to the suicide of his acquaintance Karl Jerusalem:

> The plan of Werther was instantly conceived. The elements of that composition seemed now to amalgamate, to form a whole, just as water, on the point of freezing in a vase, receives from the slightest

---

[30] Ricks (PT, 209, ll. 397–9, fn) compares the last line cited here to lines 24–5 of 'Ulysses' (and lines 388–90 of 'Voices' might also be compared to that poem). Significantly, a few lines earlier, Tennyson refers to his trances: 'mystic gleams, [. . .] I Such as no language may declare' (ll. 380, 384).
[31] For further links between the two works, see PT, 209, headnote; ll. 32–3, 284, 297, 347–9, 351, 462, fns. Compare also 'Voices', ll. 271–82, and *In Memoriam*, II, XXXIX.
[32] David Goslee, *Tennyson's Characters: 'Strange Faces, Other Minds'* (Iowa City: University of Iowa Press, 1989), p. 101. See Martin, p. 20.

concussion the form of a compact piece of ice. (FA, 1, XIV, Pt III, Bk XIII, p. 636, ll. 31–6 / Goethe, *Memoirs of Goethe*, II, Ch. XIII, p. 45)

As Elaine Jordan demonstrates, Tennyson derives inspiration from this passage in lines 11–12 of IV ('Break, thou deep vase of chilling tears, | That grief hath shaken into frost!'),[33] and a connection to *Werther* may also be discernible in XXVIII. 'How often, when I have lain down in my bed,' exclaims that novel's protagonist, 'have I wished never to wake again!' (Pt II, p. 176, ll. 20–1, 3 November [1772] / p. 159).[34] Werther – who is inconsolable at the loss of his beloved Charlotte – subsequently fulfils this wish, for he shoots himself in the head shortly after midnight on 23 December, and succumbs to his wound at noon on Christmas Eve. In XXVIII, which takes place as '[t]he Christmas bells' ring out, the similarly forlorn Tennyson is tempted by the same unseasonable wish for eternal sleep:

This year I slept and woke with pain,
  I almost wished no more to wake,
  And that my hold on life would break
Before I heard those bells again. (ll. 3, 13–16)[35]

Like 'Voices', however, IV and XXVIII effect a noticeable transformation of their Goethean sources.[36] In the earlier piece, Tennyson's basic unease with the impious act that is suicide had led him to convert the often despairing Faust into a more dauntless figure, who refuses to give in to the nihilistic counselling of the 'voice'. In both IV and XXVIII, it is almost as if this idealised Faust is now engaged in a struggle with his more pusillanimous literary sibling Werther. The former section begins: 'To Sleep I give my powers away' – but this temporary descent into oblivion leads not to the desire for a permanent one, but, instead, to a renewed dialogue with the divided self ('O heart, how fares it with thee now[?]', asks Tennyson at line 5). As in 'Voices', this internal debate concludes at daybreak, when the

---

[33] Elaine Jordan, 'Tennyson's *In Memoriam*—An Echo of Goethe', *Notes and Queries*, o.s. 213 / n.s. 15: 11 (November 1968), 414–15.
[34] See also Chapter 1, p. 60.
[35] Compare 'The Flight' (*PT*, 259), ll. 7–8.
[36] Hallam Tennyson states that XXVIII was one of 'the first written sections' (*Mem.*, I, 109; see also *PT*, 296, XXVIII, fn; S & S, p. 190). It was therefore written shortly after – or perhaps concurrently with – 'Voices'. This may also be true of IV: this section 'seems to follow from the deleted stanza at the end of 3', which 'probably dates from October 1833' (S & S, pp. 165, 164).

speaker affirms his strong commitment to life: 'With morning wakes the will, and cries, | "Thou shalt not be the fool of loss"' (ll. 15–16). This represents, I think, a deliberate contrast to *Werther*, in which a similarly 'dreadful night' leads to the opposite resolution:

> My troubled soul was agitated by a thousand ideas, a thousand different schemes! at length one thought took possession of me, and is now fixed in my heart—I will die. (Pt II, p. 224, ll. 1, 10–12, F. L. / p. 190)[37]

Turning to the concluding lines of section XXVIII, we find that they are the work of an equally 'troubled soul' – but one whose sorrows, unlike the sorrows of Werther, are not entirely unrelieved:

> [Those bells] my troubled spirit rule,
>   For they controlled me when a boy;
>   They bring me sorrow touched with joy,
> The merry merry bells of Yule. (ll. 17–20)

Here, as in section IV, a somewhat idealised Faust seems to be triumphing over Werther, for in an apparent reminiscence of 'Night' (in which the bells arouse 'child-like feeling' (l. 781 / p. 22)) the cheering sound emanating from the church transforms the speaker's yearning for the grave into fond recollections of the cradle.[38]

* * *

---

[37] See also Baynes, 'Tennyson and *Werther*', pp. 310–11.
[38] The influence of *Werther* can also be discerned in sections II and XIII of *In Memoriam*. In his letter of 6 December 1772, Goethe's protagonist refers to 'the fibres of my head'; wishes that he could be 'incorporated' with Nature; and yearningly describes 'a little spot where I had sat under a willow by the side of Charlotte' (Pt II, p. 192, ll. 28–9; p. 194, ll. 31–2 / pp. 174, 177). In *In Memoriam*, II, Tennyson – contemplating, as Werther does in his Farewell Letter, a churchyard and its trees – writes: 'Thy fibres net the dreamless head', and he seems, as he puts it, to 'grow incorporate' into an 'Old Yew' (W, Pt II, p. 262, ll. 5–7 / p. 214; *In Memoriam*, II, ll. 3, 16, 1). Also, the biblical allusion in line 6 of this section, 'And bring the firstling to the flock', could have been suggested by *Cain*, in which Byron refers to 'The firstlings of the flock' (Byron, *Poetical Works*, VI (1991), III. 1. 215). With regard to *In Memoriam*, XIII, Werther's letter of 21 August 1771 (Pt I, p. 108, ll. 16–24 / p. 93) seems to me to be just as plausible a source for lines 1–4 of this section as Ovid's *Heroides* or Milton's 'Sonnet XIX' (see S & S, p. 176). I would argue, moreover, that both II and XIII probably date (like IV and XXVIII) from 1833–4. In *Materials* (I, 127–8), Hallam Tennyson lists the former section as one of the first to be written, and Shatto and Shaw suggest that the latter is also relatively early (S & S, p. 176).

When the bells ring out again in CVI (which dates from 1846 or later), Tennyson's source is not Goethe's *Faust* but, as Hoxie N. Fairchild demonstrates, Bailey's *Festus*.[39] This shift from *Faust* to a related work is, I will argue, part of a broader pattern. In five other later-written sections of *In Memoriam* (XCV, XCVI, CX, CXXIV and the 'Prologue'), Tennyson combines the theme of religious doubt with echoes of texts that are either by, about, or inspired by Goethe. These works include Carlyle's translation of *Meister*; the same author's Goethe criticism; Austin's *Characteristics*; and two of the three 'Victorian *Fausts*' of the 1830s (*Sartor Resartus* and, once again, *Festus*).[40] Although all of these works have obvious links to *Faust*, explicit echoes of *Faust* itself are notable, in these sections, by their absence. This indicates, I think, a deepening of the nascent ambivalence that is suggested by 'Voices'. Although *In Memoriam* finds Tennyson implicitly maintaining his allegiance to the notion that *Faust* is a portrayal of the crisis of faith, he now seems to be turning away from Goethe's drama, and seeking solutions in other, closely related works.

Carlyle had portrayed Goethe as the exemplar of an individual who had successfully overcome religious doubt. In the sections of *In Memoriam* that will be discussed below, Tennyson depicts Hallam in a similar light, and I would argue that in doing so, he is likening his dead friend to the man whom Carlyle had acclaimed as 'the Wisest of our time', and whom Tennyson himself would later describe as 'among the wisest of mankind' (*WTC*, I, Bk II, Ch. IX, p. 153 / p. 142, ll. 29–30; *Mem.*, II, 288).[41] In section LXXIV, he writes:

> dearest, now thy brows are cold,
> I see thee what thou art, and know
> Thy likeness to the wise below. (ll. 5–7; see also LXI, ll. 1–4)

The Goethean element in Tennyson's portrayal of Hallam can be readily discerned in XCV, XCVI and CX (which were probably

---

[39] Hoxie N. Fairchild, '"Wild Bells" in Bailey's *Festus*?', *Modern Language Notes*, 64: 4 (April 1949), 256–8; S & S, pp. 264–5.

[40] The other 'Victorian *Faust*' of the 1830s may be drawn upon elsewhere in *In Memoriam*: Shatto and Shaw suggest that there are echoes of *Paracelsus* in LVI, CXV and CXVIII (S & S, pp. 220, 273–4, 276).

[41] The popularity of *Sartor* seems to have made it something of a Victorian commonplace to describe Goethe as 'wise' (see, for example, Ruskin, *Works*, XXVII, 485). In 1883, Tennyson's acquaintance, the *Faust* translator John Stuart Blackie, published *The Wisdom of Goethe* (Edinburgh: Blackwood, 1883).

written between 1841 and 1850).⁴² In the first-named section, a Carlylean description of Hallam as possessing 'The faith, the vigour, bold to dwell | On doubts that drive the coward back' (ll. 29–30) occurs in a context which (as Turner points out) is suggestive of Book VII, Chapter VIII of *Wilhelm Meister's Apprenticeship*.⁴³ And if, as Motter observes, XCVI⁴⁴ echoes Hallam's sonnet 'Then What is Life' (*WAH*, pp. 91–2), it may also draw on the following passage from *Characteristics*:

> [Goethe] reconciled and harmonized the jarring elements [of the world], [but] he was compelled by [his] spirit of truth to drag many a contradiction that had lain concealed, out of its dark abode, and to place it in a sharp and distinct light. (*CG*, III, 284)

Hallam, similarly, 'touched a jarring lyre at first, | But ever strove to make it true' (ll. 7–8):

> Power was with him in the night,
> Which makes the darkness and the light,
> And dwells not in the light alone. (ll. 18–20)

As Ricks observes, lines 11–12 of this section, 'There lives more faith in honest doubt, | Believe me, than in half the creeds', would appear to be influenced by a line from *Festus*, 'Who never doubted never half believed' (which, in the copy that is at the Research Centre in Lincoln, has a marginal marking next to it).⁴⁵ In section CX, Tennyson writes:

> mine the love that will not tire,
> And, born of love, the vague desire
> That spurs an imitative will. (ll. 18–20; see also LXXX, l. 1)

This draws on the words 'in all men there is a certain vague desire to imitate', from Book II, Chapter II of the *Apprenticeship* (and

---

⁴² Shatto and Shaw (pp. 253, 257) suggest that XCV was written in 1841–2, and XCVI in 1848–50. Section CX is not in the Trinity Manuscript, which may indicate composition after 1842.
⁴³ Turner, p. 122; *WM*, Vol. IX, p. 860, l. 13–p. 861, l. 23 / XXIV, 62–3.
⁴⁴ Lewes (II, 390–1) cites lines 11–17 of this section, and applies them to Goethe's own religious development.
⁴⁵ Bailey, *Festus*, p. 63; *PT*, 296, XCVI, ll. 11–12, fn. Compare also *Aids to Reflection*: 'He never truly believed, who was not made first sensible and convinced of unbelief' (Coleridge, *Collected Works*, IX (1993), 107).

perhaps also on Carlyle's assertion, in the essay 'Goethe's Works', that 'The first product of love is imitation' (*WM*, Vol. IX, p. 434, ll. 3–6 / XXIII, 111; *WTC*, XXVII, 394)).

The pattern that can be detected in XCV, XCVI and CX – a strong engagement with works and themes that are linked to *Faust*, but an avoidance of any direct engagement with *Faust* itself – is continued in CXXIV. In this pivotal section, which has been conjecturally dated to between 1845 and 1850,[46] Tennyson affirms his belief in God, amidst a plethora of Carlylean echoes, as well as a number of revealing links to 'Voices'. In line 10 – which is part of what was, as late as March 1850, the opening stanza of this section[47] – Tennyson revives the inner dialogue of the earlier poem ('I heard a voice "believe no more"'), and as Shatto and Shaw observe, there is another similarity to 'Voices' in lines 13–14 ('A warmth within the breast would melt | The freezing reason's colder part').[48] These two critics further demonstrate that the next two lines contain an echo of *Sartor*, Book II, Chapter VII, 'The Everlasting No'.[49] I propose that Tennyson turns to this chapter because it is (as Metzger points out) 'filled with echoes from *Faust*'.[50] All of these echoes relate, moreover, to the university scenes, on which Tennyson had previously drawn in 'Voices'. 'Some comfort it would have been,' declares Carlyle's protagonist Teufelsdröckh,

> could I, like a Faust, have fancied myself tempted and tormented of the Devil. [. . .] From Suicide a certain after-shine (*Nachschein*) of Christianity withheld me. [. . .] Almost since earliest memory I had shed no tear; or once only when I, murmuring half-audibly, recited Faust's Deathsong, that wild *Selig der den er im Siegesglanze findet* [*sic*] (Happy whom *he* finds in Battle's splendour). [. . .] Having no hope, neither had I any definite Fear, were it of Man or of Devil. (pp. 133, 134 / p. 124, ll. 16–17, 38; p. 125, ll. 1, 12–15, 17–18)

Rodger L. Tarr points out that the last sentence quoted here echoes Faust's monologue at the beginning of 'Night'; Metzger observes that the ending of that scene is alluded to in the reference to suicide; and

---

[46] S & S, pp. 8, 283.
[47] *PT*, 296, CXXIV, ll. 1–8, fn.
[48] S & S, p. 284; see 'Voices', l. 284, and, especially, ll. 422–3 ('My frozen heart began to beat, | Remembering its ancient heat'). Compare also 'Confessions', ll. 81–2; *WM*, Vol. IX, Bk II, Ch. XIII, p. 491, l. 34–p. 492, l. 1 / XXIII, 168.
[49] S & S, p. 284.
[50] Metzger, '*Sartor*', p. 323.

the words beginning '*Selig der*' are misquoted from 'Study [II]'.⁵¹ This proliferation of Faustian echoes is intended to prepare the reader for the chapter's climax, in which Teufelsdröckh achieves a definitive victory over religious doubt. It takes the form of an implicit confrontation with that Enlightenment *philosophe* and 'spirit of Denial' Mephistopheles (*WTC*, XXVI, 158):

> Thus had the EVERLASTING NO (*das ewige Nein*) pealed authoritatively through all the recesses of my Being, of my ME; and then was it that my whole ME stood up, in native God-created majesty, and with emphasis recorded its Protest. [. . .] The Everlasting No had said: 'Behold, thou art fatherless, outcast, and the Universe is mine (the Devil's);' to which my whole Me now made answer: '*I am not thine, but Free, and forever hate thee!*' (*SR*, p. 135 / p. 126, ll. 7–10, 12–15)

Tennyson echoes the words 'my whole ME stood up' in the lines 'And like a man in wrath the heart | Stood up and answered "I have felt"' (CXXIV, ll. 15–16). As in 'Voices' more than a decade earlier, he is associating *Faust* with religious doubt and its resolution. On this occasion, however, he turns not to the Goethean *Faust*, but to the miniature Victorian *Faust* that is 'The Everlasting No'. And in *this* text, the links to *Part One* – numerous though they are – are little more than a clothing for Carlyle's own personal philosophy: the passage cited above has no precedent in Goethe's play, but relates, instead, to a quasi-religious conversion experience that Carlyle had in Edinburgh around 1822.⁵² As in lines 379–99 of 'Voices', the receptivity to the external world that we find in *Faust* has been replaced by a Carlylean preference for inner experience.

Tennyson might well have noticed that the phrase 'my whole ME stood up, in native God-created majesty' would appear, in turn, to hark back to some words from Carlyle's translation of the *Apprenticeship* ('all that had long been gliding dimly through his soul stood up in bright distinctness before it' (Vol. IX, Bk I, Ch. IX, p. 386, ll. 14–15 / XXIII, 62)). It is to this work that Tennyson turns in lines 1–8 and 17–20 of CXXIV (which were probably added in spring 1850). The phrase 'your dreary, paltry nets which men have spun' (*WM*, Vol. IX, Bk VIII, Ch. IX, p. 965, l. 16 / XXIV, 163) would appear to be echoed at line 8: 'The petty cobwebs we have spun'.

---

⁵¹ *SR*, ed. Tarr, p. 353 (refers to *F*, l. 369 / p. 7); Metzger, '*Sartor*', pp. 323–4; *F*, ll. 1573, 1576 / p. 53.
⁵² *SR*, ed. Tarr, pp. 354–5.

Also, the following passage is a plausible source for lines 19–20, 'Then was I as a child that cries, | But, crying, knows his father near':

> 'My child!' cried [Wilhelm], 'my child! Thou art indeed mine, if that word can comfort thee. Thou art mine! I will keep thee, I will never forsake thee!' [Mignon's] tears continued flowing. At last she raised herself; a faint gladness shone upon her face. 'My father!' cried she, 'thou wilt not forsake me? [probably an allusion to Psalms 22: 1 / Matthew 27: 46 / Mark 15: 34]⁵³ Wilt be my father? I am thy child!' (Vol. IX, Bk II, Ch. XIV, p. 498, ll. 32-8 / XXIII, 175)

Tennyson's use of the *Apprenticeship* in CXXIV might be broadly compared to Carlyle's use of *Faust* in 'The Everlasting No'. The first of this section's two echoes of Goethe's novel has a certain appropriateness, for the passage on which it draws includes references to 'unbelief', and 'dreadful doubts' (Vol. IX, Bk VIII, Ch. IX, p. 964, ll. 36, 37; p. 966, l. 26 / XXIV, 162, 164). However, this passage also expresses a characteristically Goethean faith in the wisdom and beneficence of Nature – which is precisely what Tennyson is *rejecting* in lines 5–6 ('I found Him not in world or sun, | Or eagle's wing, or insect's eye' (*WM*, Vol. IX, Bk VIII, Ch. IX, p. 965, ll. 24–37 / XXIV, 163)). His second echo of *Meister* may well have been prompted by Goethe's brief biblical allusion during the tearful exchange between Wilhelm and Mignon, and the forceful contrast it presents with Christ's apparent despair on the cross. Taken as a whole, however, this scene has no real connection with religious doubt. Like 'The Everlasting No', therefore, CXXIV makes enthusiastic use of Goethe's imagery – but only as a vehicle for its author's own, very different concerns.⁵⁴

This ambivalence is also perceptible right at the start of *In Memoriam*. In the opening stanza of the first numbered section of the poem, Tennyson refers, in his own words, 'to Goethe's creed' (EE, III, 225).⁵⁵ However, the importance of this reference diminished considerably in the course of the poem's composition. As Shatto and Shaw observe, manuscript evidence suggests that this stanza was 'at

---

[53] 'My God, my God, why hast thou forsaken me?' Tennyson described these words as 'that passionate cry' (*Mem.*, I, 326).

[54] The numerous echoes of *Meister* in *In Memoriam* constitute a partial exception to the pattern for which I am arguing, for in this case, Tennyson is drawing directly on Goethe's work. It is also, however, Carlyle's work.

[55] See 'Last words', pp. 200–3.

one time intended [. . .] to be an epigraph for the entire sequence'.[56] If it did have this status at some point, this was lost when it was incorporated into section I, and its prominence was further reduced by the composition of the unnumbered section that Ricks refers to as the poem's 'Prologue'. In spite of its position at the beginning of the text, the latter was one of the last passages to be written, and the difference in spirit between it and the rest of *In Memoriam* has often been noted: here, for what is, perhaps, the only time in the whole work, 'Christian faith [. . .] is [. . .] completely triumphant' (Henry Sidgwick, cited in *Mem.*, I, 304).[57] I would suggest that this can be partly accounted for by the fact that in prefacing his reference to Goethe with the 'Prologue', Tennyson is, once again, turning away from *Faust*, and towards one of its Victorian progeny.

As discussed in the Introduction, Tennyson first read *Festus* in November 1846, and he corresponded with its author in 1848.[58] Robert Birley argues that '[t]here are certainly some Festian echoes in the introductory poem to *In Memoriam*' (which was written in 1849), but he does not provide any details.[59] In terms of the overall structure of *Festus*, the most obviously analogous passage to Tennyson's 'Prologue' is the 'Proem' (pp. v–xvi), in which Bailey writes:

O God! Thou wondrous One in Three,
   As mortals must Thee deem;
Thou only canst be said to be,
   We but at best to seem. (p. xi)

Tennyson's 'Prologue' begins with a similar contrast of divine greatness and human limitations:

Strong Son of God, immortal Love,
   Whom we, that have not seen thy face,
   By faith, and faith alone, embrace,
Believing where we cannot prove. (ll. 1–4)[60]

---

[56] S & S, p. 162; *TA*, XI, 9; XVI, 3.
[57] See also Eleanor Bustin Mattes, *'In Memoriam': The Way of a Soul. A Study of Some Influences that Shaped Tennyson's Poem* (New York: Exposition Press, 1951), pp. 90–100; S & S, pp. 159–60.
[58] See pp. 27–8; *LAT*, I, 283 ([February or March 1848]), p. 294 (12 September 1848(?)).
[59] Robert Birley, *Sunk without Trace: Some Forgotten Masterpieces Reconsidered* (London: Hart-Davis, 1962), p. 188.
[60] In a footnote, Ricks compares lines 2–3 to 1 Peter 1: 8.

In the next line ('Thine are these orbs of light and shade'), Tennyson may be fusing echoes of two phrases that can be found in later passages in *Festus* ('Thine, Lord! are all the elements and worlds', and 'orb of shade and shine' (pp. 134, 146)).[61] Returning to the 'Proem', we find that it continues with a reference to the fatal power that the Deity wields over life: 'Thou may'st slay', writes Bailey (p. xi; see also p. xii). Tennyson's 'Prologue' continues by giving expression to much the same sentiment: 'Thou madest Death', he writes (l. 7). In both texts, however, this is swiftly qualified by a recognition of divine justice: Bailey refers to 'Thy right will' (p. xii), whilst Tennyson declares that 'Thou art just' (l. 12).

In the opening scene in heaven, which follows the 'Proem' to *Festus*, Bailey writes:

Systems arise,
Or a world dies,
Each constant hour in air;
But creature mind,
In Heaven confined,
Lives on like Thee, God! there. (p. 2)

Tennyson's 'Prologue', too, evokes the ephemerality of 'systems' (albeit in a different sense), and contrasts this with the enduring greatness of God:

Our little systems have their day;
   They have their day and cease to be:
   They are but broken lights of thee,
And thou, O Lord, art more than they. (ll. 17–20)[62]

There is one further echo of *Festus* in the 'Prologue'. On pages 149–50 of his poem, Bailey describes how a 'boyish bard', working amidst 'night and stars', was greeted by a 'sunbeam', which 'swerved and grew': 'And so may sunbeams ever guide his pen,' he writes, 'And God his heart, who lights the morn of men'. He returns to this

---

[61] 'Orb[s]' is one of Bailey's favourite words; it is used in *Festus* on more than forty occasions.

[62] Compare also Carlyle, 'Signs of the Times': 'our systems and theories are but so many froth-eddies or sandbanks, which from time to time [Nature] casts up, and washes away' (*WTC*, XXVII, 71). A few pages later, he writes: 'We have our little *theory* on all human and divine things' (ibid. p. 76). This resembles Tennyson's '[o]ur little systems', as well as 'Thou seemest human and divine' ('Prologue', l. 13).

image on page 235, where he writes: 'the truth fronts us, beaming out of darkness'. Tennyson, too, refers to a growing beam of light amidst the gloom, and much as in *Festus*, it is portrayed as a link to truth and the divine: 'And yet we trust [faith] comes from thee, | A beam in darkness: let it grow' (ll. 23–4).

Tennyson appended to the 'Prologue' the date of its composition, '1849'. It may be significant that that year also marked the centenary of Goethe's birth: perhaps Tennyson, in highlighting this date, was trying to indicate that his sense of spiritual kinship with the German poet was undiminished. There is, however, no escaping the fact that in contrast to the opening stanza of section I, the 'Prologue' cannot be said to be an expression of Goethe's creed. Indeed, it could be far more accurately described as expression of Bailey's. W. H. Bruford's insight concerning the Victorian popularity of *Festus* is, I think, of considerable relevance here: 'only the longing of the age for a new religion', he writes, 'can explain how this rhetoric was ever taken for poetry'.[63] It is because Tennyson has failed to find a renewed form of Christianity in the works of Goethe that he turns, instead, to one of his imitators. So just a year before the completion of *In Memoriam*, the author of *Faust* yields priority to the author of *Festus*.

Tennyson first turns to the Carlylean view of *Faust* and its author in 'Confessions'. In all probability, he is hoping that Goethe's powerful drama of mental division – and, reputedly, of honest doubt – will help him to find a way out of his 'damnèd vacillating state', and to achieve at least some kind of rapprochement with his 'Brothers in Christ' ('Confessions', ll. 190, 29). A few years later, the composition of 'Voices' signals both a florescence and a fading of these hopes. On the one hand, the poem's numerous verbal echoes provide clear evidence of an intensified engagement with *Faust*. On the other, the divided *form* of Goethe's drama now acquires a new lease of life, as a means of expressing Tennyson's divided response to it. Two early-written sections of *In Memoriam* read almost like a continuation of 'Voices', but in five later ones (all of which deal with the crisis of faith), the picture changes once again. Here, although Goethe is, indirectly, a pervasive presence, his masterpiece is not, and one is drawn to conclude that Tennyson feels more at home with the religious outlook of works like *Sartor* and *Festus*. It looks very much as if the alleged spiritual leader is now being eschewed in favour of his disciples.

---

[63] W. H. Bruford, 'Goethe's Reputation in England since 1832', in *Essays on Goethe*, ed. Rose, pp. 187–206 (p. 197).

It is quite possible, however, that Tennyson's increasingly ambivalent attitude towards Goethe's religious outlook was never a conscious one, and that he remained at least a nominal adherent of the Carlylean view of the German poet right to the end of his life. Emily Tennyson may to some extent be reflecting her husband's opinions when, in a letter to their son Hallam in 1872, she misquotes *Faust* in support of her strong belief in the value of prayer ('That is why the "Du bist der Augenblick," is it not that Goethe calls it, is so unappreciably important' (Emily Tennyson, *Letters*, no. 273, p. 289, 3 November)).[64] As I will argue in the next chapter, a similar pattern of increasing (but largely unconscious) ambivalence is also apparent in Tennyson's response to Goethe's view of the natural world.

---

[64] In his footnote to the four German words in quotation marks, James O. Hoge writes: 'Literally, "You are the moment." In all probability she has in mind the famous lines from [the pact scene of] *Faust I*' (ibid. p. 289). Hoge then cites this passage, which is rendered by Hayward as: 'If I ever say to the passing moment—"Stay, thou art so fair!" then mayst thou cast me into chains; then will I readily perish' (ll. 1699–1702 / p. 58).

Chapter 5

'Unveil thyself!': *Faust* and the Natural World

Nature is a central theme in numerous passages in *Faust*. Tennyson draws on several of these in a lengthy series of poems that spans his entire career, and which begins with the early works 'Chorus' and 'Inscription by a Brook'. But although these two pieces are sometimes close to Faustian Nature poetry in terms of language, they are often remote from it in spirit, and the same can be said of two texts that post-date the death of Hallam: the opening stanzas of 'On a Mourner', and the conclusion to 'The Two Voices'. This striking ambivalence deepens considerably in *In Memoriam*, LIV–LVI. These three sections can be seen as exploring the conflict between contemporary science, and the view of Nature that Tennyson had absorbed (partly via Carlyle and Austin) from German literature. The closing lines of *In Memoriam* may represent – like the 1867 lyric 'The Higher Pantheism' – an attempt at rapprochement with the Goethean view of the natural world. It is possible, however, that Tennyson's deepest feelings on this subject are expressed (albeit vicariously) by the embittered speaker of the 1881 piece 'Despair'. But even that work is not quite Tennyson's last word on this subject, for he echoes Faustian Nature poetry on one final occasion shortly before his death.

Although it is hardly correct to call Goethe a Romantic, this description seems broadly applicable to his portrayal of Nature, both in *Faust* and in much of his other work. In the following passages from the Chorus of the Archangels, and Faust's 'River and rivulet' and 'Pulses of life' monologues, the natural world has – as in Wordsworth – a potently inspirational effect on the onlooker:

> Thy aspect gives strength to the angels, though none can fathom thee, and all thy sublime works are glorious as on the first day. (ll. 267–70 / p. 2)

[The countryside] is the true heaven of the multitude; big and little are huzzaing joyously. Here, I am a man—here, I may venture to be one. (ll. 938–40 / p. 29)

Thou, too, Earth, wert constant this night, and breathedst newly invigorated at my feet. Thou art already beginning to encompass me with enjoyment, thou stirrest and excitest a vigorous resolve—to aspire eternally towards the most exalted state of being. (ll. 4681–5 / Hay. 2, pp. 85–6)

Goethe also resembles Wordsworth in that he can, during most of his career, be reasonably described as a monist or pantheist (he studied the works of Spinoza, and for a brief period in the 1780s regarded himself as his disciple).[1] In his poem 'In the solemn burial-vault',[2] he refers to God and Nature as a single entity, 'Gott-Natur' (FA, 1, II, p. 685, l. 32 / Goethe, trans. Luke, p. 327), and in 'Prelude' – a translation of which is included in Austin's *Characteristics* – he expresses a deep hostility towards the Deistic separation of the two:

What were a God that impelled but from without?
That caused the All[3] to revolve mechanically?
Him it beseems to move the world from within,
To foster Nature in Himself, Himself in Nature. (FA, 1, II, p. 489, ll. 15–18 / CG, II, 198)

The dualism that Goethe is here scorning is *presupposed* in the essay by Hallam that was debated by the Apostles on 5 December 1829: 'Whether the existence of an intelligent First Cause is deducible from the phenomena of the universe' (*LAT*, I, 43). Tennyson, the record informs us, voted 'no' (ibid. I, 43). This sober view of Nature is reflected in his poetry, in much of which, the natural world provides inspiration only if it is connected with humankind, and personal experience: 'A known landskip [*sic*]', he wrote in 1838, 'is to me an old friend, that continually talks to me of my own youth and half-forgotten things, and does more for me than many an old friend that I know' (*LAT*, I, 166 [October or November(?)]). There is no 'Gott-Natur' in Tennyson: 'I believe in God,' he remarked towards the end of his life, 'not from what I see in Nature, but from what I find in man' (*Mem.*,

---

[1] Boyle, I (1991), 353, 384–5.
[2] Tennyson's admiration for this poem is recorded in *Mem.*, II, 504.
[3] Austin's over-literal translation of *All* ('universe').

II, 374). In much of his work, we can discern (in the words of Joseph Warren Beach) 'an implicit or explicit dualism', which contrasts quite sharply with the monism – or pantheism – of Goethe.[4]

This divergence of outlook is already apparent in both 'Chorus, in an Unpublished Drama, Written Very Early' (*PT*, 101, *c.* 1824(?)), and 'Inscription by a Brook' (*PT*, 191; dated 1833 (*TA*, XXIX, 33)).[5] Ricks notes that the former piece draws on Shelley's 'On Death', and also, perhaps, on his 'Epipsychidion', and *Prometheus Unbound*.[6] However, an equally strong influence is the Chorus of the Archangels from Shelley's 'Scenes' (the German text of which Tennyson 'often quoted with lavish praise' (ll. 243–70 / PBS, I, ll. 1–28; *Mem.*, II, 504, fn)).[7] Shelley's translation preserves the original's tetrameters, and, also, its rhyme scheme, which is *ababcdcd* in each of the first three sections. Both metre and rhyme scheme are duplicated by Tennyson in 'Chorus', except that he adds a final *ee* to all three stanzas (and omits the four-line '*Chorus of the Three*' at the end (ll. 267–70 /

---

[4] Joseph Warren Beach, *The Concept of Nature in Nineteenth-Century English Poetry* (New York: Pageant, 1956), p. 408.

[5] Ricks suggests that 'Chorus' was written around the same time as *The Devil and the Lady*, which dates from *c.* 1823–4 (*PT*, 101, 2, headnotes). As he points out, the phrase 'the varied earth' occurs in both (*PT*, 2, II. 1. 7; *PT*, 101, l. 1, and fn), and there are also a number of other similarities (see *The Devil*, I. 4. 49–50; II. 1. 29; 2. 63; III. 2. 78; 'Chorus', ll. 21–2, 3, 6, 22, 2). *The Devil* is based on a story set in Hildesheim in Germany, and it may have been partly inspired by Marlowe's *Dr Faustus* (*PT*, 2, headnote). Perhaps Goethe's version of the Faust legend was also an influence: as was mentioned in the Introduction, in Trinity Notebook 19, which contains one of the three surviving manuscripts of *The Devil*, Tennyson has written out, in German, the first one and a half lines of Goethe's *Hermann und Dorothea* (Alfred Lord Tennyson, Trinity Notebook 0.15.19 (Trinity College Library, Cambridge), folio 73, verso (this page is not reproduced in *TA*); FA, 1, VIII / I, p. 807, ll. 1–2). Also, the opening speech of Tennyson's play is reminiscent, once again, of the Archangels' Chorus: both passages evoke the power of Nature; both come right at the start of the text; and both are immediately followed by the appearance of the devil (compare, especially, *F*, ll. 244, 268–70 / PBS, I, second line of Shelley's fn to l. 28; ll. 26–8; *The Devil*, I. 1. 7, 21–4).

[6] *PT*, 101, headnote.

[7] Tennyson returned to the Chorus in 'This Earth is wondrous, change on change' (*PT*, 201; see Chapter 2, p. 84, fn 41), and also, I think, in lines 22–31 of 'The Golden Year' (*PT*, 276). Note that the second of Shelley's two 'Scenes' includes the proverbial phrase 'the golden age' (l. 4083 / PBS, II, l. 284). Compare also Leonard's belief in 'The Golden Year' in Tennyson's poem, and Princess Leonora's discussion of 'The Golden Age' in Goethe's play *Torquato Tasso*, which Tennyson admired (FA, 1, V, pp. 731–834, II. 1. 970–1047; *Mem.*, I, 277–8).

PBS, I, ll. 25–8)). Shelley's rhyme of 'deep' with 'sleep' becomes Tennyson's rhyme of 'sleeps' with 'deeps', and there is a considerable amount of other vocabulary that is common to both pieces (PBS, I, ll. 13, 15; 'Chorus', ll. 26, 28).[8] Also, Shelley's footnote, which refers to Goethe's original as an 'astonishing Chorus', may well have helped to suggest both Tennyson's title, and his repeated use of the word '[a]stonishment' (PBS, I, l. 28, fn; 'Chorus', ll. 10, 20, 30).

The Chorus of the Archangels portrays the natural world on the grandest of scales, its three principal stanzas describing, respectively, the universe, the earth and the elements. It represents a very pure kind of Nature poetry, for not a single human being is anywhere mentioned – and this may well explain why Tennyson's admiration for it was mixed, it would seem, with unease. Throughout this passage, Goethe depicts a natural world which – although undeniably forceful – is also orderly, purposeful and harmonious. In the 'Chorus' of Tennyson, however, the balance shifts from harmony to force, and order and purpose seem to evaporate. For example, he takes the phrase 'The sun makes music', and turns it into something more unruly: 'Each sun which from the centre flings | Grand music' (l. 243 / PBS, I, l. 1; 'Chorus', ll. 21–2). In Goethe's text, orbits are 'predestined', and 'rocks and Ocean' move swiftly '[o]nward' (ll. 245, 257 / PBS, I, ll. 3, 14–15). In Tennyson's, however, comets are 'lawless' and 'wayward', and the 'roving sea' is a 'rapid waste' (ll. 27, 29, 2). The two pieces also exhibit a broader contrast, which is, I think, no less important. The words of Goethe's Chorus can be said to form a link between God and Nature, for this vivid evocation of the earthly comes to us from the mouths of angels in heaven. In the English poet's 'Chorus', however, the natural world is implicitly secularised, the Archangels being replaced by a nameless human speaker. For Tennyson – unlike Goethe – unpeopled Nature is anarchic, and heaven, it would seem, is elsewhere.[9]

If 'Inscription by a Brook' represents a more positive response to Faustian Nature poetry, that is probably because the scene on which it draws describes a *populated* landscape. To quote Beach again, when Tennyson evokes 'rural country', it is 'almost invariably

---

[8] For example: 'rapid', 'change[s]', 'thunder', 'strength' (PBS, I, ll. 9, 24, 4, 5 (and 25); 'Chorus', ll. 2, 10 (and 20 and 30), 28, 29).

[9] Another Nature lyric that was 'written very early', 'The Dell of E—' from *Poems by Two Brothers* (PT, 9; published 1827), is broadly reminiscent of Werther's letters of 9 May and 15 September 1772 (Pt II, p. 150, l. 10–p. 154, l. 9; p. 168, l. 3–p. 170, l. 20 / pp. 137–41, 149–52).

stamped with the associations of immemorial social use. It carries accordingly the emotional freight implied in the loved humanity of which it is an expression'.[10] Humanity is abundantly represented at the beginning of the scene 'Before the Gate' in *Faust*, in which exchanges between a 'TOWNSMAN', 'ANOTHER TOWNSMAN' and a 'THIRD TOWNSMAN' are immediately followed by a dialogue between 'AN OLD WOMAN' and some 'pretty young' girls (ll. 846–83 / pp. 26–7). Shortly thereafter, as the crowd wanders into the surrounding countryside, Faust begins a monologue (which has already been referred to in Chapter 4): 'River and rivulet are freed from ice by the gay quickening glance of the spring' (ll. 903–4 / p. 28). All of these elements leave their mark on 'Inscription':

> Townsmen, or of the hamlet, young and old,
> Whithersoever you may wander now,
> Where'er you roam from, [. . .]
> [. . .]
> Pause here. The murmurs of the rivulet,
> [. . .]
> Are pleasant from the early Spring. (ll. 1–3, 5, 7)[11]

But although the peopled landscape of 'Before the Gate' seems to be much more congenial to Tennyson than the empty one of the Archangels' Chorus, 'Inscription' still does not portray the natural world as the kind of inspirational force that it is in *Faust*. The 'River and rivulet' speech describes how the townspeople are 'raised up to the open light of day. [. . .] [T]he mass is scattering itself through the gardens and fields' (ll. 928–30 / p. 29). Nature has a very different effect in Tennyson's poem:

> would you waste an hour,
> Or sleep through one brief dream upon the grass, –
> Pause here. (ll. 3–5)

Whereas Goethe's townspeople are physically and emotionally 'raised up' by the surrounding countryside, their Tennysonian counterparts

---

[10] Beach, p. 406.

[11] Tennyson might have associated 'River and rivulet' with one member of 'loved humanity' in particular, for Hayward's note on it could easily have reminded him of his recent trip to the Rhineland with Hallam: 'To understand Faust's position in this speech, the reader must fancy a town on a river, like most of those upon the Rhine' (Hay. 1, p. 221; see *LAHH*, no. 180, 16 July 1832, pp. 613–14).

are supine, the murmurous rivulet inducing lethargy and oblivion. The natural world, which in *Faust* is revivifying, is, in 'Inscription', pleasantly soporific.[12]

It was against this unpropitious background of philosophical disagreement that Tennyson, shortly after Hallam's death, turned to the scene 'A pleasant neighbourhood' in *Part Two* (already discussed in Chapter 3), in which Faust is revivified after the death of Gretchen.[13] The specific agent of his renewal is the natural world, for the sunrise that is described in his 'Pulses of life' monologue takes place amidst the mountains of the Alps:

> The pulses of life beat with renewed vigour, mildly to greet the etherial [*sic*] dawn. [. . .] The world lies already rapt in the glimmering haze of morn, the wood resounds with thousand-voiced life; within—without the vale the streaks of mist are streaming; yet heaven's clearness sinks down into the depths, and bough and branch, revivified, sprout out from the streaming abyss where they have slept immersed. [. . .] Look up!—The giant peaks of the mountains already announce the most solemn hour. They are permitted to enjoy thus early the everlasting light, which later will be turned on us down here below. Now new brilliancy and distinctness are lavished on the green-embedded Alpine meads. [. . .] The cataract roaring through the rocks—I gaze upon [it] with ever-growing transport. It rolls from fall to fall, ever and anon scattering itself into a thousand streams, whizzing foam on foam aloft into the air. But how gloriously ascending with this storm, the alternating consistency of the variegated bow expands its arch. (ll. 4679–80, 4686–91, 4695–9, 4716–22 / Hay. 2, pp. 85, 86)

Tennyson might have associated this inspirational Alpine sunrise – with its mists, mountains, forests, cataracts and rainbows – with

---

[12] The Nature imagery of another poem that can be dated to 1833 may also be influenced by Goethe. In the German author's *Memoirs*, a reference to 'poets and critics' is followed by a discussion of different types of 'minds', some of which are compared to 'shrubs' and 'flowers' (FA, 1, XIV, Pt II, Bk VIII, p. 364, l. 27; p. 365, ll. 13, 18, 19 / Goethe, *Memoirs of Goethe*, I, Ch. VIII, pp. 246, 247–8). Compare 'Poets and Critics' (*PT*, 204): 'Minds on this round earth of ours | Vary like the leaves and flowers' (ll. 3–4). Tennyson's friend Thomas Herbert Warren remarks that this poem 'always seems to me in tone and form very like Goethe' (T. H. Warren, 'Centennial Recollections', in *Interviews and Recollections*, ed. Page, pp. 154–8 (p. 157)).

[13] See pp. 97–9, 101.

two of Hallam's last letters to Somersby, which were written in the Austrian Alps on 24 and 30–31 August 1833:[14]

> I felt my spirits rise at feeling myself once more among my old favorite objects. [. . .] Next morning [. . .] began in clouds, but [. . .] the sun exerted his power, & broke them cheeringly in all directions. [. . .] First of all were discerned the dim outlines of surrounding mountains, looming through the mist; then appeared, like floating islands of the air, whole peaks & crags in clear sunlight; & in a few minutes or moments the large volumes of cloud were completely rolled away, save here & there a bright silver zone girdling the pine-forest, or some looser form of exhalation steaming slowly upwards. [. . .] This cataract [the Fall of the Traun, near Gmunden] is remarkable for [. . .] the beauty of the curve made by the principal body of water; [. . .] [and] the still greater beauty of the [Iris]; I never saw a brighter rainbow.[15]

The broad similarity between Hallam's two letters and 'A pleasant neighbourhood' means that this particular piece of Faustian Nature poetry might well have had, for Tennyson, a poignant connection with 'loved humanity'.

This may be one reason why he turned to it in late 1833. In 'On a Mourner' (*PT*, 216), which was drafted in October of that year,[16] Tennyson seems to be trying to convince himself that *his* pulses, too, can beat with renewed vigour, and that the natural world is indeed a pleasant neighbourhood:

> Nature [. . .]
> [. . .]
> [. . .] on my heart a finger lays,
>   Saying, 'Beat, mournful heart: the time
> Is pleasant & the woods & ways
>   Are pleasant. [. . .]' (*TA*, XI, 48)

The influence of 'A pleasant neighbourhood' – and of the 'Pulses of life' monologue in particular – is more unequivocal in the conclusion

---

[14] '[B]oth AT and Emily read AHH's letters from Europe' (*LAHH*, p. 785, fn 1).
[15] *LAHH*, no. 245, pp. 773, 774; no. 246, p. 782. See also no. 246, pp. 780, 781; no. 247, p. 784 (6 September 1833).
[16] Compare lines 1–2 of this poem and *DC*, Vol. I, Canto XI, p. 59 / ll. 103–4.

to 'The Two Voices' (*PT*, 209, ll. 403–62),[17] in which the speaker emerges into a 'blissful neighbourhood', where 'Nature's living motion lent | The pulse of hope to discontent' (ll. 430, 449–50).[18] It is likely that part of Goethe's opening stage direction, 'Song, accompanied by Æolian Harps', helps to prompt Tennyson's reference to 'an Æolian Harp that wakes | No certain air' (*F*, stage direction before l. 4613 / Hay. 2, p. 85; 'Voices', ll. 436–7). Faust's description of the manner in which 'the variegated bow expands its arch [. . .] diffusing all around showers' may well have suggested the words 'From out my sullen heart a power | Broke, like the rainbow from the shower' (*F*, ll. 4722, 4724 / Hay. 2, p. 86; 'Voices', ll. 443–4). Another line from the 'Pulses of life' speech, 'the wood resounds with thousand-voiced life', becomes 'The woods were filled so full with song' (*F*, l. 4687 / Hay. 2, p. 86; 'Voices', l. 455). And the lingering connection to *Part One* that is provided by Tennyson's pealing church bells (l. 408) is continued by the townspeople who

---

[17] The conclusion is generally believed to have been written later than the main body of the poem, which dates from 1833 (neither Edmund Lushington nor James Spedding had any knowledge of it until some time after that date (Hallam Tennyson, *Materials*, I, 246; Peter Allen, *The Cambridge Apostles: The Early Years* (Cambridge: Cambridge University Press, 1978), p. 168)). However, both of the two manuscripts of 'Voices' in Trinity Notebook 15 are followed by numerous stubs, as is the one in Trinity Notebook 22, and it is possible that the missing pages included drafts of the conclusion (Alfred Lord Tennyson, Trinity Notebook 0.15.15 (Trinity College Library, Cambridge); after folio 5 (six stubs); after folio 10 (seven stubs); Trinity Notebook 0.15.22 (Trinity College Library, Cambridge); after folio 14 (more than twenty stubs)). Also, when the poem was first published, it was dated simply '1833'. The conclusion's echoes of 'A pleasant neighbourhood' would be consistent with composition towards the end of that year.

[18] The influence of 'A pleasant neighbourhood' is also apparent a little earlier in 'Voices'. In a footnote to his translation of this scene, Hayward writes: 'The image, here presented, was finely applied by Mr. Macaulay in his article on Dryden, in the Edinburgh Review: "The Sun illuminates the hills whilst it is still below the horizon, and truth is discovered by the highest minds only a little before it becomes manifest to the multitude"' (Hay. 2, p. 86). Tennyson echoes these words in lines 79–81:

'The highest-mounted mind,' he said,
'Still sees the sacred morning spread
The silent summit overhead. [. . .]'

Lines 361–2 also suggest 'A pleasant neighbourhood': 'Some vague emotion of delight | In gazing up an Alpine height'.

wander through lines 409–24, for they can be plausibly traced (as in 'Inscription') to 'Before the Gate'.

In both 'Mourner' and 'Voices', however, there is perceptible discord in amongst the echoes. In 'A pleasant neighbourhood', the inspirational power of the natural world does not derive from any extraneous human associations, and Nature does not provide Faust with an ersatz for the departed Margaret (in his 'Pulses of life' monologue, there are only a couple of lines in which the earth is personified).[19] In contrast, the following passage from the 1833 draft of 'Mourner' suggests that for Tennyson, the natural world can revivify only if it is invested with *human* qualities, such as speech and sympathy:

> '[. . .] Come beat a little quicker now,
>   When all things own my quickening breath
> Thy friend is mute: his brows are low
>   But I am with thee till thy death.'
> Some such kind words to me she saith. (*TA*, XI, 48)

This human voice emanating from Nature is also heard in the conclusion to 'The Two Voices' – although there, it is considerably weaker, a mere 'whisper breathing low' (l. 434). It may not be a coincidence that this widely criticised passage is also a less distinguished piece of poetry: when Tennysonian Nature is only lightly personified, it struggles to convince. Elsewhere in the conclusion to 'Voices', further contrasts with *Faust* are revealed by the echoes of 'Before the Gate'. Goethe – a worshipper of Nature – guides his townsfolk *out* of 'the venerable gloom of churches', and *into* the 'true heaven' that is the surrounding countryside (ll. 927, 938 / p. 29). In 'Voices', however, the more dualistic Tennyson sends them back in the opposite direction: 'On to God's house the people prest', he writes (l. 409). In both this poem and 'On a Mourner', an attempt to derive emotional assuagement from Faustian Nature poetry is threatening to turn, instead, into a philosophical argument about the status of the natural world.

During the lengthy gestation of *In Memoriam* (1833–50), Tennyson's ambivalent attitude towards Goethe's view of Nature became more complicated still, for he would have been increasingly aware that the German's outlook ran counter to the findings of contemporary science. As Leonée Ormond observes, Tennyson's interest

---

[19] See ll. 4681–2 / Hay. 2, pp. 85–6 (already cited above).

in science was, ostensibly, an important area of common ground between Goethe and himself:

> Science was no stranger to poetry. Milton and Donne used discoveries in the natural world as a source of imagery, a fact of which Tennyson was well aware. Nearer to his own time, and greatly respected by Tennyson, was Goethe. Allusions to scientific theory abound in Goethe's œuvre, and the German writer also produced a notable piece of original research, *The Theory of Colours* (Tennyson owned Charles Eastlake's English translation of 1840).[20]

It is quite possible that Tennyson's numerous references to scientific ideas in *In Memoriam* were partly prompted by Goethe's example. However, the German poet's relationship with science was, in fact, a complex and difficult one. For example, his poem 'The Metamorphosis of Plants' (1798) is especially rich in allusions to scientific theory (FA, 1, I, 639–41 / Goethe, ed. Luke, pp. 147–51). But he wrote it partly because his botanical paper of the same title (1790) had met, in the words of Beach, with an 'indifferent reception. [. . .] He was [therefore] led to think of employing his great and acknowledged gift as poet for the better propagation of his views'.[21] Similarly, *The Theory of Colours* – although it was regarded by its author as his greatest achievement – was heavily criticised upon its publication in 1810. As David Luke observes:

> Goethe and the scientific establishment were and are at cross purposes. By implication and in tendency, his scientific work was essentially a protest against the materialistic presuppositions of modern science, the mathematical abstractness of its methods, its puristic departmentalism. [. . .] It was Goethe's basic conviction, expressed both in his scientific and in his literary works, that man and nature are bound to each other by a profound correlation, that nature is a whole.[22]

As Tennyson deepened his knowledge of the German poet's outlook through his reading of Austin's *Characteristics*, he would not have failed to notice that although Goethe had been acclaimed by Carlyle as 'the Wisest of our time', much of his wisdom was at odds with that of the times (*WTC*, I, Bk II, Ch. IX, p. 153 / p. 142, ll. 29–30).

---

[20] Ormond, p. 57. See Campbell (ed.), I (1971), p. 52, no. 1015.
[21] Beach, p. 292.
[22] Goethe, trans. Luke, pp. xxix–xxx.

The mediation of Austin – and, in particular, Carlyle – is, in fact, of considerable relevance here. It was partly through the writings of the latter author (who was himself at odds with the Mechanical Age) that Tennyson became familiar with what could be very loosely described as the German Romantic view of the natural world. In his essay on 'Novalis' (*WTC*, XXVII, 1–55), Carlyle had written approvingly of that poet's 'peculiar manner of viewing Nature: his habit, as it were, of considering Nature rather in the concrete, not analytically and as a divisible Aggregate, but as a self-subsistent universally connected Whole' (p. 28). This essay was published in the *Foreign Review* in July 1829, and the fact that Tennyson read it can be demonstrated by comparing it to his poem 'The Idealist' – which is dated 1829 (*PT*, 66; *TA*, XV, 254; XXIX, 8). 'Novalis' includes a lengthy discussion of Kantian philosophy, the adherents of which Carlyle personifies as 'the Idealist', who 'denies the absolute existence of Matter':

> Matter has an existence, but only as a Phenomenon: were *we* not there, neither would it be there. [. . .] [This] is true of material Nature at large, of the whole visible Universe, with all its movements, figures, accidents and qualities; all are Impressions produced on *me* by something *different from me*. [. . .] Time and Space themselves are not external but internal entities: they have no outward existence, there is no Time and no Space *out* of the mind. [. . .] [O]ur abode [is] in that Eternal City. (*WTC*, XXVII, 24–6, 29)

Tennyson satirises this passage in 'The Idealist', in which he pokes fun at what he perceives to be its solipsism, and turns Carlyle's repeated references to 'Matter' (see also ibid. XXVII, 23, 26, 29) into a mocking play on words:

> A mighty matter I rehearse,
> A mighty matter undescried;
> [. . .]
> I weave the universe,
> And indivisible divide,
> Creating all I hear and see.
> All souls are centres: I am one,
> I am the earth, the stars, the sun,
> I am the clouds, the sea.
> I am the citadels and palaces
> Of all great cities: I am Rome,
>   [. . .] I am Place
> And Time, yet is my home
> Eternity. (ll. 1–2, 5–15)

The discussion in 'Novalis' of the Kantian 'Idealist' also includes a quotation from a passage in *Faust*, which is often referred to as Faust's Credo (ll. 3457–8 / *WTC*, XXVII, 28). And although both Novalis and Kant are important influences on the conception of the natural world that is espoused in *Sartor Resartus*, 'the germ of Carlyle's whole point of view' in that work is provided – as Charles Frederick Harrold points out – by the Chant of the Earth Spirit in *Faust: Part One*.[23] This short passage of only nine lines (which will be discussed in greater detail below) is uttered by an enigmatic personification of Nature, who briefly appears to Faust in the scene 'Night'. Carlyle quotes the Chant in full in Book I, Chapter VIII of *Sartor*, and he returns to it again and again thereafter, through both allusion and direct quotation.[24] His quasi-pantheistic 'Philosophy of Clothes' is much indebted to its concluding lines, which he renders: "Tis thus at the roaring Loom of Time I ply, | And weave for God the Garment thou seest Him by.'[25]

It should be noted, however, that the crisp anapaestic rhythm of the original is not the only thing that is distorted in Carlyle's translation, for as Metzger observes:

> [The last line] is a revealing Carlylean emendation of Goethe's 'der Gottheit lebendiges Kleid [the living garment of the Godhead],' which says nothing about the garment's making visible the godhead; for Goethe nature is divine (coextensive with God), for Carlyle nature merely reflects the divine.[26]

For Tennyson, this particular aspect of Carlyle's mediation of *Faust* is likely to have been less problematic than his claim that the drama deals with religious doubt. Indeed, the Chant – which, with its personification of the natural world, might well have been of particular interest to him – was probably made a little more palatable by

---

[23] Harrold, p. 79. See also Smith, p. 51.
[24] *SR*, Bk I, Ch. VIII, p. 43; Ch. X, p. 52; Bk II, Ch. II, p. 72; Ch. VI, p. 123; Ch. IX, p. 150; Ch. X, p. 163; Bk III, Ch. VIII, p. 210; Ch. IX, p. 213 / p. 43, ll. 11–24; p. 51, ll. 19–21; p. 70, ll. 10–12; p. 115, l. 34–p. 116, l. 3; p. 140, ll. 24–6; p. 152, ll. 4–9; p. 194, ll. 5–7; p. 196, ll. 12–14.
[25] *SR*, Bk I, Ch. I, p. 4 / p. 6, l. 2; *F*, ll. 508–9; *SR*, Bk I, Ch. VIII, p. 43 / p. 43, ll. 20–1.
[26] Metzger, '*Sartor*', p. 326. See also Harrold, pp. 80–1. As Daniel Boileau pointed out in 1834, this line is also mistranslated by Hayward (Boileau, p. 7; Hay. 1, p. 12).

Carlyle's interpolation of a certain amount of distance between God and Nature.

This watering-down of the pantheism of Goethe was still not sufficient to stave off the philosophical disagreement with him that is expressed in *In Memoriam*, LIV–LVI. In the following discussion of these sections, I will make four assertions. First, it is likely that LIV–LVI date at least partly from around 1839. Second, at that time, Tennyson was reading *Sartor*, *Characteristics*, the *Apprenticeship* and *The Works of Lord Byron*, all of which left traces in these three sections. Third, the image of 'the veil' in the concluding line of LVI can be traced to another, overlapping group of sources, by writers including Goethe, Schiller, Novalis and Carlyle. Fourth, all three of these sections can be seen as exploring the opposition – so vividly delineated by the last-named author – between the German Romantic conception of Nature as a benevolent 'connected Whole', and the scientific notion of her as a 'divisible Aggregate', pitilessly indifferent to individual suffering.

For his knowledge of the latter view, Tennyson is known to have drawn on a number of recent publications, and his engagement with these provides some important clues to the dating of LIV–LVI. The most notable scientific influence on this part of the poem is generally acknowledged to be Charles Lyell's *Principles of Geology* (1830–3). Tennyson refers to this work in a letter of *c.* 1 November 1836, and he is described in the *Memoir* as having been 'deeply immersed in [it] [. . .] [d]uring some months of 1837' (*LAT*, I, 145; *Mem.*, I, 162; see also *PT*, 263, l. 3). More speculatively, Ricks compares lines 7–8 of LV to a passage from Robert Chambers's *Vestiges of the Natural History of Creation* (1844).[27] As he acknowledges, however, Hallam Tennyson states that 'The sections of "In Memoriam" about Evolution had been read by [Tennyson's] friends some years before the publication' of that book (*Mem.*, I, 223, fn; see *LAT*, I, 230 [15 November 1844]).[28] If this statement is accepted, it means that most of this part of the poem was written at some point between *c.* 1836 and *c.* 1842.

It was right in the middle of that period that Tennyson sent a revealing letter to his future wife Emily Sellwood (*LAT*, I, 174–5), which is postmarked 24 October 1839 (and which will be discussed

---

[27] *PT*, 296, LV, ll. 7–8, fn.
[28] *PT*, 296, LV, fn.

in detail below). As Lang and Shannon observe, 'there appear to be connections [in the letter] with [. . .] liv–lv', and Shatto and Shaw link it to LVI.[29] The first two critics also point out that '[t]he reference to Time and Space [in the opening sentence of the letter] and much of [its] language and subject-matter may reflect Carlyle's *Sartor Resartus*' (which had been published in book form the previous year, and whose author Tennyson had – in all probability – recently met).[30] Lang further observes that the second sentence in the letter, 'So mayst thou and I and all of us ascend *stepwise* to Perfection' (*LAT*, I, 174; italics added), is similar to the words 'men may rise on stepping-stones' from the opening stanza of *In Memoriam*, I (l. 3).[31] He also suggests that the latter text – which refers, as Tennyson himself informs us, to Goethe (*LAT*, III, 434, 3 November 1891) – dates from 'about the same time' as the letter to Emily.[32]

Lang's comments can, I think, be expanded upon. Austin's *Characteristics* (which Tennyson was given for Christmas in 1838) includes the text, in both German and English, of the poem 'The Metamorphosis of Plants',[33] in which Goethe writes:

> Werdend betrachte sie nun, wie, nach und nach sich die Pflanze,
> *Stufenweise* geführt, bilde zu Blüthen und Frucht. (FA, 1, I, p. 639, ll. 9–10 / *CG*, I, 164; italics added)

Here is Austin's English version of these lines (note her highly literal translation of the word *stufenweise*, which means 'step by step', or 'gradually'):

> Mark now the progress—how by degrees the plant
> *step-wise* led up, forms itself to blossom and to fruit. (*CG*, I, 168; italics added)

There are at least two reasons why Tennyson's phrase 'ascend stepwise to Perfection' can be confidently identified as an echo of Austin's

---

[29] *LAT*, I, 174, fn 3; S & S, p. 221.
[30] *LAT*, I, 174, fn 3; Martin, p. 241. See also the letter dated [*c*. 1 October 1839(?)] (*LAT*, I, 174).
[31] Lang, 'Introduction', in Campbell (ed.), I (1971), p. xi.
[32] Ibid. p. xi.
[33] The copy of Goethe's *Gedichte* (*Poems*) that is at TRC indicates that Tennyson studied this piece with some care: he has underlined more than a dozen words or phrases, providing marginal glosses for most of them (ET/3336, I, 199–201). He acquired this volume no later than 1837 (on the title page is the inscription 'A Tennyson | Somersby | Lincolnsh[ire]').

translation of 'Metamorphosis'. First, elsewhere in that poem, Goethe describes natural forms as gradually developing 'towards a higher perfection' (FA, 1, I, p. 640, l. 34 / CG, I, 169; German text: p. 165). And second, according to the *Oxford English Dictionary*, the word 'stepwise' did not enter the language until half a century later.[34]

Tennyson's 1838 Christmas presents also included the German copy of the *Apprenticeship* that was referred to in the Introduction, and an 1837 edition of *The Works of Lord Byron*.[35] In Book III, Chapter XII of the former volume, Goethe describes the feelings that are experienced by a writer when he is asked to make a transcript of one of his works:

> It is like the golden age of authorship: he feels transported into those centuries when the press had not inundated the world with so many useless writings, when none but excellent performances were copied, and kept by the noblest men. (Vol. IX, p. 558, l. 37–p. 559, l. 5 / XXIII, 232)

In the opening lines of an untitled poem that was first published in 1969 (*PT*, 276A), Tennyson draws an implicit contrast between this 'golden age', and the much gloomier period that has been ushered in by the invention of the press:

> Wherefore, in these dark ages of the Press
> (As that old Teuton christened them). (ll. 1–2)

The 'old Teuton' of the second line is clearly the Teutonic Goethe (who was an impressive eighty-two at the time of his death). The poem, which Ricks dates to *c.* 1839, provides evidence, therefore, that Tennyson was reading the *Apprenticeship* around that time.[36] 'Locksley Hall' (*PT*, 271) – which can be plausibly dated to *c.* 1838–9 – suggests that Tennyson might also have been studying Byron, for

---

[34] <http://www.oed.com> (last accessed 2 February 2021). In another Christmas gift from 1838 – *Rabenhorst's German Dictionary* – Tennyson has underlined the word *Stufe* ('step'), the ensuing definition of which also includes the word *stufenweise* (Noehden (ed.) (TRC, AT/1846), II, 353).

[35] *The Works of Lord Byron: Complete in One Volume* (London: Murray, 1837), TRC, AT/688; inscribed 'A. Tennyson Xmas day 1838'. This gift is likely to have been prompted by the fact that the fiftieth anniversary of the poet's birth had fallen on 22 January of that year. For Tennyson's copy of the *Apprenticeship*, see Introduction, p. 31, and ibid. fn 135.

[36] *PT*, 276A, headnote.

Ricks and Winnick find echoes of his work in lines 106 and 123.[37] Also, Tennyson's discussion of theological issues in his 1839 letter to Emily reads, at times, like a wary critique of the apparently blasphemous *Cain* (which is included in his copy of *The Works of Lord Byron* (pp. 316–40)).

It seems almost certain, therefore, that when Tennyson wrote that letter, he had recently been reading *Sartor*, *Characteristics*, the *Apprenticeship* and Byron. And it is probable that he had also been writing – or would soon begin to write – *In Memoriam*, LIV–LVI.

In the first of these three sections, Tennyson is drawing, I think, on the holistic view of Nature that is propounded in *Sartor*. But he is also beginning to draw away from it. '[N]othing hitherto was ever stranded, cast aside,' writes Carlyle; '[. . .] The withered leaf is not dead and lost' (*WTC*, I, Bk I, Ch. XI, p. 56 / p. 55, ll. 18–19, 22).[38] Tennyson expresses a comparable sentiment when he writes: 'not one life shall be destroyed, | Or cast as rubbish to the void' (LIV, ll. 6–7). Tellingly however, whereas Carlyle uses the past and present tenses, Tennyson employs the future. His basic dualism is thereby asserting itself: for him, present-day earthly reality, and the eventual administration of divine justice, are two different things. Indeed, he sounds a little like Byron's Cain when he remarks, in his letter to Emily: 'one might ask why has God made one to suffer more than another, why is it not meted equally to all'.[39] However, *unlike* Cain, he is quick to add, more resignedly: 'Let us be silent for we know nothing of these things' (*LAT*, I, 175). Similarly, LIV continues: 'Behold, we know not anything',[40] and it goes on to express the tentative hope that 'good shall fall | At last – far off – at last, to all' (ll. 13–15).

This nascent conflict between God and Nature is intensified in LV, in which an initial echo of the pantheistic Goethe (and of his British mediators) is quickly drowned out by the more sombre language of the scientist Lyell. *Sartor* asserts that 'Nature [is] not an Aggregate but a Whole', and that 'Nature is one, and a living indivisible whole',

---

[37] Baynes, 'Three New Sources'; *PT*, 271, l. 123, and fn; Winnick, p. 125.
[38] As Tarr observes (*SR*, ed. Tarr, p. 298, endnote) – and as Tennyson might have recognised – these words would appear to draw on a passage in the *Apprenticeship* (Vol. IX, Bk II, Ch. I, p. 429, ll. 13–21 / XXIII, 106). Also, the paragraph in *Sartor* from which they are taken begins: 'Detached, separated! I say there is no such separation' (*SR*, Bk I, Ch. XI, p. 56 / p. 55, l. 18). This, in turn, echoes *Werther*: 'detached, separated—perhaps for ever!—No, Charlotte, no! we now exist, how can we be annihilated!' (Pt II, p. 249, ll. 17–19, F. L. / p. 203).
[39] Compare Byron, *Poetical Works*, VI (1991), *Cain*, I. 1. 64–79.
[40] This comparison is made, implicitly, in *PT*, 296, LV, ll. 7–8, fn.

whilst *Characteristics* includes such phrases as 'a great living Whole'; 'the life-abounding Whole'; 'that the Whole may have life'; and 'a more living breath now moved through and vivified the Whole'.[41] Tennyson is probably thinking of this German Romantic conception of the natural world in the opening line of LV – but he quickly goes on to identify the Deity not with Nature, but, instead, with the human soul:

> The wish, that of the living whole
>   No life may fail beyond the grave,
>   Derives it not from what we have
> The likest God within the soul? (ll. 1–4)

For Goethe, of course, the Deity lies both within *and* without. As he declares in *Characteristics*: 'my manner of viewing things [. . .] had taught me to see God in Nature, and Nature in God, indissolubly, so that this mode of conception was become the basis of my whole existence' (FA, 1, XVII, p. 246, paragraph 797 / CG, II, 197; see also CG, III, 267, fn; p. 271). Tennyson – faced with the compelling arguments of *Principles of Geology* – is led to ask whether this mode of conception might not be threatened with dissolution: 'Are God and Nature then at strife, | That Nature lends such evil dreams?' (ll. 5–6). His subsequent meditations on this theme in lines 7–20 – which are heavily influenced by Lyell – are profoundly gloomy.[42] And although the section concludes by invoking 'the larger hope' (comparable to 'the hope that conquers all things', or 'great hope of universal good' that is mentioned in his letter to Emily (LV, l. 20; *LAT*, I, 174, 175)),[43] even this is circumscribed by the despair with which the poet is inclined to contemplate the natural world.

In section LVI, Tennyson gives vivid poetic expression to a rapid intensification of that despair. He draws, once again, on Lyell, as well as Goethe, and his British admirers: Byron, Carlyle and Austin. However, when he echoes the last four of these five authors, he appears to gravitate towards passages that are congruent with the works of the first. It is almost as if Goethe – and those who stand close to him – are being summoned to testify *against* the

---

[41] SR, Bk I, Ch. XI, p. 55 / p. 54, ll. 13–14 (adapted from a line in 'Novalis', cited earlier); Bk III, Ch. VII, p. 196 / p. 182, l. 4; CG, I, 310, 99; FA, 1, I, 'The Metamorphosis of Plants', p. 640, l. 62 / CG, I, 170; CG, III, 271.
[42] Killham, pp. 248–9.
[43] This comparison, too, is implicitly made in PT, 296, LV, ll. 7–8, fn.

Goethean view of the natural world, and to vindicate, instead, the Lyellean one.

As Eleanor Bustin Mattes observes, the latter is strikingly encapsulated in the quotation on the title page of the second volume of *Principles of Geology*: 'The inhabitants of the globe, like all the other parts of it, are subject to change. It is not only the individual that perishes, but whole species'.[44] Tennyson might have felt that there was a broad compatibility between these sentiments and the Chant of the Earth Spirit in *Faust* and *Sartor*, which evokes, in the words of Carlyle, 'Nature, with its thousandfold production and destruction':

> 'In Being's floods, in Action's storm,
> I walk and work, above, beneath,
> Work and weave in endless motion!
> Birth and Death. [. . .]' (*F*, ll. 501–4; *SR*, Bk I, Ch. VIII, p. 43 / p. 43, ll. 9–10, 13–16)

In a similar passage in *Characteristics*, Goethe's friend Johannes Falk evokes 'the violence of the whirlwind, the lightning, and the earthquake,'

> by which the mother of all things quickly puts an end to those somewhile contradictions which are found in her works, in a manner which to us appears utterly lawless, though, in truth, conformably to her own immutable laws, by which she brings destruction out of life, and life out of destruction. (*CG*, I, 32; see also p. 31)

It is probable that all three sources – Lyell, the Chant and *Characteristics* – leave their mark on Tennyson's memorable personification of 'Nature, red in tooth and claw' (LVI, l. 15) in the second stanza of LVI:

> 'I bring to life, I bring to death:
> The spirit does but mean the breath:
> I know no more.' (ll. 6–8)[45]

---

[44] Charles Lyell, *Principles of Geology*, 4th edn, 4 vols (London: Murray, 1835); Mattes, pp. 58–9.

[45] These lines – and the subsequent evocation of 'Man, her last work' (l. 9) – should also be compared to lines 5–13 of Coleridge's poem 'Human Life, On the Denial of Immortality' (1817) (Coleridge, *Collected Works*, XVI: *Poetical Works: Poems (Reading Text)*, ed. J. C. C. Mays (2001), I. 2, pp. 886–7). Line 9 of section LVI of *In Memoriam* resembles a passage from that 'English *Faust*', *Paracelsus* (see S & S, p. 220; refers to Browning, *Poems*, I (1991), *Paracelsus*, V, ll. 681–711).

In the penultimate stanza of this section, Tennyson would seem to be drawing, once again, on three different sources, which are, on this occasion, *Sartor*, the *Apprenticeship* and *Cain*. In Book II, Chapter VII of the first-named work, the beleaguered protagonist Teufelsdröckh declares:

> it seemed as if all things in the Heavens above and the Earth beneath would hurt me; as if the Heavens and the Earth were but boundless jaws of a devouring monster, wherein I, palpitating, waited to be devoured. (p. 134 / p. 125, ll. 23–5)

This image of a 'monster' can also be found in the concluding words of Book VI of the *Apprenticeship* – although here, it refers not to Nature, but to a godless, unguided humanity:

> I have seen too well what a monster might be formed and nursed in every human bosom, did not a higher Influence restrain us. (Vol. IX, p. 793, ll. 16–18 / XXIII, 459)

The last of the three sources for the penultimate stanza of LVI is identified by Shatto and Shaw, who observe that in *Cain*, Act II, scene 2, Lucifer reveals to the protagonist the ghosts of a long-extinct species, 'Reptiles engender'd out of the subsiding | Slime of a mighty universe' (Byron, *Poetical Works*, VI (1991), ll. 44–105, esp. 97–8).[46] Tennyson would appear to be entwining these three literary threads in his bleak portrayal of 'Man, [Nature's] last work' (l. 9):

> No more? A monster then, a dream,
>   A discord. Dragons of the prime,
>   That tare each other in their slime,
> Were mellow music matched with him. (ll. 21–4)

Of the three sources for this stanza, the passage from *Sartor* – which is much indebted, as Tennyson would have recognised, to a passage from *Werther*[47] – is certainly an appropriate influence here, for the

---

[46] S & S, p. 221. Shatto and Shaw also note that 'The idea of the extinction of species originated with Georges Cuvier' (p. 219), who is referred to by Byron in his prefatory 'Note' to *Cain*, a passage which Tennyson had already echoed in 'The Two Voices' (Byron, *Poetical Works*, VI (1991), p. 229, ll. 54–6); see Chapter 4, p. 138, fn 25.

[47] See *W*, Pt I, p. 108, ll. 9–14, 18 August 1771 / p. 92. The abruptly shifting perceptions of the natural world in this letter should also be compared to 'Nothing Will Die' and 'All Things Will Die' (*PT*, 93, 94).

image of a 'monster' in the opening line seems to emerge from the grim portrayal of Nature that has been offered at the beginning of this section. However, as in the *Apprenticeship*, the term is applied, in fact, to a spiritually forlorn humanity – and it is powerfully reinforced through the Byronic evocation of antediluvian 'slime'.

In the final stanza of LVI, Tennyson's personification of a creative-destructive Nature – and his portrayal of her comfortless progeny Man – are brought into conjunction with the evocative, mysterious image of 'the veil' (l. 28). Once again, the poet would appear to be drawing on an extremely wide range of sources, including, on this occasion, Schiller, Novalis, Carlyle, the *Apprenticeship* and *Faust*.[48] Indeed, it is almost as if Tennyson, in lamenting the absence of a heavenly 'voice to soothe and bless' (l. 26), is marshalling a host of literary ones in its stead.

The combined insights of A. C. Bradley, T. H. Vail Motter, Eleanor Bustin Mattes and Louise Dugas Wiggins suggest that in both this stanza and, also, in lines 11–15 of CIII, Tennyson is thinking of the myth of the veiled statue of Sais in Egypt.[49] The last three critics all point out that Hallam had referred to this in his writings, and they argue that he took this theme from a poem by Schiller, 'The Veiled Image at Sais' (which is included, it should be noted, in the second volume of Gower's *Faust* translation (Schiller, *Werke und Briefe*, I, 242–4 / Gower, pp. 137–41)). 'Tennyson', argues Mattes, '[. . .] probably came to the image [of the veil] by way of Hallam'.[50]

It could, however, have been transmitted in the opposite direction, from Tennyson to his friend, and Schiller may or may not have been its ultimate source. The most plausible scenario is that 'The Veiled Image at Sais' caught Hallam's attention because he had recently read Carlyle's essay 'Novalis', which includes translations of two lengthy passages from that author's fragmentary novel, *The Disciples at Sais* (*WTC*, XXVII, 30–5; see also XXVI, 149). In Schiller's poem, the veil is the cloak of Truth, but in 'Novalis' it becomes – as it would be, much later, in *In Memoriam*, LVI – a symbol of the natural world. 'Nature', enthuses Carlyle, 'is no longer dead, hostile Matter, but the

---

[48] See also A. C. Bradley, *A Commentary on Tennyson's 'In Memoriam'*, 3rd edn (London: Macmillan, 1910), p. 153, and *PT*, 296, LVI, l. 28, fn.

[49] Bradley, p. 153 (refers also to *Maud*, I. 4. 144); *WAH*, p. 83, and fn; Mattes, pp. 62–3, endnote 14; Louise Dugas Wiggins, 'Tennyson's Veiled Statue', *English Studies*, 49 (1968), 444–5. See also S & S, pp. 221–2.

[50] Mattes, p. 63, endnote 14.

veil and mysterious Garment of the Unseen' (*WTC*, XXVII, 29). As has already been noted above, 'Novalis' was published in July 1829 – and the writings of both Tennyson and Hallam provide evidence that they read it within six months of its appearance. The former, as we have seen, responded to it with his poem 'The Idealist', the manuscript of which bears the date of 1829. In December of that year, Hallam made his first recorded reference to the veil-theme, which can be found in a lyric that is addressed, significantly perhaps, to Emily Tennyson, the sister of the poet: 'Art thou not She | Who in my Sais-temple wast a light | Behind all veils of thought, and fantasy [?]', he asks (*WAH*, p. 83; see also pp. 144, 154).[51] And as Mattes points out, in February of the following year, Tennyson used the words 'He lifts the veil' in an essay that he wrote on the subject of 'Ghosts' (*Mem.*, I, 497).[52]

The image of 'a veil' can also be found, some two decades later, in Tennyson's letter to Emily Sellwood of October 1839 (*LAT*, I, 175). As with the 'monster' of the penultimate stanza of LVI, this could reflect his reading of the *Apprenticeship*, Book V of which includes – in a narrative context of recent bereavement – a number of references to a 'veil', or 'Spirit's veil' (Vol. IX, Ch. XII, p. 696, l. 9; Ch. XIII, p. 697, l. 12–13 / XXIII, 365, 366). And in a passage in Book III of that novel, we even find the phrase 'behind the veil' (Vol. IX, Ch. X, p. 550, l. 10 / XXIII, 223), the very words that Tennyson uses in the concluding line of LVI.[53]

It seems likely, however, that the Earth Spirit in *Faust* is of equal importance here, for shortly before it appears, Goethe's restless,

---

[51] It was also in December 1829 that Hallam read out to the Apostles the essay that has been mentioned above: 'Whether the existence of an intelligent First Cause is deducible from the phenomena of the universe.' This, too, suggests the influence of Carlyle's 'Novalis', whose passage on 'the Idealist' includes a discussion of the relationship between 'the great First Cause' and the 'visible Universe' (the latter being 'only [. . .] a Phenomenon' (*WTC*, XXVII, 25, 24)). See also *TA*, XV, 254, and compare *WTC*, XXVII, 26–7 to *LAHH*, no. 76, p. 312 (1 September [1829]); no. 78, p. 322 ([16 September 1829]).

[52] Mattes, p. 63, endnote 14; Pinion, *Tennyson Chronology*, p. 12. Like Hallam's essay of December 1829, this, too, was intended to be read out to the Apostles, which could be seen as indicating that the two friends had been studying 'Novalis' together.

[53] See also *WM*, Vol. IX, Bk V, Ch. XIII, p. 698, l. 15; Ch. XVI, p. 726, l. 15 / XXIII, 367, 395, as well as Bk VII, Ch. I, p. 801, l. 14; Bk VIII, Ch. V, p. 932, l. 9 / XXIV, 5, 131. As John Beer observes, Coleridge uses the words 'behind the veil' in *Aids to Reflection* (Coleridge, *Collected Works*, IX (1993), 358, and fn).

impetuous protagonist exclaims: 'Unveil thyself!' (l. 476 / p. 11).[54] It is this urgent need to penetrate the secrets of Nature that Tennyson is expressing in the final stanza of LVI:

> O life as futile, then, as frail!
>   O for thy voice to soothe and bless!
>   What hope of answer, or redress?
> Behind the veil, behind the veil. (ll. 25–8)

Like *Sartor*, however, section LVI represents a noticeably selective response to *Faust* and its related texts. Taken as a whole, the Chant of the Earth Spirit places more emphasis on Nature's creativity than it does on her destructiveness, and it is, in any case, an early and somewhat untypical Goethean text.[55] This sense of the broader

---

[54] The first complete English translation of Faust's encounter with the Earth Spirit was made by Shelley (*Shelley Manuscripts*, XXI (1995), p. 137, ll. 296–331; p. 139, ll. 332–68), who echoes this passage in 'Alastor' (Shelley, *Complete Works*, I (1927), pp. 175–98, ll. 719–20; refers to *F*, ll. 504, 506 / p. 12), and who introduces a 'Spirit of the Earth' into Act III, scene 4 of *Prometheus Unbound* (Shelley, *Complete Works*, II (1927), 236–42). In their comments on *In Memoriam*, LVI, Mattes, Ricks and Shatto and Shaw all point out that the word 'veil' is common in his work (Mattes, p. 62, endnote 14; *PT*, LVI, l. 28, fn; S & S, p. 221). His predilection for it can be partly traced to *Faust*, for he often uses it (together with closely related terms) in contexts that are suggestive of 'Night' (Shelley, *Complete Works*, I (1927), p. 177, l. 18–p. 178, l. 49 (esp. p. 178, l. 38); p. 197, ll. 719–20; IV (1928), p. 129, l. 15 and preceding stage direction– p. 130, l. 27 (esp. p. 129, l. 24); V (1928), pp. 180–2 (esp. p. 180); Leland R. Phelps, 'Goethe's *Faust* and the Young Shelley', in *Wege der Worte. Festschrift für Wolfgang Fleischhauer anläßlich seines 65. Geburtstages*, ed. Donald C. Riechel (Cologne: Böhlau, 1978), pp. 304–12 (p. 306); Stokoe, p. 155). Tennyson might have been aware of this connection (see Hay. 1, p. 217).

[55] Something similar might be said of the poem 'Divinity' (1783), for as Boyle observes, its argument is not based 'on any assumption of union with Nature', and it can therefore be seen as a 'betrayal of Goethe's poetic identity' (Boyle, I (1991), 279). It begins: 'Let man be noble, generous and good! For this alone distinguishes him from all beings known to us. [. . .] For Nature is unfeeling; the sun shines on the evil and on the good' (FA, 1, I, p. 333, ll. 1–6, 12–15 / Goethe, trans. Luke, p. 67; alludes to Matthew 5: 45). Tennyson may be thinking of these lines (which, to quote Boyle again, deal with 'the relation of man [. . .] to animals' and his 'moral distinctness' from them) in his letter to Emily: 'Man', he writes, 'is greater than all animals because he is capable of moral good and evil' (Boyle, I (1991), 350, 279; *LAT*, I, 174; Bradley (p. 107) suggests a link to *In Memoriam*, XXVII — and beyond to section I, which refers to Goethe). Tennyson would later describe 'Divinity' as 'one of the noblest of all poems' (*Mem.*, II, 288; see also I, 491), and Emily would call it 'one of our great favorites' (Emily Tennyson, *Journal*, p. 234, 22 September 1865; see also p. 186, 12 May 1863; p. 192, 17 December 1863).

context is also important to a proper understanding of the hubris that Faust displays towards the Spirit. A little later on in 'Night', he already sounds more reverential: 'Inscrutable at broad day,' he muses, 'nature does not suffer her veil to be torn from her' (ll. 672–3 / p. 18). And in 'A pleasant neighbourhood', he comes to accept that he will never be able to get behind 'the veil' that is the natural world (l. 4714 / Hay. 2, p. 86).[56] For Tennyson, however, this relaxed acceptance of Nature and her mysteries is far more problematic. Indeed, if the argument of *Principles of Geology* is correct, the German Romantic view of the natural world is – like everything else on earth – threatened with extinction.

In the very last stanza of *In Memoriam*, Tennyson seems to be trying to contain this potential crisis. As Mattes observes, the words 'That God, which ever lives and loves' ('Epilogue', l. 141) would appear to draw on the following passage from the chapter 'The Everlasting Yea' in *Sartor*:

> what is Nature? Ha! why do I not name thee GOD? Art not thou the 'Living Garment of God?' [*F*, Chant of the Earth Spirit, l. 509] O Heavens, is it, in very deed, HE, then, that ever speaks through thee; that lives and loves in thee, that lives and loves in me? (Bk II, Ch. IX, p. 150 / p. 140, ll. 25–8)[57]

Tennyson's response to the Chant has by this point been through almost as many shifts as the Earth Spirit itself, which 'Work[s] and weave[s] in endless motion'. This final, valedictory echo suggests, however, that even as he is describing the 'divine event' as 'far-off', he is also seeking to maintain at least some degree of contact with the contrary view of Goethe – for whom the Deity is synonymous, instead, with 'the whole creation' (*In Memoriam*, 'Epilogue', ll. 143–4).

As Metzger observes, it is likely that in the passage from 'The Everlasting Yea' that has been cited above, Carlyle is thinking not only of the Chant of the Earth Spirit, but also of the monologue that is often referred to as Faust's Credo (a couple of lines from which are quoted, as we have seen, in 'Novalis').[58] Both *Sartor* and the

---

[56] Compare the conclusion of 'Voices', ll. 445–7.
[57] Mattes, pp. 85–6.
[58] Metzger, '*Sartor*', p. 327. The passage later on in 'The Everlasting Yea' which Mattes (pp. 69–70) suggests as an influence on *In Memoriam*, CXXIV also includes echoes of the Credo (compare *SR*, Bk II, Ch. IX, p. 155 / p. 144, ll. 14–19, and *F*, ll. 3451–6 / p. 144).

Credo are, in turn, probable influences on 'The Higher Pantheism' (*PT*, 353), which Tennyson wrote in December 1867. In the Credo, Faust – to quote the rather tendentious summary of P. J. Bailey – is 'teaching and preaching a sensuous and impure Pantheism':[59]

> The All-embracer, the All-sustainer, does he not embrace and sustain thee, me, himself? Does not the heaven arch itself there above?—Lies not the earth firm here below?—And do not eternal stars rise, friendlily twinkling, on high?—Are we not looking into each other's eyes, and is not all thronging to thy head and heart, and weaving in eternal mystery, invisibly—visibly, about thee?—Fill thy heart with it, big as it is, and when thou art wholly blest in the feeling, then call it what thou wilt! Call it Happiness! Heart! Love! God! (ll. 3438–54 / p. 144)

If Carlyle's long series of questions about the relationship between God and Nature in 'The Everlasting Yea' is the child of this passage, 'The Higher Pantheism' would appear to be both child and grandchild:

> The sun, the moon, the stars, the seas, the hills and the plains—
> Are not these, O Soul, the Vision of Him who reigns?
>
> Is not the Vision He? though He be not that which He seems?
> Dreams are true while they last, and do we not live in dreams?
>
> Earth, these solid stars, this weight of body and limb,
> Are they not sign and symbol of thy division from Him? (ll. 1–6)[60]

But although the family likeness of these three texts is readily apparent in their similarities of theme, form and imagery, it is much less pronounced with regard to sentiment. In Faust's self-confident Credo, the questions are merely rhetorical, but those of Carlyle are suggestive, at times, of genuine uncertainty. And if the confidence

---

[59] Philip James Bailey, 'The Author of *Festus* and the Spasmodic School', in *Literary Anecdotes of the Nineteenth Century: Contributions towards a Literary History of the Period*, ed. W. Robertson Nicoll and Thomas J. Wise, 2 vols (London: Hodder & Stoughton, 1895–6), II (1896), 411–18 (p. 416).
[60] See also *Mem.*, I, 315, 514; II, 68.

of the father-text returns in Tennyson's poem, that is because the creed espoused by Goethe has now been substantially modified. The incipient dualism of *Sartor* (in which God is not quite identical with Nature, but merely 'speaks through' her) is taken a good deal further in 'The Higher Pantheism', with its emphasis, in the last line quoted above, on the 'division' between heaven and earth. It is not easy to see how this abiding sense of separation can be meaningfully reconciled with the poem's title.

Similar complexities can be discerned in 'Despair' (*PT*, 389). This piece is dated 9 June 1881 (*TA*, VIII, 117), and was written, therefore, just four months after the death of Carlyle on 5 February that year. In it, Tennyson returns to 'Signs of the Times' (on which he had drawn quite heavily in 'Mechanophilus' in 1833).[61] The poem bids farewell not just to the author of that essay, but also, it would seem, to the hopes that he had raised – most notably, the expectation that with the help of German literature and philosophy, a new, more positive view of Nature could be developed. 'Despair' deals with 'A man and his wife [. . .] [who] resolve to end themselves by drowning' (Tennyson's headnote). Lines 21–34 draw on a passage towards the end of 'Signs', in which Carlyle makes reference to 'suicide'; declares that 'our creed is Fatalism'; and ponders the 'dark features' of the age – although he maintains, nevertheless, that 'we [have not] at any time despaired of the fortunes of society':

> Despair, or even despondency, in that respect, appears to us, in all cases, a groundless feeling. [. . .] This deep, paralysed subjection to physical objects comes not from Nature, but from our own unwise mode of *viewing* Nature. [. . .] [These] are clear possibilities; nay, in this time they are even assuming the character of hopes. [. . .] [I]t is a wise adage that tells us, 'the darkest hour is nearest the dawn.' (*WTC*, XXVII, 79, 80–1)[62]

It is likely that this passage provided Tennyson with the title of 'Despair', in which he also harks back to Carlyle's reference to a

---

[61] See Chapter 2, pp. 77–8.
[62] This passage also includes a quotation from the *Apprenticeship* (which Tennyson would probably have recognised (*WTC*, XXVII, 81; refers to *WM*, Vol. IX, Bk VI, p. 750, ll. 22–3 / XXIII, 418)).

dark, fatalist creed. The hoped-for dawn, however, has proven to be false:

> See, we were nursed in the dark night-fold of your fatalist creed,[63]
> And we turned to the growing dawn, we had hoped for a dawn indeed,
> [. . .]
>
> Hoped for a dawn and it came, but the promise had faded away;
> We had past from a cheerless night to the glare of a drearier day.
> (ll. 21–2, 27–8)

The next two lines are an oblique reference to the once-fiery – but now extinguished – Carlyle (who, in 'The Everlasting No' in *Sartor*, had made use of the biblical images of the 'Pillar of Cloud' and the 'Pillar of Fire' (*SR*, Bk I, Ch. VII, p. 130 / p. 122, ll. 20, 21; Exodus 13: 21–2)):

> He is only a cloud and a smoke who was once a pillar of fire,
> The guess of a worm in the dust and the shadow of its desire –
> (ll. 29–30)

The four lines that follow might be seen as suggesting that the German Romantic view of Nature has died with him, for the damage done to it by Lyell has been compounded, it would seem, by Darwin:

> Of a worm as it writhes in a world of the weak trodden down by the strong,
> Of a dying worm in a world, all massacre, murder, and wrong.
>
> O we poor orphans of nothing – alone on that lonely shore –
> Born of the brainless Nature who knew not that which she bore!
> (ll. 31–4)

It should be emphasised, however, that these deeply antagonistic lines are addressed not from Tennyson to Goethe, but from the speaker of this 'Dramatic Monologue'[64] to his interlocutor – and, implicitly, to the late Carlyle. Whether the poet whose work Carlyle had done so much to promote was also in Tennyson's mind can only be guessed at. It would appear, therefore, that right to the end of his long life, Tennyson was reluctant to reject openly the German Romantic view of Nature. Indeed, in 'The Dreamer' (*PT*, 461), which was the very

---

[63] The word 'dark' was changed to 'drear' in 1885 (*PT*, 389, l. 21, fn). In Tennyson's manuscript, the first reading of the word 'fatalist' is 'Calvinist' (the faith in which Carlyle had been raised (*TA*, VIII, 114)).

[64] That was the poem's original subtitle (see *PT*, 389, headnote).

'last poem he finished' before his death in 1892 (*Mem.*, II, 419), the midnight visit of an anapaestic 'Voice of the Earth' (l. 3) (or, to quote from one of the drafts of the poem, 'the Spirit of Earth' (*TA*, XIV, 283)) is almost certainly a final echo of the Spirit of the Earth in 'Night'.[65]

Tennyson's response to Goethe's portrayal of Nature in *Faust* can be usefully compared to his treatment of the related theme of religious doubt. The two poets' spiritual views were overlapping but distinct: both of them believed in God, but Goethe – unlike Tennyson – did not have even the slightest belief in Christ. The contrast between the two men was more unequivocal with regard to the natural world, for Goethe believed in 'Gott-Natur', but the dualistic Tennyson did not. For the latter poet, Nature possessed no inherent divinity, and was more congenial, therefore, when linked to humanity, or invested with human characteristics. This outlook – which was apparent from a very early stage of Tennyson's career – was reinforced by the sudden loss of the human being whom he had valued above all others.

In the case of religious doubt, Tennyson's increasing ambivalence towards this aspect of *Faust* can be largely attributed to the differences between himself, Goethe and Carlyle. With regard to Nature, however, there is another triangle, which is, I think, of greater relevance: Tennyson, Goethe and Lyell. *In Memoriam* suggests that Tennyson's sometimes deep disagreements with Goethe on these two topics were mingled with an equally deep need to avoid an open rupture. It is entirely possible, moreover, that these mixed and complex feelings stayed with him to the end of his life.

In conclusion, it seems fair to say that Tennyson's often ambivalent view of Nature was paralleled by his often ambivalent view of the Goethean conception of her. But although he questioned and modified the German poet's notion of the natural world on several occasions, he never openly and comprehensively rejected it. Tennyson's only truly *antagonistic* responses to *Faust* can be found, instead, in the small number of poems in which he engages with Goethe's portrayal of sexuality. It is these works that will be discussed in the final chapter.

---

[65] Ricks remarks of 'The Dreamer': 'Apparently T[ennyson] first wrote the song (ll. 17–32)' (*PT*, 461, headnote). What is probably the initial draft of this passage is in Trinity Notebook 34, on the verso of folio 4 (*TA*, XIV, 260). On the recto of this folio, and on folio 3, is a revised version of 'Mechanophilus' (ibid. XIV, 257–9). As I argued in Chapter 2, pp. 74–7, this youthful, visionary poem is influenced by Faust's pursuit of the setting sun in 'Oh, happy he'. In lines 4–5 of 'The Dreamer', the elderly Tennyson writes, 'I am losing the light of my Youth | And the Vision that led me of old', and in the refrain of the poem's song, he proposes a noticeably Faustian solution to this malaise: 'follow the Sun!' (ll. 20, 24, 28, 32; see also l. 14).

Chapter 6

'The kiss of heavenly love': Saints and Sinners

Tennyson wrote four Faustian poems on saints and sinners: 'St Simeon Stylites', 'St Agnes' Eve', 'Forlorn' and 'The Vision of Sin'. All but the first of these would appear to indicate that he was deeply uncomfortable with Goethe's attitude towards sexuality, and that he felt a similar unease with regard to the German poet's morality more generally.

Whilst staying at her family home near Plymouth in 1848, Tennyson conversed with the young Miss Rundle (later the novelist Elizabeth Rundle Charles), who recorded his views on German literature:

> [it] was the influential literature of the day; Goethe, the most influential man; [. . .] [Tennyson] [f]elt the grand intellectual power of Faust, but threw it aside in disgust at the first reading, why he hardly knew, thought the whole tone low. (Hallam Tennyson, *Materials*, I, 358)

In nineteenth-century Britain, this kind of reaction to Goethe's writings was very common, and could often be attributed to a dislike of their bawdier passages. Whilst translating the *Apprenticeship* in 1823, Carlyle complained of its 'libidinous actresses and their sorry pasteboard apparatus for beautifying and enlivening the "moral world"', and declared: '[I] could sometimes fall down and worship [Goethe]; at other times I could kick him out of the room' (Carlyle, *Letters*, II (1970), 437, 21 September). Ten years later, Wordsworth told Emerson that *Meister* was 'full of all manner of fornication. [. . .] He had never gone farther than the first part; so disgusted was he that he threw the book across the room'.[1]

---

[1] *The Collected Works of Ralph Waldo Emerson*, ed. Alfred R. Ferguson and others, 10 vols (Cambridge, MA: Harvard University Press, 1971–2013), V: *English Traits*, ed. Philip Nicoloff, Robert E. Burkholder and Douglas Emory Wilson (1994), p. 11.

Goethe's portrayal of sexuality (in, for example, the following exchange from the scene 'Martha's Garden' in *Faust*) could be more neutrally described as frank:

FAUST.
Ah, can I never recline one little hour undisturbed upon thy bosom, and press heart to heart and soul to soul?

MARGARET.
Ah, did I but sleep alone! I would gladly leave the door unbolted for you this very night. (ll. 3502–6 / pp. 146–7)

Passages such as these stand in noticeable contrast to the work of Tennyson, who never portrays an extra-marital relationship in this open and sympathetic manner. Indeed, as discussed in Chapter 1, in *In Memoriam*, XCVII, he transforms Faust and Margaret into 'Two partners of a married life' (l. 5), and when he makes use of the Gretchen tragedy in *Maud*, he discreetly skips over 'Martha's Garden' and the adjacent scenes.[2] Of course, his large output does include a number of erotic poems, but even here, desire is rarely allowed to burst the bounds of convention (it seems significant that the love of Schiller's Raimond for Joan of Arc – which helps to inspire 'Come down, O maid' – is that of a would-be husband). In their views on sexuality, Tennyson and Goethe differed widely – far more than they did with regard to religion, or even Nature. Like many of his contemporaries, Tennyson's admiration for *Faust* would appear to have been qualified by profound moral reservations about its licentious passages.

Faust might also have struck Tennyson as being morally questionable in a more general sense – and this reaction, too, was a common one. Notwithstanding the medieval roots of its subject matter, Goethe's drama is not a didactic portrayal of the struggle between light and darkness. It explores, instead, the elusive 'grey areas' in between: the sometimes reckless Faust can hardly be described as a hero, and the witty and urbane Mephistopheles is certainly not a conventional villain. The often strong feeling that they are both really two sides of a single individual is an expression of Goethe's nuanced moral outlook, in which evil is inseparable from – but firmly subordinate to – goodness. In other words, the monism that

---

[2] See pp. 57–8, 65.

informs his view of Nature is (as Luke observes) equally characteristic of his morality:

> [Goethe] accepts evil as necessary but does not ponder it particularly deeply or assign to it any very effective role in his essentially monistic cosmos; his Devil, as we see in [the 'Prologue in Heaven' in] *Faust*, is on friendly visiting-terms with God. Sin, as a concept, apparently scarcely existed for him. He refused to think of man or nature as fallen or radically corrupt.[3]

This humanistic outlook was a frequent source of disquiet amongst Goethe's nineteenth-century British readers, who often expressed a preference for a more didactic – and morally polarised – kind of literature. Writing in the *Dublin Review* in 1840, Charles William Russell speaks for many when he argues that the protagonist's redemption at the end of *Part Two* 'destroys the existence of *Faust* as a moral poem. Had Faustus [. . .] been prepared by repentance and purified by martyrdom, [. . .] we might see in his ultimate deliverance [. . .] the realization of some moral lesson'.[4] Russell's need to conventionalise Goethe's morality is also apparent in his comments on *Part One*:

> with all its wildness and levity, [it] contains many passages replete with the most sublime conceptions of religion. [. . .] We need only refer to the hymn of the archangels in the Prologue, deformed as it is by its juxta-position with the revolting levity of Mephistopheles, [. . .] and [. . .] to that exquisitely touching prayer in which [Margaret] pours out her soul to the Mother of Sorrows, in her own hour of sorrow, and alas! of sin. (Russell, p. 495)

Tennyson's moral outlook was, I think, much closer to that of critics such as Russell than it was to Goethe's: he certainly believed in the reality of sin, and he regarded good and evil as being in opposition. It is notable that although he wrote three different poems that echo the 'Prologue in Heaven', he confined his attention to the Chorus of the Archangels, and chose (like several of the work's British translators) to ignore the 'revolting levity' of the ensuing dialogue between Mephistopheles and the Lord. A similar disquiet can be detected in

---

[3] Goethe, trans. Luke, p. xxxvi.
[4] [Charles William Russell], 'ART. VIII.—1. *Faust: A Tragedy*. By J. Wolfgang von Goethe', *Dublin Review*, 9: 18 (November 1840), 477–506 (pp. 494–5).

'The Two Voices', for although this piece draws on the dialogues of Mephistopheles and Faust, Tennyson is careful to heighten the contrast between them, by debasing the one and ennobling the other. In his morality, as in his attitude to Nature, Tennyson is a good deal more dualistic than Goethe.

This difference of outlook is strongly reflected in three of the four poems that will be discussed in this chapter: 'St Agnes' Eve', 'Forlorn' and 'The Vision of Sin'. The first two of these pieces date, I will argue, from the 1833–4 period, whilst the third is believed to have been written around 1839. In all three of these poems, Tennyson is expressing his antagonism towards passages in *Faust* that deal with sexuality. He repeatedly subordinates these earthly pleasures to more spiritual ones, emphasising not physical gratification, but, instead, what one might call 'the kiss of heavenly love' (*F*, l. 771 / p. 22). He also exhibits a pervasive tendency to bifurcate Goethe's monism, replacing his moral 'greyness', wherever possible, with bold, confident strokes of black and white.

It was probably a short time before he composed the first of these three works that Tennyson wrote another poem on a saint, 'St Simeon Stylites' (*PT*, 210). This piece fits only loosely into the framework of the present chapter, for it does not deal directly with sexuality, and its speaker is a saint in name only, who insists (repeatedly, but disingenuously) that he is a sinner. There are, however, at least two reasons why 'Simeon' deserves to be discussed here in detail: first, its distinction as a poem, and second, the perceptible influence upon it of *Faust*.

In his note on 'Simeon', Hallam Tennyson remarks that its speaker is '[t]o be read of in Gibbon's *Decline and Fall*, [. . .] and [William] Hone's *Every-Day Book* [1826–7]' (EE, I, 394). But if Tennyson consulted the former work, he did not take anything specific from it,[5] whilst the latter, I will argue, was just one of a number of different sources. These include Carlyle's essay 'Schiller', Byron's *Deformed Transformed* and *The Giaour*, and Hayward's *Faust*. There is a web of interconnections that links these works to one another – and

---

[5] The only possible exception is the information contained in lines 108–10 of 'Simeon' – but this is also provided by Hone (Edward Gibbon, *The History of the Decline and Fall of the Roman Empire*, ed. David Womersley, 3 vols (Harmondsworth: Penguin, 1994), Vol. II, Ch. XXXVII, p. 427; William Hone, *The Every-Day Book; or: Everlasting Calendar of Popular Amusements*, 2 vols (London: Hunt and Clarke, 1826–7), I (1826), 37–8).

which links them, in turn, to Tennyson's poem. First, the glossary relating to *Faust* that is in Harvard Notebook 13 (which was cited in the Introduction) comes immediately after a draft of 'Simeon' (*TA*, II, 263–6), which suggests that Tennyson was reading Goethe's drama around the same time as he wrote this piece. Second, as was mentioned in Chapter 2, the editorial material in Hayward's translation of *Part One* makes a number of references to the works of Byron, including *The Deformed Transformed* (Hay. 1, pp. 207, 214). Third, Hayward also refers, on two separate occasions, to the *Correspondence between Schiller and Goethe*, of which Carlyle's essay is, ostensibly, a review (ibid. p. lxxxiv, fn; p. 276; see also Hay. 2, p. 105). I propose that Hayward's comments led Tennyson to read or reread 'Schiller', and that his attention was drawn to the following passage (which is part of a discussion of the playwright's ill-health):

> it is a shame for the man of genius to complain. Has he not a 'light from Heaven'[6] within him, to which the splendour of all earthly thrones and principalities is but darkness? And the head that wears such a crown grudges to lie uneasy?[7] If that same 'light from Heaven,' shining through the falsest media, supported Syrian Simon through all weather on his sixty-feet Pillar, or the still more wonderful Eremite who walled himself, for life, up to the chin, in stone and mortar; how much more should it do, when shining direct, and pure from all intermixture? Let the modern Priest of Wisdom either suffer his small persecutions and inflictions, though sickness be of the number, in patience, or admit that ancient fanatics and bedlamites were truer worshippers than he. (*WTC*, XXVII, 189–90)[8]

The religious language of this passage is typical of the essay as a whole. Mindful, perhaps, of the still-lingering British view that the author of *The Robbers* was an advocate of revolution, immorality

---

[6] Presumably a reference to Acts 9: 3 and 26: 13 (the conversion of Paul on the road to Damascus in Syria). As Ricks observes (*PT*, 209, ll. 222–5, fn), Tennyson echoes Acts 7: 55 in 'The Two Voices', on which he may have been working at the same time as 'Simeon' (see below).

[7] Tennyson would have recognised Carlyle's allusion to *2 Henry IV*, III. 1. 31 (*New Oxford Shakespeare*, pp. 1359–436), to which he himself alludes in *In Memoriam*, CXXVII, l. 9.

[8] A number of details in this passage suggest that Carlyle's knowledge of St Simeon was derived from Gibbon's *Decline and Fall*, which he had first read in 1817 (Mark Cumming, 'Gibbon, Edward', in *The Carlyle Encyclopedia*, ed. Mark Cumming (Madison: Fairleigh Dickinson University Press, 2004), pp. 191–3).

and atheism, Carlyle adopts a heavily sermonising tone. As in his Goethe criticism, he seems, at times, to be presenting his subject as a candidate for canonisation:

> We might say, there is something priest-like in that Life of [Schiller's]: [. . .] it has a priest-like stillness, a priest-like purity; nay, if for the Catholic Faith we substitute the Ideal of Art, and for Convent Rules, Moral or Æsthetic Laws, it has even something of a monastic character. [. . .] Thus immured, not in cloisters of stone and mortar, yet in cloisters of the mind, which separate him as impassably from the vulgar, he works and meditates only on what we may call Divine things. (*WTC*, XXVII, 175)

Carlyle argues, however, that the irreproachable 'Holy Man' Schiller was very much an anomaly:

> That high purpose after spiritual perfection, which with him was a love of Poetry, [. . .] is [. . .] the necessary parent of good conduct, as of noble feeling. [. . .] [H]ow seldom is it the sincere and highest purpose, how seldom unmixed with vulgar ambition, and low, mere earthly aims, which distort or utterly pervert its manifestations! (ibid. XXVII, 175, 185)

This passage, too, may well have played a role in the genesis of Tennyson's poem: it is precisely this disquieting mixture of high and low that characterises the speaker of 'Simeon'.

I would suggest that Tennyson's pillar-hermit inherits much of his contradictory personality from Faust. In tracing these connections, it is helpful, I think, to read the poem in conjunction with 'The Two Voices'. There are at least three reasons for linking these two pieces. First, Tennyson may well have worked on them simultaneously (there are drafts of both in Trinity Notebook 22 (*TA*, XII, 223–30, 237–48)). Second, like 'Voices', 'Simeon' draws on the university scenes of *Faust: Part One* ('Night', 'Before the Gate' and the two 'Study' scenes). And third, both poems are products of an intense involvement with Goethe's play, which is offset, however, by an equally strong sense of distance. As discussed in Chapter 4, 'Voices' appropriates the tense dialogue form that characterises much of *Part One*, but it uses it as a means of questioning the play itself. In a sense, the resultant poem is actually a monologue: the monologue of a single, deeply divided mind. This description can also be applied, with equal justice, to 'Simeon'. In this poem, Tennyson takes echoes of the tempestuous Faust, and puts them into the mouth of a supposedly beatific saint, thus forging an unlikely – and often repugnant – hybrid figure. In the words of Martin, 'Simeon' is 'a strong statement on the dual nature of man', and like 'Voices', it may well have been influenced by the 'Two souls' speech: Tennyson's pillar-hermit shares Faust's contradictory tendencies towards self-abasement and self-aggrandisement.[9]

The former characteristic is evident right from the poem's opening line: 'Although I be the basest of mankind'. This would appear to echo the Faustian protagonist of *The Deformed Transformed*: 'But even thus, the lowest, | Ugliest, and meanest of mankind' (Byron, *Poetical Works*, VI (1991), I. 1. 348–9). The possibility that Byron was somewhere in Tennyson's mind would appear to be confirmed by line 3, 'Unfit for earth, unfit for heaven', which is a fairly clear reminiscence of line 436 of *The Giaour*: 'Unfit for earth, undoom'd for heaven' (Byron, *Poetical Works*, III (1981), no. 205, p. 53).

Another likely influence on 'Simeon' is 'Before the Gate' in *Part One*. In this scene, Faust is offered gifts by an almost genuflecting crowd, who praise him and his late father for their feats of healing. In his monologue 'Only a few steps further', he responds to this acclaim with scorn, and speaks, instead, of self-mortification, prayer and fasting:

OLD PEASANT.
Doctor, [. . .] [t]ake [. . .] the fairest jug, which we have filled with fresh liquor: I pledge you in it. [. . .] *(The people come round [Faust].)* [. . .] You have been our friend in evil days, too, before now. Many a one stands here alive whom your father tore from the hot fever's rage, when he stayed the pestilence. You too, at that time a young man, visited all the houses of the sick. [. . .]

WAGNER.
What a feeling, great man, must you experience at the honours paid you by this multitude. [. . .] [T]hey all but bend the knee as if the Host were passing.

---

[9] Martin, p. 264. At one point in the 'Two souls' speech, Faust invokes 'spirits hovering [. . .] 'twixt earth and heaven' (l. 1118–19 / p. 35). His assistant Wagner assumes that this is a reference to demons, and tells him to '[i]nvoke not the well-known troop' (l. 1126 / p. 35; see also l. 1302 / p. 43). This exchange may have helped to suggest Tennyson's 'betwixt the meadow and the cloud', and his 'troops of devils' ('Simeon', ll. 14, 4; compare also *F*, l. 1135 / p. 36, and 'Simeon', l. 161).

FAUST.
Only a few steps further, up to that stone yonder. Here we will rest from our walk. Here many a time have I sat, thoughtful and solitary, and mortified myself with prayer and fasting. [. . .] The applause of the multitude now sounds like derision in my ears. Oh! couldst thou read in my inmost soul, how little father and son merit such honour![10]

The words of Simeon – who is, like Faust, atop a lofty stone – describe a very similar scenario:

> The silly people take me for a saint,[11]
> And bring me offerings of fruit and flowers:
> [. . .]
>   Good people, you do ill to kneel to me.
> What is it I can have done to merit this?
> I am a sinner viler than you all.
> It may be I have wrought some miracles,
> And cured some halt and maimed; but what of that?
> [. . .]
>   [. . .] Mortify
> Your flesh, like me, with scourges and with thorns;
> Smite, shrink not, spare not. If it may be, fast
> Whole Lents, and pray. (ll. 125–6, 131–5, 176–9; see also ll. 79–81)

The self-aggrandising side of Faust's personality may also leave traces in Simeon. For example, in 'Night', Goethe's protagonist asks 'Am I a god?', and he tells the Earth Spirit: 'I am he, am Faust, thy equal. [. . .] [T]he image of the Deity [. . .]!' (ll. 439, 500, 516 / pp. 9, 12). Tennyson's pillar-hermit exhibits a similar hubris in his relationship with the Lord, for he lobbies Him for canonisation, and bluntly declares: 'I have some power with Heaven' (ll. 17–20, 45–53, 127–30, 136–7, 148–51, 189–94, 141). Indeed, as William E. Fredeman observes, in

---

[10] Lines 981, 985–7, stage direction before l. 993; ll. 995–1002, 1011–12, 1020–5, 1030–3 / pp. 31–3.

[11] The phrase 'the silly people' can be found in *Werther*, and in 'Night' Faust refers bitterly to 'The few [. . .] who sillily enough [. . .] published what they had felt and seen to the multitude' (*W*, Pt II, p. 130, ll. 3–4, 24 December [1771] / p. 115; *F*, ll. 590–2 / p. 15). These words are immediately followed by: '—these, time immemorial, have been crucified and burnt' (l. 593 / p. 15). Compare 'Simeon': 'they were stoned, or crucified, / Or burned' (ll. 50–1).

the latter part of the poem, 'he addresses God not as a supplicant but as an equal'.[12]

For both Faust and Simeon, self-abasement and self-aggrandisement are mingled in their desire for death, for their surrender to extinction is also a defiant display of will-power. When Faust reaches for the poison at the end of 'Night', he declares:

> Why, of a sudden, is all so exquisitely bright [. . .]? [. . .] I hail thee, thou precious phial. [. . .] [V]ouchsafe thy master a token of thy grace! [. . .] I grasp thee. [. . .] Now is the time to show by deeds that man's dignity yields not to God's sublimity. [. . .] [C]ome down, pure crystal goblet. [. . .] You glittered at my father's festivities. (ll. 688, 690, 695, 697, 712–13, 720, 723 / pp. 19, 20; see also ll. 1570–1 / p. 53)

In what Ricks describes as Simeon's 'suicide-martyrdom',[13] the phial of poison is replaced, it would seem, by the crown of sainthood. Although the verbal similarities to 'Night' are few and inconclusive, the uneasy mixture of splendour, determination and irreverence is much the same:

> A flash of light. Is that the angel there
> That holds a crown? Come, blessèd brother, come.
> I know thy glittering face. I waited long;
> My brows are ready. What! deny it now?
> Nay, draw, draw, draw nigh. So I clutch it. Christ! (ll. 200–4; see also ll. 17–18, 36, 198–9)[14]

---

[12] William E. Fredeman, '"A Sign Betwixt the Meadow and the Cloud": The Ironic Apotheosis of Tennyson's "St. Simeon Stylites"', *University of Toronto Quarterly*, 38: 1 (October 1968), 69–83 (p. 79).

[13] Ricks, *Tennyson*, p. 103.

[14] The central image of these lines may be partly inspired by Carlyle's mention of 'a crown' in the passage from 'Schiller' quoted above (see also 'Study [II]', ll. 1803–5 / p. 61; for an alternative source, see *PT*, 210, l. 205, fn). As we have seen, Carlyle also describes the saint as surviving 'through all weather', and this, too, has its counterpart in Tennyson's poem, in which the 'weather-beaten' speaker endures 'Rain, wind, frost, heat, hail, damp, and sleet, and snow' (ll. 19, 16). The poet's friend W. E. H. Lecky recalled that '[h]e once confessed to me that when he wrote his "Simeon Stylites" he did not know that the story was a Syrian one, and had accordingly given it a Northern colouring which he now perceived to be wrong' (Hallam Tennyson, *Materials*, III, 324). However, it is difficult to see how Tennyson's profession of ignorance can have been genuine: both Carlyle and Gibbon explicitly describe the saint as 'Syrian', whilst Hone mentions 'Antioch' (Gibbon, Vol. II, Ch. XXXVII, p. 427; Hone, I, 38, 39; for Carlyle, see above). I would suggest that Tennyson sprinkled his poem with damp Germanic

Once again, it may be helpful to compare 'Simeon' to 'The Two Voices'. In the latter piece, the life-affirming determination that the speaker achieves just before the bells ring out contrasts strongly with the suicidal despair of Faust at the analogous moment in 'Night'. Simeon, however, embraces the oblivion that the conclusion of 'Voices' eschews, and Tennyson can therefore be seen to be using him as a monitory counterpart to the exemplary speaker of the other poem.

Indeed, although Simeon's ambiguous character might appear to belie my contention that Tennyson had a stronger sense of the contrast between good and evil than Goethe did, a recognition of the poem's links to *Faust* may serve to qualify this judgement. In the latter work, the moral status of the protagonist is never explicitly spelled out, and is open, therefore, to debate. In 'Simeon', however, Tennyson blends a somewhat exaggerated version of Faust with a Christian saint, and in doing so, he circumscribes the reader's possible responses. Although Simeon's self-abasement resembles that of Faust, it is both more extreme and less sincere. Self-aggrandisement, meanwhile, can be seen, in Faust, as anything from Titanism to blasphemy, but in the seemingly pious pillar-hermit, it cannot be anything but the latter. Similarly, Faust's deeply un-Christian desire for death becomes grossly inappropriate when it is echoed by Simeon. The latter character certainly possesses qualities that his creator admired (most notably, an unwavering belief in God and immortality). Ultimately however, he is a manifest hypocrite, a deeply flawed individual who falls far short of the probity implied by his title. And in exposing him as such, Tennyson is displaying a much more clear-cut sense of good and evil than the author of *Faust*.

This moral dualism is, I think, still more apparent in 'St Agnes' Eve', 'Forlorn' and 'The Vision of Sin'. The first of these three works is dated 'Sept. 1833' (*PT*, 212; *TA*, XXIX, 29). Like 'Simeon', our understanding of it can be enhanced if we read it in conjunction with another poem that was written that year. In this case, the related text is 'Inscription by a Brook' (*PT*, 191) – and equally relevant, I will argue, is Cary's translation of *The Divine Comedy*. As discussed in

---

weather because *his* Simeon inhabits the imaginative world of *Faust* (specifically, the outdoor scene 'Before the Gate': the words 'hail', 'mist' and 'chill' are common to both texts (*F*, ll. 909, 1143 / pp. 28, 36; 'Simeon', ll. 16, 74, 112; see also *DC*, Vol. III, Canto XXI, pp. 112–13 / ll. 95–115, esp. p. 112 / ll. 105–7)). Note, also, that lines 168–75 of 'Simeon' are almost certainly inspired by *Faust*, ll. 1216–322 / pp. 40–3.

the previous chapter, 'Inscription' draws on the exchanges between *'Promenaders of all kinds'* (stage direction before l. 808 / p. 24) at the beginning of 'Before the Gate', so it is reasonable to assume that Tennyson devoted a considerable amount of attention to that passage. Parts of it are openly sexual, with 'pretty lads [. . .] running after [. . .] the prettiest girls' (one of the former remarks: 'Quick, lest we lose the game. The hand that twirls the mop on a Saturday, will fondle you best on Sundays' (ll. 832, 835, 815, 843–5 / pp. 25, 24, 26)). Towards the end of these exchanges, an 'OLD WOMAN' approaches two 'CITIZENS' DAUGHTERS', and remarks: 'Who would not fall in love with you? Only not so proud! [. . .] [W]hat you wish, I should know how to put you in the way of getting' (dialogue cue before l. 872; ll. 873–5 / p. 27). The indignant response of one of the girls may have helped to suggest the subject of 'St Agnes': 'Come along, Agatha. I take care not to be seen with such witches in public; true, on Saint Andrew's eve she showed me my future lover in flesh and blood' (ll. 876–9 / p. 27).[15]

Tennyson's treatment of this theme suggests that he felt it necessary to offset Goethe's earthiness with echoes of another, less bawdy poet. Edward FitzGerald relates the following anecdote:

> once[,] looking with A. T. at two busts of Dante and Goethe in a shop window in Regent Street, I said, 'What is there wanting in Goethe which the other has?' 'The Divine!' [replied Tennyson.] (*Mem.*, I, 121; see also II, 287–8)

In 'St Agnes', Tennyson supplies this want by combining *Faust* (as he does in a number of other poems of 1833) with *The Divine Comedy*. Cary offers the following summary of Canto III of *Paradise* – the setting of which is a familiar symbol of sexual restraint:

> In the moon Dante meets with Piccarda, [. . .] who tells him that this planet is allotted to those, who, after having made profession of chastity and a religious life, had been compelled to violate their vows. (*DC*, p. 14 / p. 444)

This former nun tells Dante how she was 'snatch'd [. . .] from the pleasant cloister's pale' by a group of men, and thereafter, 'The

---

[15] 'A maiden who fasted on [St Agnes's] Eve might see a vision of her destined lover' (*PT*, 212, headnote).

saintly folds [...] with [...] violence were torn' from her (ibid. p. 18 / ll. 109, 116, 115). There are two possible connections here to Tennyson's poem. First, this dead 'virgin sister' (ibid. p. 16 / l. 46) resembles St Agnes, whose 'refusal to marry', explains Ricks, was followed by her being 'violated before execution'.[16] Second, in 'St Agnes' Eve', 'the legend', Tennyson informs us, 'is told by a nun' (cited in *PT*, 212, headnote). His speaker's opening lines suggest, moreover, that upon her death, her soul will follow a similar trajectory to that of Piccarda:

> Deep on the convent-roof the snows
>   Are sparkling to the moon:[17]
> My breath to heaven like vapour goes:
>   May my soul follow soon! (ll. 1–4)

Piccarda describes how those who remain faithful to the 'pure laws [...] | [...] e'en till death [...] keep watch, or sleep | With their great bridegroom' (*DC*, Vol. III, Canto III, p. 17 / ll. 100, 102–03). Tennyson's speaker employs the same image:

> For me the Heavenly Bridegroom waits,
>   To make me pure of sin. (ll. 31–2)[18]

In these lines, the 'future lover in flesh and blood' of 'Before the Gate' has been transformed into an ethereal vision of Christ. This far-reaching sanctification of *Faust* is rounded off by the poem's echoes of Corinthians, Hebrews and Revelation (all of which are noted by Ricks).[19] Indeed, the contrast between 'St Agnes' and 'Before the Gate' could hardly be greater: Goethe's flirtatious young men and women are nowhere to be found in Tennyson's lyric, which transports its abstemious speaker up to the very brink of heaven.

---

[16] *PT*, 212, headnote.

[17] See also line 16 ('yonder argent round'), and one of the drafts of the poem that are in Harvard Notebook 16, in which 'The moon' is mentioned in the first reading of line 25 (*TA*, III, 13). Four pages earlier in this notebook is the Faustian poem 'This Earth is wondrous, change on change', in which Tennyson, like Dante, embarks on an imaginary journey to the moon (ibid. III, 9–10; *PT*, 201). Between these two pieces is 'Ulysses' (*PT*, 217), with its 'echo of Dante' – *and* of *Faust* (*TA*, III, 10–11; *Mem.*, II, 70).

[18] Compare also *DC*, Vol. III, Canto X, p. 56 / ll. 135–6, and 'St Agnes', l. 36.

[19] *PT*, 212, ll. 19, 31, 33, 35, fns.

In the first of his two Faustian poems on sinners, 'Forlorn' (*PT*, 314), Tennyson effects a contrary transformation: in this piece, a licentious character – far from being raised up – is, instead, sent perilously close to hell. Drafts of 'Forlorn' are in Harvard Notebook 20, which also includes a fragment of *Maud* (1854–5), so Ricks dates 'Forlorn' to *c*. 1854 (*TA*, III, 66–80, 82).[20] However, Hallam Tennyson describes it as '[a]n early poem' (*EE*, VII, 365), and if we trace its connections with *Faust*, we realise that it is linked not just to *Maud*, but also to 'Oh! that 'twere possible', 'Love's latest hour is this' and 'The Flight' (1833–4).[21] All five of these works draw on the Gretchen tragedy (in particular, the scenes 'Dungeon' and 'Night.—Street Before Margaret's Door'). The manner in which they do so is, however, notably diverse. Although 'Forlorn', 'Oh! that 'twere possible' and 'Love's latest hour' make use of plot elements from this episode, they also echo specific phrases from Hayward's translation (as does 'The Flight'). In contrast, *Maud* uses plot elements only, which reflects the fact that by the 1850s, Tennyson was reading Goethe's drama in German. I would argue, therefore, that the surviving drafts of 'Forlorn' are revisions of a now-lost earlier version, which was written during Tennyson's absorption in Hayward's *Faust* in 1833–4.[22]

In 'Night.—Street Before Margaret's Door', the emissary of hell Mephistopheles is seen 'slinking' towards Gretchen's home (l. 3646 / p. 154). From the street below her window, he mocks her by serenading her with a song that tells a monitory tale of pre-marital relationships. It begins: 'What are you doing here, Catherine, before your lover's door at morning dawn?' (ll. 3682–5 / p. 156). The main body

---

[20] *PT*, 314, headnote.
[21] See Chapter 1, pp. 58–63.
[22] The drafts of 'Forlorn' that are in Harvard Notebook 20 include earlier versions of lines 72 and 18: 'When [or: While] the dogs are howling', and 'While the winds are blowing' (*TA*, III, 67, 76, 80, 73). These resemble the opening line of a Faustian poem from *c*. October 1833: 'Hark! the dogs howl! the sleetwinds blow' (*PT*, 214). Harvard Notebook 20 also includes fragments of 'The Brook' (*PT*, 313; *TA*, III, 62–5, 81, 84), in which the words 'a wizard pentagram' (l. 103) suggest *Faust*: 'MEPHISTOPHELES. | [. . .] [A] small obstacle prevents me from walking out—the wizard-foot upon your threshold. | FAUST. | The Pentagram embarrasses you?' (ll. 1393–6 / p. 46). Henry van Dyke argues that 'The Brook' 'takes its theme [. . .] from Goethe', although he does not name any specific work; he may be thinking of the poem 'The Youth and the Mill-brook' (Henry van Dyke, *Studies in Tennyson*, 2nd edn (New York: Scribner, 1921), p. 39; *FA*, 1, I, 672–4).

of 'Forlorn' (which takes place 'In the night, O the night, | While the Fiend is prowling' (ll. 65–6)) begins:

> Catherine, Catherine, in the night,
>   What is this you're dreaming?
> There is laughter down in Hell
>   At your simple scheming . . . (ll. 13–16)[23]

Tennyson's Catherine has fallen into the trap that threatens her Faustian namesake: like Gretchen in 'Dungeon', she has been seduced, made pregnant and abandoned; her 'mind is failing', her heart is full of 'madness', and she is '[w]aiting for [her] summons' (ll. 3–4, 7–10, 19–34, 1, 9, 36, 82, 22). *Unlike* Margaret, she has *not* committed infanticide – but she effectively tries to do so by attempting to commit suicide: 'Mother, dare you kill your child? | [. . .] Murder would not veil your sin' (ll. 37, 49; see also ll. 61–4).[24]

This marked emphasis on Catherine's sinfulness is suggestive, once again, of Tennyson's antagonism towards the sexually open and morally nuanced aspects of *Faust*. To be sure, in the latter stages of the Gretchen tragedy, the heroine is overcome by a deep feeling of remorse for the evil that has been caused by her liaison with the protagonist. However, throughout these scenes, we sense, also, that Goethe's own morality is less severe than that of this simple Catholic girl, whom he portrays without condescension, but with prodigious sympathy. Tennyson's Catherine seems, by contrast, to be truly forlorn, forsaken not just by her lover, but also by the poet himself. It is not easy to find anything in this piece that might indicate compassion for her.

This moral contrast between the two works is also a formal one. In *Faust*, Gretchen's tragedy – agonising though it is – can at least be said to be *hers*, for it is *her* psychological state that provides the focus of the drama ('Margaret's Room' and 'Place Devoted to Religious Exercises' are lyrical solo pieces, and even 'Dungeon' – to quote Williams – 'is in almost all respects her scene').[25] In contrast, Catherine in 'Forlorn' is

---

[23] Tennyson would not have needed to read Hayward's 'Notes' in order to realise that Mephistopheles' song is, in turn, 'obviously imitated from Ophelia's.— (*Hamlet*, Act 4, Scene 5.)' (Hay. 1, p. 249; refers to *New Oxford Shakespeare*, pp. 1997–2099, IV. 2. 46–53). There is, however, no 'Catherine' in the latter.

[24] Compare also *Faust*, ll. 4579, 4600 / p. 202 and 'Forlorn', ll. 12, 83. 'The Mother's Ghost' (*PT*, 221; 1833) could be another moralistic transformation of the Gretchen tragedy: whereas Margaret deliberately kills her baby, this poem depicts a baby that has inadvertently killed its mother (by being born).

[25] Williams, p. 118.

pushed to the peripheries of the poem: she speaks the first two stanzas, and the concluding stanza describes her actions, but the fourteen stanzas in between consist of bitter reproaches directed against her. In this, the main body of the poem, Tennyson marshals a number of insulting, reproachful or impatient voices from *Faust*, and directs them at the erring Catherine. At the end of 'Night.—Street Before Margaret's Door', Gretchen's dying brother Valentine fiercely criticises her for her sexual licence, and calls her a 'whore' – much as Catherine, in drafts of line 37 of 'Forlorn', is denounced as a 'Harlot' (*F*, ll. 3722–75, esp. 3730 / pp. 158–60, esp. p. 158; *TA*, III, 75, 79). Margaret's neighbour Martha responds to Valentine's invective by telling him not to commit 'the sin of slander' as he dies, and in 'Forlorn', this warning is redirected at Catherine: 'Do not die with a lie in your mouth' (*F*, l. 3765 / p. 159; 'Forlorn', l. 57). An echo of Mephistopheles' exhortation to Faust and Gretchen at the end of 'Dungeon' ('Up! or you are lost. Profitless hesitation!') also finds its way into the poem: 'Up, get up, the time is short' (*F*, ll. 4597–8 / p. 202; 'Forlorn', l. 73). When read in conjunction with *Faust*, the words of the principal speaker of 'Forlorn' seem almost polyphonic: Tennyson's antipathy towards Catherine's conduct is expressed through a veritable chorus of disapproval.

Much *less* emphatic is the salvation that this sinner eventually finds. In the poem's concluding stanza, Catherine writes a letter to the man who was to have become her husband, in which she informs him that she is carrying the child of another. This confession will enable her, it seems, to narrowly escape the fires of hell: 'Tell him all before you die,' the principal speaker urges her, 'Lest you die forever' (ll. 75–76). For a truly redemptive conclusion, however, we must turn, instead, to 'Happy: The Leper's Bride' (*PT*, 424), which appeared as a pendent to 'Forlorn' when that poem was belatedly published in 1889.[26] As Ricks observes, 'Happy' emphasises 'marriage, religion, and morality', for its speaker is a woman who remains faithful to her husband Ulric despite the fact that he

---

[26] *PT*, 314, headnote. It seems likely that when Tennyson wrote 'Happy' in early 1888 (*Mem.*, II, 345), *Faust* was somewhere in his mind. Shortly before, he had composed 'To Ulysses' (*PT*, 423), which could easily have reminded him of his Faustian poem of 1833. Immediately *after* 'Happy', he wrote 'To Mary Boyle: With the Following Poem' (*PT*, 425), in which Winnick identifies two echoes of *Part One* (Winnick, pp. 214–15; refers to *F*, ll. 716, 3457 / Gower, I, 39; Hay. 1, p. 144). That work, in turn, was written as a preface to 'The Progress of Spring' (*PT*, 193), which dates, like 'Ulysses', from 1833, and which may owe something to *Faust*'s springtime monologue 'River and rivulet' (ll. 903–48 / pp. 28–9) (discussed in Chapter 5, pp. 156–8.

has contracted leprosy.[27] She provides, in fact, a saintly contrast to the sinful Catherine, for Ulric's grim physical condition ensures that her love for him is spiritual rather than sexual (she denigrates the body as a 'Satan-haunted ruin, [a] little city of sewers' (l. 34; see also ll. 29–36)). Although she had once been tempted by infidelity, *she* was able to resist: 'See, I sinned but for a moment. I repented and repent, | And trust myself forgiven by the God to whom I kneel' (ll. 85–6). In the poem's concluding lines, the devoted speaker expresses her gratitude to the priest who wedded her to Ulric. Here (as in the conclusion of 'St Agnes'), Tennyson places considerable emphasis on the *spiritual* character of the union of man and woman: 'I thank him. I am happy, happy. Kiss me. In the name | Of the everlasting God, I will live and die with you' (ll. 107–8).

The kiss of heavenly love is felt more tentatively in the conclusion to 'The Vision of Sin' (*PT*, 277; *c*. 1839). In this poem, as in 'Forlorn', Tennyson is implicitly reprimanding a character from *Faust* – although on this occasion, the sinner in question is not Margaret but her lover. As Ricks notes, 'A few details [in "The Vision"] suggest Shelley's *The Triumph of Life*', an unfinished poem which was written between May and July of 1822 (Shelley, *Complete Works*, IV (1928), 167–85).[28] Earlier that year, Shelley had been 'reading over and over again Faust', and translating his two 'Scenes' (Shelley, *Complete Works*, X (1926), Letter no. DLXXXIV, 10 April 1822, p. 371). This is reflected in 'The Triumph': Tennyson would certainly have recognised the allusion to 'Before the Gate' at lines 26–8,[29] and he might also have spotted the similarity between lines 138–224 and 'May-Day Night'. Shelley's translation of the latter scene (on which Tennyson had drawn in at least two poems in 1833) provided, I will argue, an important source for 'The Vision'.

'May-Day Night' is set in the Harz region of eastern Germany, which consists of a 'black wall of mountains | That hems us in'; the highest point of the range, the Brocken, is variously described as a 'mountain | [. . .] all enchanted', and a 'wizard mountain' (ll. 3930–1, 3868, 4093 / PBS, II, ll. 112–13, 36–7, 294). Similarly, parts of 'The Vision' are set within a 'mountain-tract, | That girt the region', which is also referred to as a 'mystic mountain-range' (ll. 46–7, 208). In

---

[27] *PT*, 424, headnote.
[28] *PT*, 277, headnote; Shelley, *Major Works*, p. 815.
[29] This is identified by the editors of Shelley, *Major Works* (p. 816; see *F*, ll. 1087–8 / p. 34).

'May-Day Night', as Faust and Mephistopheles ascend the Brocken, they hear music:

> The sound of song, the rushing throng!
> Are the screech, the lapwing, and the jay,
> All awake as if 'twere day? (ll. 3890–1 / PBS, II, ll. 66–8)[30]

In 'The Vision of Sin', Tennyson writes:

> the music [. . .]
> [. . .]
> Stormed in orbs of song, a growing gale;
> Till thronging in and in, to where they waited,
> As 'twere a hundred-throated nightingale. (ll. 23, 25–7)[31]

Tennyson's ensuing description of dissipation (ll. 28–45) also draws on 'May-Day Night' (which evokes the 'revelry' of 'young rioters', who are 'Dancing and drinking, jabbering, [and] making love' (ll. 4073–4, 4058 / PBS, II, ll. 273, 272, 256)). And as well as resembling one another in their subject matter, the two texts also exhibit some formal similarities: both employ a mixture of tetrameters and pentameters, with intermittent use of couplets.[32]

It is likely that Tennyson would have felt considerable unease about 'May-Day Night' – which, in the words of Williams, 'conveys more than vividly an orgiastic, obscene, blasphemous, grotesque, filthy, seething, stinking, screaming throng'.[33] Goethe himself seems to have been wary of his readers' possible reactions to this scene, for as Albrecht Schöne argues, he appears to have discarded the deeply irreverent conclusion to it that he originally envisaged.[34] In

---

[30] The first line cited here is interpolated by Shelley; it is a modified reiteration of line 3883.

[31] See also 'The Ruined Kiln' (*PT*, 192; written 1833): 'And sparrows in a jangling throng | Chirped all in one – a storm of song' (ll. 6–7). This poem is in Harvard Notebook 16, three pages after 'This Earth is wondrous' – which is also influenced by Shelley's 'Scenes' (*TA*, III, 12; see Chapter 2, p. 84, fn 41).

[32] There is also some shared vocabulary, including 'fountain[s]', '[p]recipitate', 'heath', 'trunks' and 'moss' (PBS, II, l. 105 (and l. 138), l. 9, l. 82 (and l. 210), l. 132, l. 82; 'The Vision', l. 8 (and l. 21), ll. 37, 61 (and l. 72), ll. 93, 212). Both texts also include descriptions of intense colours (*F*; l. 3901 (and l. 4034); l. 3922 / PBS, II, l. 79 (and l. 231); l. 104 (mistranslation); 'The Vision', ll. 31–2).

[33] Williams, p. 112.

[34] Albrecht Schöne, *Götterzeichen Liebeszauber Satanskult. Neue Einblicke in alte Goethetexte* (Munich: Beck, 1982), pp. 107–230.

the published version, therefore, Mephistopheles diverts Faust from his intended meeting with the lord of the witches Urian at the summit of the Brocken, and draws his attention, instead, to four '[o]ld gentlemen' (l. 4072).[35] Each one of these briefly utters a few cynical or reactionary sentiments (ll. 4076–91 / PBS, II, ll. 275–92), and the ensuing stage direction informs us that Mephistopheles, too, *'appears to have grown very old'*. This short episode provides Tennyson with a means of expressing his antagonism towards the surrounding licentiousness, for when a similar shift from debauchery to decrepitude is described in section IV of 'The Vision' (ll. 63–206), it acquires perceptible moral overtones. As Tennyson explains, in this part of the poem, his protagonist – who had previously 'given himself up to pleasure and Epicureanism' – becomes 'worn out', and 'grows into a cynical old man' (EE, II, 353–4). It seems significant that in contrast to the mere handful of lines that are accorded to Goethe's '[o]ld gentlemen', section IV of 'The Vision' takes up almost two-thirds of the piece. As in 'Forlorn', Tennyson is altering the balance of his Faustian source, by abbreviating sensual pleasures, and lengthening their unwelcome aftermath.[36]

Like the pendent to that poem, however, 'The Vision' goes on to suggest that a 'crime of sense' (l. 215) can yet give way to redemption. In section V, Tennyson takes the *'Voices above'* and *'Voices below'* of 'May-Day Night', and transforms them into an exchange between 'a voice upon the slope', and another that peals down 'from that high land' (*F*, ll. 3986–89, 3994–9 / PBS, II, ll. 180–3, 189–95; 'The Vision', ll. 219, 221). This represents, once again, a far-reaching sanctification of *Faust*: in Goethe's drama, the voices belong to participants in the Satanic revelries, but in 'The Vision', they are clearly intended to suggest communication with the Deity (who in the last line of the poem, makes Himself 'an awful rose of dawn' (l. 224)). Tennyson is straying much farther from the infernal summit of the Brocken than Goethe had done in 'May-Day Night'. In his own

---

[35] This correct translation of 'alten Herrn' is taken from Hay. 1 (p. 173); Shelley mistranslates this phrase as '[o]ld gentlewomen' (PBS, II, l. 271). Tennyson would probably have spotted this mistake (which Hayward had pointed out in his 'Preface' (Hay. 1, p. lxiii)).

[36] At the end of 'May-Day Night', Faust sees an apparition of Margaret (who is soon to be decapitated for killing their child): she has a 'blood-red line' across her neck, and 'can carry | Her head under her arm' (ll. 4204, 4207 / PBS, II, ll. 404, 406–7). This image recurs in section IV of 'The Vision': 'In her left [hand] a human head' (l. 138).

words, he is leading the reader into a 'landscape which symbolizes God, Law and the future life', and expressing (to quote his son) the hope that 'the whole human race would [. . .] be at length purified and saved' (EE, II, 354). It is likely that the expression of that hope was occasioned by Tennyson's disappointment with regard to certain aspects of *Faust*. The conclusion of 'The Vision of Sin' suggests, in fact, that like many of his contemporaries, he was not without reservations about the apparent ease with which salvation is achieved by Goethe's impure protagonist.

Within the quartet of Faustian poems on saints and sinners that has been discussed in this chapter, 'Simeon' – with its complex, contradictory speaker – stands somewhat apart. Tennyson's transformation of Goethe's unholy protagonist into a Christian saint results in a characterisation that does not sit easily with received notions of good and evil. It should be noted, however, that although this poem is certainly less moralistic than the other three, it is, nevertheless, somewhat *more* moralistic than *Faust*.

This disparity between text and source is even more striking in 'St Agnes' Eve', 'Forlorn' and 'The Vision of Sin'. These poems represent Tennyson's only truly antagonistic responses to Goethe's drama, and they can, therefore, be usefully contrasted with the works that were discussed in Chapters 1 and 2. It would appear that in order to feel the warm sympathy with Gretchen that informs such pieces as 'Oh! that 'twere possible', Tennyson also needed to express the cold disapproval of her licentiousness that marks 'Forlorn'. Equally revealing contrasts can be drawn between 'St Agnes' and 'The Vision' on the one hand, and 'Ulysses' on the other. In the last-named work, Tennyson is turning the Ulisse of the *Inferno* into a redemptive figure, by fusing his voyage with the visionary flight of Faust in 'Oh, happy he'. In 'St Agnes', however, it is not the Dantean text that is redeemed, but the Goethean one, for in this poem, a more earth-bound, earthier passage from 'Before the Gate' is mingled with the celestial *Paradise*. And although 'Ulysses' suggests that Tennyson would have been basically sympathetic towards the entry of Faust into the after-life at the end of *Part Two*, 'The Vision' indicates that he had some important reservations about the circumstances under which that redemption is achieved.

'St Agnes', 'Forlorn' and 'The Vision' all reveal, then, a marked antagonism towards certain aspects of Goethe's drama. It is, however, this very hostility which ensures that in one respect, they merit – more than any of the other pieces that have been discussed in this book – the description 'a Victorian *Faust*'. They all suggest that Tennyson shared the widespread nineteenth-century unease with the sexual openness and moral complexity of Goethe's drama, and that he also shared the concomitant need to transform it into something more conventional. These three poems belong, therefore, with works such as Bailey's *Festus*, W. S. Gilbert's *Gretchen* and Roden Noel's *A Modern Faust*. In all of these texts, a character with traceable Faustian ancestry attains – to quote Coleridge's comments on his unwritten drama on Michael Scott – 'the conviction of Redemption of Sinners through God's grace' (Coleridge, *Collected Works*, XIV (1990), I, 338).

'Last words'

The first numbered section of *In Memoriam* begins:

> I held it truth, with him who sings
>   To one clear harp in divers tones,
>   That men may rise on stepping-stones
> Of their dead selves to higher things. (ll. 1–4)

When Tennyson was asked in the autumn of 1891 to whom he had referred in these lines, he replied: 'I believe I alluded to Goethe. Among his last words were these: "Von Aenderungen zu höheren Aenderungen," "from changes to higher changes"' (*LAT*, III, 434, 3 November 1891; see also ibid. fn 2). He quotes the same words in the note on this stanza in the Eversley Edition of his *Works*, and describes them as an expression of 'Goethe's creed' (EE, III, 225).[1] As Winnick observes:

> the *Goethe Jahrbuch* for 1891 [. . .] report[ed] the existence of a letter from Jenny von Pappenheim (1811–90) in the possession of her granddaughter, Lily von Kretschmann, in which von Pappenheim says that among Goethe's last words, to her, clear and distinct—words later slightly misquoted by T[ennyson]—were 'Nun kommt die Wandelung zu höheren Wandelungen' [Now comes the change to higher changes].[2]

---

[1] See also *LAT*, III (1990), 179 (19 August 1879) (and fn 2); Alfred Gatty, *A Key to Tennyson's 'In Memoriam'* (London: Bell, 1882), (TRC, no catalogue number), p. 1; [Anon.], 'Tennyson's "In Memoriam"', *The Times*, 5 October 1887, p. 10; Alfred Gatty, 'Tennyson and Goethe', *The Times*, 14 October 1887, p. 13; *Mem.*, II, 391–2, fn.

[2] Winnick, p. 150.

Tennyson would not, however, have been familiar with this quotation when he composed the Goethe-stanza (as I will refer to it) about half a century earlier. There is still some room for speculation, therefore, as to what was in his mind at the time.

It is probable for at least four reasons that the stanza was written around 1839. First, this would be consistent with the evidence that is provided by the poet's notebooks, for these four lines make their first appearance towards the beginning of the Trinity and Lincoln Manuscripts, which were begun, respectively, in 1840 and 1842 (*TA*, XI, 9; XVI, 3). Second, as I argued in the Introduction, it was around 1839 that Tennyson went through a period of renewed interest in German literature. Third, as was mentioned in Chapter 5, Lang makes a connection between the 'stepping-stones' of the Goethe-stanza, and Tennyson's use of the word 'stepwise' in the letter that he sent to Emily Sellwood in October of that year, and he suggests, therefore, that the two texts were written at 'about the same time'.[3] Fourth, as was also mentioned in Chapter 5, it was in *c.* 1839 that Tennyson penned the only other passage in his œuvre in which he refers to Goethe as an individual: the first two lines of 'Wherefore, in these dark ages of the Press' (*PT*, 276A). These words draw on a passage in the *Apprenticeship*, a German copy of which was given to Tennyson for Christmas in 1838.

The *Apprenticeship* may also have been an influence on the Goethe-stanza. Turner argues that '[t]he harp image [in line 2] clearly alludes' to the melancholy Harper, who is a prominent character in the novel, and whose beautiful songs were greatly esteemed by Tennyson.[4] This assertion finds some support, I think, in a passage in Book V, Chapter XII, in which the Harper sings 'a multitude of songs', to the accompaniment of his daughter Mignon on the tambourine (Vol. IX, p. 694, l. 20 / XXIII, 363). From this 'simple [. . .] instrument', writes Goethe, she is able to elicit 'a great variety of tones' (Vol. IX, p. 694, ll. 35–6 / XXIII, 364).

Tennyson's 1838 Christmas presents also included *The Works of Lord Byron* and Austin's *Characteristics*. In these volumes, too, we find passages which might well have exerted an influence on the Goethe-stanza. As George G. Loane observes, in 'The Siege of Corinth'

---

[3] Lang, 'Introduction', in Campbell (ed.), I (1971), p. xi (refers to *LAT*, I, 174).
[4] Turner, p. 122. 'In his smaller poems such as those in *Wilhelm Meister*', said Tennyson, 'Goethe shows himself to be one of the great artists of the world' (*Mem.*, II, 422–3).

(Byron, *Poetical Works*, III (1981), 322–56), which is included in Tennyson's copy of the *Works* (pp. 120–31), Byron writes:

> Or pave the path with many a corse,
> O'er which the following brave may rise,
> Their stepping-stone—the last who dies! (Section 10, ll. 194–6)[5]

Also, as I argued in Chapter 5, Tennyson's use of the word 'stepwise' in his October 1839 letter to Emily (*LAT*, I, 174) can be traced to the poem 'The Metamorphosis of Plants', which is included in *Characteristics*.

Austin's compendium also includes an account of its subject's death in Weimar on 22 March 1832. This passage may well be of relevance to Tennyson's reference, in his comments on the Goethe-stanza, to the German poet's 'last words':

> Just before he expired the grand duke [. . .] expressed a strong desire [. . .] to speak some last words of love and consolation to him. A few moments afterwards [Goethe's secretary] Dr. Eckermann quoted to the friends assembled in the adjoining room the two last lines of Faust [in *Part Two*, Act V].[6] [. . .] At that moment Goethe breathed his last. (*CG*, III, 93–4)

Elsewhere in *Characteristics*, we read:

> Faust may be considered as the first and last song of the poet. Two of the acts of the second part were written very recently, and it was not till a few weeks before his death that he beheld the completion of his work. (ibid. III, 44–5)

It is worth speculating, therefore, whether Tennyson, in *c.* 1839, was thinking not of the 'last words' that would be attributed to Goethe by Jenny von Pappenheim's granddaughter more than half a century later, but of the last words he had uttered *as a poet*: the closing scene of *Faust: Part Two*, the ethereal 'Mountain Defiles' (ll. 11844–12111 / Macdonald, pp. 340–51). As is hinted at by the two quotations from *Characteristics*, this can be said to be Goethe's 'last words' in the

---

[5] See George G. Loane, *Echoes in Tennyson and Other Essays* (London: Stockwell, [1928]), p. 9.
[6] Lines 11583–4 are cited (although Faust speaks, in fact, a further two lines before he dies).

same way as 'Crossing the Bar' (*PT*, 462) has traditionally been regarded as the last words of Tennyson. This scene was speculatively linked to the Goethe-stanza by David Asher as long ago as 1888, and both Lore Metzger and Jerome Hamilton Buckley made similar points in the mid-twentieth century.[7] Their arguments are lent greater credibility by the fact that (as we saw in Chapters 1 and 3) it was around 1839 that Tennyson conceived *The Princess*, which is heavily influenced by *Part Two*, and a decade and a half later, he would draw on 'Mountain Defiles' in the concluding part of *Maud*.

As Williams observes, in this scene, 'Faust's soul, his immortal self [. . .] rises through successive stages towards "higher spheres" ["höhern Sphären" (l. 12094)]'.[8] He is passing, one might say, 'Von Aenderungen zu höheren Aenderungen', 'from changes to higher changes'. Goethe is thereby expressing his strong belief in an afterlife of progressive development, a belief he is said to have reiterated just a short time later on his deathbed. That same belief was also of enormous importance to Tennyson: as we saw in Chapter 2, he once remarked that he could 'hardly understand [. . .] how any great, imaginative man [. . .] can doubt of the Soul's continuous progress in the after-life' (*Mem.*, I, 321). This outlook is central to 'Ulysses', and it is even more prominent in that other great poetic response to Hallam's death, *In Memoriam*. It seems likely, therefore, that it was to this belief that Tennyson was referring when he spoke of 'Goethe's creed', and he might also have been thinking of his last words as a poet, the closing scene of *Part Two*, in which the selfsame creed finds powerful lyrical expression.

---

[7] David Asher, 'Lord Tennyson and Goethe', *Publications of the English Goethe Society*, o.s. 4 (1888), 114–17 (pp. 116–17); Lore Metzger, 'The Eternal Process: Some Parallels between Goethe's *Faust* and Tennyson's *In Memoriam*', *Victorian Poetry*, 1: 3 (August 1963), 189–96 (pp. 190–1, 193); Jerome Hamilton Buckley, *The Victorian Temper: A Study in Literary Culture* (London: Cass, 1966), pp. 87, 88–9.

[8] Williams, p. 208. The scene includes two other uses of the word *höher* ('higher') (l. 11918; stage direction before l. 11934).

Conclusion

The influence of *Faust* on Tennyson began around 1824; reached a remarkable level of intensity in 1833–4; and continued, intermittently, until 1855. Goethe's drama was of considerable importance for the direction that Tennyson's career took, for he drew on it in at least three of his extended works, as well as all four of his earliest dramatic monologues.

In addition to the crucial 1833–4 period (discussed below), a number of other significant dates in the story of Tennyson and *Faust* can be identified: *c*. 1824; 1827–31; *c*. 1839; *c*. 1845–7; March–May 1850; and 1854–5. It was probably in 1824 that Tennyson wrote his earliest Faustian lyric, 'Chorus, in an Unpublished Drama' (*PT*, 101). His time at Cambridge (1827–31) was marked by a strong preoccupation with both *Werther* and *Wilhelm Meister* (chiefly the *Apprenticeship*). This period produced, however, only one poem that is indubitably influenced by *Faust*, 'Refulgent Lord of Battle' – although a few faint echoes of Goethe's drama may also be discernible in 'Supposed Confessions', and the two Mariana lyrics (*PT*, Vol. III, p. 608; *PT*, 78, 73, 160). The books that Tennyson was given for Christmas in 1838, and the letter that he sent to Emily Sellwood in October of the following year (*LAT*, I, 174–5), suggest a resurgence of his interest in Goethe. This is confirmed by 'The Golden Year' (*PT*, 276), 'Wherefore, in these dark ages' (*PT*, 276A) and 'The Vision of Sin' (*PT*, 277), all of which have been dated either wholly or partly to 1839. It is probable that the Goethe-stanza from *In Memoriam* was also written around that time (*PT*, 296, I, ll. 1–4), as well as sections LIV–LVI (which echo *Faust, Meister, Sartor, Cain* and *Characteristics*). It is likely that it was also in 1839 that Tennyson conceived *The Princess* (*PT*, 286) – although most of the composition of this Faustian-Schillerian poem would appear to have been carried out in 1845–7. In March 1850, Emily Sellwood was given a copy of *Part One*, and her fiancé published the trial edition of

In Memoriam. This conjunction of events is an intriguing one, for of the seven sections of Tennyson's elegy that were not included in that limited first printing – and which can, therefore, be speculatively dated to between March and May 1850 – four are influenced by Goethe (as are lines 1–8 and 17–20 of CXXIV, which may also have been written at this time). Specifically, Turner links VII to the *Apprenticeship* (and I have argued the same for CXXIV); its companion-piece, CXIX, is adapted from the Faustian fragment 'Let Death and Memory keep the face' (*PT*, Vol. III, pp. 596–7), whilst XCVI suggests the influence of *Characteristics*, and XCVII draws on the Gretchen tragedy.[1] Tennyson returned to the last-named text in *Maud* (*PT*, 316), which was written in 1854–5. That poem effectively marks the end of his creative engagement with *Faust*, for of all the works that he wrote in the remaining thirty-seven years of his life, only three can be confidently said to have been influenced by Goethe's drama: 'The Higher Pantheism' (*PT*, 353), 'To Mary Boyle' (*PT*, 425) and 'The Dreamer' (*PT*, 461).

The twelve-month period from March 1833 to around February 1834 may well be more important than all of these other phases put together. Indeed, the majority of the Faustian poems discussed in this book date from that year, which was a pivotal one for Tennyson for at least three reasons. First, it was marked by a defining personal experience, the death of Arthur Hallam. Second, it witnessed what was possibly the greatest burst of creativity in Tennyson's entire career. Third, the many poems that he wrote at this time include seven that would affect the whole course of his artistic development.

There can be little doubt that of all the texts that Tennyson read during 1833–4, Hayward's translation of *Part One* and his article on *Part Two* were the second most important (the *most* important was, of course, the letter from Henry Elton, informing him that Hallam was 'no more' (*LAT*, I, 93, 1 October 1833)). The editorial material in these two works includes references to *The Sorrows of Young Werther*; the *Memoirs of Goethe*; *Cain*; *The Deformed Transformed*; Shelley's 'Scenes'; and Carlyle's 'Goethe's "Helena"' (Hay. 1, pp. vi, fn; lix–lxiv; 207, 214, 220, 228, 235, 237, 238, 241, 244, 253–4; Hay. 2, p. 96). It seems likely that these remarks led Tennyson to read, re-read or recollect these works, and Hayward's repeated suggestions of a link between *Faust* and *The Divine Comedy* could have had much the same effect (Hay. 1, pp. lxxiii, lxxviii, lxxviii–lxxix, fn; Hay. 2, p. 105). Similarly, Hayward's two references to the *Correspondence*

---

[1] Turner, p. 122.

between Schiller and Goethe might well have led Tennyson to Carlyle's essay 'Schiller', which is, ostensibly, a review of that volume (Hay. 1, pp. lxxxiv, fn; 276; see also Hay. 2, p. 105).

Of the roughly forty poems that Ricks dates to the 1833–4 period (*PT*, 191–230, excluding 225), more than half have either definite or possible links to Goethe's drama, and to the closely related works that have been cited above. Ricks dates eight of these poems – either wholly or partly – to *c.* spring 1833: 'Inscription by a Brook' (*PT*, 191); 'The Ruined Kiln' (*PT*, 192); 'Mechanophilus' (*PT*, 197); 'Stanzas' (*PT*, 198); 'This Earth is wondrous, change on change' (*PT*, 201); 'Poets and Critics' (*PT*, 204); 'Sir Launcelot and Queen Guinevere' (*PT*, 205); and 'The Gardener's Daughter' (*PT*, 208). It is, however, from around June onwards that the influence on Tennyson of Goethe's drama becomes especially intense. Indeed, of the nineteen poems that Ricks dates to between then and early 1834, no less than *fifteen* would appear to be influenced by *Faust* and related works: 'The Two Voices' (*PT*, 209); 'St Simeon Stylites' (*PT*, 210); 'The Beggar Maid' (*PT*, 211); 'St Agnes' Eve' (*PT*, 212); 'Hark! the dogs howl!' (*PT*, 214); 'On a Mourner' (*PT*, 216); 'Ulysses' (*PT*, 217); 'Tithon' (*PT*, 218); 'Tiresias' (*PT*, 219); 'Semele' (*PT*, 220); 'The Mother's Ghost' (*PT*, 221); 'Love's latest hour is this' (*PT*, 224); 'Morte d'Arthur' (*PT*, 226); 'Oh! that 'twere possible' (*PT*, 227); and 'Break, break, break' (*PT*, 228). I would add to this list a further seven pieces (all of which, I have argued, are influenced by *Faust* and its author, and which may well date from 1833–4): 'The Flight' (*PT*, 259); *In Memoriam*, II, IV, XIII and XXVIII (*PT*, 296); 'Forlorn' (*PT*, 314); and 'Let Death and Memory keep the face' (*PT*, Vol. III, pp. 596–7).[2]

As is clear from the numerous sources that are cited in Ricks's *Poems of Tennyson* and Winnick's *New Textual Parallels*, the literary influences on these thirty pieces are both copious and wide-ranging. They include a number of texts (the Bible, *The Odyssey*, *The Aeneid*, Horace's *Odes* and *Hamlet*) that are echoed in several different poems. But Hayward's *Faust* translations – and the closely related works that are referred to therein – would appear to provide the only common thread.

It is possible, moreover, that this small group of interrelated texts helped to suggest some of the other sources on which Tennyson drew

---

[2] The other early sections of *In Memoriam* constitute an exception to the pattern for which I am here arguing, for none is influenced by Goethe. Also, of the 1833–4 fragments (*PT*, Vol. III, pp. 619–25), only 'What did it profit me' is at all suggestive of *Faust* (ibid. Vol. III, p. 620).

in the poems of 1833–4. The reference to 'Syrian Simon' in Carlyle's 'Schiller' (*WTC*, XXVII, 190) – and also, perhaps, the mention of 'Saint Andrew's eve' in 'Before the Gate' (*F*, ll. 878–9 / p. 27) – could have led Tennyson to consult the relevant entries in Hone's *Every-Day Book*. The presence in *The Divine Comedy* of Ulysses, Tithonus and Tiresias (and a recognition of these characters' similarities to Faust, and to Lynceus in 'Helena') might well have prompted him to re-read or recollect the classical sources for these three poems.[3] The theme of 'Semele' was probably suggested either by Canto XXX of the *Inferno* (p. 157 / l. 2); by Canto XXI of *Paradise* (p. 109 / l. 5); or by the quotation from Marlowe's *Dr Faustus* in Hayward's article on *Part Two* (Hay. 2, p. 94). Tennyson might even have been led from the death of the King of Thule in *Part One* (ll. 2759–82 / p. 108) to Malory's *Morte d'Arthur*. It was, I think, with some prescience that Shelley remarked: 'Faust may furnish the germ of other poems' (Shelley, *Complete Works*, X (1926), Letter no. DLXXXIV, p. 371, 10 April 1822).[4]

Three of Tennyson's Faustian poems of 1833–4 would subsequently furnish their author with the 'germs' of longer works. Hallam Tennyson calls 'Hark! the dogs howl!' 'the germ of "In Memoriam"', whilst Ricks describes 'Oh! that 'twere possible' as '[t]he germ of *Maud*', and 'Morte d'Arthur' has a comparable relationship to the *Idylls*.[5] Although there is no known 'seed poem' for *The Princess*, that work, too, draws extensively on *Faust*. Goethe's drama might be said, therefore, to have played a significant role in Tennyson's gradual move towards larger structures.[6] In the seventeen years that separate 'Hark! the dogs howl!' from the publication of *In Memoriam*, he went from the raw depiction of an individual tragedy, to an ambitious attempt to give artistic expression to the age in which he was living. This might be seen as a largely unwitting recapitulation of Goethe's even longer journey, which had taken him from the brief *Original Faust*, to the 12,111 lines of *Faust: Parts One and Two*. Similarly, Tennyson's awareness of the disparities of scale and genre

---

[3] *DC*, Vol. I, Canto XXVI, pp. 140–1 / ll. 85–135; Vol. II, Canto IX, p. 45 / l. 1; Vol. I, Canto XX, p. 104 / p. 436; p. 105 / l. 37; Vol. II, Canto XXII, p. 122 / l. 112.
[4] See *Mem.*, I, 268; II, 496, 497.
[5] *Mem.*, I, 107; *PT*, 316, headnote. Hallam Tennyson's comment is somewhat opaque: 'Hark!' is not in the *abba* stanza, and unlike 'Oh! that 'twere possible' and 'Morte d'Arthur', it was not incorporated into the work for which it furnished the 'germ'.
[6] The earliest of Tennyson's long poems, *The Lover's Tale* (*PT*, 153), is loosely modelled on *Werther* (see Baynes, 'Tennyson and *Werther*', pp. 302–16).

between the brief lyric 'Oh! that 'twere possible' and its principal source – Hayward's lengthy *Faust: A Dramatic Poem* – could well help to explain why he developed it into the much more substantial *Maud: A Monodrama* (the earlier piece 'was really intended', he is said to have remarked retrospectively, 'to be part of a dramatic poem').[7] The poetic 'seed' of *Maud* was the offspring of a full-grown plant, so there might have seemed to be something natural about its incremental expansion to proportions more commensurate with those of its parent.

The poems of 1833–4 also include four that are usually regarded as Tennyson's earliest dramatic monologues: 'St Simeon Stylites', 'Ulysses', 'Tithon' and 'Tiresias'. All of these works draw (to varying extents) on the themes, language and imagery of *Faust*. But Hayward's two translations may also have been a *formal* influence on these poems. As Luke observes, although *Faust* is ostensibly a drama, it includes numerous passages that read almost like self-contained lyrics:

> its lyricism is exceptionally pervasive, even seeming [. . .] to predominate over dramatic functionality; its dialogue is less integrated and indivisible than that of [Goethe's plays] *Iphigenie* or *Tasso*, and indeed often reads rather like two or more lyrical monologues at cross purposes.[8]

As one might expect, the passages in *Faust* to which the description 'lyrical monologue' is most applicable were of especial interest for the lyric poet Tennyson. The influence on his work of 'Margaret's Room' (ll. 3374–413 / pp. 141–2) may have made itself felt as early as the Mariana poems, and there can be little doubt that this scene would later provide a source for 'Hark! the dogs howl!' and 'Let Death and Memory keep the face'. Also, Tennyson ended all of the early versions of 'Oh! that 'twere possible' with a clear echo of Gretchen's other solo piece, 'Place Devoted to Religious Exercises' (*PT*, 227, ll. 63–4; *F*, ll. 3606–7 / p. 153). One of Faust's most lyrical monologues, 'River and rivulet' (ll. 903–40 / pp. 28–9), was an influence on 'Inscription by a Brook' and 'The Two Voices', and his 'Two souls' speech (ll. 1110–25 / p. 35) would appear to have left its mark on both the latter poem and 'Supposed Confessions'.

---

[7] *The Works of Tennyson: With Notes by the Author*, ed. Hallam, Lord Tennyson (London: Macmillan, 1913), p. xxxix.

[8] Goethe, trans. Luke, p. xviii.

It was, however, three other passages that are spoken by Goethe's protagonist – 'Oh, happy he' (ll. 1064–99 / pp. 33–4), 'The pulses of life' (ll. 4679–727 / pp. 85–6) and, to a much lesser extent, 'Only a few steps further' (ll. 1022–55 / pp. 32–3) – which had the greatest consequences for Tennyson's work, for it was these that influenced his first four dramatic monologues. When read in isolation, these three Faustian speeches could themselves be fairly described as dramatic monologues (as could 'River and rivulet'). Indeed, they fulfil, by and large, even the most proscriptive of the various definitions that have been proposed for that form, for they include 'speaker, audience, occasion, revelation of character, interplay between speaker and audience, dramatic action, and action which takes place in the present'.[9] It should be observed, first of all, that speaker and audience – and the interplay between them – are highly characteristic of these passages.[10] During those which occur in the scene 'Before the Gate', Faust's assistant Wagner is onstage with him, and there are a number of lines in which he is addressed (ll. 1031–3, 1070–1 / pp. 32–3, 34; see also ll. 916–17, 929–30 / pp. 28, 29). And although the protagonist *is* alone in 'The pulses of life', his intense engagement with Nature, and his occasional use of the imperative, make him sound, at times, as if he were speaking to an audience ('Thou, too, Earth, wert constant this night'; 'Look up!'; 'Meditate upon it, and you will conceive more accurately' (ll. 4681, 4695, 4726 / Hay. 2, pp. 85, 86)).[11] Revelation of character is another key feature of these passages: there is Faust's vehement self-abasement in 'Only a few steps further'; his unremitting striving in 'Oh, happy he'; and his new, less hubristic attitude towards Nature in 'The pulses of life' (whilst in 'River and rivulet', he is emotionally revivified by the coming of spring). Also, all of these monologues include dramatic action unfolding in the present (and the Easter festivities of 'River and rivulet' create a noticeable sense of occasion). Admittedly, that action is, by and large, very limited: in 'The pulses of life', for example, almost the only thing that can be said to *happen* is that the sun rises, whilst

---

[9] Ina Beth Sessions, 'The Dramatic Monologue', *PMLA*, 62: 2 (June 1947), 503–16 (p. 508).

[10] The same might be said of many of Goethe's other works, most notably *Werther* (see Baynes, 'Tennyson and *Werther*', p. 307). As Boyle observes: 'Goethe's mind was a dialogue, certainly: to exist it needed reaction. [. . .] His forte was the letter, the monologue with an addressee' (Boyle, I (1991), pp. 264, 661).

[11] Note that in 'Tithon' (which is influenced by this monologue), the 'audience', once again, is not a human being, but a natural phenomenon.

in 'Oh, happy he' it sinks, and the speaker gives vivid expression to his desire to pursue it. This constitutes, however, a further resemblance to Tennyson's dramatic monologues, for these brief descriptions can be applied, with equal justice, to the action of 'Tithon' and of 'Ulysses', the two poems that these passages helped to inspire.[12]

In sum, the formal similarities between these three or four speeches from *Faust*, and Tennyson's first four dramatic monologues, are strikingly numerous. What is more, these close affinities must be evaluated in combination with the more specific similarities of theme, language and imagery which have been discussed in the preceding chapters ('Simeon' draws on 'Only a few steps further'; 'Ulysses' on 'Oh, happy he'; 'Tithon' – and perhaps also 'Tiresias' – on 'The pulses of life'). It does not seem entirely fanciful, therefore, to suggest that in these four pieces, Tennyson imported the dramatic qualities of the Faustian monologue into the English lyric poem, and invented, thereby, a major new literary genre.[13]

In Victorian Britain, *Faust* was a central text, which ranked alongside the works of Homer, Dante, Shakespeare, Milton and the Romantics. It need not surprise us, therefore, that Goethe's drama had a similar status for the pre-eminent Victorian poet. It was of crucial importance to him in the months before (and, in particular, after) the defining event of his life, the death of Arthur Hallam. He also turned to *Faust* when dealing with themes such as God, Nature and morality – although his attitude towards Goethe's stance on these topics was often ambivalent and occasionally hostile. *Faust* can nevertheless be said to have exercised a far-reaching influence on Tennyson's achievement. It helped to inspire at least three of his extended works, as well as all four of his earliest dramatic monologues. Indeed, apart from the Bible, *The Divine Comedy* and a small number of Shakespearean texts, it is not easy to think of an individual work of literature that exerted a greater influence on Tennyson than *Faust*.

---

[12] 'Ulysses', observes Martin (p. 186), '[. . .] is full of the *need* of going forward not progress itself; there is much exhortation, little action.'

[13] It may even be that Browning's independent invention of the dramatic monologue had a comparable background. His earliest works in the form, 'Porphyria' and 'Johannes Agricola', were written shortly after the Faustian *Paracelsus* (Browning, *Poems*, I (1991), 328–37).

Bibliography

(For abbreviated items, see pages xv–xvii.)

Unpublished Sources

(N.B.: the published books in this section are included because of their marginal markings and annotations.)

Anon., 'Catalogue of Books in Tennyson's Library. 1856–59' (TRC, N/20).
Bailey, Philip James, *Festus: A Poem* (London: Pickering, 1845) (TRC, AT/481).
[Dante Alighieri], *The Vision; or Hell, Purgatory, and Paradise, of Dante Alighieri: Translated by the Rev. Henry Francis Cary, A.M.*, 3rd edn, 3 vols (London: Taylor, 1831) (TRC, AT/826).
Ellis, Susie, 'The Influence of Goethe's *Faust* on the Fiction of Henry James' (unpublished doctoral thesis, University of Ulster, 1992).
[Elvin, Lawrence(?)], 'Catalogue of the Library of Alfred Lord Tennyson, C-GRE', "Robin" Binder No. 582½ R (*c.* 1963) (TRC, no ref. no.).
Gatty, Alfred, *A Key to Tennyson's 'In Memoriam'* (London: Bell, 1882) (TRC; no ref. no.).
Goethe, Johann Wolfgang, *Conversations of Goethe with Eckermann and Soret*, trans. John Oxenford, 2 vols (London: Smith, Elder, 1850) (TRC, AT/1008).
—, *Faust: A Dramatic Poem, by Goethe; Translated, with Notes, by the Translator of Savigny's "Of the Vocation of our Age for Legislation and Jurisprudence."* [Abraham Hayward] (London: Moxon, 1833) (TRC, AT/3274).
—, *Gedichte*, 2 vols (Stuttgart: Cotta'schen, 1829) (TRC, ET/3336).
—, *Goethe's Werke. Vollständige Ausgabe letzter Hand*, vols 5 and 6 (Stuttgart: Cotta'schen, 1828) (TRC, AT/1016).
—, *Wilhelm Meisters Lehrjahre. Ein Roman*, 4 vols (Berlin: Unger, 1795–6) (TRC, AT/1017).
Hallam, Julia Maria, [*Travel Journal*, 17 May–1 September 1822] (British Library, *Hallam Papers*, Additional Manuscripts, 81293–305 (81295A)).

Noehden, G. H. (ed.), *Rabenhorst's Pocket Dictionary of the German and English Languages, in Two Parts*, 3rd edn (London: Longman, 1829) (TRC, AT/1846).

[Schiller, Johann Christoph Friedrich], *Schiller's sämmtliche Werke in einem Bande* (Stuttgart: Cotta'schen, 1834) (TRC, AT/1947).

Smith, David Francis, 'English Response to Goethe, 1824–1865' (unpublished doctoral thesis, University of Oxford, Exeter College, 1981).

[Tennyson, Alfred Lord], 'Catalogue of my Books' (TRC, N/25).

—, Trinity Notebook 0.15.19 (Trinity College Library, Cambridge).

—, Trinity Notebook 0.15.20 (Trinity College Library, Cambridge).

—, Trinity Notebook 0.15.22 (Trinity College Library, Cambridge).

[Tennyson, Audrey], 'Farringford Library Catalogue 1887' (TRC, N/23).

[Tennyson, Emily], 'Catalogue of Books in Alfred Tennyson's Library 1874' (TRC, N/22).

[Tennyson, Emily, and Alfred Lord Tennyson], 'Loose Sheets from a Catalogue of Tennyson's Library 1855–56' (TRC, N/19).

Trollope, William (ed.), *Pentalogia Græca* (London: Rivington, 1825) (TRC, AT/3550).

Trout, R. Ridgill, 'Inventory of the Library, the Property of Hallam, Lord Tennyson Trust Ltd. Stored at Messrs Shoolbred's Depository Harrow Road. W. June 1957. R. Ridgill Trout. F.V.I. 37 Tavistock Square. London. W.C.I.' (TRC, no ref. no.).

Primary Sources

[Allen, Thomas], *The History of the County of Lincoln: From the Earliest Period to the Present Time*, 2 vols (London: Saunders, 1834).

Allingham, William, *William Allingham's Diary: 1847–1889*, ed. H. Allingham and D. Radford (London: Macmillan, 1907; repr. London: Centaur Press, 2000).

Anon., 'Anthology for 1839', *Athenæum*, 634 (21 December 1839), 958–9.

Anon., 'Art. IV. *Festus, A Poem*. London: Pickering. 8vo. pp. 360', *Eclectic Review*, 6 (December 1839), 654–64.

Anon., 'ART. VI.—*Cours de Littérature Dramatique*. Par A. W. Schlegel. Traduit d'Allemand', *Quarterly Review*, 12: 23 (October 1814), 112–46.

Anon., 'Drama: The Week', *Athenæum*, 3042 (13 February 1886), 241.

Anon., 'The Drama. ART. VIII.—*Manfred: A Dramatic Poem*. By Lord Byron. 8vo. pp. 80. London, Murray, 1817', *Critical Review*, 5: 6 (June 1817), 622–9.

Anon., '*Faust: A Dramatic Poem, by Goethe*', *Athenæum*, 287 (27 April 1833), 260–1.

Anon., '*Faust and Loose*', *Saturday Review*, 61: 1581 (13 February 1886), 229.

Anon., '*Faust up to Date*', *Saturday Review*, 66: 1724 (10 November 1888), 554.

Anon., 'Funeral of Mr. Hayward, Q.C.', *The Times*, 7 February 1884, p. 7.
Anon., 'The Literary Examiner. *Faust: A Dramatic Poem, by Goethe*', *Examiner*, 1312 (24 March 1833), 180–1.
Anon., 'Miscellaneous Literary Notices, No. XXII: Germany', *Foreign Quarterly Review*, 11: 22 (April 1833), 531–5.
Anon., 'Our Omnibus-Box', *The Theatre*, n.s. 8 (July 1886), 47–58.
Anon., 'Scene from *Faust and Loose*', *Judy, or the London Serio-Comic Journal* (14 April 1886), 170.
Anon., 'Tennyson's "In Memoriam"', *The Times*, 5 October 1887, p. 10.
Arnold, Matthew, *The Complete Prose Works of Matthew Arnold*, ed. R. H. Super, 11 vols (Ann Arbor: University of Michigan Press, 1960–77).
—, *The Letters of Matthew Arnold*, ed. Cecil Y. Lang, 6 vols (Charlottesville: University Press of Virginia, 1996–2001).
—, *The Poems of Matthew Arnold*, ed. Kenneth Allot, 2nd edn, ed. Miriam Allott (London: Longman, 1979).
Asher, David, 'Lord Tennyson and Goethe', *Publications of the English Goethe Society*, o.s. 4 (1888), 114–17.
[Bädeker, Karl], *Die Schweiz. Handbüchlein für Reisende, nach eigener Anschauung und den besten Hülfsquellen bearbeitet* (Koblenz: Bädeker, 1844).
Bailey, Philip James, 'The Author of *Festus* and the Spasmodic School', in *Literary Anecdotes of the Nineteenth Century: Contributions towards a Literary History of the Period*, ed. W. Robertson Nicoll and Thomas J. Wise, 2 vols (London: Hodder & Stoughton, 1895–6), II (1896), pp. 411–18.
—, *Festus: A Poem* (London: Pickering, 1845).
Blackie, John Stuart, *The Wisdom of Goethe* (Edinburgh: Blackwood, 1883).
Boileau, D., *A Few Remarks on Mr. Hayward's English Prose Translation of Goethe's 'Faust'* (London: Treuttel, Würtz, Richter, and Wacey, 1834).
Browning, Robert, *The Complete Works of Robert Browning: With Variant Readings & Annotations*, ed. Roma A. King, Jr and others, 17 vols (Athens: Ohio University Press, 1969–2012).
—, *The Poems of Browning*, ed. John Woolford, Daniel Karlin and Joseph Phelan (London: Longman, 1991–).
Browning, Robert, and Elizabeth Barrett Browning, *The Brownings' Correspondence*, ed. Philip Kelley and Ronald Hudson (Winfield: Wedgestone Press, 1984–).
Bulwer Lytton, [Edward], *Falkland*, ed. Herbert van Thal (London: Cassell, 1967).
Byron, George Gordon Lord, *Byron's Letters and Journals*, ed. Leslie A. Marchand, 13 vols (London: Murray, 1973–94).
—, *The Complete Poetical Works*, ed. Jerome J. McGann and Barry Weller, 7 vols (Oxford: Clarendon Press, 1980–93).
—, *The Works of Lord Byron: Complete in One Volume* (London: Murray, 1837).

Callimachus, *Hymns and Epigrams; Lycophron; Aratus*, with translations by A. W. Mair and G. R. Mair, 2nd edn (Cambridge, MA: Harvard University Press; London: Heinemann, 1955).

[Carlyle, Thomas], 'ART. II.—*Faustus: from the German of Goethe*. London. Boosey and Sons. 1821, 8vo. pp. 86', *New Edinburgh Review*, 2: 4 (April 1822), 316–34.

Carlyle, Thomas, and Jane Welsh Carlyle, *The Collected Letters of Thomas and Jane Welsh Carlyle*, ed. Charles Richard Sanders, Duke-Edinburgh Edition (Durham, NC: Duke University Press, 1970–).

Carroll, Lewis, 'The Stage and the Spirit of Reverence', *The Theatre*, n.s. 11 (June 1888), 285–94.

Clough, Arthur Hugh, *The Poems of Arthur Hugh Clough*, ed. F. L. Mulhauser, 2nd edn (Oxford: Oxford University Press, 1974).

Coleridge, Samuel Taylor, *The Collected Works of Samuel Taylor Coleridge*, ed. Kathleen Coburn, Bollingen Edition, 16 vols (London: Princeton University Press, 1969–2002).

— (trans.), *Faustus: From the German of Goethe*, ed. Frederick Burwick and James C. McKusick (Oxford: Clarendon Press, 2007).

Conan Doyle, Arthur, *The Sign of the Four*, ed. Christopher Roden (Oxford: Oxford University Press, 1993).

Cross, J. W. (ed.), *George Eliot's Life: As Related in her Letters and Journals*, 3 vols (Edinburgh: Blackwood, 1885).

Disraeli, Benjamin, *Vivian Grey*, ed. Herbert van Thal (London: Cassell, 1968).

Eliot, George, *Daniel Deronda*, ed. Graham Handley (Oxford: Clarendon Press, 1984).

—, *The George Eliot Letters*, ed. Gordon S. Haight, 9 vols (New Haven, CT: Yale University Press, 1954–78).

—, 'The Lifted Veil', in *The Lifted Veil; Brother Jacob*, ed. Helen Small (Oxford: Oxford University Press, 1999), pp. 1–43.

Emerson, Ralph Waldo, *The Collected Works of Ralph Waldo Emerson*, ed. Alfred R. Ferguson and others, 10 vols (Cambridge, MA: Harvard University Press, 1971–2013), V: *English Traits*, ed. Philip Nicoloff, Robert E. Burkholder and Douglas Emory Wilson (1994).

[Empson, William], 'ART. VI.—*Faust: A Dramatic Poem, by Goethe*', *Edinburgh Review*, 57: 115 (April 1833), 107–43.

Gatty, Alfred, 'Tennyson and Goethe', *The Times*, 14 October 1887, p. 13.

Gibbon, Edward, *The History of the Decline and Fall of the Roman Empire*, ed. David Womersley, 3 vols (Harmondsworth: Penguin, 1994).

Gilbert, W. S., *Gretchen: A Play, in Four Acts* (London: Newman, 1879).

Goethe, Johann Wolfgang, *Auswahl von Goethes lyrischen Gedichten* [ed. Edward Craven Hawtrey], 2nd edn (Eton: Williams, 1834).

—, *Conversations of Goethe with Eckermann and Soret*, trans. John Oxenford, 2 vols (London: Smith, Elder, 1850).

—, *Faust: A Tragedy by J. W. Goethe. Part II, as Completed in 1831* [trans. William Bell Macdonald], 2nd edn (London: Pickering, 1842).
—, *Memoirs of Goethe: Written by Himself* [n. trans.], 2 vols (London: Colburn, 1824).
—, *Selected Verse: With Plain Prose Translations of Each Poem*, ed. and trans. David Luke (Harmondsworth: Penguin, 1964).
Gower, Lord Francis Leveson (trans.), *Faust: A Drama, by Goethe. With Translations from the German*, 2nd edn, 2 vols (London: Murray, 1825).
[Hayward, Abraham], 'ART. II.—*Lord Byron. Von Karl Elze. Berlin, 1870*', *Quarterly Review*, 131: 262 (October 1871), 354–92, repr. as 'Byron and Tennyson', in A. Hayward, *Sketches of Eminent Statesmen and Writers: With Other Essays*, 2 vols (London: Murray, 1880), II, 305–59.
— (trans.), *Faust: A Dramatic Poem, by Goethe. Translated into English Prose, with Remarks on Former Translations, and Notes*, 2nd edn (London: Moxon, 1834).
—, *A Selection from the Correspondence of Abraham Hayward, Q.C. from 1834 to 1884: With an Account of his Early Life*, ed. Henry E. Carlisle, 2 vols (London: Murray, 1886).
Heinemann, William, 'Goethe on the English Stage', *Publications of the English Goethe Society*, o.s. 4 (1888), 24–7.
—, 'The Lyceum *Faust*: A List of Press Notices and Reviews', *Publications of the English Goethe Society*, o.s. 2 (1887), 112–14.
[Heraud, John Abraham], 'Hayward's Translation of Goethe's *Faust*', *Fraser's Magazine*, 7: 41 (May 1833), 532–54.
H[erschel], J[ohn] F[rederick] W[illiam], W[illiam] W[hewell], J[ulius] C[harles] H[are], E[dward] C[raven] H[awtrey], and J. G. L. (unidentified; probably John Gibson Lockhart) (trans.), *English Hexameter Translations from Schiller, Goethe, Homer, Callinus, and Meleager* (London: Murray, 1847).
Hone, William, *The Every-Day Book; or: Everlasting Calendar of Popular Amusements*, 2 vols (London: Hunt and Clarke, 1826–7).
James, Henry, *The Scenic Art: Notes on Acting and the Drama 1872–1901*, ed. Allan Wade (London: Hart-Davis, 1949).
Keats, John, *The Poems of John Keats*, ed. Jack Stillinger (Cambridge, MA: Belknap Press of Harvard University Press, 1978).
Koller, W. H., *'Faust' Papers: Containing Critical and Historical Remarks on 'Faust' and its Translations* (London: Black, Young, and Young, 1835).
Lewes, G. H., *The Life and Works of Goethe: With Sketches of his Age and Contemporaries, from Published and Unpublished Sources*, 2 vols (London: Nutt, 1855).
[Lockhart, John Gibson], 'ART. VII.—1. *Faust: A Drama, by Goethe. With Translations from the German*', *Quarterly Review*, 34: 67 (June 1826), 136–53.
Lyell, Charles, *Principles of Geology*, 4th edn, 4 vols (London: Murray, 1835).

Malory, Sir Thomas, *La Morte d'Arthur: The Most Ancient and Famous History of the Renowned Prince Arthur, and the Knights of the Round Table*, 3 vols (London: Wilks, 1816).

Medwin, Thomas, *Medwin's Conversations of Lord Byron*, ed. Ernest J. Lovell, Jr (Princeton: Princeton University Press, 1966).

Moore, Thomas, *Letters and Journals of Lord Byron: With Notices of his Life* (London: Murray, 1830).

—, *Memoirs, Journal, and Correspondence of Thomas Moore*, ed. Lord John Russell, 8 vols (London: Longman, Brown, Green and Longmans, 1853–6).

Noel, Roden, *A Modern Faust and Other Poems* (London: Kegan Paul, Trench, 1888).

Page, Norman (ed.), *Tennyson: Interviews and Recollections* (Basingstoke: Macmillan, 1983).

Pater, Walter, *The Renaissance: Studies in Art and Poetry*, ed. Adam Phillips (Oxford: Oxford University Press, 1986).

Robinson, Henry Crabb, *Diary, Reminiscences, and Correspondence of Henry Crabb Robinson*, ed. Thomas Sadler, 2nd edn, 3 vols (London: Macmillan, 1869).

Rossetti, Dante Gabriel, *Collected Poetry and Prose*, ed. Jerome McGann (New Haven, CT: Yale University Press, 2003).

—, *Dante Gabriel Rossetti: His Family-Letters. With a Memoir by William Michael Rossetti* [ed. William Michael Rossetti], 2 vols (London: Ellis and Elvey, 1895).

Ruskin, John, *The Works of John Ruskin*, ed. E. T. Cook and Alexander Wedderburn, Library Edition, 39 vols (London: Allen, 1903–12).

[Russell, Charles William], 'ART. VIII.—1. *Faust: A Tragedy*. By J. Wolfgang von Goethe', *Dublin Review*, 9: 18 (November 1840), 477–506.

Salvin, Rev. H. (trans.), *Mary Stuart, A Tragedy; The Maid of Orleans, A Tragedy: From the German of Schiller, with a Life of the Author* (London: Longman, 1824).

Schiller, Friedrich, *Werke und Briefe*, ed. Otto Dann, Axel Gellhaus and others, 12 vols (Frankfurt am Main: Deutsche Klassiker, 1988–2004).

Shakespeare, William, *The New Oxford Shakespeare: The Complete Works, Modern Critical Edition*, ed. Gary Taylor, John Jowett and others (Oxford: Oxford University Press, 2016).

Shelley, Percy Bysshe, *The Bodleian Shelley Manuscripts: A Facsimile Edition, with Full Transcriptions and Scholarly Apparatus*, ed. Donald H. Reiman, 23 vols (New York: Garland, 1986–2002), XXI: *Miscellaneous Poetry, Prose and Translations from Bodleian MS. Shelley adds. c. 4, etc.*, ed. E. B. Murray (1995).

—, *The Complete Works of Percy Bysshe Shelley*, ed. Roger Ingpen and Walter E. Peck, Julian Edition, 10 vols (London: Benn; New York: Scribner, 1926–30).

—, *The Major Works*, ed. Zachary Leader and Michael O'Neill (Oxford: Oxford University Press, 2003).

—, 'Stanzas by Percy Bysshe Shelley: To * * * * *', *Fraser's Magazine*, 6: 34 (November 1832), 599–600.

Staël Holstein, Mme la Baronne de, *De l'Allemagne*, 3 vols (Paris: Nicolle, 1810; repr. London: Murray, 1813).

—, *Germany* [trans. Francis Hodgson(?)], 3 vols (London: Murray, 1813).

[Taylor, William], 'Faust, &c.; i. e. *Faustus: A Tragedy*, by Goethe. 16mo. pp. 312. Tubingen [*sic*]. 1808', *Monthly Review*, 62 (August 1810), 491–5.

Tennyson, Alfred Lord, *Selected Poems*, ed. Aidan Day (London: Penguin, 2003).

—, *The Works of Tennyson: With Notes by the Author*, ed. Hallam, Lord Tennyson (London: Macmillan, 1913).

Tennyson, Emily, *Lady Tennyson's Journal*, ed. James O. Hoge (Charlottesville: University Press of Virginia, 1981).

—, *The Letters of Emily Lady Tennyson*, ed. James O. Hoge (University Park: Pennsylvania State University Press, 1974).

[Tennyson, Hallam Lord], *Materials for a Life of A. T.: Collected for my Children*, 4 vols ([n.p., n. pub., 1895].

Thackeray, William Makepeace, *The History of Pendennis*, ed. Peter L. Shillingsburg (New York: Garland, 1991).

Weathercock, Janus, 'Sentimentalities on the Fine Arts: To be Continued When he is in the Humour', *London Magazine*, 1: 2 (February 1820), 136–40.

Wilde, Oscar, *The Complete Letters of Oscar Wilde*, ed. Merlin Holland and Rupert Hart-Davis, (London: Fourth Estate, 2000).

—, *The Complete Works of Oscar Wilde*, ed. Russell Jackson and Ian Small (Oxford: Oxford University Press, 2000–), III: *The Picture of Dorian Gray: The 1890 and 1891 Texts*, ed. Joseph Bristow (2005).

[Wills, W. G.], *Faust, in a Prologue and Five Acts: Adapted and Arranged for the Lyceum Theatre by W. G. Wills, from the First Part of Goethe's Tragedy* ([n.p., n. pub, 1886]).

Wordsworth, William, and Dorothy Wordsworth, *The Letters of William and Dorothy Wordsworth*, ed. Ernest de Selincourt, 2nd edn, ed. Chester L. Shaver, Mary Moorman and Alan G. Hill, 8 vols (Oxford: Clarendon Press, 1967–93).

Secondary Sources

Allen, Peter, *The Cambridge Apostles: The Early Years* (Cambridge: Cambridge University Press, 1978).

Ashton, Rosemary, *George Eliot: A Life* (London: Hamilton, 1996).

—, *The German Idea: Four English Writers and the Reception of German Thought, 1800–1860* (Cambridge: Cambridge University Press, 1980).

Bailey, J. O., 'Hardy's "Mephistophelian Visitants"', *PMLA*, 61: 4 (December 1946), 1146–84.

Batchelor, John, *Tennyson: To Strive, to Seek, to Find* (London: Chatto & Windus, 2012).

Baum, Paull F., *Tennyson Sixty Years After* (Chapel Hill: University of North Carolina Press, 1948).

Baumann, Lina, *Die englischen Übersetzungen von Goethes 'Faust'* (Halle: Niemeyer, 1907).

Baynes, Tom, 'Alfred Tennyson, Bulwer's *Falkland*, and Graves's *Werther*', *Notes and Queries*, o.s. 265 / n.s. 67: 4 (December 2020).

—, 'The Authorship of the First English Translation of Goethe', *Publications of the English Goethe Society*, 90: 2 (September 2021), 91–108.

—, 'The Spirit of Goethe Looks Forth: Hallam, Carlyle, and *In Memoriam*', *Tennyson Research Bulletin*, 11: 5 (November 2021).

—, 'Tennyson and *Werther*', *Essays in Criticism*, 70: 3 (July 2020), 302–25.

—, 'Three New Sources for "Locksley Hall": Goethe, Byron, and Dickens', *Notes and Queries*, o.s. 266 / n.s. 68: 4 (December 2021).

Beach, Joseph Warren, *The Concept of Nature in Nineteenth-Century English Poetry* (New York: Pageant, 1956).

Birley, Robert, *Sunk without Trace: Some Forgotten Masterpieces Reconsidered* (London: Hart-Davis, 1962).

Black, Greta A., 'P. J. Bailey's Debt to Goethe's *Faust* in his *Festus*', *Modern Language Review*, 28: 2 (April 1933), 166–75.

Blocksidge, Martin, '*A Life Lived Quickly*': *Tennyson's Friend Arthur Hallam and his Legend* (Brighton: Sussex Academic Press, 2011).

Bluhm, H. S., 'The Reception of Goethe's *Faust* in England after the Middle of the Nineteenth Century', *Journal of English and Germanic Philology*, 34: 2 (April 1935), 201–12.

Boyle, Nicholas, *Goethe: The Poet and the Age* (Oxford: Clarendon Press, 1991–).

Bradley, A. C., *A Commentary on Tennyson's 'In Memoriam'*, 3rd edn (London: Macmillan, 1910).

Brewer, William D., *The Shelley-Byron Conversation* (Gainesville: University Press of Florida, 1994).

Buckley, Jerome Hamilton, *Tennyson: The Growth of a Poet* (Cambridge, MA: Harvard University Press; London: Oxford University Press, 1960).

—, *The Victorian Temper: A Study in Literary Culture* (London: Cass, 1966).

Bush, Douglas (ed.), 'Alfred, Lord Tennyson', in *Major British Writers*, ed. G. B. Harrison, 2nd edn, 2 vols (New York: Harcourt, Brace, 1959), II, 369–466.

—, *Mythology and the Romantic Tradition in English Poetry* (New York: Pageant, 1957).

Butler, E. M., *Byron and Goethe: Analysis of a Passion* (London: Bowes & Bowes, 1956).

Campbell, Nancie (ed.), *Tennyson in Lincoln: A Catalogue of the Collections in the Research Centre*, 2 vols (Lincoln: Tennyson Society, 1971–3).

Carré, Jean-Marie, *Gœthe en Angleterre: étude de littérature comparée* (Paris: Plon-Nourrit, 1920).
Cazamian, Louis, *Carlyle*, trans. E. K. Brown (New York: Macmillan, 1932).
Chambers, D. Laurance, 'Tennysoniana', *Modern Language Notes*, 18: 8 (December 1903), 227–33.
Chiasson, E. J., 'Tennyson's "Ulysses" – A Re-interpretation' (1954), in *Critical Essays on the Poetry of Tennyson*, ed. John Killham (London: Routledge & Kegan Paul, 1960), pp. 164–73.
Cronin, Richard, 'Goethe, the Apostles, and Tennyson's "Supposed Confessions"', *Philological Quarterly*, 72: 3 (Summer 1993), 337–56.
Culler, A. Dwight, 'Monodrama and the Dramatic Monologue', *PMLA*, 90: 3 (May 1975), 366–85.
—, *The Poetry of Tennyson* (New Haven, CT: Yale University Press, 1977).
Cumming, Mark, 'Gibbon, Edward', in *The Carlyle Encyclopedia*, ed. Mark Cumming (Madison, NJ: Fairleigh Dickinson University Press, 2004), pp. 191–3.
Day, Aidan, 'Notable Acquisitions by the Tennyson Research Centre: Tennyson's Annotated Copy of William Trollope's *Pentalogia Graeca* and an Unlisted MS Poem', *Tennyson Research Bulletin*, 3: 5 (November 1981), 203–8.
Douglas-Fairhurst, Robert, 'Introduction', in *Tennyson Among the Poets*, ed. Robert Douglas-Fairhurst and Seamus Perry (Oxford: Oxford University Press, 2009), pp. 1–13.
Douglas-Fairhurst, Robert, and Seamus Perry (eds), *Tennyson Among the Poets* (Oxford: Oxford University Press, 2009).
Droop, Adolf, *Die Belesenheit Percy Bysshe Shelley's nach den direkten Zeugnissen und den bisherigen Forschungen* (Weimar: Wagner, 1906).
Dyke, Henry van, *Studies in Tennyson*, 2nd edn (New York: Scribner, 1921).
Ellis, David, *Byron in Geneva: That Summer of 1816* (Liverpool: Liverpool University Press, 2011).
Ellmann, Richard, *Oscar Wilde* (London: Hamilton, 1987).
Elze, Karl, *Lord Byron: A Biography. With a Critical Essay on his Place in Literature* [n. trans.], (London: Murray, 1872).
Fairchild, Hoxie N., '"Wild Bells" in Bailey's *Festus*?', *Modern Language Notes*, 64: 4 (April 1949), 256–8.
Forker, Charles R., 'Tennyson's "Tithonus" and Marston's *Antonio's Revenge*', *Notes and Queries*, o.s. 204 / n.s. 6: 11 (December 1959), 445.
Frantz, Adolf Ingram, *Half a Hundred Thralls to Faust: A Study Based on the British and the American Translators of Goethe's 'Faust' 1823–1949* (Chapel Hill: University of Carolina Press, 1949).
Fredeman, William E., '"A Sign Betwixt the Meadow and the Cloud": The Ironic Apotheosis of Tennyson's "St. Simeon Stylites"', *University of Toronto Quarterly*, 38: 1 (October 1968), 69–83.

Garland, H. B., *Schiller* (London: Harrap, 1949; repr. Westport, CT: Greenwood, 1976).
Gatty, Alfred, *A Key to Lord Tennyson's 'In Memoriam'*, 4th edn (London: Bell, 1894).
Gerhardt, Hans-Peter, 'Oscar Wildes *Dorian Gray* als Faustdichtung', *Faust-Blätter*, 25 (1973), 669–75.
Goslee, David F., *Tennyson's Characters: 'Strange Faces, Other Minds'* (Iowa City: University of Iowa Press, 1989).
—, 'Three Stages of Tennyson's "Tiresias"', *Journal of English and Germanic Philology*, 75 (1976), 154–67.
Grant, Stephen Allen, 'The Mystical Implications of *In Memoriam*', *Studies in English Literature, 1500–1900*, 2: 4 (Autumn 1962), 481–95.
Haber, Grace Stevenson, 'Echoes from Carlyle's "Goethe's 'Helena'" in *The Mayor of Casterbridge*', *Nineteenth-Century Fiction*, 12: 1 (June 1957), 89–90.
Hammerton, J. A., 'Philip James Bailey and his Work', *Sunday Magazine*, 27: 4 (January 1898), 45–52.
Harrold, Charles Frederick, *Carlyle and German Thought: 1819–1834* (New Haven, CT: Yale University Press, 1934).
Hauhart, William Frederic, *The Reception of Goethe's 'Faust' in England in the First Half of the Nineteenth Century* (New York: Columbia University Press, 1909).
Hewitt, Ben, *Byron, Shelley, and Goethe's 'Faust': An Epic Connection*, Studies in Comparative Literature 33 (Oxford: Legenda, 2015).
Holmes, Richard, *Shelley: The Pursuit* (London: Harper Perennial, 2005).
Irving, Laurence, *Henry Irving: The Actor and his World* (London: Faber and Faber, 1951).
Jordan, Elaine, 'Tennyson's *In Memoriam*—An Echo of Goethe', *Notes and Queries*, o.s. 213 / n.s. 15: 11 (November 1968), 414–15.
Kennedy, Ian H. C., 'Alfred Tennyson's *Bildungsgang*: Notes on his Early Reading', *Philological Quarterly*, 57: 1 (Winter 1978), 82–103.
Killham, John, *Tennyson and 'The Princess': Reflections of an Age* (London: Athlone Press, 1958).
Klapper, M. Roxana, *The German Literary Influence on Shelley*, Salzburg Studies in English Literature: Romantic Reassessment, 43 (Salzburg: Universität Salzburg, 1975).
Knowles, James, 'Aspects of Tennyson: II (A Personal Reminiscence)', *Nineteenth Century*, 33: 191 (January 1893), 164–88.
Kohl, Norbert, *Oscar Wilde: The Works of a Conformist Rebel*, trans. David Henry Wilson (Cambridge: Cambridge University Press, 1989).
Krüger, Eva, *Bilder zu Goethes 'Faust'. Moritz Retzsch und Dante Gabriel Rossetti* (Hildesheim: Olms, 2009).
Leggett, B. J., 'Dante, Byron and Tennyson's Ulysses', *Tennessee Studies in Literature*, 15 (1970), 143–59.

Levin, Harry, 'A Faustian Typology', in *Faust through Four Centuries: Retrospect and Analysis. Vierhundert Jahre Faust. Rückblick und Analyse*, ed. Peter Boerner and Sidney Johnson (Tübingen: Niemeyer, 1989), pp. 1–12.

Loane, George G., *Echoes in Tennyson and Other Essays* (London: Stockwell, [1928]).

Luke, David, '"Vor deinem Jammerkreuz": Goethe's Attitude to Christian Belief', *Publications of the English Goethe Society*, n.s. 59 (1989), 35–58.

McKay, Kenneth M., *'Many Glancing Colours': An Essay in Reading Tennyson, 1809–1850* (Toronto: University of Toronto Press, 1988).

McKillop, Alan D., 'A Victorian *Faust*', *PMLA*, 40: 3 (September 1925), 743–68.

Martin, Robert Bernard, *Tennyson: The Unquiet Heart* (Oxford: Clarendon Press, 1980).

Mattes, Eleanor Bustin, *'In Memoriam': The Way of a Soul. A Study of Some Influences that Shaped Tennyson's Poem* (New York: Exposition Press, 1951).

Metzger, Lore, 'The Eternal Process: Some Parallels between Goethe's *Faust* and Tennyson's *In Memoriam*', *Victorian Poetry*, 1: 3 (August 1963), 189–96.

—, '*Sartor Resartus*: A Victorian *Faust*', *Comparative Literature*, 13: 4 (Autumn 1961), 316–31.

Mustard, Wilfred P., *Classical Echoes in Tennyson* (New York: Macmillan, 1904).

Ormond, Leonée, *Alfred Tennyson: A Literary Life* (Basingstoke: Macmillan, 1993).

Paden, W. D., 'Tennyson and Persian Poetry, Again', *Modern Language Notes*, 58: 8 (December 1943), 652–6.

—, *Tennyson in Egypt: A Study of the Imagery in his Earlier Work* (Lawrence: University of Kansas, 1942).

Parker, Fred, '"Much in the mode of Goethe's Mephistopheles": *Faust* and Byron', in *International Faust Studies: Adaptation, Reception, Translation*, ed. Lorna Fitzsimmons (London: Continuum, 2008).

Pettigrew, John, 'Tennyson's "Ulysses": A Reconciliation of Opposites', *Victorian Poetry*, 1: 1 (January 1963), 27–45.

Phelps, Leland R., 'Goethe's *Faust* and the Young Shelley', in *Wege der Worte. Festschrift für Wolfgang Fleischhauer anläßlich seines 65. Geburtstages*, ed. Donald C. Riechel (Cologne: Böhlau, 1978), pp. 304–12.

Pick, R., *Schiller in England 1787–1960: A Bibliography* (London: [n. pub.], 1961).

Pinion, F. B., *A Tennyson Chronology* (Basingstoke: Macmillan, 1990).

—, *A Thomas Hardy Dictionary: With Maps and a Chronology* (Basingstoke: Macmillan, 1989).

Pniower, Otto, 'Goethes *Faust* und das hohe Lied', *Goethe-Jahrbuch*, 13 (1892), 181–98.
Proescholdt-Obermann, Catherine Waltraud, *Goethe and his British Critics: The Reception of Goethe's Works in British Periodicals, 1779 to 1855* (Frankfurt am Main: Lang, 1992).
Ray, Gordon N., *Thackeray*, 2 vols (London: Oxford University Press, 1955–8).
Rea, Thomas, *Schiller's Dramas and Poems in England* (London: Unwin, 1906).
Reid, T. Wemyss, *The Life, Letters, and Friendships of Richard Monckton Milnes, First Lord Houghton*, 2 vols (London: Cassell, 1890).
Richards, Jeffrey, *Sir Henry Irving: A Victorian Actor and his World* (London: Hambledon and London, 2005).
Ricks, Christopher, *Allusion to the Poets* (Oxford: Oxford University Press, 2002).
—, *Tennyson*, 2nd edn (Basingstoke: Macmillan, 1989).
Robbins, Tony, 'Tennyson's "Ulysses": The Significance of the Homeric and Dantesque Backgrounds', *Victorian Poetry*, 11: 3 (Autumn 1973), 177–93.
Robinson, Charles E., 'The Devil as Doppelgänger in *The Deformed Transformed*: The Sources and Meaning of Byron's Unfinished Drama', in *The Plays of Lord Byron: Critical Essays*, ed. Robert Gleckner and Bernard Beatty (Liverpool: Liverpool University Press, 1997), pp. 321–45.
Roloff, Walter, Morton E. Mix and Martha Nicolai, *German Literature in British Magazines 1750–1860*, ed. Bayard Quincy Morgan and A. R. Hohlfeld (Madison: University of Wisconsin Press, 1949).
Roppen, Georg, '"Ulysses" and Tennyson's Sea-quest', *English Studies*, 40: 2 (April 1959), 77–90.
Rose, William (ed.), *Essays on Goethe* (London: Cassell, 1949).
Rossi, Dominick, 'Parallels in Wilde's *The Picture of Dorian Gray* and Goethe's *Faust*', *CLA Journal*, 13: 2 (December 1969), 188–91.
Schöne, Albrecht, *Götterzeichen Liebeszauber Satanskult. Neue Einblicke in alte Goethetexte* (Munich: Beck, 1982).
Sessions, Ina Beth, 'The Dramatic Monologue', *PMLA*, 62: 2 (June 1947), 503–16.
Simpson, James, *Matthew Arnold and Goethe*, Texts and Dissertations, 2 (London: Modern Humanities Research Association, 1979).
Spivey, Ted R., 'Damnation and Salvation in *The Picture of Dorian Gray*', *Boston University Studies in English*, 4: 3 (Autumn 1960), 162–70.
Stokoe, F. W., *German Influence in the English Romantic Period 1788–1818* (Cambridge: Cambridge University Press, 1926).
Templeman, William Darby, 'Tennyson's "Locksley Hall" and Thomas Carlyle', in *Booker Memorial Studies: Eight Essays on Victorian Literature in Memory of John Manning Booker 1881–1948*, ed. Hill Shine (Chapel Hill: University of North Carolina Press, 1950), pp. 34–59.

Thomas, Jayne, *Tennyson Echoing Wordsworth* (Edinburgh: Edinburgh University Press, 2019).
Thwaite, Ann, *Emily Tennyson: The Poet's Wife* (London: Faber and Faber, 1996).
Trilling, Lionel, *Matthew Arnold*, 2nd edn (New York: Columbia University Press; London: Allen & Unwin, 1949).
Turner, Paul, *Tennyson* (London: Routledge & Kegan Paul, 1976).
Waller, John O., 'Tennyson and Philip James Bailey's *Festus*', *Bulletin of Research in the Humanities*, 82: 1 (Spring 1979), 105–23.
Walters, J. Cuming, *Tennyson: Poet, Philosopher, Idealist* (London: Kegan Paul, Trench, Trübner, 1893).
Wiggins, Louise Dugas, 'Tennyson's Veiled Statue', *English Studies*, 49 (1968), 444–5.
Williams, John R., *Goethe's 'Faust'* (London: Allen & Unwin, 1987).
Winnick, R. H., *Tennyson's Poems: New Textual Parallels* (Cambridge: Open Book Publishers, 2019).
Wright, Walter F., *The Shaping of 'The Dynasts': A Study in Thomas Hardy* (Lincoln: University of Nebraska Press, 1967).

Index

Aeschylus, 96
after-life *see* religion
Alexander, Sir George, 38
Alexandra, Queen of the United Kingdom, 38
Allen, Dr Matthew, 63
Allingham, William, 108
Alton Locke, 64
Ampère, Jean-Jacques, 128
Anster, John, 11, 24
Apostles, the, 15, 22n, 154, 173n
Arnold, Matthew, 1, 27, 29, 30–1, 127, 129–30
Asher, David, 203
Ashton, Rosemary, 36
atheism *see* religion
Athenæum, 18, 28
Austin, Sarah, 5, 32, 66, 69n, 106, 144, 153, 154, 162–3, 166–7, 169, 201, 202
Austria, 36
  Alps, 159
  Gmunden, 159
  Vienna, 22, 55, 82, 102, 115

Bädeker, Karl, 109, 113
Bailey, James Osler, 37
Bailey, Philip James, 1, 25, 27–9, 64n, 144, 145, 149–51, 176, 199
Balfour, John, 31n
Baum, Paull F., 140
Beach, Joseph Warren, 155, 156–7, 162
Beer, John, 173n
Bible, the, 50, 139, 206, 210
  Acts, 139n, 184n
  Corinthians, 74, 191
  Exodus, 92n, 178
  Genesis, 85n
  Hebrews, 191
  Mark, 148
  Matthew, 148, 174n
  Peter, 149n
  Psalms, 148
  Revelation, 191
  Song of Songs, 56n
Birley, Robert, 149
Blackie, John Stuart, 24, 144n
Blackwood's Edinburgh Magazine, 11
Bluhm, H. S., 40
Boileau, Daniel, 17n, 164n
Boyle, Nicholas, 88n, 98, 174n, 209n

Bradley, Andrew Cecil, 172, 174n
Brewer, William D., 7
Browning, Robert, 1, 25, 26–7, 40, 59n, 144n, 170n, 210n
Bruford, Walter Horace, 151
Buckley, Jerome Hamilton, 106, 203
Bulwer, Edward, 16, 27
Burwick, Frederick, 4, 5
Bush, Douglas, 90, 106n, 119
Byron, George Gordon, Lord, 1, 7–11, 43, 53n, 97, 105, 109, 127, 129, 167–8, 169, 184, 186
  'Alpine Journal', 109, 110n
  Cain, 9, 22, 56n, 92, 93n, 101n, 118n, 138n, 143n, 168, 171, 172, 204, 205
  Childe Harold's Pilgrimage, 56n, 92n
  Deformed Transformed, The, 10, 22, 91, 129, 137, 183, 184, 186, 205
  Don Juan, 9, 10
  Giaour, The, 183, 186
  Manfred, 8, 9, 10, 92, 109
  Marino Faliero, 9
  Sardanapalus, 9, 10
  'Siege of Corinth, The', 201–2
  Vision of Judgment, The, 9–10
  Werner, 10
  Works of Lord Byron, The (1837), 165, 167, 168, 201

Callimachus, 101–2
Cambridge, 14–15, 22n, 30, 47, 51n, 95, 96, 204
Carlyle, Thomas, 1, 12–13, 16, 23, 25–6, 29, 30, 32, 34, 35, 40, 48, 54, 67, 72, 79–80, 92, 94, 98, 102, 127, 128, 130–4, 135, 136, 137, 139, 141, 144, 146–8, 151, 152, 153, 162–5, 166, 169, 172, 177–8, 179, 180
  'Death of Goethe', 13, 131
  'Faustus', 12–13, 81, 89, 93, 130, 136
  'Goethe', 13, 15, 54, 131, 134, 136, 141
  'Goethe's "Helena"', 13, 15, 22, 37–8, 81, 87, 89, 93, 95, 96–7, 100, 101, 105, 114, 130, 205
  'Goethe's *Works*', 13, 131, 146
  'Novalis', 15, 163–4, 169n, 172–3, 175
  Sartor Resartus, 1, 25–6, 79–80, 144, 146–7, 151, 164, 165, 166, 168, 170, 171, 174, 175, 176, 177, 178, 204
  'Schiller', 183, 184–5, 188n, 206, 207
  'Signs of the Times', 77–8, 84n, 141, 150n, 177–8
  Wilhelm Meister's Apprenticeship (trans.), 13, 15, 18, 30, 53, 54, 55, 65, 74, 80n, 133, 144, 145, 147–8, 165, 168, 171, 172, 173, 177n, 180, 201, 204, 205
  Wilhelm Meister's Travels (trans.), 13, 15, 18, 40n, 109n, 131, 132–3, 136, 204
Carracci, Annibale, 88n
Carré, Jean-Marie, 7, 26, 108n
Carroll, Lewis, 39
Cary, Henry Francis, 22–3, 74, 77, 82–3, 98n, 189, 190
Cauteretz, Valley of, 113, 118n
Chambers, D. Laurance, 96
Chambers, Robert, 165
Chamisso, Adelbert von, 17

Charles, Elizabeth Rundle, 180
Chaucer, Geoffrey, 18
Christ and Christianity *see* religion
Cicero, 83
Clairmont, Claire, 7n
Clough, Arthur Hugh, 1, 29–30, 127, 129, 136n
Coleridge, Samuel Taylor, 1, 3–5, 15, 18, 28, 48, 134
   Aids to Reflection, 134n, 145n, 173n
   Death of Wallenstein (trans.), 121
   Faustus: From the German of Goethe (trans., attributed), 4–5, 12, 53n, 129
   'Human Life, On the Denial of Immortality', 170n
   Michael Scott (projected drama), 4, 28, 199
Conan Doyle, Arthur, 40–1
conversations, literary, 51–5
Crimean War, 67
Cross, John Walter, 36
Culler, A. Dwight, 68, 127n, 136–7
Cuvier, Georges, 171n

Dante Alighieri, 18, 22–3, 210
   Banquet, The, 82–3
   Divine Comedy, The, 22–3, 42, 74, 97–8, 139n, 189, 190, 205, 207, 210
   Inferno, 22, 23, 72, 77–8, 80, 81, 82–3, 84, 85, 93, 94, 98n, 100n, 139n, 198, 207
   Paradise, 98n, 190–1, 207
   Purgatory, 74, 98n, 139n
Darwin, Charles, 178
Day, Aidan, 96
de Vere, Aubrey, 64
death, 58, 59, 60, 63, 73–4, 81, 82, 83, 85, 87, 88, 89, 90, 91, 93, 99, 103, 106, 107, 112, 113, 114n, 115, 117, 118, 119, 120–1, 122, 123, 134–5, 150, 170
   desire for, 53, 81, 100, 104, 140, 188, 189
   fear of, 84, 85, 94
Deism *see* religion
devil, the *see* religion
Disraeli, Benjamin, 15–16
Dodgson, Charles Lutwidge *see* Carroll, Lewis
Donne, John, 162
Donne, William Bodham, 62, 136
doubt *see* religion
dramatic monologues, 86, 178, 204, 209–10
Droop, Adolf, 7n
Dryden, John, 160n
Dublin Review, 182
Dumfries, 33

Eastlake, Charles, 162
Eckermann, Johann Peter, 34, 67n, 202
Eclectic Review, 28
Edinburgh, 11, 147
Edinburgh Review, 18, 160n
Edward VII, King of the United Kingdom, 38
Eliot, George, 1, 36, 43, 64, 65
Elizabeth I, Queen of England, 116
Ellis, Susie, 37
Emerson, Ralph Waldo, 180
Enlightenment, the, 13, 29, 130, 147
Euripides, 96
Evans, Mary Ann *see* Eliot, George
Examiner, 18

Fairchild, Hoxie N., 144
Falk, Johannes, 170

Faust
  characters: Baucis, 101; Earth Spirit, 25, 164, 170, 173, 174–5, 179, 187; Emperor, 66, 120; Euphorion, 11, 96–7, 103, 104–6; Faust, 6, 27, 58, 61, 66, 75–6, 87, 88–9, 93, 98, 100, 101, 103, 104, 114, 115–16, 118–19, 122, 128, 129, 130, 132, 136, 137, 138, 139, 140, 141, 142, 143, 157, 158, 160, 161, 174n, 175, 176, 181, 182, 185–9, 192n, 196, 197, 198, 202, 203, 207, 209; Helena, 96, 100, 101, 102, 114, 116, 119, 120n, 122; Lynceus, 99–101, 207; Margaret ('Gretchen'), 15–16, 30–1, 36, 38, 42n, 47, 52, 53, 55–6, 58–66, 67, 68–70, 99, 122, 132, 158, 161, 181, 192, 193, 194, 195, 197n, 198, 208; Mephistopheles, 3, 7, 10, 13, 27, 29, 36, 37, 38, 39, 51, 61, 88, 89, 93, 101, 114, 118, 128–9, 130, 137, 138, 139, 147, 181, 182–3, 192, 193n, 194, 196, 197; old gentlemen, 197; old peasant, 186; Philemon, 101; Valentine, 65, 194; Wagner, 75, 76, 89, 90, 128, 136, 186, 209
  composition of, 2, 58, 88n, 98, 102, 196–7, 202–3, 207
  influence of, 1, 6–8, 9–10, 11, 15–16, 21–2, 25–31, 33, 36–8, 40–2, 43, 52, 64, 92, 128–30, 174n, 199
  moral and religious criticisms of, 3–4, 12, 13, 25, 39, 43, 180, 181–3, 199, 210
Original Faust, 2, 98, 207

Part One, episodes, scenes and passages from: 'Before the Gate', 10, 28, 74, 80, 137, 140, 157, 161, 185, 186, 189n, 190, 191, 195, 198, 207, 209; Chant of the Earth Spirit, 25, 164–5, 170, 174, 175; Chorus of the Archangels, 7, 12n, 28, 84n, 153, 155–6, 157, 182; 'Dedication', 113n; 'Dungeon', 47, 52, 58–62, 63, 66n, 98, 99, 100, 192, 193, 194; 'Evening', 58, 64, 68, 69–70; Faust's Credo, 164, 175–6; 'Forest and Cavern', 57–8, 70n; 'Garden', 56n, 65; Gretchen tragedy, 41–2, 47, 55, 57–8, 59n, 62–3, 64–6, 68, 70, 181, 192, 193, 205; 'Margaret's Room', 31, 53, 55–6, 62–3, 69n, 193; 'Martha's Garden', 181; 'May-Day Night', 6, 10, 57; 137, 138, 139, 195–7; 'Night', 6, 20n, 25, 28, 87–8, 137, 138, 140, 141, 143, 146, 164, 174n, 175, 179, 185, 187, 188, 189; 'Night.—Street before Margaret's Door', 65, 192, 194; 'Oh, happy he, who can still hope', 8, 74, 75–7, 78, 80, 84, 87, 88, 89, 90, 93, 179n, 198, 209, 210; 'Only a few steps further', 186, 187, 209, 210; 'Place Devoted to Religious Exercises' ('Zwinger'), 53, 62, 193, 208; 'Prologue in Heaven', 3, 5, 6, 7, 10, 24, 122, 182; 'Prologue on the Theatre', 20; 'River and rivulet are freed from ice', 140, 153, 154, 157, 194n,

Faust (cont.)
    208, 209; 'Street, The', 47, 65, 66n, 69n; 'Study [I]', 41, 80, 89, 185; 'Study [II]', 28, 32, 80, 92, 137, 138, 147, 152n, 185, 188n; 'There was a King in Thule', 58, 64, 68–9, 70, 207; 'Two souls, alas, dwell in my breast', 128, 130, 136–7, 186, 208; university scenes, 137, 139, 146, 185; 'Witches' Kitchen', 80, 88
    Part Two, acts, scenes and passages from: Act I, 2, 99, 114, 116, 118–19; Act II, 114, 120n; Act III ('Helena'), 13, 15, 22, 38, 66, 95, 96–7, 99–100, 101, 102, 114, 115–16, 205, 207; Act IV, 11, 66, 119–20; Act V, 66, 100, 101, 103, 202–3; 'Mountain Defiles', 67, 202–3; 'Pleasant neighbourhood, A', 99, 101, 158, 159–61, 175; 'Pulses of life beat with renewed vigour, The', 98, 99, 153, 154, 158, 159–61, 209, 210
    performance of, 38–40, 41–2
    reception of, 1, 3–4, 11–13, 16, 18, 21n, 24–5, 28–9, 30, 37, 39–40, 42–3, 95, 97, 128, 130–1, 152, 176, 180, 181–2, 210
    translation of, 1, 3, 4–6, 7, 8, 11, 12n, 16–18, 20n, 21, 24–5, 26, 33, 34–5, 36, 39, 43, 52, 55, 62, 98, 100, 114n, 135–6, 155, 164, 174n, 182, 195, 197n
Faust, Johann Georg, 1, 26
Filmore, Lewis, 36
FitzGerald, Edward, 29, 78, 190

Foreign Quarterly Review, 21, 35, 94, 95, 137
Foreign Review, 13, 15, 163
forward movement *see* progress
Fouqué, Friedrich de la Motte, 17
Fraser's Magazine, 7n, 18, 26n
Fredeman, William E., 187–8

Germany, 2, 4, 17, 19, 36, 38, 108, 116
    Bonn, 50
    Göttingen, 16
    Harz Mountains, 138, 195
    Heidelberg, 50
    Hildesheim, 155n
    Jena, 50
    Mannheim, 109
    Rhineland, the, 15n, 108, 157n
    Weimar, 10, 16, 36, 102, 107, 108, 202
Gibbon, Edward, 183, 184n, 188n
Gilbert, William Schwenck, 39, 199
Gladstone, William Ewart, 23, 38
God *see* religion
Goethe, Johann Wolfgang
    life: discovers Faust legend, 2; visits Bernese Alps, 109; grieves for Schiller, 107; death of, 2, 16, 102, 167, 202
    character: monistic outlook, 154, 155, 181–2, 183; morality, 12, 13, 180, 181–2, 183, 189, 193; Nature, view of, 148, 153–4, 156, 161–2, 164, 169–70, 175, 176, 179, 181–2; religious beliefs, 131–2, 154, 155, 161, 164, 169, 176, 179, 182, 203; sexuality, view of, 180–1
    writings: *Conversations of Goethe*, 34, 67;

Correspondence between Schiller and Goethe, 184, 205–6; 'Divinity', 174n; 'Do you know the land', 32n; *Götz von Berlichingen*, 11; *Hermann and Dorothea*, 14, 31, 155n; 'Higher and Highest Things', 74; 'In the solemn burial-vault', 108, 154; *Iphigenia in Tauris*, 55n, 208; 'Keep not standing fix'd and rooted', 109n; 'Lili's Park', 98n; *Memoirs of Goethe* (1824 translation of *Poetry and Truth*), 22, 59n, 141–2, 158n, 205; 'Metamorphosis of Plants, The' (1790 scientific essay), 162; 'Metamorphosis of Plants, The' (1798 poem), 162, 166–7, 202; 'Nature and Art', 33n; *Notes and Essays for a Better Understanding of the West-eastern Divan*, 113n; 'Permanence in Change', 119n; 'Prelude', 154; 'Song of the Spirits over the Waters', 109; *Sorrows of Young Werther, The*, 2, 14, 16, 18, 22, 25, 50n, 53, 58–60, 64–5, 66n, 67, 68, 83n, 131, 134–5, 136, 141–3, 156n, 168n, 171, 187n, 204, 205, 207n, 209n; *Theory of Colours, The*, 162; *Torquato Tasso*, 155n, 208; 'To the Favoured', 55n; *West-eastern Divan*, 113n; *Wilhelm Meister's Apprenticeship*, 13, 15, 18, 25, 30, 31, 53, 54, 55, 65, 74, 80n, 133, 144, 145, 147–8, 165, 167, 168, 171, 172, 173, 177n, 180, 201, 204, 205; *Wilhelm Meister's Travels*, 13, 15, 18, 25, 40n, 131, 132–3, 136, 204; 'Youth and the Mill-brook, The', 192n
see also Faust
Goethe, Ottilie von, 17
Goslee, David F., 95n, 101n, 141
Gower, Lord Francis Leveson, 5, 15, 18, 135–6, 172
Gozzi, Carlo, 114–15n
Grant, Alexander, 35
Graves, Richard, 2, 14, 16, 53
Greece, 10, 92n, 95, 114, 116
  Cephalonia, 10–11
  Eleusis, 120n
  Ithaca, 88, 92n
  Missolonghi, 103
Grimm, Jacob and Wilhelm, 16

Haber, Grace Stevenson, 37–8
Hallam, Arthur Henry, 14–15, 19, 22, 47–62, 68–72, 80–7, 90–1, 92n, 95, 99, 102, 103–4, 106, 108–10, 112–13, 115, 118, 119, 121, 122, 134n, 137n, 139, 144–5, 157n, 159, 172, 205, 210
  'Four Translations from the German', 55, 91
  'Lines Addressed to Alfred Tennyson', 52–3, 59
  'On Some of the Characteristics of Modern Poetry', 53–4
  'Oration, on the Influence of Italian Works of Imagination', 48–9
  Poems (1830), 52–3
  'Sonnet [How is't for every glance of thine I find]', 173
  'Sonnet [Then What is Life]', 145
  'Whether the existence of an intelligent First Cause', 154, 173n
Hallam, Ellen, 51n, 69

Hallam, Henry, 19n, 86, 110, 112n
Hallam, Julia, 110, 112
Hardenberg, Friedrich von *see* Novalis
Hardy, Thomas, 37–8
Harrold, Charles Frederick, 164
Hauhart, William Frederic, 17–18, 24
Hawtrey, Edward Craven, 51n
Hayward, Abraham, 16–22, 23–4, 26, 32, 37, 62n
  'ART. II.—*Lord Byron*', 23
  'ART. IV.—*Goethe's nachgelassene Werke*', 21, 22, 35, 69n, 94, 97, 98, 100, 160n, 183, 205, 206, 207, 208
  Faust: A Dramatic Poem, 1, 16–21, 22–3, 24, 26, 30, 32, 37, 54, 55, 56n, 57, 69n, 70n, 76, 91, 92n, 137, 152n, 157n, 164n, 184, 192, 193n, 197n, 205, 206, 208
Heath, John, 31, 68–9, 82
Heinemann, William, 39
Hewitt, Ben, 9
Hoge, James O., 152n
Hohenheim, Theophrastus *see* Paracelsus
Holmes, Richard, 128
Homer, 42, 81n, 88, 89, 99n, 206, 210
Hone, William, 183, 188n, 207
Horace, 81n, 99n, 139, 206
Howitt, Mary, 27

immortality *see* religion
infanticide, 52, 58, 65, 66, 193
Irving, Henry, 38–40, 42
Italy, 23, 48n, 86
  Florence, 9
  Livorno, 10
  Pisa, 5, 129
  Rome, 88n, 163
  Trieste, 82, 85, 92n

James, Henry, 37, 39
Jean Paul, 23
Jerusalem, Karl, 141
Joan of Arc, 111–12, 114, 116–17, 120, 122, 181
Jordan, Elaine, 142
Judy, or the London Serio-Comic Journal, 38

Kant, Immanuel, 51, 163, 164
Karl Friedrich, Grand Duke of Saxe-Weimar-Eisenach, 202
Keats, John, 52, 99
Kemble, John Mitchell, 51n, 62, 68, 136
Kennedy, Ian H. C., 15, 53, 65, 74, 132
Killham, John, 114–15n, 116, 120n
Kinglake, Alexander William, 23
Klapper, M. Roxana, 6
Körner, Karl Theodor, 50
Kretschmann, Lily von, 200

Lamb, Lady Caroline, 9
Lang, Cecil Y., 23, 33, 63n, 68–9, 80n, 166, 201
Lecky, William Edward Hartpole, 188n
Leggett, Bobby Joe, 92n
Leighton, David Hillcoat, 96
Leighton, Robert, 134n
Lewes, George Henry, 1, 24, 35–6, 42, 43, 66, 95n, 145n
Lewis, Matthew, 8
Liberal, The, 6
Lincolnshire, 14, 77, 78
  Mablethorpe, 72, 76, 78, 80
  Somersby, 13, 51, 63n, 69, 76n, 77n, 87n, 96, 109n, 159, 166n

Lippincott's Magazine, 41
Liszt, Franz, 38
Livy, 51
Loane, George G., 201
Locke, John, 49n
Lockhart, John Gibson, 11–12, 51n
London, 16, 23, 26, 33, 38, 39, 51, 190
London Magazine, 3
Luke, David, 119n, 162, 182, 208
Lushington, Edmund, 160n
Lushington, Ellen, 57
Luther, Martin, 50
Lyceum Theatre, 38–40, 40–1, 41–2
Lyell, Charles, 165, 168, 169–70, 178, 179

Mablethorpe *see* Lincolnshire
Macaulay, Thomas Babington, Baron Macaulay, 160n
Macdonald, William Bell, 33
Mackenzie, Henry, 11
McKillop, Alan D., 28
McKusick, James C., 4
madness, 50n, 52, 58, 59, 62, 63, 66, 93, 193
Malory, Sir Thomas, 70, 207
Malthus, Daniel, 2n
Marlowe, Christopher, 2, 63n, 155n, 207
Martin, Robert Bernard, 69, 82, 90, 113, 186, 210n
Martin, Theodore, 34
Mattes, Eleanor Bustin, 170, 172, 173, 174n, 175
Maturin, Charles Robert, 11
Medwin, Thomas, 10, 129
Metzger, Lore, 26, 146, 164, 175, 203
Milnes, Richard Monckton, 14, 63n

Milton, John, 18, 162, 210
  Paradise Lost, 42, 139
  Sonnet XIX, 143n
Molière, 22n, 67n
money, 65, 66
monodrama, 68
Moore, Thomas, 11, 92n
morality, 2, 3, 4, 12, 13, 25, 27, 39, 43, 49, 123, 130, 133, 174n, 180, 181–3, 185, 189, 193, 194, 197, 198, 199, 210
  good and evil, 174n, 181–2, 189, 198
  sin, 25, 39, 182, 191, 193, 194
  see also religion
Motter, T. H. Vail, 47–8, 91n, 145, 172
mountains, 67, 75, 77, 92n, 202, 203
  Alps, 109–10, 112, 158–9, 160n
  Brocken, 38, 57, 65, 70n, 195, 196, 197
  Harz, 138, 195
  Jungfrau, 112, 113
  Mount Ida, 118
  Pyrenees, 113
  Scottish, 12
  Silver Horn, 112n
Moxon, Edward, 19, 23, 28
Murray, John, 9

Napoleon III, 34n
Nature, 6, 57, 118, 123, 137, 138n, 143n, 148, 150n, 153–79, 181, 182, 183, 209, 210
  humanity and, 154, 156–8, 159, 161, 179
  pantheism, 153, 154, 155, 164–5, 168, 176–7, 205
  science and, 153, 161–2, 165, 168–70, 175, 178

Nature (*cont.*)
  sea, the, 75–6, 77, 81–4, 85–6, 88, 89n, 90, 92n
  see also mountains
New Edinburgh Review, 12
Newton, Sir Isaac, 49n
Nibelungenlied, 50
Noehden, George Henry, 110
Noel, Roden, 40, 127, 130, 199
Novalis, 15, 163, 164, 165, 172–3, 175

Ormond, Leonée, 112n, 127n, 161–2
Outlines, Illustrative of 'Faust', 5, 128, 129
Ovid, 101, 143n
Oxenford, John, 34

Paden, William Doremus, 127
Palgrave, Francis Turner, 107–8
pantheism *see* Nature
Pappenheim, Jenny von, 200
Paracelsus, 26
Parker, Fred, 10
Pater, Walter, 37
personification, 15, 106, 130, 161, 163, 164, 170, 172
Petrarch, Francesco, 51, 102
Pettigrew, John, 86, 92n
Plato, 51, 102
Proescholdt-Obermann, Catherine Waltraud, 24–5
progress, 72, 76–7, 78, 79–80, 81, 83–4, 84–6, 87–9, 166–7, 203, 210n

Quarterly Review, 3, 12

Racine, Jean, 22n
Raphael Sanzio da Urbino, 51, 102

religion, 2, 3, 4, 6, 12, 13, 39, 43, 49n, 123, 181, 182, 184, 190, 194
  atheism, 130, 132n, 185
  Christ and Christianity, 7, 29, 30, 81, 114, 127, 131–2, 135, 146, 148, 149, 151, 179, 188, 189, 191, 198
  Deism, 154
  devil, the, 6, 9, 10, 14, 28, 56n, 129, 138n, 146, 147, 155n
  doubt, 29, 30, 40n, 127–52, 164, 179
  God, 27, 28, 30, 92n, 132, 146, 148n, 149–50, 154, 156, 164–5, 168–9, 175, 176–7, 179, 182, 188, 189, 197–8, 210
  immortality and the after-life, 34n, 71, 72, 81, 84, 87, 88, 90, 94, 103, 104, 127, 170n, 189, 198, 203
  pantheism *see* Nature
  see also Bible, the; morality
Retzsch, Moritz, 4–5, 17, 36
Rice, Stephen Spring, 22n
Richards, Jeffrey, 38
Richter, Johann Paul Friedrich *see* Jean Paul
Ricks, Christopher, 52, 53, 59n, 60, 76, 84, 85, 86, 92n, 99, 101n, 104, 121n, 139n, 141n, 145, 149, 155, 165, 167–8, 174n, 179n, 184n, 188, 191, 192, 194, 195, 206, 207
Robbins, Tony, 88
Robertson, Robert, 50
Robinson, Charles E., 129
Robinson, Henry Crabb, 4
Rogers, Samuel, 18
Romanticism, 11, 15, 42, 136, 153, 163, 169, 175, 178, 210

Roppen, Georg, 89
Rossetti, Dante Gabriel, 27, 36–7, 43
Ruskin, John, 37, 144n
Russell, Charles William, 182
Russell, Elizabeth, 76n

St Paul, 74, 184n
Salvin, Rev. H., 111n, 116n
Schelling, Friedrich Wilhelm, 23
Schérer, Edmond, 30
Schiller, Johann Christoph Friedrich, 51n, 54–5, 107–9, 110–14, 116–17, 118, 119, 120, 122, 165, 172, 183, 184–5, 188n, 204, 205–6, 207
Bride of Messina, The, 55
Complete Works (1834), 110, 115n, 116n
Correspondence between Schiller and Goethe, 184, 205–6
Death of Wallenstein, The, 121n
Demetrius, 107
'Division of the Earth, The', 91n
Maid of Orleans, The, 54, 110–14, 116–17, 120, 181
Mary Stuart, 116
'On the Sublime', 54
Robbers, The, 184
'Veiled Image at Sais, The', 172
William Tell, 109
Schlegel, August Wilhelm, 50
Schöne, Albrecht, 196
science, 37, 49n, 78, 153, 161–2, 165, 168–70
Scott, Michael, 4, 28, 199
Scott, Walter, 11, 64
sea, the *see* Nature
Sellwood, Emily *see* Tennyson, Emily Lady
sexuality, 36, 65, 179–81, 183, 189–99

Shakespeare, William, 18, 36, 42, 50, 81n, 99, 210
Hamlet, 42, 64, 129, 139, 193n, 206
2 Henry IV, 184n
Measure for Measure, 53
Romeo and Juliet, 64
Sonnets, 56n
Shannon, Edgar F., Jr, 23, 63n, 68–9, 166
Shatto, Susan, 82, 143n, 144n, 145n, 146, 148–9, 166, 171, 174n
Shaw, Marion, 82, 143n, 144n, 145n, 146, 148–9, 166, 171, 174n
Shelley, Percy Bysshe, 1, 5–8, 9–10, 11, 12n, 43, 81n, 128, 129, 207
'Alastor', 128–9, 174n
'Epipsychidion', 155
Faust, fragmentary prose translation of, 6, 174n
'Ode to Heaven', 7
'On Death', 155
Posthumous Poems, 6, 14
'Prologue to *Hellas*', 7
Prometheus Unbound, 155, 174n
'Scenes from the Faust of Goethe', 6, 12n, 14, 18, 22, 80, 84n, 137, 138, 139n, 155–6, 195–7, 205
'To—' ('O! there are spirits in the air'), 128
'To Edward Williams' ('The serpent is shut out from Paradise'), 7
'Triumph of Life, The', 195
Sidgwick, Henry, 149
Smiles, Samuel, 27
Smith, David Francis, 35, 133
Somersby *see* Lincolnshire

Southey, Robert, 18
Spasmodic School, 64
Spedding, James, 160n
Spinoza, Baruch, 154
Staël Holstein, Germaine de, 3, 13, 48, 49n
Stanford, Charles Villiers, 32n
Stewart, Duggald, 49n
Stokes, Henry Sewell, 32n
Stokoe, Frank Woodyer, 7
'Storm and Stress', 58
suicide, 2, 8, 10, 58, 60, 87–8, 136, 138, 140, 141–3, 146, 177, 188, 193
Sunday Magazine, 29
Switzerland, 31, 108, 109, 110
  Bernese Alps, 109, 110, 112
  Grindelwald, 109
  Lauterbrunnen, 109, 110, 112, 113
  Lucerne, 109
  Meiringen, 109, 110
  Reichenbach Falls, 109, 110
  Staubbach Falls, 109, 110
  Thun, 31n

Tarr, Rodger L., 146, 168n
Taylor, Bayard, 34
Taylor, William, 3, 43
Tennyson, Alfred Lord
  life: studies at Cambridge, 14–15, 30, 47, 51n, 95–6, 204; friendship with Arthur Hallam, 14–15, 47, 51–2, 53–4, 70, 113, 172–3; visits Cauteretz, 113, 118n; visits Mablethorpe, 72, 76, 78, 80; death of Arthur Hallam, 22, 54–5, 70–1, 72, 80, 81–4, 86, 91n, 92n, 102, 106, 112–13, 115, 119, 158–9, 205, 210; learns German, 13, 19–21, 31–2, 33–4, 68n, 110, 192; visits Switzerland, 108–9, 110, 112–13; engagement and marriage, 57; visits Weimar, 108; attends Lyceum *Faust*, 42; death of, 1, 42, 179
  character: admiration for Goethe, 13–15, 18–19, 21, 31–5, 68n, 81, 137, 144, 155, 162, 174n, 201; belief in immortality and the after-life, 72, 81–4, 127, 203; Nature, view of, 153, 154–5, 156–8, 159, 161, 168–75, 176–7, 178–9, 181, 183; sexuality, view of, 181, 190, 193–5, 196–7, 198–9; visions and trances, 72–5, 76, 79, 80, 84, 85–6, 87n, 89, 90, 91, 127, 141n, 179n, 198
  writings: 'All Things Will Die', 171n; 'Ancient Sage, The', 73; 'Armageddon', 72, 74–5, 76, 90, 91; 'Beggar Maid, The', 69n, 206; 'Break, break, break', 56, 206; 'Britons, Guard Your Own', 34n; 'Brook, The', 192n; 'Chorus, in an Unpublished Drama, Written Very Early', 14, 153, 155–6, 204; 'Come down, O maid, from yonder mountain height', 95, 108, 109, 111–13, 114, 118, 120, 181; 'Crossing the Bar', 203; 'Dell of E—, The', 156n; 'Despair', 153, 177–8; *Devil and the Lady, The*, 14, 56n, 155n; 'Dreamer, The', 42, 178–9, 205; 'Dream of Fair Women, A', 116n; 'English Warsong', 50n; 'Flight, The', 59, 60,

61, 63n, 82, 86n, 142n, 192, 206; 'Forlorn', 180, 183, 189, 192–4, 197, 198, 206; 'Gardener's Daughter, The', 56n, 206; 'Ghosts', 173; 'Golden Year, The', 155n, 204; 'Happy: The Leper's Bride', 194–5; 'Hark! the dogs howl!', 47, 56, 57, 70, 74, 84, 85, 192n, 206, 207, 208; 'Higher Pantheism, The', 153, 176–7, 205; 'Idealist, The', 163, 173; *Idylls of the King*, 70, 207; *In Memoriam A. H. H.*, 25, 33, 47, 52n, 57–8, 70n, 82, 84–6, 87, 89, 90, 91, 92n, 103, 115, 118, 119n, 121–2, 127, 128, 130, 131, 132, 141–51, 153, 161, 162, 165–6, 168–75, 179, 181, 200–3, 204, 205, 206, 207; 'Inscription by a Brook', 153, 155, 156–8, 161, 189–90, 206, 208; 'In the Valley of Cauteretz', 113n; 'Let Death and Memory keep the face', 56–7, 70, 205, 206, 208; 'Lines [Here often, when a child, I lay reclined]', 76; 'Locksley Hall', 64n, 72, 78–80, 81, 87n; *Lover's Tale, The*, 14, 64n, 72n, 207n; 'Love's latest hour is this', 58, 60–3, 70, 192, 206; 'Mariana', 53, 204, 208; 'Mariana in the South', 15, 53, 204, 208; *Maud: A Monodrama*, 1, 33, 47, 63–8, 172n, 181, 192, 203, 205, 207, 208; 'Mechanophilus (In the Time of the First Railways)', 72, 76–80, 83n, 89, 90, 177, 179n, 206; 'Morte d'Arthur', 69–70, 206, 207; 'Mother's Ghost, The', 59n, 193n, 206; 'Mystic, The', 74; 'Nothing Will Die', 171n; 'Now sleeps the crimson petal', 113n; 'Ode to Memory: Addressed to—', 83; 'Œnone', 15, 118; 'Oh! that 'twere possible', 47, 59, 60–1, 62, 63–4, 66, 70, 192, 198, 206, 207, 208; 'On a Mourner', 153, 159, 161, 206; 'On Sublimity', 57n; 'Palace of Art, The', 51, 102; 'Pierced through with knotted thorns of barren pain', 84n, 85n; *Poems* (1832), 19; *Poems by Two Brothers*, 14, 156n; *Poems, Chiefly Lyrical*, 15, 53, 132n, 136; *Princess: A Medley, The*, 33, 95, 105–22, 123, 181, 203, 204, 207; 'Progress of Spring, The', 194n; 'Refulgent Lord of Battle tell me why', 96, 97, 204; 'Rosebud, The', 59n; 'Ruined Kiln, The', 196n, 206; 'St Agnes' Eve', 180, 183, 189–91, 195, 198, 206; 'St Simeon Stylites', 180, 183–9, 198, 206, 208, 210; 'Semele', 102n, 206, 207; 'Sir Launcelot and Queen Guinevere', 96, 206; 'Sonnet [Alas! how weary are my human eyes]', 14; 'Stanzas [What time I wasted youthful hours]', 77n, 206; 'Supposed Confessions of a Second-Rate Sensitive Mind', 14, 127, 130, 131, 132–6, 137, 146n, 151, 208; 'Tears, idle tears', 119; 'This Earth is wondrous, change on change', 74, 84n, 91, 191n, 196n,

Tennyson, Alfred Lord (*cont.*) 206; 'Timbuctoo', 86n, 91; 'Tiresias', 95, 96, 97, 98n, 99, 101–2, 103, 104–5, 106, 123, 206, 207, 208, 210; 'Tithon', 59n, 95, 97–8, 99–101, 102, 103–4, 106, 123, 206, 207, 208, 209n, 210; 'Tithonus', 95n, 207; 'To Mary Boyle: With the Following Poem', 194n, 205; 'To Ulysses', 194n; 'Two Voices, The', 127, 130, 131, 132n, 136–41, 142, 144, 146, 147, 151, 153, 160–1, 171n, 175n, 183, 184n, 185–6, 189, 206, 208; 'Ulysses', 72, 80–94, 97, 103, 104, 113, 121, 123, 137, 141n, 191n, 194n, 198, 203, 206, 207, 208, 210; 'Vision of Sin, The', 180, 183, 189, 195–8, 204; 'Voyage, The', 85–6; 'What did it profit me that once in heaven', 84n, 87n, 206n; 'Wherefore, in these dark ages of the Press', 167, 201, 204

Tennyson, Edward, 63
Tennyson, Emily (the poet's sister), 48n, 50–1, 68–9, 110n, 121n, 159n, 173
Tennyson, Emily Lady (the poet's wife), 32, 33, 35, 57, 66, 67n, 68n, 76n, 108, 152, 165, 166, 168, 169, 173, 174n, 201, 202, 204
Tennyson, Hallam Lord, 40, 42, 57, 76n, 142n, 143n, 165, 183, 207

Tennyson, Mary, 68
Tennyson, Matilda ('Maud'), 19
Tennyson, Septimus, 63
Tennyson Research Centre, 19, 22n, 26, 28, 34, 82, 96, 110, 145
Terry, Ellen, 38, 42
Thackeray, William Makepeace, 16, 27
Tieck, Ludwig, 17, 50, 55, 91n
Tintern Abbey, 119
Trelawny, Edward John, 10n
Trench, Richard Chenevix, 15
Tribute, The, 63
Trilling, Lionel, 30
Trollope, William, 96
Turner, Paul, 112n, 118, 145, 201, 205

van Dyke, Henry, 192n
Victoria, Queen of the United Kingdom, 81, 113n
Virgil, 53, 81n, 206

Waller, John O., 28
Warren, Thomas Herbert, 158n
Whewell, William, 14, 23, 51n
Wiggins, Louise Dugas, 172
Wilde, Oscar, 1, 41–2, 43, 64, 127, 130
Williams, John R., 67, 193, 196, 203
Wills, William Gorman, 39
Winnick, R. H., 139n, 168, 194n, 200, 206
Wordsworth, William, 15, 18, 64, 81n, 139, 153, 154, 180

Young, Edward, 136n

EU representative:
Easy Access System Europe
Mustamäe tee 50, 10621 Tallinn, Estonia
Gpsr.requests@easproject.com